UNPACKING NORMATIVITY

This book provides a new and wide-ranging study of law's normativity, examining conceptual, descriptive and empirical dimensions of this perennial philosophical issue. It also contains essays concerned with, among other issues, the relationship between semantic and legal normativity; methodological concerns pertaining to understanding normativity; normativity and legal interpretation; and normativity as it pertains to transnational law. The contributors come not only from the usual Anglo–American and Western European community of legal theorists, but also from Latin American and Eastern European communities, representing a diversity of perspectives and points of view – including essays from both analytic and continental methodologies. With this range of topics, the book will appeal to scholars in transnational law, legal sociology, normative legal philosophy concerned with problems of state legitimacy and practical rationality, as well as those working in general jurisprudence. It comprises a highly important contribution to the study of law's normativity.

Unpacking Normativity

Conceptual, Normative, and Descriptive Issues

Edited by
Kenneth Einar Himma,
Miodrag Jovanović
and
Bojan Spaić

•HART•
OXFORD • LONDON • NEW YORK • NEW DELHI • SYDNEY

HART PUBLISHING

Bloomsbury Publishing Plc

Kemp House, Chawley Park, Cumnor Hill, Oxford, OX2 9PH, UK

HART PUBLISHING, the Hart/Stag logo, BLOOMSBURY and the Diana logo are trademarks of Bloomsbury Publishing Plc

First published in Great Britain 2018

A catalogue record for this book is available from the British Library.

Library of Congress Cataloging-in-Publication data

Names: Legal Normativity and Language (Conference) (2015 : Univerzitet u Beogradu. Pravni fakultet). | Himma, Kenneth Einar, editor. | Jovanović, Miodrag A., editor. | Spaić, Bojan, editor. | Univerzitet u Beogradu. Pravni fakultet, organizer.

Title: Unpacking normativity : conceptual, normative, and descriptive issues / edited by Kenneth Einar Himma, Miodrag Jovanović and Bojan Spaić

Description: Oxford, UK ; Portland, Oregon : Hart Publishing, 2018. | Includes index. | "Unpacking Normativity is a follow-up to the international conference "Legal Normativity and Language", which was organised at the Faculty of Law, University of Belgrade, on 19 October 2015."—ECIP introduction.

Identifiers: LCCN 2018022053 | ISBN 9781509916269 (Epub) | ISBN 9781509916245 (hardback : alk. paper)

Subjects: LCSH: Law—Philosophy—Congresses. | Normativity (Ethics)—Congresses. | Social norms—Philosophy—Congresses.

Classification: LCC K225 .L44 2015 | DDC 340/.01—dc23 LC record available at https://lccn.loc.gov/2018022053

ISBN: HB: 978-1-50991-624-5
ePDF: 978-1-50991-625-2
ePub: 978-1-50991-626-9

Typeset by Compuscript Ltd, Shannon
Printed and bound in Great Britain by TJ International Ltd, Padstow, Cornwall

To find out more about our authors and books visit www.hartpublishing.co.uk. Here you will find extracts, author information, details of forthcoming events and the option to sign up for our newsletters.

TABLE OF CONTENTS

PART IV
NORMATIVITY AND LEGAL REASONING

PART V
LEGAL NORMATIVITY BEYOND THE STATE

LIST OF CONTRIBUTORS

Dimitrios Kyritsis is an Associate Professor in Law at the University of Reading. Prior to joining Reading he was a Lecturer in Law at the University of Sheffield and Hauser Global Law Research Fellow at New York University. He holds a DPhil from the University of Oxford. His publications include his monographs *Shared Authority: Courts and Legislatures in Legal Theory* (Hart Publishing, 2015) and *Where Our Protection Lies: Separation of Powers and Constitutional Review* (Oxford University Press, 2017). He is currently on a research fellowship at the Centre for Law and Public Affairs, Institute of State and Law, the Czech Academy of Sciences. He serves on the editorial board of *Jurisprudence: An International Journal of Legal and Political Thought* and *Problema*.

Triantafyllos (Tria) Gkouvas is a former Postdoctoral Research Fellow at Monash University (2016–17) and the University of Antwerp (2015–16). He obtained his doctoral degree from the University of Antwerp. His doctoral thesis defends the possibility of metajurisprudential disagreement about the existence and the normative force of legal norms. His current research is part of a project funded by the Australian Research Council entitled 'Construing Statutes: The Interaction Between a Statute's Linguistic Content and Principles of Statutory Interpretation', focusing on the role of statutory canons as avenues for implementing constitutional and statutory rights instruments.

Brian H Bix is the Frederick W. Thomas Professor of Law and Philosophy at the University of Minnesota. He holds a D Phil (doctorate) from Balliol College, Oxford University and a JD (Law degree) from Harvard University. He writes and teaches in the areas of Jurisprudence, Contract Law, Family Law, and Constitutional Law. His publications in the area of Jurisprudence include *A Dictionary of Legal Philosophy* (Oxford, 2004), *Jurisprudence: Theory and Context*, 7th edn (Sweet & Maxwell, 2015) and *Law, Language, and Legal Determinacy* (Oxford, 1993).

Kenneth Einar Himma is a continuing visiting professor at the University of Belgrade. He is the author of more than a hundred articles in legal philosophy, information ethics, philosophy of religion, and applied ethics, as well as the volumes *Morality and the Nature of Law* and *Coercion and the Nature of Law* (forthcoming Oxford University Press). He is also an associate editor for the *Oxford Handbook of Jurisprudence and Philosophy of Law*, with Jules Coleman and Scott Shapiro (eds), as well as an editor for *Law as an Artifact*, with Luka Burazin and Corrado Roversi (forthcoming Oxford University Press), *The Rule of Recognition and the*

Constitution, with Matthew Adler (Oxford University Press, 2009), *The Handbook of Information and Computer Ethics*, with Herman Tavani (Wiley, 2008).

George Pavlakos is the Professor of Law and Philosophy and Director of Research at the School of Law, University of Glasgow. From 2007 to 2016 he was Research Professor of Globalisation and Legal Theory and director of the Centre for Law and Cosmopolitan Values at the University of Antwerp. From this position he attracted and managed a number of substantial research grants with a combined budget of €1.9 million. Since 2012 he has been consulting director of the Centre for Law and Public Affairs, Institute of State and Law, The Czech Academy of Sciences. His personal research awards include two Alexander von Humboldt Fellowships, an FWO-Odysseus grant, a JE Purkyne Senior Research Fellowship (Czech Academy of Sciences) and a Fernand Braudel Senior Fellowship (EUI, Florence). In recent years he has held visiting and part-time positions at the Universities of Antwerp, Glasgow, Kiel, the UCLA Law School, the Cornell Law School and the Beihang Law School (Beijing). His published work includes the monograph *Our Knowledge of the Law* (Hart Publishing, 2007) and he has recently edited (with Veronica Rodriguez-Blanco) *Reasons and Intentions in Law and Practical Agency* (Cambridge University Press, 2015). He is also general editor of the book series *Law and Practical Reason* at Hart Publishing and joint general editor of the journal *Jurisprudence*, published by Routledge.

Andrei Marmor is the Jacob Gould Schurman Professor of Philosophy and Law at Cornell University. Prior to joining Cornell in 2015, he was Professor of Philosophy and Maurice Jones Jr Professor of Law at the University of Southern California. His research interests span philosophy of law, moral, social and political philosophy, and philosophy of language. Marmor has published dozens of articles, six book monographs and a number of edited volumes. His most recent books include *Social Conventions: from Language to Law* (Princeton, 2009), *Philosophy of Law* (Princeton, 2011) and *The Language of Law* (Oxford, 2014). His books and articles have also appeared in numerous translations, including in Chinese, Spanish, Portuguese, Hebrew, and Italian.

Wil Waluchow is a Professor of Philosophy and Senator William McMaster Chair in Constitutional Studies at McMaster University. His main research interests are general jurisprudence and the philosophy of constitutional law. Among Waluchow's most notable publications are *Inclusive Legal Positivism* (Oxford University Press, 1994); *The Dimensions of Ethics* (Broadview, 2003) and *A Common Law Theory of Judicial Review: The Living Tree* (Cambridge University Press, 2008).

Horacio Spector is Professor of law at the School of Law of the University of San Diego and Universidad Torcuato Di Tella in Buenos Aires, and member of the Research Faculty in the Center for the Philosophy of Freedom at the University of Arizona. He was founding dean of the Torcuato Di Tella School of Law

(1996–2008) and held fellowships from the Alexander von Humboldt and the John Simon Guggenheim Memorial foundations. He was visiting scholar at the University of Heidelberg, the University of Mannheim, Oxford University and the Humboldt University of Berlin, and visiting professor at the University of Toronto, Louisiana State University, and the Hebrew University of Jerusalem, where he also held the Visiting Chair in Latin American Studies. He is the author of *Autonomy and Rights. The Moral Foundations of Liberalism* (Oxford University Press, 1992), *Analytische und Postanalytische Ethik. Untersuchungen zur Theorie moralischer Urteile* (Alber, 1993), and co-editor of *Rights: Concepts and Contexts* (Ashgate, 2012). He has published numerous papers in peer-reviewed journals on legal, moral, and political philosophy.

Bojan Spaić is Professor in Introduction to Law and Philosophy of Law at the University of Belgrade Faculty of Law, and Alexander von Humboldt Research Fellow on the Institute for Public Law, Constitutional Law and Legal Philosophy of the University of Heidelberg. He is the coeditor of numerous books in English and Serbian including *Jurisprudence and Political Philosophy in the 21st Century: Reassessing Legacies*, with Miodrag Jovanović (Peter Lang, 2012), *Fundamental Rights: Justification and Interpretation*, with Kenneth Einar Himma (Eleven International Publishing, 2016). He has published two books in Serbian and papers in Serbian and English on legal interpretation, ontological and methodological hermeneutics, pragmatism.

Andrej Kristan is Juan de la Cierva fellow at the University of Girona, Spain, and a visiting lecturer at the University of Ljubljana, Slovenia. He also serves as the co-editor in chief of *Revus. Journal for Constitutional Theory and Philosophy of Law*. His interests are mainly in the fields of jurisprudence and philosophy of language, though he also holds degrees in history of legal institutions and in law. He earned his PhD from the University of Genoa. In 2015, he received the European Award of Legal Theory for his doctoral dissertation on the semantics of legal discourse. His recent publications include the monograph *Derecho y otros enigmas* (Marcial Pons, 2017) and the article 'Assessment Sensitivity in Legal Discourse' (co-authored with M Vignolo and published in *Inquiry: An Interdisciplinary Journal of Philosophy*).

Katharina Stevens is an Assistant Professor of Philosophy at the University Lethbridge. She studied legal philosophy and argumentation theory at McMaster University and has published on argumentation-theory and philosophy of law. Her research for this chapter has been supported through the Dworkin-Balzan Fellowship at NYU School of Law she held in 2016/2017.

Veronica Rodriguez-Blanco is the inaugural Chair in Moral and Political Philosophy (Jurisprudence) at the University of Surrey Centre for Law and Philosophy, UK. She studied law and legal philosophy in Oxford and Cambridge and is the author of numerous articles in peer-reviewed journals. She is the author of the monograph *Law and Authority under the Guise of the Good* (Hart Publishing, 2014) and co-editor of the volumes *Reasons in Intentions and Law in Practical Agency* (Cambridge University Press, 2015) and *Dignity in the Legal and Political Philosophy of Ronald Dworkin* (Oxford University Press, 2018). Her research has been funded by the British Council, Cambridge Overseas Trust, Alexander Von Humboldt Fellowship and the Fernand Braudel Fellowship (EUI, Italy). She has been a Visiting Professor at the University of Stockholm and the University of Vienna and is the co-editor of the peer-reviewed journal *Jurisprudence: An International Journal of Legal and Political Thought.*

Miodrag A Jovanović is a Full Professor in Jurisprudence, Faculty of Law, University of Belgrade. His areas of interest are jurisprudence, philosophy of international law, legal theory of collective rights, political theory of multiculturalism, federalism and legal and political nature of the EU. He is a fellow of the Alexander von Humboldt Foundation and the 2016 Brandon Fellow of the Lauterpacht Centre for International Law (Cambridge). His internationally published books include: *Collective Rights – A Legal Theory* (Cambridge University Press, 2012); *Constitutionalizing Secession in Federalized States: A Procedural Approach* (Eleven International Publishing, 2007). His forthcoming book is *The Nature of International Law* (Cambridge University Press, 2018).

TABLE OF CASES

References are to page number.

TABLE OF LEGISLATION

References are to page number.

INTRODUCTION

The function of law is, as the matter is frequently put, to guide human behaviour. To accomplish this objective, law must perform a couple of functions. First, to successfully guide behaviour, the law must be reasonably contrived to inform subjects of what acts are required or proscribed of subjects. Second, to ensure that law is efficacious in regulating behaviour, the law must attempt to provide subjects with what they are likely to treat in their deliberation as reasons for conforming their behaviour to the law – at least in cases in which they are strongly inclined to do otherwise. Accordingly, the law is characteristically, if not necessarily, structured to perform both an epistemic and a normative function: the epistemic function is to inform subjects of their obligations under the law while the normative function is to provide something that would motivate them to comply with those obligations (ie something subjects regard as a reason for action).

It seems plausible to think, then, that it is part of the very nature of law that it either is or purports to be normative – whether we are speaking of laws as mandatory norms or of legal systems as institutional normative systems. That law is contrived to provide reasons for subjects to do as it requires is a paradigmatic feature of law that must be explicated – or unpacked – if we are to develop a comprehensive understanding of the institution of law. Understanding the putative normativity of law involves a host of problems that range from explaining how law could provide reasons for action to understanding the very nature of normativity itself.

Unpacking Normativity is a collection of essays that attempt to explicate the notion of normativity and to understand whether and how law is normative. The volume is divided into five major sections that approach the issue of legal normativity from different vantage points. Some are concerned with conceptual issues while others are concerned with more practical issues having to do with how to understand the role of normativity in legal reasoning and, more generally, in the normative theory of practical rationality.

The first section is concerned with identifying various methodological approaches to understanding normativity in law. In 'Is Moralised Jurisprudence Redundant?' Dimitrios Kyritsis considers whether what Julie Dickson characterises as an *indirectly evaluative* methodology can produce an adequate philosophical explication of the normativity of law. Kyritsis concedes that an indirectly evaluative methodology plays an important role in explicating the nature of law, but argues that there are significant limits with respect to what it can tell us about law. A moralised methodology that is agnostic between positivism and anti-positivism, on Kyritsis's view, is needed to supplement the indirectly evaluative approach and enable us to achieve a comprehensive understanding of the normative institution of law.

In 'The Metric Approach to Legal Normativity', Triantafyllos Gouvas calls attention to a methodological assumption that, he argues, is common to positivist and anti-positivist theories. Gouvas takes Raz's normative/explanatory *Nexus* as a basis for advancing a functionalist account of how to evaluate what he terms the 'robustness' of any theory that purports to explain a source of practical normativity in terms of reasons for action. More precisely, Gouvas argues that a theory's normative robustness depends on the capacity of the facts to which a theory assigns normative relevance to jointly perform three distinct functions: metaphysical, evaluative and explanatory. The resulting picture, as Gouvas puts it, 'animates a metanormative taxonomy capable of tracking affinities and divergences between foundational theories of law which the traditional positivist/non-positivist divide seems to suppress'.

The second section of the volume is concerned with the nature of legal normativity and legal obligation. In 'The Nature of Legal Obligation', Brian Bix argues for two provocative claims. First, Bix defends a volunteerist account of legal obligation and normativity according to which the normativity of law depends on whether citizens choose to regard law as normative or obligatory. Second, he argues that the manner in which the notion of normativity applies in law is logically independent of the manner in which that notion applies in morality; thus, on Bix's view, legal normativity should be understood as *sui generis* and not merely as a form of or subset of morality.

In 'The Problems of Legal Normativity and Legal Obligation', Kenneth Einar Himma takes a position at odds with Bix's voluteerist conception of legal normativity. In particular, Himma argues that the only plausible account of legal obligation is a non-volunteerist one that holds that legal obligations bind all putative subjects by providing prudential reasons for action. Any other account of legal normativity, he argues, implies that mandatory legal norms merely purport to define legal obligations and hence merely purport to provide reasons for action – a view that Himma believes is inconsistent with the legal practices and self-conceptions of practitioners that construct the content of our very concepts of law and legal obligation.

In 'Non-Naturalism, Normativity and the Meaning of Ought: Some Lessons from Kelsen', George Pavlakos argues that Kelsen is committed to certain non-naturalist presuppositions that are incompatible with what Pavlakos characterises as 'a strict separation between the legal and the moral domain'. As he understands it, non-naturalism 'is synonymous with, or at least constitutes a condition of', practical normativity in general. Pavlakos argues that insofar as normativity pertains to the moral as well as the legal domain, one cannot consistently treat legal obligation in a non-naturalistic manner and concludes by attempting to sketch an alternative account of normativity that does not, as he believes Kelsen's does, entail an artificial distinction between law and morality that 'condemn[s] law to inertness'.

The third section of the volume is concerned with norms as reasons for action. In 'Norms, Reasons and the Law', Andrei Marmor argues that it is a mistake to think that there is something unique to the normativity of law. He argues that different kinds of norms provide reasons for action in different ways, identifying four different classes of norms: (1) norms that function to codify preexisting reasons for action; (2) norms that instantiate, or complete, reasons for action that underdetermine the modes of conduct which would be responsive to the reasons; (3) norms that constitute various human activities; and (4) authoritative directives. Having explored how these different types of norms bear on our reasons for action, Marmor argues that these four kinds of norms are present in law as well, suggesting that the normativity of law is both complex and multifarious. Normativity in law, he concludes, is not fundamentally different from normativity in other practical domains.

Wil Waluchow's 'Normative Reasoning from a Point of View' defends the idea that judges can interpret and apply the law while taking a detached point of view that does not endorse, so to speak, the point of view that is expressed in the law. Waluchow argues that the Razian view that judges who accept law's claim to moral force cannot interpret and apply the law from a detached point of view is mistaken. If, on Waluchow's view, (1) the judge accepts and endorses her legal system as reasonably just and effective; (2) accepts and endorses her moral obligation to decide a case according to law's demands; and (3) that moral obligation demands is an interpretation of a constitutional provision constructed from the point of view of the legal system and its history of prior moral commitments, then the judge will consider herself morally bound (in a fully committed way) to accept a constructive interpretation she would ideally prefer to reject. Such commitments, he points out, are not anti-democratic in character.

Horacio Spector's 'Legal Reasons and Upgrading Reasons' is, like Gouvas's contribution, concerned with the Nexus Thesis, according to which law gives its addressees reasons for action only insofar as its norms track, trigger, or are otherwise related to prior reasons. Authoritative legal norms track pre-existing reasons, according to the Nexus Thesis as Spector understands it, only insofar as they partially or totally reproduce pre-existing reasons. Spector concedes that the Nexus Thesis is generally true, but argues that law's main function is to *create* reasons that do not necessarily track or trigger prior reasons but are rather, as he puts it, *plugged into* such reasons. According to Spector, people in complex societies have higher-order reasons ('upgrading reasons') for recognising authoritative mechanisms of reason-giving into which the lower-order reasons generated by these authoritative mechanisms are plugged.

The fourth section is concerned with the role of normativity in understanding legal reasoning. In 'The Normativity of Basic Rules of Legal Interpretation, Bojan Spaić considers a number of theoretical questions that arise in connection with different classes of rules of interpretation and their role in guiding and justifying ascriptions of meaning to legal texts. Spaić identifies and explicates certain shared commitments that are presupposed by three different conceptions of basic norms of interpretation: (1) those that are presupposed by viewing basic norms of interpretation as *constitutive*; (2) those that are presupposed by viewing basic norms of interpretation as *regulative*; and (3) those that are presupposed by viewing basic norms of interpretation as *instrumental*. He concludes by posing something of a theoretical dilemma for the theory of legal interpretation: if, one the one hand, basic norms of interpretation are conceived as constitutive or instrumental in character, they cannot justify guide interpretative ascriptions of meaning; but if, on the other, such norms are conceived as regulative in character, they lend themselves to a problematic indeterminacy that they are supposed to solve.

Andrej Kristan's 'Another Way to Meet Hart's Challenge' is concerned to show that legal realism can meet the Hartian challenge of being able to distinguish law from what he called the game of scorer's discretion. Hart argued that legal realism is unable to distinguish law from the game of scorer's discretion because it defines law so as to include the contents of final judicial decisions and thus gives rise to a presumptively problematic form of rule-scepticism. Kristan concedes for the sake of argument that legal realism leads to such rule-scepticism and argues that the same considerations that lead Hart to believe legal realism implies such scepticism also problematise his theory. If such a rule-scepticism is sufficient to refute legal realism, it is also, Kristan concludes, sufficient to refute Hart's own positivist theory of law.

Katharina Stevens's contribution, 'The Constraining Force of Analogies and the Role of the Judge', explicates and defends the role that reasoning by analogy plays in common-law reasoning. In particular, Stevens is concerned to rebut the claim that analogical reasoning fails to constrain judicial decision-making insofar as it can be used to justify any conclusion a judge might be predisposed to reach. She argues that judges typically regard themselves as interlocutors who have the task of understanding and evaluating arguments and are therefore properly disposed to evaluate the argumentative force the analogy might have. For judges so disposed, arguments from analogy can provide epistemically legitimate normative guidance, even when judges cannot find applicable rules that would determine the outcomes of their decisions.

The fifth section of the book is concerned with the notion of legal normativity as it extends beyond the law of states. In 'What Makes a Transnational Rule of Law? Understanding the Logos and Values of Human Action in Transnational Law', Veronica Rodriguez-Blanco argues for two related theses concerning coercion and the rule of law as it pertains to transnational law. First, she argues that, once the notion of coercion is properly understood, the 'coercion question' does, contrary to initial appearances, arise in transnational legal contexts. Second, she argues for a 'thick' conception of the rule of law as it pertains to transnational law that would enable us to understand how participants of a legal practice comply with regulations, rules, directives, and principles (RRDPs). A satisfactory account of how human beings comply with RRDPs, on her view, paves the way to properly understanding the role of coercion at the transnational level.

Closing out the volume is 'Theorising "Unidentified Normative Objects" of Global Regulatory Regimes', by Miodrag Jovanović. Jovanović's concern is with certain regulatory instruments ('unidentified normative objects' or UNOs) that are poorly understood through the framework of existing conceptual theories of law. Jovanović distinguishes two problems: (1) the *epistemological* question of how to identify and distinguish normative statements from 'is-statements'; and (2) the normative question of how to explain how, from the standpoint of practical rationality, norms provide us with reasons for action. Jovanović argues that law's normative force competes with the normative force of other classes of orders and that law's higher level of efficiency should be attributed, not to some special sort of normativity, but to the combined effects of law's institutionalisation and its coercive guarantees. He concludes by applying these findings to two paradigmatic cases of UNOs – regulatory instruments of the World Health Organization and the Basel Committee on Banking Supervision.

Unpacking Normativity is a follow-up to the international conference 'Legal Normativity and Language', which was organised at the Faculty of Law, University of Belgrade, on 19 October 2015. The conference was organised within the project 'Constitutionalism and the Rule of Law in the Nation-State Building Process – The Case of Serbia', which is financed by the Ministry of Education, Science and Technological Development of the Republic of Serbia.

Ken Himma
Miodrag Jovanović
Bojan Spaić
Seattle, Belgrade, Heidelberg, March 2018

PART I

Methodological Approaches to Understanding Normativity

1

Is Moralised Jurisprudence Redundant?*

DIMITRIOS KYRITSIS

I. Introduction

In recent years questions about legal normativity have spilled over into the debate about the methodology of jurisprudence. In fact, it has been thought by some that the resolution of the methodological issue can give us a decisive reason for siding with either positivism or non-positivism. Thus, it has been argued by some anti-positivists that jurisprudence cannot be fully descriptive. Rather, it must necessarily make judgments about which view of law is morally appealing in a suitable sense. The jurisprude, it is said, is not a detached observer but an engaged participant who takes sides in first-order legal disputes.

This suggestion has been challenged by Julie Dickson, who claims that jurisprudence may still be evaluative without being moralised.[1] All it need do in order to sift through the data of legal practice is make judgments of importance, or *indirectly evaluative judgments* in Dickson's terminology. The idea of indirect evaluation is used not only as a shield but also as a sword. If it can help us identify essential truths about law, then the invocation of moral value, far from essential to jurisprudential method, appears to be redundant, a dispensable extra.

This chapter criticises the use of indirect evaluation in legal theory. It does not go so far as to suggest that such evaluation is unsound. Rather, it aims to cast some doubt on the alleged priority of indirectly evaluative jurisprudence over moralised jurisprudence. In particular, it criticises the claim that this priority is grounded in

*I am grateful to the organisers of the conference on Legal Normativity and Language at the University of Belgrade and participants for their helpful comments. I would also like to acknowledge the financial support of the Grant Agency of the Czech Academy of Sciences through a project on 'The Role of the Principle of Proportionality in the Decision-making of Courts' (grant ID: 15-23955S) awarded to the Institute of State and Law of the Academy of Sciences of the Czech Republic, created under subsidies for a long-term conceptual development (RVO: 68378122).

[1] Henceforth, I shall use the terms moralised jurisprudence and anti-positivism more or less interchangeably. However, I shall avoid the term 'normative jurisprudence', which does not readily convey the conviction that jurisprudential method must be morally laden.

the fact that law is crucially shaped by the understandings, attitudes, and beliefs of those who use it. This is one of the features of law that both sides have sought to exploit to tilt the methodological debate in their favour. Non-positivists like to zero in on the normative character of participants' understandings, attitudes, and beliefs towards law and argue that jurisprudence should be continuous with them, whereas positivists like Dickson insist that, being *about* those understandings, attitudes and beliefs, jurisprudence need not be normatively committed in the same way that they are.

Here I shall put forward a set of arguments for doubting the superiority of the indirectly evaluative methodology in the philosophical study of the concept of law. Their combined thrust is to question the ability of judgments of importance to ground our theoretical choices, as we navigate the complexity of people's understandings of law. Of course, there are other arguments that have as their point of departure the dependence of the concept of law on participants' understandings. Their assessment will have to await another occasion. My suspicion is that, as a general matter, this dependence does not provide a shortcut in the debate between positivism and anti-positivism. Given the limited scope of the present inquiry, however, it will have to remain a suspicion. But at the very least I hope that the arguments I present will encourage participants in the debate to sharpen their use of this dependence so as to effectively engage the opposing view.

The chapter will be structured as follows: I shall first explain what Dickson takes the dialectic between moralised and non-moral jurisprudence to be. I shall show that this decisively frames her own brand of indirectly evaluative jurisprudential method, but that it also risks missing the gist of moralised jurisprudence. I shall then test how well indirectly evaluative jurisprudence can explicate the concept of law in light of the latter's dependence on participants' understandings compared to its moralised opposite number. I shall conclude that, if indirectly evaluative jurisprudence is indeed a sword, it is a rather blunt one.

II. Indirect Evaluation and Theories of Law

Legal practice presents us with a vast collection of data. Hardly anyone maintains that jurisprudence must simply report those data; instead, it must 'systematize, clarify and sieve [them] for importance and relevance'.[2] How can it evaluate which ones are important and relevant? What criteria should it employ? Anti-positivists maintain that these criteria must include moral considerations: for them, a sound philosophical explication of legal practice is one that is in an appropriate sense morally appealing. Dickson construes the anti-positivist method as follows:

> … to evaluate something is to ascribe real value or worth to it, and this univocal meaning is the only one which the term will bear. We just do not count something

[2] J Dickson, *Evaluation and Legal Theory* (Oxford, Hart Publishing, 2001) 43.

> as being an evaluation, unless it consists of an ascription of such worth or entails such an ascription.[3]

Dickson argues that this method is underpinned by what she calls the 'no place to stop' argument.[4] She takes John Finnis and other proponents of moralised jurisprudence to claim something like the following: once we have mounted on the evaluative track, there is no stopping short of full-blown moral evaluation. According to the 'no place to stop' argument unless jurisprudence is to be reduced to an arid reporting exercise, stripped from any ability to make judgments of relative importance about its database, it cannot but be moralised. The anti-positivist wins by default.

Notice two things about this argument. First, it has a 'my way or the highway' air to it. It allows room for only one type of jurisprudential inquiry, one that necessarily involves evaluation. Second, it crucially shapes the dialectical position of methodological positivism. It suggests that all its proponents ought to do is come up with a way of making evaluations that does not involve recourse to moral considerations. This is the ambition of Julie Dickson's well-known indirectly evaluative legal philosophy (IELP).[5] IELP resists the starkly binary choice between moralised and descriptive jurisprudence. According to it, there is more than one type of evaluation. More specifically, there is evaluation according to moral as well as non-moral standards. It is this kind of evaluation that undergirds methodological positivism. For Dickson it is a mistake to say that positivists aim to describe some phenomena, report regularities of behaviour and the prevalence of certain attitudes and beliefs in the community. They aspire to accomplish more than just articulate contingent truths about a certain social institution that may hold in some community but not somewhere else. Rather, they seek to capture necessary truths that help us understand law's distinctive 'mode of operation': its central characteristics that make it the kind of institution it is. This requires discarding what is merely contingent and focusing on what is crucial and fundamental. Though this exercise will inevitably involve evaluation of some sort,[6] it does not – according to Dickson – necessitate full-blown moral evaluation. Arguably, indirect evaluation provides the stopping point between mere description typical of sociological inquiries and moral evaluation. Note that Dickson does not deny that there is room for a moralised jurisprudence; legal philosophy, she says, is a broad church.[7] Still, she insists on the priority of the non-moral inquiry. We must, she writes, 'postpone, and approach cautiously, *morally* evaluating and certainly morally justifying law

[3] ibid 48.
[4] ibid 43.
[5] ibid.
[6] There are traces of such a view in later work by Hart as well. See HLA Hart, 'Comment' in R Gavison (ed), *Issues in Contemporary Jurisprudence: Essays in Honor of HLA Hart* (Oxford, Oxford University Press, 1986) 39.
[7] J Dickson, 'Ours is a Broad Church: Indirectly Evaluative Philosophy as a Facet of Jurisprudential Inquiry' (2015) 6(2) *Jurisprudence* 207.

until we have a non-morally-evaluative – or morally commendatory – account of law's most significant and important properties, and the relevance of those properties to our social, political and moral lives'.[8]

This understanding of the relationship between the study of the nature of law and morality echoes HLA Hart's famous assertion in the Postscript to *The Concept of Law* that the type of theoretical inquiry he is engaging in is not antagonistic to Dworkin's.[9] For Hart, whereas the former is in the business of describing the essential features of all legal systems, the latter determines the conditions under which this or that legal system can be morally justified. It is implicit in his argument that the two types of jurisprudence, the descriptive and the normative, operate on parallel levels. There may be important interrelations between moralised and what he calls descriptive accounts of law, but their success is tested independently; they strive, that is, for different kinds of truths.

In this sense, both Dickson and Hart think moralised jurisprudence is redundant. It is redundant not because it is not significant, but because it comes to the scene at an analytically second stage, which presupposes and relies on the prior identification of law, the object of its moral assessment. Only after we have determined what is X, are we justified in judging whether that X is also a good or a bad thing.

So, what does indirect evaluation mean more precisely? At times, the distinction between direct and indirect evaluation is presented as a philosophical discovery about methodology in general. To make such a claim convincing, Dickson would have to show that indirect and direct evaluations track different classes of philosophical truths: that there are philosophical truths we arrive at by means of direct evaluation and ones we do by means of indirect evaluation. If she were right about this distinction, she would have indeed come up with a middle ground, a place for jurisprudential theories to stop, without in this way compromising their theoretical aims. But it is not entirely clear which philosophical truths indirect evaluation aims at. Consider the following passages:

(1) 'An indirectly evaluative proposition of the form "X is an important feature of the law" is thus a proposition which attributes some evaluative property to that feature of the law, but which does not entail a directly evaluative proposition to the effect that the feature of the law in question is good or bad'.[10]

(2) 'In the case of a proposition like "X is an important feature", the evaluation concerned does not go to the substance or content of the subject of the proposition in the same way as is the case as regards a directly evaluative proposition'.[11]

[8] ibid 215.

[9] HLA Hart, *The Concept of Law*, 2nd edn with a new Postscript (Oxford, Oxford University Press, 1994).

[10] Dickson, *Evaluation and Legal Theory* (n 2) 53.

[11] ibid.

(3) 'In asserting a proposition like "X is an important feature", we are accounting the existence of some X as significant and hence worthy of explanation, not directly evaluating as good or bad the substance or content of that X'.[12]

Now, it is true by stipulation that indirect evaluation is different from direct evaluation. The former does not employ moral tests while the latter does. It is more difficult to make out by virtue of what Dickson thinks the questions they answer belong to separate philosophical domains. What about the idea that indirect evaluation shies from the 'substance or content of the subject of the proposition'? But what precisely is the substance or content of a proposition to which an indirectly evaluative judgment is juxtaposed? If by 'content' Dickson means its moral merit, then, again, the statement is not particularly informative. So, it must be something else. What about the different idea that indirect evaluation merely asserts the existence of a certain feature? Yet, this idea does not seem to get us much further either. For the idea that, say, a legal norm can *exist* irrespective of its moral merits, is already built into the statement. But that is what is in dispute between positivists and anti-positivists.

Perhaps, we can get guidance from an example Dickson appears to rely on more heavily. Often, we say of an event that it is the most important thing that has happened to someone, without committing ourselves to a particular view about its moral value, about whether it made one's life a good or a bad one. Now, this is undeniable, but we must be careful to determine the precise import of the example. For one thing, something can be important in all sorts of ways, for various reasons. But Dickson is interested in a particular sense of importance. Something is important in this latter sense, if it points to a feature of a social or physical phenomenon that is part of its very nature. If a physical or social phenomenon lacks that feature or ceases to possess it, it is not (or no longer) the same thing. Hence, it may be important that white wine be served chilled, but warm white wine is no less wine, whereas something whose chemical composition is not H_2O is not water, even if it is transparent and we drink it to quench our thirst.[13] So the claim that some events in our life are important – though not morally so – does not by itself establish the appropriateness of indirect evaluation as a philosophical, or more narrowly jurisprudential, methodology. It would have to be supplemented by an account whereby the occurrence of such events makes one's life the life that it is, whatever their consequences upon its moral quality.

More fundamentally, as the example of water and wine shows, it is quite true that in many cases the evaluation needed to pin down the essential features of some object or phenomenon, either physical or social, will not require recourse to

[12] ibid.

[13] I am assuming here that there is a possible world with H_2O but no creatures with our biological characteristics that need H_2O to quench their thirst and our sensory apparatus to perceive it as transparent. See S Kripke *Naming and Necessity*, Lecture III (Oxford, Blackwell Publishers, 1981) esp 127–34.

morality. It would be absurd to suggest that scientists determining the nature of water or wine should go about making moral judgments. By virtue of what would it be absurd? Plausibly, the kind of evaluations needed to determine the concepts we employ to mark objects of our social and physical environment should trace the nature of that object. On this view, there is something in the nature of water and wine that makes moral considerations irrelevant to the determination of their fundamental characteristics.

These thoughts bring Dickson back to square one. There are various things we mean when we make judgments of importance. That is why such judgments normally invite the further question: 'with respect to what?' Furthermore, things are important in moral or non-moral ways. In this sense the distinction between direct and indirect evaluation is sound. Indeed, it must be rather uncontroversial. But this does not suffice to shield Dickson from the anti-positivist challenge. In addition, she bears the burden of supplying a link between her preferred mode of inquiry and the philosophical study of law. This is a burden that all theory shoulders. Our example was water. We are inclined to say that its chemical composition is important to the concept of water, meaning that nothing without that composition counts as water, even though we obviously do not imply that it is also of moral significance that things be so. A more general way of putting the same point is that the appropriateness of one or the other mode of evaluation is to be judged by appeal to the kind of thing our inquiry is directed to or the kinds of features that belong to its essence.

III. A Wrong Turn

Before turning to assess how the finding of the previous section bears on the explanatory potential of indirect evaluation, I want to show how it opens up the possibility of understanding moralised jurisprudence in a different way from Dickson. Recall that she sets herself to refute the 'no place to stop' argument, which she takes to be central to the moralised jurisprudence of John Finnis and Ronald Dworkin. According to it there is only one mode of philosophical evaluation, the moral mode; if jurisprudence has to be evaluative, then it must be morally laden. However, this strikes me as too strong a reformulation of Finnis and Dworkin's position. To my mind, neither author need deny the existence of other non-moral modes of evaluation, nor their appropriateness for certain inquiries.[14] In line with the lesson of the preceding section, we can say instead that they are making the

[14] For instance, Dworkin acknowledges that non-moral evaluation may be appropriate for examining the 'sociological concept of law', which he distinguishes from the doctrinal concept of law, the target concept of legal theory. See R Dworkin, *Justice in Robes* (Harvard, Harvard University Press, 2006) ch 8.

narrower claim that it is something about the nature of law, and not the nature of philosophical evaluation in general, that makes moral principles pertinent to legal theory.

Take Finnis as an example. For him, the study of law must be morally laden because law is taken by members of the community to provide standards of conduct. He writes: 'If there is a point of view in which legal obligation is treated as at least presumptively a moral obligation … then such a viewpoint will constitute the central case of the legal viewpoint'.[15] But since nothing can be binding, unless it conforms to right reason, then the primary task of the legal philosopher is to explain how the law is the sort of thing that can impose moral obligations. This exercise will furnish focal instances of law. Of course, actual social orders do not always live up to this aspiration. Despite their moral defects they may still be thought of as law, though only in a peripheral sense. Even then they are law in virtue of their similarity to the focal, morally justifiable instances. Hence, Finnis would insist that moralised jurisprudence is antagonistic with and on the same terrain as descriptive jurisprudence, in the sense that the truth of one entails the falsity of the other. For him we cannot reach conclusions about the nature of law other than by means of moral evaluation of the sort just sketched. Such moral evaluation is not, so to speak, parasitic upon other evaluations that supposedly fully determine the concept of law.

Of course, Finnis may be wrong. But that is beside the point. What is more significant for present purposes is that he has come to propound a version of moralised jurisprudence, because he thinks moral considerations can make best sense of the obligatory nature of law. For all we know, practices that lack this feature might call for a non-moral methodology. Therefore, in order to adjudicate between his position and Dickson's there is no avoiding looking at legal practice to see which methodology is best suited to explicate it.

In fact, elsewhere Dickson herself endorses this line of thought. She claims that

> if we are to learn something interesting about the role of evaluation in legal theory, then we must seek to understand whether, and in what sense, the particular data with which legal theory deals has a special bearing upon the kinds of evaluative judgments a successful theorist must make.[16]

In the following sections we shall examine some of the reasons she gives for thinking that the exercise described in this passage will pick out indirect evaluation as the one appropriate for legal theory. As announced, these reasons turn on the fact that the concept of law depends on the understandings, beliefs and attitudes of participants. We shall conclude that this fact does not put moralised jurisprudence at a disadvantage from the very beginning.

[15] See also J Finnis, *Natural Law and Natural Rights* (Oxford, Clarendon Press, 1980) 14–15.
[16] See Dickson, *Evaluation and Legal Theory* (n 2) 35.

IV. Law and Participants' Self-Understanding

Dickson starts from the observation that those who participate in legal practice employ the concept of law to shape their perception of the social world.[17] Arguably, this means that its analysis must be different from other concepts in the social sciences, which are in a way superimposed on the social world, but do not figure in the thoughts and beliefs of ordinary members of society. An example of the latter type of concept is 'ideology', as used for example in Marxist accounts of society. People under the bourgeois ideology will typically be unaware of the fact that their moral claims are ultimately grounded in class interest and struggle. How do we know then that there is such a thing? Simplifying grossly, we can say that sociologists construct concepts like ideology on the basis of stipulations and general assumptions about how society (or a society) functions. They subsequently go out in the world and make empirical observations, which enable them to test whether those concepts can adequately explain various phenomena and patterns of social behaviour. It makes sense to speak of 'ideology' if this concept improves our understanding of social behaviour, even though it is not part of the conceptual scheme of those people whose behaviour we seek to understand.

At first sight, the concept of 'law' does not work this way at all. One of HLA Hart's key contributions to the theory of law is the idea that law is normative. In *The Concept of Law* Hart distanced himself from Austin, who explicates law in terms of habits and sanctions, and instead gave prominence to what he called the internal point of view of officials. The internal point of view, he contends, is that of someone who takes law to provide a standard of conduct. Those who adopt it justify their behaviour by appeal to that standard and criticise deviations from it in others. An adequate theory of law must account for this internal point of view and the practices of justification and argumentation built around it. From this Hart concluded that jurisprudence ought not to take a purely external perspective, focusing solely on regularities of behaviour and the effectiveness of sanctions in securing compliance. Rather, it needs to take the internal point of view at face value. Perhaps Hart was wrong to think that the internal point of view can be accommodated by his theory. But that does not detract from the value of his insight, namely that, unlike concepts such as water, law is largely constituted by what people think about it. And this, so the argument goes, has considerable impact on the methodology of jurisprudence.

In fact, this has been taken to be the point of departure for much moralised jurisprudence. Arguably, a value-laden methodology makes better sense of the internal point of legal practitioners and thus vindicates law's normativity, because it helps identify which standards genuinely justify conduct. Thus, it

[17] For a similar starting point see J Raz, 'Two Views of the Nature of the Theory of Law: A Partial Comparison' (1998) 4 *Legal Theory* 249, and M Giudice, *Understanding the Nature of Law: A Case for Constructive Conceptual Explanation* (Cheltenham, Edward Elgar Publishing, 2015) ch 8.

might be said that Ronald Dworkin radicalises Hart's insight. He suggests that, in order to account for the normative character of law, we ought to accept that the theory of law is not neutral with respect to the competing concrete claims of legal practitioners; it does not strive to describe our attitudes in a detached manner. Rather, it takes sides in ordinary legal discourse. As Dworkin characteristically puts it in a famous passage from *Law's Empire*, 'no firm line divides jurisprudence from adjudication or any other aspect of legal practice … Jurisprudence is the general part of adjudication, silent prologue to any decision at law'.[18]

There is a prima facie reason why the mere fact that legal practice is normative does not automatically provide an argument in favour of moralised jurisprudence. It does not go without saying – indeed it strikes some jurisprudes as odd – that the philosopher's task should be on the same level as the participant's. The latter takes the practice as reason-giving. But arguably the philosopher merely intends to analyse this feature; to carry out this task she need not be taking part in the practice. According to this view, the claims we make as part of the philosophical analysis of law are neutral with regard to the 'first-order' claims that are put forward in the course of taking part in the practice like the claim that the defendant has a duty in law to pay damages to the claimant. They are neutral in the sense that they do not validate some first-order legal claim – except perhaps strike out the most outlandish ones that defy our conceptual framework, such as the claim that the defendant must pay damages because a tree said so. They occupy, so to speak, an Archimedean standpoint. Whether you take one or the other view of what the law requires, your claim still has the same deep structure, and it is that deep structure that legal philosophers seek to elucidate.

In fact, the philosopher need not take the law to be morally justified at all. Perhaps she thinks it is iniquitous and should be modified. Still, on the view under discussion this is a distinct issue, with no bearing on the study of law as it is experienced by those who treat it as reason-giving. Seen from this perspective, moralised jurisprudence appears indeed superfluous. No doubt, legal norms can be morally evaluated, and moralised jurisprudence will be essential to that task. However, when it comes to understanding what makes those norms legal, their moral assessment is an unnecessary – and potentially misleading – extra. Considerations of moral merit will inevitably filter out some norms that are immoral but are treated by a society as binding. Thus, they will impede our understanding of the concept of law actually used in that society.

If considerations of moral merit are out of the question, which considerations should we rely on instead? This question reintroduces the challenge of sifting through the immense and varied database of legal practice, 'that Everest of data',[19] in order to arrive at a unified theory of its essential features. At least, proponents of moralised jurisprudence can use moral considerations to discard some elements

[18] R Dworkin, *Law's Empire* (Oxford, Hart Publishing, 1998) 90.
[19] Dworkin, *Justice in Robes* (n 14) 166.

from that database and focus on others.[20] Dickson, by contrast, anchors judgments about the theoretical importance of some feature of law in 'the prevalence of certain beliefs on the part of those subject to law concerning X, and the consequences which those beliefs have'.[21] The first characteristic she often explains as what the law 'invariably'[22] possesses. By 'consequences' of some belief she primarily has in mind its effect on our deliberations or its role as a point of focus for our direct evaluations.

Let us start with the first characteristic. 'Invariably' can be taken to mean one of two things: first, it may denote some feature that law possesses by virtue of its very nature. Invariable then would mean necessary. But that would trivialise Dickson's thesis by making it tautological. What is necessary, part of the very nature of law, is supposed to be what a theory of law ends up with. Hence, it cannot figure as a criterion for sorting out through the data on pain of circularity. Or else it might imply an empirical observation: that wherever and whenever there is law, social scientists have discovered that the surface behaviour of those subject to law is the same.[23] For one thing, that would be a tremendously ambitious project, on which no philosopher has ever embarked.[24] More to the point, this construal of Dickson's thesis would be saddled with a rather implausible view of error. It would presuppose that people never have mistaken beliefs about the concepts they use. It would also be exposed to the familiar challenge from disagreement. If what makes something important for legal theory is its prevalence, how come people disagree in the way Dworkin thinks they do in pivotal cases? What is it they disagree about? And how can we tell the beliefs of which side we should trust to reveal the important features of law?

To this set of questions legal philosophers have given a wide range of answers. Some say that even when two people disagree about the concept 'law', they still implicitly rely on the conventional meaning of that concept.[25] For others, philosophical explanations are extrapolations from paradigmatic applications of the concept and are thus inherently controversial.[26] These are both prima facie plausible suggestions. However, it is questionable whether they support anything like the indirectly evaluative methodology. The second suggestion is especially hard to square with it. Paradigmatic applications may well serve to signal what practitioners deem important, but they do not by themselves determine how and why they are important, unless they are supplemented by a philosophical account that

[20] S Perry, 'Hart's Methodological Positivism' in J Coleman (ed), *Hart's Postscript* (Oxford, Oxford University Press, 2001) 311.

[21] Dickson, *Evaluation and Legal Theory* (n 2) 59.

[22] ibid.

[23] This is the approach advocated in W Waluchow, *Inclusive Legal Positivism* (Oxford, Oxford University Press, 1994).

[24] Dworkin, *Justice in Robes* (n 14) 166–67.

[25] See, for instance, J Coleman, *The Practice of Principle: In Defence of a Pragmatist Approach to Legal Theory* (Oxford, Oxford University Press, 2001).

[26] T Endicott, 'Herbert Hart and the Semantic Sting' in J Coleman (ed), *Hart's Postscript: Essays on the Postscript to the Concept of Law* (Oxford, Oxford University Press, 2001) 39.

is built on them. The fact that, though answerable to paradigms, such an account is controversial is strong evidence that indirect evaluation can at best be part of a much bigger methodological story. What about the first suggestion? This one at least gives us comfort that legal theory aims at uncovering the shared understanding of the concept rather than advancing a partisan conception with which many practitioners disagree. Still, this metaphysical view requires, at the methodological level, that we cut through the surface disagreements of practitioners. A methodology that insists on a numerical standard of prevalence is of little help in this task.

Some of the criticisms mentioned above also apply to Dickson's second proposal. It is doubtful that we can come up with an unequivocal account of the role legal norms play in our practical lives just by looking at the attitudes of practitioners. For one, Hart acknowledged that some people abide by the law out of fear of sanction. They thus adopt an external perspective toward law, heeding it only when it can hurt them, not because they take themselves to be bound by it. To accommodate this dimension of legal practice, Hart famously maintained that for law to exist it suffices that legal officials adopt the internal point of view, whereas the rest of the population need only by and large conform to legal norms without necessarily taking the law as a normative standard. But this focus on the internal point of view, however reasonable, exposes Hart to a methodological challenge that Dickson also faces. The challenge can be put in the following general form: Which attitudes, beliefs and dispositions should legal theorists focus on? Is it those of the 'bad man' or of the law-abiding citizen? Or is it perhaps those of the official?[27] Given that all of these perspectives are rather salient, it is not clear we can answer this question solely by appeal to indirect evaluations.

In making these observations, I do not mean to endorse the view that the concept of law itself is fraught with indeterminacy, and therefore that the task of legal theory is not to reflect how that concept is being used, but to produce accounts of that concept that suit our practical, including moral, goals.[28] Rather, my aim is the more modest one of pointing out that the existence of disparate perspectives towards the law recommends adopting a methodology that will often have to go beyond the surface behaviour of the participants. For Dickson, legal theory may 'systematise, sieve and clarify' the self-understandings of the participants in legal practice, but it is not clear whether in her view it can discard any part thereof as simply misguided. And even if she thinks it can, the preceding analysis has demonstrated that 'the prevalence and consequences' of certain attitudes cannot yield a determinate philosophical criterion. As a result, what we are probably left with is a range of considerably divergent sets of beliefs, attitudes and dispositions that share too little in terms of a highest common factor for the theorist to construct a 'modest' account of law out of them.

[27] Notably, this point has been pressed by Stephen Perry in S Perry, 'Hart's Methodological Positivism' (n 20) 324ff.

[28] L Murphy, 'Concepts of Law' (2005) 30 *Australian Journal of Legal Philosophy* 1; D Priel, 'Jurisprudence and Necessity' (2007) 20 *Canadian Journal of Law and Jurisprudence* 173.

V. Conclusion

In her critique of Dworkin, Dickson contends: '[his] approach results in [him] foreclosing the issue of whether law is an inherently moral phenomenon more or less from the outset of his discussion, thus restricting considerably the remit of legal theoretical inquiry'.[29] This point can be generalised to moralised jurisprudence as a whole. But if the foregoing analysis is correct, there is reason to think that this complaint may not be entirely warranted: Dworkin and other proponents of moralised jurisprudence must of course provide their arguments for why we should treat law as an 'inherently moral phenomenon'. Having done so, they are perfectly justified in foreclosing the methodological issue 'from the outset'. They may be wrong on substantive grounds but they do not beg the methodological question. In this regard, they are in no better or worse position than their opponents. Any theory of law will have to adopt a methodology that is appropriate for the kind of thing that it takes law to be.

Some may regard this as an alarming proposition. Methodology is there to discipline and guide our search for the nature of law. But then I go on to argue that the methodology is itself sensitive to what we take the nature of law to be, which presumably we should only discover at the end of the process. Arguably, we are left with no place to anchor at least some of our beliefs, say about methodology, and to use them as a basis for assessing the truth of our further beliefs, say about the nature of law. Finnis may think that the methodology of jurisprudence must be capable of vindicating the obligatory character of law, but surely Austin would disagree. It is no surprise, then, that they end up with very different respective substantive theories of law. But, surely, we want our methodology to adjudicate between them rather than presuppose them.

While this understanding of methodology as internal to a given legal theory surely poses challenges, I do not think it involves us in a vicious circle. I cannot argue for this bigger claim now. Still, what I have said in this chapter points to a more modest but still interesting thought: we should not expect that methodological considerations by themselves, unhinged from law, will deliver outright victory to either positivism or anti-positivism. Our assessment of Dickson's indirectly evaluative methodology vindicates this thought: indirect evaluation cannot get off the ground if not supported by arguments to the effect that it has a good fit with the nature or the concept of law. In this chapter I have given some reasons to doubt that. The complex and multi-layered character of legal participants' understandings, attitudes and beliefs seems to defy judgments of importance.

To be sure, I do not preclude that, once the notion of such judgments is further developed, they may be found to be up to the task. Nor do I mean to say that,

[29] See Dickson, *Evaluation and Legal Theory* (n 2) 129.

if Dickson's solution is wanting, this automatically qualifies moral considerations as fit for the job. What I wanted to point out was that successful methodological proposals must take a certain shape and address certain puzzles. Effectively to engage with moralised jurisprudence, positivists have to show what it is about law (or perhaps more generally about philosophical accounts of concepts) that makes it the case that theories of law need not have resort to moral arguments. It is not enough to say that explication of a thing or concept (or, more specifically, law) is one thing and moral justification is quite another. For the soundness of this distinction is precisely what their opponents are disputing. In this debate there are no defaults.

2

The Metric Approach to Legal Normativity

TRIANTAFYLLOS GKOUVAS

I. Introduction

A recurring idea in this essay will be that despite their irreconcilable ideas on the nature of legal normativity, prominent analytic legal positivists and non-positivists share a methodological premise that merits greater visibility. This premise can be epitomised by the claim that any account of the normativity of law is answerable to the standards of robustness that govern ascriptions of ordinary reasons for action. I will venture to showcase this premise with a view to, hopefully, adding some depth to available metanormative disagreements in law. What I intend to argue is that discussions about the normative import of the law tend to measure the robustness of legal normativity by assessing its proximity to an ideal relation between normative reasons and the explanation of intentional action. Even for legal philosophers who favour a very thin account of legal normativity, the grounds of their deflationary approach are a function of their distance from the region of normative space featuring a synergy between the normative guidance of action, the evaluation of agents and the explanation of action.

In the first part of this essay I will associate this ideal standard of normative agency with what Joseph Raz has aptly described as the normative/explanatory *Nexus*. I will try to demonstrate how the *Nexus*, instead of mapping the entire domain of practical normativity, points to a specific region of normative space whose 'gravitational pull' attracts theories of legal normativity which postulate the existence of legal facts atop a stratified ontology featuring moral and/or social facts in its lower strata. To codify my argument I will be referring to this tendency as the *metric approach* precisely with a view to accentuating the role of the *Nexus* as a comparative standard of normative robustness. The metric approach will be presented as a *metanormative* thesis about the determinants of a legal theory's normative robustness.

To illustrate the specificity of the region of normative space occupied by *Nexus* reasons I will provide an anatomy of *Nexus* reasons by breaking them down into three distinct component functions (metaphysical, evaluative and explanatory). These functions will also provide the metrics of normative robustness of a theory of normativity. A genuine *Nexus* reason-giving fact will be further analysed as a fact that performs all three functions in a given context and, consequently, a theory of normativity will be maximally robust when and because the facts it identifies as normatively relevant are genuine *Nexus* reasons. Raising awareness about the 'demandingness' of the *Nexus* as a habitat for competing metanormative theories will serve as the background for making better sense of how and why available theories of legal normativity can be classified as thinner or more robust by reference to their approximation of the *Nexus* entanglement between action-guidance, evaluation and normative explanation.

In the next two parts I will try to associate the robustness of particular theories of legal normativity with the degree of their proximity to the *Nexus* space of reason-giving facts. A theory of legal normativity will be modelled as maximally robust if the facts it singles out as legal perform all the *Nexus* functions in a given context. More specifically, the second part will sample out Mark Greenberg's moral impact theory of law and Joseph Raz's theory of legal authority as the two theories of law which are metrically closest to the *Nexus* region. The third and final part will feature Ronald Dworkin's argument about the force of law and Scott Shapiro's account of the inner rationality of law as two distinct, yet metrically 'deviant' responses to the pressure to emulate the normativity of *Nexus* reasons.

II. The Three Functions of the *Nexus*

Joseph Raz's account of the *Nexus* is a remarkable leap forward thanks to the switch he endeavours from talk about the dependence of normativity on our beliefs about reasons to talk about *Reason* or, equivalently, our capacities *qua* rational agents. By allowing this switch Raz replaces the challenge of accounting for the mind-dependence of reasons with the challenge of accounting for the dependence of reasons on our rational functioning. It is precisely in the context of this switch that Raz's concept of the normative/explanatory *Nexus* becomes operative. Whereas traditional externalists about reasons affirm and internalists deny that there is always a reason to do what would in some respect be *right*,[1] Raz's *Nexus* provides a negative answer to the question of whether there is always a reason to do what would in some respect be *good*.[2] Reasons, according to Raz, must be

[1] The crux of the relevant controversy lies in identifying the relevance of facts about our actual or counterfactual motivational states for the grounding of facts about what reasons we have or what reasons there exist. Despite their strikingly conflicting internal divisions internalists hold that part of what it is for something to be a reason for action is that it must bear some relation to a motivational fact, whereas externalists model their position on the rejection of this schematic premise.

[2] By sharp contrast with the possibility of motivation the possibility of correctly exercising our rational powers does not track but limits the extension of the concept of a normative reason.

capable of guiding us, but not every fact that would make our actions good in a certain respect is a reason to act because there are values that we may not be able to recognise or respond to.

The *Nexus* is presented as an explanation of the occasional mismatch between response-dependent reasons and response-independent values by operating as a filter on what could count as a reason: reasons are such that they are capable of guiding our actions by virtue of our awareness of them. In Raz's own words,

> [t]he point is that normative reasons must be capable of providing an explanation of an action: If that R is a reason to φ then it must be possible that people φ for the reason R and when they do, that explains (is part of an explanation of) their action.[3]

The concepts of normative action-guidance, (the exercise of our) rational capacity and explanation of intentional action are the three components of the *Nexus* which I plan to recast in functional terms for the sake of rendering more intelligible their methodological relevance for a theory's normative robustness.

More precisely, I will suggest that what explains the eligibility of *Nexus* reasons for serving as a marker of normative robustness is the fact that *Nexus* cases are cases where one and the same reason-giving fact manages to simultaneously perform three distinct metanormative functions, each one corresponding to the three elements noted above, namely, normative action-guidance, the evaluation of the exercise of our rational capacities, and the explanation of actions done for reasons. Consequently, I will suggest that to say that a theory of legal normativity is robust with respect to the *Nexus* standards of reasonhood is to say that law-given reasons are such that they figure, within a given context, in three distinct metanormative claims about the performance of each function: (a) a metaphysical claim about which facts favour or mandate a particular response; (b) an evaluative claim about which facts serve as standards for appraising an agent's exercise of her rational capacities; and (c) an explanatory claim about which facts make normatively intelligible an event of intentional action.

To obtain a better view of how *Nexus* functions play out I suggest we take an ordinary descriptive fact like the fact that John's friend Mark is sick at the hospital as what could be eligible to perform all the functions associated with acting for a *Nexus* reason. The first function that a reason-giving fact can perform is metaphysical in the sense that the fact that Mark is sick at the hospital stands in a *normative relation of favouring* to John's act of visiting him. This relation could be easily reparsed as the claim that the fact that John's friend is sick at the hospital *is a reason* for John to visit him regularly. This is perhaps the most prominent function associated not just with ordinary descriptive facts but also with other types of normative fact like thin deontic facts or thick evaluative facts.

Our rational capacities perform this limiting task by way of indicating which values are apt for serving as a standard of our appraisal *qua* agents. For an elucidation of Raz's departure from a standard internalist conception of the normativity of reasons see U Heuer, 'Guided by Reasons: Raz on the Normative-Explanatory *Nexus*' (2012) 2 *Jurisprudence* 353.

[3] J Raz, *From Normativity to Responsibility* (Oxford, Oxford University Press, 2011) 27.

A second role that is frequently assigned to normatively salient facts is that of *being treated by an agent as a reason for action*. To treat a fact as reason-giving just is to exercise one's rational capacities in a certain way. Holding our exemplary fact about John's friend Mark fixed, we also care to ask what it is for John to treat the fact that Mark is sick at the hospital as a reason to visit Mark. What is distinctive of this kind of treating-as relation is its critical, evaluative function. For it to be the case that an agent treats a fact as a reason for action is for it to be the case that her action becomes *evaluatively* reflective of her in the sense that she can be characterised as being *responsive to reasons* or being *held accountable* in a more robust sense on the basis of the facts she *treated as* counting in favour of acting. Returning to John's example, his actually *treating* the fact that Mark is sick at the hospital as a reason to visit him entails that he merits to be evaluated as being properly responsive to the existence of normative reasons.[4]

Finally, we don't only care to justify our actions or attitudes and evaluate ourselves as agents but we also care to explain a series of event types like acting for a normative reason.[5] In our example, the fact that Mark is sick at the hospital will additionally stand in an *explanatory* relation to the event of 'John's having visited Mark at the hospital on Thursday evening'. Again there arises the question of how this explanatory role assumed by facts is normative in any informative sense. To adopt the view that facts can causally explain an action is to go back to a point where a conception of facts *as* reasons for action is dispensable unless one is willing to re-conceptualise the normative pressure exercised by reasons as a type of causation. In order to preserve the irreducibly normative relevance of reason-giving facts we need to accept that such facts can operate as *normative grounds* of atomic facts about what one did, thought or felt. On this approach, the same facts that favour a prospective action can rationalise, make normatively intelligible or right actual instances of acting for reasons, such that the link between the actual acting and the question of whether the action was called for in the first place remains unsevered.

In the remainder of this essay I will treat the case of reason-giving facts that perform these three functions as a specification of Joseph Raz's claim that

> every normative reason can feature in an explanation of the action for which it is a reason, as a fact that, being recognised for what it is, motivated the agent to perform the action, so that the agent guided its performance in light of that fact.[6]

[4] Thomas Scanlon makes a similar point about the evaluative function of moral principles. In his words, '[c]riticism of the way an agent decided what to do is unavoidably predicated on assumptions about the agent's state of mind – in particular about what he or she took into account in deciding what to do and took as reasons for and against acting as he or she did': TM Scanlon, *Moral Dimensions: Permissibility, Meaning, Blame* (Harvard MA, Belknap Press, 2008) 23.

[5] For two competing treatments of this question, see P Hieronymi, 'Reasons for Action' (2011) 111 *Proceedings of the Aristotelian Society* 407 and C Korsgaard, 'Acting for a Reason' in C Korsgaard, *The Constitution of Agency: Essays on Practical Reason and Moral Psychology* (Oxford, Oxford University Press, 2008) 207.

[6] Raz, *From Normativity to Responsibility* (above n 3) at 28.

In other words I shall shoulder the hypothesis that, barring cases of epistemic error or akratic will,[7] a reason-giving fact attains the normative/explanatory *Nexus* when and because it performs all three functions. A fact such as Mark's stay at the hospital performs the functions of favouring John's visit (metaphysical function), serving as a standard of John's rational evaluation (evaluative function) and making normatively intelligible the event of John's visit to the hospital (explanatory function).

III. Legal Reasons as *Nexus* Reasons

Following this digression into the functions composing a *Nexus* reason I will resume the progress of my argument and focus on the way in which the metanormative commitments of contemporary accounts of legal normativity – both non-positivist and positivist – can be taxonomised by reference to how closely they can afford to associate their account of legal facts with what could qualify as a proper *Nexus*-type reason for action. My contention will be that despite their radically opposed premises the exemplary theories of law I plan to examine converge with respect to how they measure the robustness of their metanormative commitments. For the sake of showcasing this metanormative convergence I will employ the functional analysis of the *Nexus* as a jurisprudentially neutral standard for positioning a theory of legal normativity on the normative/explanatory plane. The jurisprudential neutrality of the *Nexus* consists in the fact that it serves as a metanormative standard for measuring the normative robustness of a *theory* of legal normativity, not as an normative criterion for the individuation of a fact as a *legal* fact. This normative robustness will be a function of the capacity of a legal fact *as identified* by a given theory to perform in a given context the three functions I have associated with the *Nexus*.

Crucially, it will be a further, substantive issue whether a particular theory of law chooses to make the normative force of legal facts a condition of their existence. What matters is that from a methodological viewpoint the normativity and the existence of the law can be kept apart in the narrow sense that a *theory* of legal normativity can be normatively robust without premising the identity of legal facts on moral facts. In the light of these qualifications, the convergence I plan to attribute to my exemplary cases should not be considered as a sign of doubt about the extent to which legal positivism actually departs from the basic tenets that circumscribe non-positivist theories. This is a platitude I have no intention to

[7] An additional reason why this type of event – acting for a reason – merits special attention is that in a series of cases the reasons that actually explain and/or favour an action and the agent's own reasons for acting, ie the facts or putative facts the agent herself treats as normative reasons, seem to diverge. For a committed response to this puzzle see, among others, P Hieronymi, 'Reasons for Action' (n 5) and M Schroeder, 'Having Reasons' (2008) 139 *Philosophical Studies* 57.

refute precisely because I take it to be fairly uncontroversial that a legal positivist and a legal non-positivist do engage in a substantive and deep disagreement about the nature of law.

In what follows I will employ the tripartite distinction between the metaphysical, the evaluative and the explanatory functions of reason-giving facts in order to give a general description of when and how, by the lights of the metric approach, legal facts emulate the normative robustness of *Nexus* reasons for action. Given the reconstructive nature of this taxonomy my argument is in constant need of appeals to licensing evidence provided by recent debates in legal philosophy. Therefore, I carry the burden of locating those segments of actual jurisprudential discussions that purport to make a point similar to the ideas suggested by the 'functions jargon' I introduced in the previous part. From a first-order, jurisprudential viewpoint the legal facts of the kind envisaged by Joseph Raz's theory of authoritative directives and Mark Greenberg's theory of binding legal obligations cannot be subsumed under a single category. For Raz, legal facts are descriptive facts about the existence of legal norms whose content corresponds to the content of directives issued by a legal authority, whereas for Greenberg legal facts are normative facts that obtain by virtue of the fact that the actions of legal institutions have changed the morally relevant circumstances in 'the legally proper way'.

For the sake of registering this difference my claim about the metanormative convergence of these two theories will derive its force from available 'jurisprudential cues' encountered in contemporary debates. These cues are such that they register the first-order difference between these theories and also provide hints as to their metanormative convergence. In this part I will associate each of the three metanormative functions (metaphysical, evaluative, explanatory) of *Nexus* reasons with these jurisprudential cues in three respective sections. Each section will provide exegetical evidence of how Joseph Raz's theory of authority-based reasons and Mark Greenberg's theory of binding legal obligations conceptualise their common metanormative commitment to legal facts as genuine *Nexus* reasons.

A. The Metaphysical Function of Legal Facts

In this section I shall argue that Joseph Raz's understanding of legal directives as sources of content-independent reasons and Mark Greenberg's understanding of non-defective legal systems as the locus of genuinely binding legal obligations are jurisprudential 'cues' pointing to the metaphysical function of *Nexus* reasons. Beginning with the concept of content-independence[8] it should be noted that

[8] The term was coined by HLA Hart, see his 'Legal and Moral Obligation' in AI Melden (ed), *Essays in Moral Philosophy* (Seattle, University of Washington Press, 1958) 102, and *Essays on Bentham* (Oxford, Oxford University Press, 1982) 254–255. For a critical discussion of this notion *cf* P Markwick, 'Law and Content-Independent Reasons' (2000) 20(4) *Oxford Journal of Legal Studies* 579 and S Sciaraffa, 'On Content-Independent Reasons: It's Not in the Name' (2009) 28 *Law and Philosophy* 233.

it has acquired the shell of a technical term used by analytic legal philosophers to describe the broadly positivist claim that the obtaining of a reason relation between a legal fact and an act-type is independent of the directive's specific content and/or consequences. On pain of absurdity this claim does not entail the further claim that the obtaining of this relation is independent of the obtaining of any normative fact whatsoever. The only constraint it imposes is that *the normative fact* that a legal (descriptive) fact is a reason to φ is grounded in normative facts that are not about the *content* or the *essential function* of legal requirements. On this construal, the fact that it is legally obligatory to φ is a content-independent reason to φ in the sense that the reason why this fact and not another one is normatively salient has nothing to do with its constituent items – that is, with the moral merit of φ-ing or the consequences of its being authoritatively prescribed.[9]

Joseph Raz explicitly embraces content-independence as a prominent feature of the way in which legal facts, ie facts about the existence of legal norms, stand in a reason-giving relation to actions. Raz proceeds to incorporate the notion of content-independence into his theory of authority by noting that

> [a] reason is content-independent if there is no direct connection between the reason and the action for which it is a reason. The reason is in the apparently 'extraneous' fact that someone in authority has said so, and within certain limits his saying so would be reason for any number of actions, including (in typical cases) for contradictory ones. A certain authority may command me to leave the room or to stay in it. Either way, its command will be a reason. This marks authoritative reasons as content-independent. By this feature they can be distinguished from many reasons, including various other kinds of utterances that are reasons.[10]

At the same time Raz is cautious enough to add that it is not an exclusive mark of guidance by legal reasons, mainly because there are other groups of concepts like promises and vows, offers and threats or requests and commands that also operate on the model of content-independence.[11] Provided that legal authority is not the only type of authority capable of providing external guidance, Raz associates the notion of practical authority, ie the normative power of a person or institution to impose duties on others, with content-independent reasons precisely because their bindingness or, alternatively, the fact that they favour or require action is not grounded in the value of the content of these reasons but in the fact that they are proper manifestations of one's practical authority.

[9] I have deliberately chosen to avoid scholarly variations of the term 'content-independent reason' with a view to showcasing the core idea on which competing positivist theories seem to converge. For instance, in Raz's account of legal positivism the 'exegetical' analogue of content-independence would be the *first-order* component of a protected reason. In Raz's own unpacking of the term '[r]ules and commitments are what I call protected reasons, ie a systematic combination of a reason to perform the act one has undertaken to perform, or the one required by the rule, and an exclusionary reason not to act for certain reasons': J Raz, *Practical Reason and Norms*, with a new postscript (Oxford, Oxford University Press, 1999) 191.

[10] J Raz, *The Morality of Freedom* (Oxford, Oxford University Press, 1986) 35.

[11] ibid 35–37.

A non-positivist route for performing the metaphysical function of standing in a reason-giving relation to an agent and an action or attitude can be traced in the vocabulary used by Mark Greenberg in his elaboration of the 'bindingness hypothesis'. According to Greenberg, the bindingness hypothesis is a hypothesis about the way in which legal obligations are related to all things considered moral obligations. He proceeds to formulate this hypothesis by remarking that

> a legal system is supposed to operate by arranging matters in such a way as to reliably ensure that its legal obligations are all-things-considered morally binding (or, equivalently, that a legal system is *defective* to the extent that it does not so operate)' (emphasis added).[12]

Greenberg attempts to illustrate this claim by offering the example of the relation between the legal obligations about tax payment and the moral obligations about the redistribution of resources. If, in a particular legal system, there is a legal obligation to pay tax on one's income in accordance with a certain scheme the legal system will be morally defective to the extent that it remains morally permissible not to pay the income tax. Greenberg explicitly associates this remark with legal normativity when he clarifies that '[a]n intuitive way of putting the point is that the law is supposed to be binding, where that means genuinely binding all things considered – not just legally binding (which the law trivially is)'.[13]

Keeping this connection in mind we can see how his theory of legal normativity can be read as carrying a generic[14] claim about the way in which facts about the obtaining of legal obligations provide distinct reasons for action *by virtue of* their association with the institutional activity of a *non-defective* legal system. The crucial link in this analysis is to be found in Greenberg's choice to disassociate his own account of bindingness from general accounts of political legitimacy that purport to explain how we come to acquire a general moral obligation to obey the laws of our political community. Greenberg acknowledges that the bindingness hypothesis is amenable to an alternative formulation that features in its antecedent the possession of legitimate authority, and a general moral obligation to obey the law (political obligation) in its consequent. To avoid this route he draws a distinction between two putative ways in which the operations of legal systems can change the content of our moral reasons.

On the first approach which Greenberg explicitly associates with authority-based theories of law, legal systems achieve bindingness by possessing legitimate authority, that is, by arranging matters so that citizens have a general moral obligation to obey legally authoritative pronouncements.[15] This approach does not

[12] M Greenberg, 'The Standard Picture and Its Discontents' in L Green and B Leiter (eds), *Oxford Studies in Philosophy of Law*, vol I (New York, Oxford University Press, 2011) 39, 84.

[13] ibid.

[14] Genericity is used in the technical sense of denoting the cluster of properties associated with instances of a *kind* (natural, social, normative etc).

[15] ibid 97–100.

endow legal facts *themselves* with the power of generating particular reasons for action but rather switches their role into that of merely enabling conditions for the instantiation of a general moral obligation to obey what becomes part of the content of the law of a given system. By contrast, Greenberg's favoured approach purports to turn bindingness into a property of legal facts in the sense that a legal system operates properly when the actions of its institutions change the circumstances that in combination with the most fundamental moral truths or principles determine the content of our moral obligations. On this understanding, legal facts *just are* the moral impact of these new circumstances.

B. The Evaluative Function of Legal Facts

Moving to the second, evaluative standard for measuring a theory's responsiveness to the *Nexus* standards, the question we care to ask is how agents are evaluatively reflected in their law-conforming behaviour. As evidenced by the relevant literature, the most appealing option for the legal positivist is to associate one's treating a legal fact as a reason for action with one's being *rational* in following a legal directive. Arguments about the inner rationality of law or the rationality of being guided by authoritative rules are commonly used by positivist philosophers who want to keep their normative vocabulary free of thick moral terms like being law-abiding. On the other side of the spectrum, non-positivist appeals to the virtue of law-abidance or the praiseworthiness of giving weight to how the actions of legal institutions affect what we ought to do are, as expected, more apposite to the role assigned to morality by non-positivist theories of law. In this section I will follow the same pattern of exposition by illustrating how, despite differences in their conceptual vocabulary, the same two exemplary theories converge in their metanormative commitment to legal facts as standards of agential evaluation.

Joseph Raz's revisionist approach[16] to rule-guided behaviour is the main source of information as to how he prefers to model the evaluative impact of facts about the existence of legal norms. The gist of this approach is that under certain conditions it is rational to follow a rule even if the balance of reasons suggests otherwise. This general idea about how rules impact our practical reasoning is further specified by Raz's notion of authoritative *pre-emption*. In Raz's own words this model

[16] I borrow the term from Edward McClennen's taxonomy of theories of rule-based rationality. According to McClennen, '[t]he revisionist agrees with the compatibilist that rule-guided behavior does have a real place within an instrumental theory of justification, but one that forces us to revise the standard account of practical reasoning. The revisionist, then, denies that if the rule gives the wrong result it would be irrational to follow it' in EF McClennen, 'The Rationality of Being Guided by Rules' in A Mele and P Rawling (eds), *The Oxford Handbook of Rationality* (Oxford, Oxford University Press, 2004) 222, 225. He then immediately proceeds to classify Raz as a paradigmatic revisionist noting that revisionism has attracted a significant following in recent years.

states that 'an authoritative directive is not simply one reason to be added to the balancing of reasons in determining how to act', but 'should exclude and take the place of some of them.'[17] Reparsed as a principle of rationality, pre-emption can be also understood as stipulating that it is irrational not to take the directive as excluding certain first-order reasons[18] from the process of balancing because that would amount to counting the reasons behind the directed action twice: once in the balancing done by the agent herself, and again in establishing the reason backing the authoritative directive.[19]

My reconstructive intervention consists in my proposing an understanding of Raz's notion of pre-emption and the auxiliary concept of an exclusionary reason as elements of an evaluative account of what it is to be 'legally' rational rather than as elements of a metaphysical account of how legal reasons exclude other reasons by virtue of their kind and not by virtue of their weight. There is an abundant secondary literature that purports to make sense of how reasons of authority are endowed with this exceptional capacity of excluding other reasons from being part of the case for an action.[20] A promising way to see that, despite his occasionally ambiguous prose, Raz treats exclusionary reasons not as a literal addition to the metaphysical inventory of normative entities but as an account of what it is *for an agent* to reason with rules is to focus on his distinction between the behaviour of *conforming* and the behaviour of *complying* with a reason. In the postscript to the second edition of *Practical Reason and Norms* Raz sets out to clarify how he purports to use the concept of an exclusionary reason by employing an informative distinction between conforming with a reason simply by way of acting as it dictates, and complying with a reason by way of treating the relevant consideration as what makes one's action worthy of being performed.[21] With this distinction at

[17] Raz, *The Morality of Freedom* (n 10) 58.

[18] There has been a gradual shift in Raz's view about the type of first-order reasons that are subject to exclusion. In the second edition of *Practical Reason and Norms*, Raz suggests that 'one ought to exclude all the reasons both for and against [the prescribed act] which were within the jurisdiction of the authority': J Raz, *Practical Reason and Norms*, with a new postscript (Oxford, Oxford University Press, 1999) 191; see also J Raz, 'Facing Up: A Reply' (1989) 62 *Southern California Law Review* 1153, 1194. In later work he confines the scope of exclusion to first-order reasons against an act prescribed by a rule claiming that '[t]he service conception [of authority] expresses that thought by the thesis that authoritative directives preempt those reasons against the conduct they require that the authority was meant to take into account in deciding to issue its directives': 'The Problem of Authority: Revisiting the Service Conception' (2006) 90 *Minnesota Law Review* 1003, 1018. For a critical account of Raz's oscillation with regard to the scope of exclusion see C Essert, 'A Dilemma for Protected Reasons' (2012) 31 *Law and Philosophy* 49.

[19] Raz, *The Morality of Freedom* (n 10) 58.

[20] Kenneth Ehrenberg locates the same ambivalence when he remarks that, literally speaking, authoritative directives purport to track the *reasons* that apply to those subject to legal authority, rather than the *reasoning* that leads an agent to act in conformity with those reasons. Ehrenberg frames this distinction as holding between law's claiming authority and law's demanding that we treat authoritative directives as preemptive: see K Ehrenberg, 'Law's Authority is not a Claim to Preemption' in W Waluchow and S Sciaraffa (eds), *Philosophical Foundations of the Nature of Law* (Oxford, Oxford University Press, 2013) 51.

[21] Raz, *Practical Reason and Norms* (n 18) 178–90.

hand Raz proceeds to label exclusionary reasons as negative second-order reasons whose distinctive mark is that they count against complying (rather than just conforming) with other reasons to act in particular ways. It is the latter association that lends definitive support to the evaluative (rather than metaphysical) function of exclusion.

Consequently, it is possible to argue that whereas the only thing that happens from a strictly metaphysical point of view is the fact that a legal norm exists or provides a first-order, content-independent reason to act as the norm stipulates, there is a another, evaluative level at which an agent is required *not to treat* (or equivalently *not to comply with*) competing first-order reasons as bearing on the question of whether to act in conformity with a legal norm. This second level is not meant to qualify what it is for a legal fact *to be* a reason for action but rather what it is for an agent to *treat a legal fact as a reason for action.* To treat a legal fact as a reason to φ just is to treat it as an exclusionary reason which further entails that one must not treat other facts as reasons for not φ-ing.

On this approach it is easy to see how pre-emption can be understood as Raz's preferred specification of the evaluative role of legal facts. What marks the evaluative dimension of pre-emption is precisely the evaluative property of *irrationality* attached to agents who fail to appreciate the exclusionary force of legal reasons. In the present context, the rationality of being guided by legal rules is supposed to be evidenced by the fact that law-conforming agents are more likely to conform with reasons that apply to them independently of the legal authority's say-so by treating a legal fact as an exclusionary reason, namely, *by not treating other non-legal facts as reasons not to act in conformity with a legal norm.*[22] Consequently, a positivist like Raz could claim that legal facts perform the evaluative function of the *Nexus* in the sense that treating them as (exclusionary) reasons for action constitutes an instance of rational behaviour.

On the opposite side of the jurisprudential spectrum rationality gives way to moral standards of appraisal that fit better with the pivotal role non-positivist philosophers accord to morality. There are at least two ways in which a non-positivist can explain what it is to treat a legal fact as a reason for action. The first and perhaps most prominent way is virtue-ethical in spirit as it features law-abidance as the primary evaluative property. John Finnis attempts to locate a solution to the problem of 'how an obligation-imposing law provides a reason for action which would not exist independently of that law'[23] in the idea that

[22] Raz's own distinction between mere conformity and compliance with reasons counts in favour of this reparsing of exclusionary reasons as a rational property which agents can be possessed of if they choose not to act on competing first-order reasons. In this vein, exclusionary reasons – as opposed to the first-order reasons they purport to protect – are such that they can only be complied with (not conformed) precisely because their function becomes apparent as soon as the agent acts in recognition of the value involved in authoritative guidance.

[23] J Finnis, *Natural Law and Natural Rights*, revised edition (Oxford, Oxford University Press, 2011) 314.

a correct way to identify 'the law-abiding subject's practical reasoning'[24] is to reason as follows:

A We need for the sake of common good, to be law-abiding.

B But where φ is stipulated by law as obligatory, the only way to be law-abiding is to do φ.

C Therefore, we need [it is obligatory for us] to do φ where φ has been legally stipulated to be obligatory.[25]

On this broadly natural law-inspired conception, legal facts perform an evaluative function to the extent that they serve as standards for the attribution of the virtue of law-abidance. Crucially, law-abidance as a virtue does not amount to a disposition to obey the law *qua* law regardless of its moral merits. As William Edmundson explains, '[t]he law-abiding regard the law as invariably a reason for action, but they are not generally disposed to obey regardless of their own assessments of the moral and rational merits'.[26]

On a more deontological approach the normative impact of treating legal facts as reasons for action need not involve the attribution of a virtuous disposition to agents. The same evaluative task can be carried out in relational terms in the sense that agents who treat their legal obligations as generating reasons for action are considered as morally praiseworthy by their fellow-citizens. I must confess that I lack sufficient textual evidence for positioning Greenberg's account of legal bindingness within the thick-thin spectrum of moral evaluation. That being said, there are occasions in his writings where he talks about our 'abiding concern'[27] with law remarking that 'the way in which the law is supposed to generate an obligation for a person to act is not by giving the person extremely strong prudential reasons, in particular by threatening that person with sanctions'.[28] Greenberg contrasts this legally improper way of ensuring bindingness with what he calls the *legally proper* way of giving agents reasons for action. Part of what makes this reason-giving legally proper is that legal requirements are not treated as merely prudential reasons for action.

On Greenberg's account properly generated legal obligations are those that are morally binding all things considered. In that sense we are allowed to assume that what it is for an agent to treat a legal fact as reason for action must be similar to what it is for the same agent to treat a moral fact, that is, a fact about her all things considered moral obligation, as a reason for action. Consequently, it would make sense to attribute to Greenberg the view that treating one's binding legal obligations as reasons for action serves as a standard of moral praise much in the same

[24] ibid 315.
[25] ibid 316.
[26] WA Edmundson, 'The Virtue of Law-Abidance' (2006) 6 *Philosophers' Imprint* 1, 3.
[27] M Greenberg, 'The Moral Impact Theory of Law' (2014) 123 *Yale Law Journal* 1288, 1341.
[28] Greenberg, 'The Standard Picture and Its Discontents' (n 12) 83.

way that acting in recognition of one's moral obligations makes a person morally praiseworthy.

C. The Explanatory Function of Legal Facts

For a complete view of what it is for a legal fact to operate as a *Nexus* reason we need to fix one more parameter. What we have seen so far is that both Raz's and Greenberg's theories of law are robust enough to allow legal facts to operate as reasons for action and also be evaluatively relevant. What remains is a positive answer to the question of whether legal facts can also serve as normative explanations of law-conforming behaviour. In this regard, I shall argue that both positivist and non-positivist *Nexus* variants of the metric approach have a strongly similar conception of how normative explanations of law-conforming behaviour are to be modelled. I shall argue that whereas both positivist and non-positivist simulations of the *Nexus* model are committed to a subsumptive model of normative explanation,[29] they differ with respect to how they define the counterfactual 'tenacity' of legal facts.

In the positivist framework the counterfactual stability of legal facts is commonly cashed out in terms of a 'general efficacy' condition on legal systems. The latter term can be understood in dispositional terms such that the norms constituting the content of the law of a legal system at a particular time are such that they are normally obeyed.[30] On this construal a legal fact can enjoy the status of an explanatory generalisation so long as it can exhibit a sufficient degree of invariance under counterfactual perturbations. This scope of invariance may include platitudes to the effect that a legal norm would have still been complied with even if law-subjects do not actually attach any moral value to it. The latter counterfactual can be supported by a legal fact for as long as it remains conceptually consistent with what is conceptually entailed by one's jurisprudential theory.

Joseph Raz's specification of the efficacy of legal norms involves a shift of focus from the practices of law-enforcing institutions to the practices of law-applying institutions. In his own words,

> Efficacy … is relevant only insofar as it affects the practices of the law-applying institutions. If, for example, the courts consistently refuse to act on a law, that law is

[29] Mark Schroeder informatively associates representatives of the British moral rationalist movement of the 18th century like Ralph Cudworth, Samuel Clarke and Richard Price with what he describes as the standard model of normative explanation. In Schroeder's reconstructive definition of the subsumptive model of normative explanation '[t]he explanation that *X* ought to do *A* because *P* follows the *Standard Model* just in case it works because there is (1) some further action *B* such that *X* ought to do *B* and (2) not just because P and (3) P explains why doing *A* is a *way* for *X* to do *B*' in M Schroeder, 'Normative Explanations' (2005) 1 *Journal of Ethics & Social Philosophy* 1, 11.

[30] S Shapiro, *Legality* (Cambridge MA, Harvard University Press, 2011) 202. More traditional accounts of the notion of efficacy can be found in the work of HLA Hart and John Austin. Hart thought that general conformity is a necessary but not sufficient condition of efficacy, noting that an attitude of

> not part of the legal system the courts operate, despite the fact that it was lawfully enacted and was never repealed … According to this approach, then, the existence of the law is logically related to the practice of the law-applying organs.[31]

Raz proceeds to associate this conception of efficacy in application with what he takes to be the proper type of counterfactual supported by facts about the existence of legal norms. The definition he stands up for serves to mitigate the demandingness of general efficacy by focusing on the counterfactual attitude of recognition of the validity of a legal norm by the courts. He notes that

> [t]he condition of a law's membership in a legal system is, however, a counterfactual: if presented with the appropriate case the courts would act on the law.[32] This may be true even though they are never- or seldom-presented with the appropriate case. Prosecutions in criminal cases may seldom be made, and civil cases may always be settled out of court in a way contrary to the law. Therefore a law may be valid even though it is largely inefficacious.[33]

By sharp contrast, a non-positivist cannot avail herself of the counterfactual stability of generally efficacious legal systems as a basis for the explanatory potency of legal facts. The reason is that for a non-positivist the explanatory potency of legal facts is not a function of their attachment to a legal system which enjoys general obedience, but rather a function of their normative force or, equivalently, bindingness. Mark Greenberg makes this point when he claims that the actions of legal institutions are supposed to make the moral situation better by ensuring that the legal obligations they create provide decisive reasons for action. Greenberg makes this point explicit by combining two claims about the nature of legal systems. The first claim is already familiar; it states that legal systems are supposed to ensure that the actions of legal institutions generate legal obligations that are morally binding. The second claim is that

> it is part of the nature of law that a legal system is supposed to change our moral obligations in order to improve our moral situation – not, of course, that legal systems always improve our moral situation, but that they are defective as legal systems to the extent that they do not.[34]

acceptance of the system's secondary rules is what ultimately determines the quality of a legal system's efficacy through time. See his *The Concept of Law*, 2nd edn with postscript by J Raz and P Bulloch (eds), (Oxford, Oxford University Press, 1994) 100–101. Given his reductive view on law John Austin, on the other hand, was led to associate the efficacy of law not just with the degree of actual conformity with the law (the habit of obedience as he calls it), but with the upholding of sovereignty. See his *Lectures on Jurisprudence or the Philosophy of Positive Law*, 4th edn, revised and edited by Robert Campbell, vol 1 (London, John Murray; reprint, Bristol, Thoemmes Press, 2002) 220–21.

[31] J Raz, 'The Identity of Legal Systems' (1971) 59 *California Law Review* 795, 803–804.

[32] At a later point Raz introduces a probabilistic criterion that can be authentically determined by the law-applying institutions of a given system. According to this criterion, a legal system and consequently its norms remain efficacious 'if a certain ratio of cases of obedience to its laws to the total number of opportunities to obey them obtains': J Raz, *The Concept of a Legal System: An Introduction to the Theory of the Legal System*, 2nd edn (Oxford, Clarendon Press, 1980) 203.

[33] Raz, 'The Identity of Legal Systems' (n 31) 804.

[34] Greenberg, 'The Moral Impact Theory of Law' (n 27) 1294.

The combination of these two claims results in the view that a legal system is supposed not merely to produce binding legal obligations, but to do so in a way that improves the moral situation. With this combined claim at hand we may proceed to formulate a condition of counterfactual stability for legal facts that does not depend on a general efficacy clause, but rather invokes the bindingness of legal facts as the basic criterion of counterfactual tenacity. In other words, the idea is that legal facts will be capable of explaining atomic instances of law-conforming behaviour to the extent that, *despite their violability*, they remain morally binding in what Greenberg calls the *legally proper way*.[35] Much in the same way that the explanatory status of moral principles is not affected by their actual violation, general legal obligations do not lose their explanatory potency just because they are violated in practice. So long as they are binding in a way that makes the moral situation better, they retain their capacity to serve as normative explanations of actual conduct.

IV. Loosing the *Nexus*

In the remainder of this essay I would like to steer the discussion back to its original claim that the metric approach to legal normativity also applies to jurisprudential theories that choose to resist to some degree the gravitational pull of the *Nexus*, yet remain answerable to its constraints. The way for a 'deviant' jurisprudential theory to remain 'metrically' answerable to the *Nexus* standards is to explicitly or implicitly acknowledge that legal facts may, either occasionally or systematically, need supplementation by extra-legal facts in order to account for the performance of one the three functions that constitute a *Nexus* reason. Occasional supplementation may be necessary when, for instance, despite its proper grounding in legal practice a legal fact fails to perform its *evaluative* function because it fails to make its violation a ground for holding someone all-things-considered responsible for not being legally compliant. Conversely, systematic supplementation may be needed when legal facts are modelled in a way that premises their *explanatory* potency on their being contextually coupled with other reasons, prudential and/or moral, such that legally compliant actions can never be rendered normatively intelligible solely by reference to legal facts. In what follows I will associate Ronald Dworkin's account of the force of law with the occasional variant of normative supplementation and

[35] In a footnote to 'The Moral Impact Theory of Law' Greenberg acknowledges the strong connection between the notion of the legally proper way of changing the moral profile and the improvement of the moral situation. He notes that 'it is part of the Moral Impact Theory that the legal institutions that are relevant for its purposes – the ones that generate those moral obligations that are legal obligations – are ones that are supposed to improve the moral situation … this point is really an elaboration of the notion of the legally proper way of changing the moral profile … That is, in order for a change in the moral profile to come about in the legally proper way, it must be the result of action by a legal institution that, by its nature, is supposed to improve the moral situation' (ibid 1324).

Scott Shapiro's account of the inner rationality of law with the systematic variant of normative supplementation. What matters for our present purpose is that both theories provide evidence for taking them to be partial departures from a robust, *Nexus*-based conception of legal normativity.

Starting with Dworkin's account of the force of law I will try to demonstrate how his main concern about the normative demands of law can be recast as a metanormative objection to theories of legal normativity that relate the reason-giving force of legal facts to their capacity to guide civilian conduct. Our first acquaintance with the concept of the force of law takes place in *Law's Empire*, where Dworkin illustratively divides the path to law's imperial realm into two main routes, the grounds of law which regard the grounds of legal facts, and the force of law,[36] which Dworkin defines as 'the relative power of any true proposition of law to justify coercion in different sorts of exceptional circumstances'.[37] Dworkin appeals to ordinary legal practice to justify this distinction, noting that '[o]ur lawyers and citizens recognise a difference between the question what the law is and the question whether judges or any other official or citizen should enforce or obey the law'.[38] The same point is presented as being verified on theoretical grounds. In this regard, Dworkin supplements his phenomenological claim with the claim that 'conceptions of law, which are theories about the grounds of law, commit us to no particular or concrete claims about how citizens should behave or judges should decide cases'.[39]

As already evidenced by these textual references, Dworkin clearly associates the normative force of 'true legal propositions', or, in more precise language, of legal facts, with their capacity to justify the enforcement of a right or obligation on demand. Dworkin repeats that same point in his latest work when he remarks that 'legal rights [and their correlative duties] are those that people are entitled to enforce on demand, without further legislative intervention, in adjudicative institutions that direct the executive power of sheriff or police'.[40] This association between legal facts and reasons for enforcement on demand is accompanied by a distinction between the institutional reasons for enforcement provided by legal facts and the reasons for action provided by the obtaining of a political obligation, namely a general moral obligation to obey the law.

[36] Dworkin locates the bond between these two components in the fact that the grounds of law are also part of what grounds the normative fact that law provides reasons for enforcement upon demand. In his words, '[t]hese two parts must be mutually supportive. The attitude a full theory takes up on the question how far law is commanding, and when it may or should be set aside, must match the general justification it offers for law's coercive mandate, which in turn is drawn from its views about the controversial grounds of law': R Dworkin, *Law's Empire* (Cambridge MA, Belknap Press, 1986) 110.

[37] ibid 110. In a similar vein Dworkin intensifies the connection between legal facts and reasons for enforcement when he remarks that 'in a flourishing legal system the fact of law provides a case for coercion that must stand unless some exceptional counterargument is available' (ibid).

[38] ibid 109.

[39] ibid 112.

[40] R Dworkin, *Justice for Hedgehogs* (Cambridge MA, Harvard University Press, 2011) 406.

Dworkin frames this distinction as being between the problem of the legitimacy of coercive power and the problem of political obligation. In this regard he notes that the former problem

> rides on the back of another classical problem: that of political obligation. Do citizens have genuine moral obligations just in virtue of law? Does the fact that a legislature has enacted some requirement in itself give citizens a moral as well as a practical reason to obey?[41]

Dworkin is willing to assert that there is such a thing as a general moral obligation to obey the law, which he further unpacks as a kind of associative obligation. At this level the morality of political association tracks the content of the law by requiring whatever the law requires at a particular instance. As he remarks,

> [t]hese two issues – whether the state is morally legitimate, in the sense that it is justified in using force against its citizens, and whether the state's decisions impose genuine obligations on them – are not identical. No state should enforce all of a citizen's obligations. But though obligation is not a sufficient condition for coercion, it is close to a necessary one.[42]

What enables Dworkin to separate these two questions and associate only the former question of legitimate coercion with the subject matter of legal normativity is the contrast he implies between the facts that provide reasons for enforcement and the facts that provide reasons for conformity. In virtue of their more specific meaning as facts about the instantiation of principles of political morality by obligations or rights, legal facts are facts that purport to guide a state's adjudicative and executive institutions in realising, ie enforcing on demand, the content of rights and duties that best justify both past instances of coercive enforcement as well as current announcements about the future use of force or the imposition of sanctions.

It is because of Dworkin's disassociation of reasons for enforcement – or legal reasons proper – and reasons for compliance – political associative reasons – that his theory of the force of law resists the full grip of the *Nexus* quadrant. More specifically, the reason is that for Dworkin legal facts *qua* reasons purport to perform the metaphysical and explanatory functions of requiring and making normatively intelligible a particular response (enforcement) in a given context (upon official demand), but fall short of always providing the basis for a sufficient *evaluation* of official actors who are tasked with enforcing the law and of citizens who are bound by legal duty. From the viewpoint of law as integrity, facts that provide standards for evaluating the merit or demerit of official or civilian compliance or non-compliance are occasionally furnished by extra-legal considerations.

[41] Dworkin, *Law's Empire* (n 36) 191.

[42] ibid. Venturing a guess, I believe that Dworkin thought that one is entitled to preserve both aspects of bindingness so long as she disassociates the concept of authority understood as the normative power to impose duties on others from the theory of what brings legal obligations and rights into existence.

In Dworkin's assessment integrity in the enforcement of claims of legal right will often be realised in such a way that the same legally relevant concerns will point in the same direction, both with respect to whether law-subjects are politically obligated to obey the law and with respect to whether the coercive direction of their action by the state is permissible. That being said, there will be cases where the reasons that settle the question of whether to enforce the law all things considered are provided by facts that lack morally relevant institutional pedigree. This was the case with the Fugitive Slave Act, where what determined *what the law was* before the American Civil War failed to also give *normative force* to this law. In Dworkin's words,

> [t]he structuring fairness principles that make law a distinct part of political morality – principles about political authority, precedent, and reliance – gave the slaveholders' claims more moral force than they would otherwise have had. But their moral claims were nevertheless and undoubtedly undermined by a stronger moral argument of human rights. *So the law should not have been enforced*' (emphasis added).[43]

In such cases and, perhaps, in other less morally egregious ones, facts about what the law requires will need to be supplemented by other, morally relevant facts in order to reach a final verdict as to whether state officials who are tasked with enforcing the law are answerable for deciding not to enforce it, as well as whether the responsibility of citizens who decide to resist the enforcement of a morally questionable legal requirement is mitigated by the fact that the coercive direction of their action is not – all things considered – permissible. It is precisely in this sense that Dworkin's argument about the force of law remains metrically answerable to the *Nexus even though* it purports to loosen its grip on the reason-giving force of legal facts. In other words, insofar as legal facts are not supposed to be intrinsically capable of unexceptionally governing the evaluation of legally relevant actions, there will occasionally be competing concerns about whether legal officials merit an exonerating evaluation for declining to perform their duty to enforce the law, or whether citizens are less or not responsible for revolting against the enforcement of laws.

The second instance of metanormative divergence from the *Nexus* is lucidly represented by Scott Shapiro's planning account of legal normativity. In what follows I will be referring to his account as a thesis about the inner rationality of law, a term which Shapiro describes as the body of rational requirements applicable in a given legal system.[44] Shapiro is willing to acknowledge that his account of legal normativity is rather thin, claiming that '[t]he inner rationality of law, of course, is a limited *set of constraints* because the rational norms of planning

[43] Dworkin, *Justice for Hedgehogs* (n 40) 411.

[44] Shapiro attributes the ownership of this term to Michael Bratman, who in turn has adapted Lon Fuller's famous phrase 'the inner morality of law' (see M Bratman, 'Reflections on Law, Normativity and Plans' in S Bertea and G Pavlakos (eds), *New Essays on the Normativity of Law* (Oxford, Hart Publishing, 2011) 73, 81).

only apply to those who accept plans' (emphasis added).[45] Moreover, his way of associating the normativity of law with the normativity of rational constraints is indicative of the way he implements the metric approach, in the sense that he presents the rational normativity of 'legal' plans as a token of weaker normativity in comparison to the reason-giving normativity of moral facts. In his words,

> the normativity of the master plan of a legal system is of *a very limited sort. While legal officials are rationally required to conform to their shared plan, it is also true that those who do not accept the law are not similarly bound.* Furthermore, the master plan of a legal system may be morally illegitimate and hence not capable of imposing a moral obligation on anyone to obey' (emphasis added).[46]

The model Shapiro employs to describe the normative function of the practice of legal officials strongly resembles the type of normative pressure involved in ordinary instrumental reasoning. Legal officials adopt a master plan as a very general means of rectifying the moral deficiencies associated with the circumstances of legality.[47] Shapiro is willing to accept that there is clear evidence of normative pressure with regard to the activity of legal planning. In particular, he associates this normativity with the normativity of facts about the adoption of plans. According to Shapiro, the latter type of planning normativity piggybacks on the obtaining of two attitudinal facts: (a) the fact that the legal officials *believe* that a given sub-plan is a means of serving the purposes set out in the legal system's master plan; and (b) the fact that legal officials *represent* the system's master plan as a morally legitimate solution for what has been identified as morally problematic or contentious in a given community. Consequently, the normative pattern that plays out bifurcates in two consecutive theses:

(i) *Authorisation Thesis:* The fact that the legal officials of *S* represent the Master Plan *M* of *S* as a morally legitimate response to the circumstances of legality gives rise to a rational requirement to [intend to plan for others, if they represent M as morally legitimate].

(ii) *Inner Rationality of Law Thesis*: The fact that the legal officials of *S* believe that plan *P* is a means to implement the Master Plan *M* of *S* gives rise to a rational requirement to [intend to fulfil, monitor and readjust *P* if the legal officials of *S* represent *M* as morally legitimate].

The first normative thesis makes a general claim about what type of normative requirement flows from another metaphysical thesis, which Shapiro calls the 'Moral Aim Thesis'. According to the latter thesis, 'the fundamental aim of legal activity is to remedy the moral deficiencies of the circumstances of legality'.[48] The *Authorisation Thesis* just states the normative consequences of the *Moral Aim Thesis.*

[45] Shapiro, *Legality* (n 30) 183.
[46] ibid 170.
[47] ibid 213.
[48] ibid 213.

What it says is that facts about the representation of the master plan of a legal system as serving a moral aim are normatively relevant by virtue of their giving rise to a rational requirement of instrumental consistency. This rational requirement should be read as taking wide scope over a conditional featuring the acceptance of the system's master plan as its content.[49] In this way we can say that the rational requirement to plan for others can be satisfied in two normatively asymmetrical ways. One way is for the group of high-ranking legal officials to abandon their commitment to representing this particular master plan as morally legitimate. The other way is for the same group to engage in the activity of producing plans for law-subjects. The only state of affairs that this type of requirement prohibits is the simultaneous preservation of a moral representation of the master plan and an akratic reaction towards the activity of planning for others. Beyond this negative prohibition nothing about this requirement per se can provide decisive guidance as to how to run a legal system.

Moving to the second thesis, it is fairly obvious that its function is ancillary to the foundational function of the rational requirement to plan for others. All it says is that there must be a rational pattern in realising the legal activity of planning for others. In this regard it appears that the inner rationality of law consists in a set of rational requirements whose object is again a conditional rather than a particular response or course of action. This is a typical instance of a law-specific wide-scope principle of instrumental rationality which by itself fails to provide robust guidance as to how to proceed all things considered. The reason is that the above requirement can be satisfied in at least two ways that mark a distinct normative asymmetry. More precisely, a legal official can satisfy this requirement either by intending to fulfil the plan or by ceasing to sincerely or professedly represent the plan as morally necessitated by the system's master plan. From the point of view of planning rationality, the only normative constraint that obtains is that a legal official is necessary irrational if she persists in combining the following pair of attitudes: representing the system's master plan as morally legitimate *and* failing to intend to fulfil the plan that facilitates the master plan's implementation.

The upshot of these exegetical remarks is that, whereas Dworkin's departure from the *Nexus* is licensed by his choice not to reserve a robust *evaluative* role for legal facts, Shapiro's account reserves a robust role for the evaluation of the instrumental rationality of legal officials at the expense, however, of the *explanatory potency* of legal plans. In other words, according to plan positivism, facts about the existence of legal plans are sufficiently dispositive of how the behaviour of legal officials is constrained and evaluated within the scope of a legal system's master plan but they remain systematically incapable of making normatively intelligible particular choices within the scope of a plan. The reason is that by the lights of

[49] For a more extensive defence of the wide-scope account of rational requirements see, among many, J Brunero, 'The Scope of Rational Requirements' (2010) 60 *Philosophical Quarterly* 28; J Way, 'Defending the Wide-Scope Approach to Instrumental Reason' (2010) 147 *Philosophical Studies* 213.

plan positivism the activity of legal officials is subject to constraints and evaluative[50] standards solely from the viewpoint of instrumental rationality. Beyond the avoidance of rational inconsistencies legal plans have no *explanatory* normative role to play in the sense that they cannot themselves settle the question of which way of responding to a plan is the normatively optimal one. Legal plans as such can never figure autonomously in what renders legal activity normatively intelligible precisely because their existence merely prohibits inconsistencies in the attitudes that give rise to these plans. Consequently, legal plans *systematically* necessitate their supplementation by moral facts in order to provide a full explanation of actions that purport to count as implementations of these plans.

[50] This is clearly evidenced by Shapiro's comment that 'an official who accepts her position within an authority structure will be rationally criticisable if she disobeys her superiors, fails to flesh out their orders so that she may take the means necessary to satisfy their demands, adopts plans that are inconsistent with these orders, or reconsiders them without a compelling reason to do so' Shapiro (n 30) 183.

PART II

On the Nature of Legal Normativity/ Legal Obligation

3

The Nature of Legal Obligation*

BRIAN H BIX

I. Introduction

In this paper, I want to explore two basic questions about the nature of law and legal obligation. First, to what extent is legal obligation or legal normativity 'optional', a matter of choice? This is an indirect way of exploring the claims scholars have made about law – and also about the role of the legal scholar. Legal theorists claim that they must 'explain the normativity of law', the way that law gives us reasons for action. I think it worth considering, first, whether – or when – law gives us reasons for action. Hans Kelsen's legal theory (or at least one reading of it) will be used as a useful starting point for this discussion.

Secondly, the paper will consider to what extent legal obligation is *sui generis*, its own distinctive form of normativity, as contrasted to being a form or subset of moral obligation. To put the point a different way: does a statement like 'X has a *legal obligation* to do A' reduce to statements of a different normative form (for example, regarding X's *moral* obligations)?[1] Here, works by HLA Hart and Mark Greenberg will be the starting points, with Hart exemplifying the idea of law as a distinct form of obligation, and Greenberg portraying law as a subset of morality.

* An earlier version of this paper was presented at the Singapore Symposium in Legal Theory, National University of Singapore, and at Magna Graecia University, Catanzaro, Italy, and I am grateful to the participants at those presentations for their comments and suggestions. This paper further develops ideas first presented at Conferences on Rules in Krakow and on Kelsen in Chicago, and I also want to thank those present at those gatherings for their comments and suggestions. Those papers were subsequently published as: BH Bix, 'Kelsen in the US: Still Misunderstood' in J Telman (ed), *Hans Kelsen in America – The Anxieties of Non-Influence* (Dordrecht, Springer, 2016) 17; BH Bix, 'Rules and Normativity in Law' in T Gizbert-Studnicki, K Płeszka, M Arszkiewicz and P Banas (eds), *Problems of Normativity, Rules and Rule Following* (Dordrecht, Springer, 2015) 125.

[1] In other contexts, the question would be whether a statement of legal obligation reduces to a factual claim – eg, a prediction of what judges and other legal officials will do. That is a different (though still important) debate, for another occasion.

II. The Nature of Legal Obligation – Question 1: Normativity as a Matter of Choice?

Is law generally normative for all citizens, or only for those citizens who so choose? I want to approach this question through the works of Hans Kelsen. Kelsen's legal theory emphasises the normative and systemic nature of law. Kelsen focuses on David Hume's insight that normative conclusions could not be grounded on non-normative (empirical) premises – no deriving 'ought' from 'is', ie no conclusion about what one ought to do can be derived from statements regarding what is the case. Thus, every normative conclusion requires a normative premise, and any normative system would require a hierarchy leading to a foundational axiom.[2] Validity and authorisation can be traced, ultimately to the most basic norm of the system, which, in the case of legal systems, Kelsen calls the *Grundnorm* – the Basic Norm. In Kelsen's theory of (legal) norms, every 'ought' claim implies the (presupposition of the) Basic Norm. As Kelsen notes, the likely content of a legal system's *Grundnorm* will be something like 'act according to the norms of the historically first constitution'.[3]

Again, I cannot emphasise strongly enough: much of Kelsen's work, and much of the argument I am presenting here, is grounded on this separation of is and ought, on the inability to derive normative conclusions (like 'one ought to do X') from statements of what is the case or what happened (like 'certain legal officials acted in a certain way'). This is a matter we will, necessarily, return to again later in the paper.

Under one reading of Kelsen's work (which I have elaborated at greater length elsewhere),[4] whether citizens presuppose the Basic Norm for their community's legal system is, in a basic sense, optional.[5] For example, Kelsen notes that

[2] H Kelsen, *Introduction to the Problems of Legal Theory*, BL Paulson and SL Paulson trans (Oxford, Clarendon Press, 1992) 55–56. Once one views normative systems as hierarchical structures that are grounded ultimately on a foundational norm that (by definition – as a foundational norm) is not subject to any further (direct) proof, the implications are potentially significant, and potentially sceptical. If the important normative systems of one's life, like morality, religion, and law, are perhaps grounded on an ultimate norm that cannot be proven and can be accepted or rejected with seemingly equal legitimacy, then those important guideposts of our life suddenly seem less sturdy. However, these implications must be left to others to discuss, or for other occasions.

[3] Kelsen, *Introduction to the Problems of Legal Theory* (n 2) 56–57.

[4] Bix, 'Kelsen in the US: Still Misunderstood' (n *); BH Bix, 'Rules and Normativity in Law' (n *) 125.

[5] For a good overview of the different tenable readings of Kelsen's writings on the Basic Norm, see SL Paulson, 'A "Justified Normativity" Thesis in Hans Kelsen's Pure Theory of Law? Rejoinders to Robert Alexy and Joseph Raz' in M Klatt (ed), *Institutionalized Reason: The Jurisprudence of Robert Alexy* (Oxford, Oxford University Press, 2011) 61. I should emphasise that nothing in my argument depends on whether my reading of Kelsen is 'right' or 'best'; this article is ultimately about the right way to think about the nature of law, not about the exegetically best understanding of Kelsen's intentions.

anarchists need not, and would not, perceive the actions of legal officials as anything other than 'naked power',[6] like a gangster's order. Kelsen clarifies:

> The fact that the basic norm of a positive legal order *may* but *need not* be presupposed means: the relevant interhuman relationships may be, but need not be, interpreted as 'normative', that is, as obligations, authorizations, rights, etc. constituted by objectively valid norms. It means further: they can be interpreted without such presupposition (ie without the basic norm) as power relations .... (emphasis added)[7]

Kelsen emphasises that in legal cognition one starts with the *facts* of actions by officials and interprets or understands those facts in a normative way (or, to change the metaphor, projects onto those facts a normative understanding).[8] He speaks about those who perceive official actions as norms, in some places noting, in other places simply implying, that one can also choose *not* to perceive such actions in a normative way. In HLA Hart's terms, it is the difference between an 'internal' and 'external' view of the actions of officials, and also the difference between 'accepting' and not 'accepting' the legal system.[9]

With the help of Joseph Raz's idea of 'detached normative statements', one can speak of what a normative rule or system requires without thereby endorsing or accepting that rule or system.[10] Thus, someone who is not a vegetarian can say to a vegetarian friend, 'you should not eat that (because it has meat in its ingredients)', and a non-believer can say to an Orthodox Jewish friend, 'you should not accept that speaking engagement (because it would require you to work on your Sabbath)'. Analogously, the (radical) lawyer or (anarchist) scholar can make claims

[6] Kelsen, *Introduction to the Problems of Legal Theory* (n 2) §16 at 36. In a later edition of the same text, he clarifies that an anarchist who was also a law professor 'could describe positive law as a system of valid norms, without having to approve of this law': Kelsen, *Pure Theory of Law*, Max Knight trans (Berkeley, University of California Press, 1967) 218 fn 82.

[7] Kelsen, *Pure Theory of Law* (n 6) 218 Kelsen also states: 'For the Pure Theory strongly emphasises that the statement that the subjective meaning of the law-creating act is also its objective meaning – the statement, that is, that law has objective validity – is only a *possible* interpretation of that act, not a necessary one': H Kelsen, 'A "Realistic" Theory of Law and the Pure Theory of Law: Remarks on Alf Ross's *On Law and Justice*' in LD d'Almeida, J Gardner and L Green (eds), *Kelsen Revisited: New Essays on the Pure Theory of Law* (Oxford, Hart Publishing, 2013) 218–219. Later in the same passage, Kelsen adds, helpfully: 'The concept of normative validity is, rather, *an interpretation*; it is an interpretation made possible only by the presupposition of a basic norm', and that such an interpretation is well-grounded '*if* one presupposes the ... basic norm': Kelsen, 219. Elsewhere, Kelsen writes: 'This presupposition [of the Basic Norm] is possible but not necessary. ... Thus, the Pure Theory of Law, by ascertaining the basic norm as the logical condition under which a coercive order may be interpreted as valid positive law, furnishes only a conditional, not a categorical, foundation of the validity of positive law': H Kelsen, 'What is the Pure Theory of Law?' (1960) 34 *Tulane Law Review* 269, 276.

[8] The perception or interpretation of empirical events in a normative way is not confined to law. For example, some look at the world around them, and see norms of etiquette or norms from a religious system, while others look at the same world and do not see, or perceive, or interpret the world in this normative way.

[9] HLA Hart, *The Concept of Law*, 3rd edn (Oxford, Oxford University Press, 2012) 87–91; see also T Morawetz, 'Law as Experience: Theory and the Internal Aspect of Law' (1999) 52 *SMU Law Review* 27.

[10] J Raz, *Practical Reason and Norms* (Princeton, Princeton University Press, 1990) 170–77; J Raz, *The Authority of Law*, 2nd edn (Oxford, Oxford University Press, 2009) 156–57.

about what one ought to do if one accepted the legal system (viewed the actions of legal officials in a normative way), even if that lawyer or scholar saw the actions of legal officials only in a non-normative way, as mere acts of power.[11]

Some have explored the question of whether legal normativity is optional by considering the analogy of games. One might say to a person playing chess that she ought not (for example) to move the bishop a certain way, or that she is required to move her king out of 'check'. However, that person could easily have decided simply not to play chess, in which case prescriptions about how she ought to move the bishop or the king would have no application.[12] The statement of what one ought to do only makes sense once one has taken up the practice.

However, the game analogy is at best imperfect, and it is important to focus on the ways in which it and other proffered analogies differ from law. If someone said that she was not playing chess and did not want to play in the future, it would be clear that 'chess rules' and 'chess reasons' would not apply to her. By contrast, consider etiquette: someone might reasonably insist that its rules and reasons apply even to those people who insist that they do not 'accept' or 'participate in' etiquette.[13] As for religion, our ideas about voluntariness of affiliation have changed significantly over time. On one hand, in many societies today, including most so-called 'Western' countries, the normative rules of a particular religion are not thought to be binding on those who are not (self-identified) members of that religious group. However, the way we think about religion today is far different from the way people thought about it in the past. As Jacques Barzun pointed out,

> in earlier times people rarely thought of themselves as 'having' or 'belonging to' a religion. … Everybody 'had' a soul, but did not 'have a God', for God and all that pertained to Him was simply what is, just as today nobody has 'a physics'; there is only one and it is automatically taken to be the transcript of reality.[14]

And similarly, true believers even today (especially in countries in which fundamentalist views have significant social and political influence) perceive the dictates of their religion not as something chosen, but as 'the Truth', binding on all.

We certainly *say* that the law of a country 'applies' to its citizens (and often non-citizens resident in the country) whether those individuals 'accept' the law or not. By this, we mean in part that if those individuals act contrary to law's prescriptions, they may be subjected to sanctions. However, while law's *coercion* may be inescapable, its *normativity* is not. And while law may *claim* normative

[11] When one says that one can *choose* to view the (legal) actions of officials normatively or not, it is important to note that this does not mean that this 'choice' is always or necessarily a *conscious* choice. The reference to 'choice' indicates primarily that there is an option; one could do (or think) otherwise.

[12] *cf* A Marmor, *Law in the Age of Pluralism* (Oxford, Oxford University Press, 2007) 153–81, comparing law and chess.

[13] P Foot, *Virtues and Vices* (Oxford, Basil Blackwell, 1978) 160.

[14] J Barzun, *From Dawn to Decadence: 500 Years of Western Cultural Life, 1500 to the Present* (New York, HarperCollins, 2000) 24.

status, the position of this article is that law only has this normative status *as a general matter*[15] for those citizens who so choose.

It may seem absurd to claim that citizens do not (in a sense) have 'legal obligations' – even as regards legal systems that are efficacious and are generally just – unless and until those citizens have (in a sense) so chosen. However, I think that the conclusion seems less absurd when one focuses on the problem of deriving 'ought' from 'is', and the need to posit or presuppose foundational axioms for the validity of any normative system – including, or especially, legal systems.

III. The Nature of Legal Obligation: Question 2: *Sui Generis*?

A question that relates to the optional status of legal normativity, but which is nonetheless a distinct inquiry, is whether legal normativity is *sui generis*, or whether, instead, it is best thought of as a kind of moral obligation.

For this inquiry, it might be useful to start with a basic question: What does it mean to say that there is *a valid legal obligation*? The immediate and simple answer is that this means that there is an obligation that derives from the legal materials, from a particular legal system. This is (trivially) true, but it only pushes the question back one step. What is *the nature* of this legal obligation? A growing number of theorists – from a variety of perspectives and jurisprudential 'schools' – assert or assume (but rarely argue at any length for) that legal obligations are a kind of moral obligation.

Some have argued that the reason (or one reason, among many) that law should be understood as a kind of morality, or a subset of morality, is that law uses moral terminology: right, duty, permission, etc.[16] As already discussed in the first part of this paper, law undoubtedly is, or purports to be, normative: to inform citizens what they should do, what they should not do, what they are authorised to do, and what they are empowered to do. However, the difficulty with an argument based on purportedly moral language is that these terms are not exclusive to morality, but most can be found with any of a large number of normative practices, including games and language use.

A different line of argument has come from theorists like Mark Greenberg, who argue that law is basically a subset of morality. One thing that is said to motivate or justify this approach is the complicated relationship between the actions of (legal) officials and the resulting legal rules. As Greenberg has pointed out in a number

[15] As will be discussed in the next section, individual legal rules can affect our *moral* duties by triggering existing moral obligations.

[16] NE Simmonds, 'Value, Practice, and Idea' in J Keown and RP George (eds), *Reason, Morality, and Law: The Philosophy of John Finnis* (Oxford, Oxford University Press, 2013) 317–18.

of publications,[17] the relationship (for example) between what a legislature enacts and the rule(s) that are added to the legal system is not as direct or as straightforward as most non-lawyers (and probably many lawyers and judges, too) suspect. An enactment may be rendered invalid by its inconsistency with a constitutional provision, or its meaning may be affected by efforts to incorporate it with existing adjoining or overlapping statutes and existing common law case law, etc. However, while the observation about the effect (or lack thereof) of legislation on the list of legal rules may warrant a more nuanced understanding of the nature of legal norms, it is not enough, on its own, to justify equating legal and moral obligation.

In thinking about the nature of legal obligation, it is useful to return to HLA Hart's legal theory. Hart, like Kelsen, emphasised the normativity of law in his criticism of earlier legal theorists (particularly John Austin), and in the development of his own, more hermeneutic theory of law. Hart argued that Austin's command theory did not sufficiently distinguish a community acting out of fear, the 'gunman situation writ large',[18] from a community where the officials and at least some portion of the citizens 'accepted' the law as giving them reasons for action – what Hart called 'the internal point of view'.

As part of the legal positivist separation of law and morality that he advocated, Hart (a) is careful not to claim that citizens *must* accept the law as giving them reasons for action (he does not even discuss the circumstances under which citizens *should* do so); and (b) offers a broad and open-ended set of reasons for why citizens *might* accept the law as giving them reasons for action. Hart writes that a citizen 'may obey it [the law] for a variety of different reasons and among them may often, though not always, be the knowledge that it will be best for him to do so'.[19] And later: '[A]dherence to law may not be motivated by it [moral obligation], but by calculations of long-term interest, or by the wish to continue a tradition or by disinterested concern for others'.[20]

The question still remains for Hart: what is the nature of this normativity of or in law? The law prescribes behaviour – to act in certain ways, and to avoid acting in other ways – and also empowers citizens to use legal institutions and processes for their own purposes (through wills, contracts, incorporation, and the like). If under a Hartian analysis someone accepts the legal system as giving reasons for action, what kind of reasons are those? Is there any alternative to understanding these reasons as moral reasons?

As noted, people often obey the law for purely prudential reasons: to avoid the financial penalties, potential loss of liberty, or public humiliation that can come

[17] eg M Greenberg, 'The Standard Picture and its Discontents' in L Green and B Leiter (eds), *Oxford Studies in Philosophy of Law*, vol I (Oxford, Oxford University Press, 2011) 39–106; M Greenberg, 'The Moral Impact Theory of Law' (2014) 123 *Yale Law Journal* 1288.

[18] HLA Hart, 'Positivism and the Separation of Law and Morals' (1958) 71 *Harvard Law Review* 593, 603.

[19] Hart, *The Concept of Law* (n 9) 114.

[20] Hart, *The Concept of Law* (n 9) 232.

from being adjudicated as a law-breaker. However, recall that Hart's critique of Austin's command theory is that for many people law is more than (that phrase again) the 'gunman situation writ large' – that a perception of (legal) obligation can frequently be something different from merely feeling obliged (coerced).[21] Hart clearly intends an understanding of legal normativity where legal reasons are something distinct from (mere) prudential reasons.

So, if for Hart legal obligation (legal reasons for action) is not to be equated with either moral or prudential reasons, what is left? Many commentators interpret Hart as treating law as a *sui generis* form of normativity, a form of normativity distinct from all others; there is certainly support for this position in his writings.[22]

As mentioned, Hart, as a legal positivist, does not explore whether there are good moral reasons for accepting a particular legal system (or all legal systems) as giving reasons for action. Analogously, Hart does not explore at any length what kind of reasons people might think that the law gives them. It is sufficient for Hart that some people treat the law as giving reasons for action (and this is a fact for which the descriptive or conceptual theorist still needs to account).[23] However, as Hart sees it, it is not for the theorist of law to be too concerned about what sort of reasons these might be, and whether they are well grounded. Elsewhere (as part of his debate with Lon Fuller), Hart emphasises that one should not confuse 'ought' with morality – that there were many forms of 'ought', many sorts of reasons for action.[24]

Along the same lines, one could read Hart as saying that for the person who accepts the law, the sort of reason the law gives is a *legal* reason, just as those who make other choices might consider themselves as subject to *chess* reasons (while playing that game – for example, reasons within the game for moving the bishop diagonally rather than otherwise, and to this square rather than

[21] Hart, *The Concept of Law* (n 9) 82–91

[22] See eg HLA Hart, *Essays on Bentham: Jurisprudence and Political Theory* (Oxford, Oxford University Press, 1982) 262–68; *cf* J Finnis, *Philosophy of Law: Collected Essays Volume IV* (Oxford, Oxford University Press, 2011) 248–56; KE Himma, 'A Comprehensive Hartian Theory of Legal Obligation: Social Pressure, Coercive Enforcement, and the Legal Obligations of Citizens' in W Waluchow and S Sciaraffa (eds), *Philosophical Foundations of the Nature of Law* (Oxford, Oxford University Press, 2013) 152. Hart stated that 'legal right and legal duty [have] meanings which are not laden with any … connection [to morality]': *Essays on Bentham*, 263. It should be noted that in this section, with Hart, as in the prior section, with Kelsen, it is not crucial for my purposes that my reading of those theorists is the only tenable one, that it is the best one, or that it is the right one. What is important are the merits of the ultimate arguments, whether they are fairly attributable to those theorists or not.

[23] There is relevance to the fact that legal rules purport to be *social* rules, binding on a whole community. As Hart points out, those who accept law view those rules as binding not just *them* (those who accept the rules), but everyone else in the community, just as those who decide to play chess accept the rules governing the movement of chess pieces as binding all who play the game: Hart, *The Concept of Law* (n 9) 56–57. The complication there is that all who see themselves as playing the game already have (implicitly) accepted the rules of the game, while all those who live in a community do not necessarily accept that community's legal and political rules (and here we get back to an argument like Locke's notion of tacit consent).

[24] Hart 'Positivism and the Separation of Law and Morals' (n 18) 612–14.

another one), *etiquette* reasons, *fashion* reasons, etc. There is, to be sure, something a little strange about this line of analysis – one can understand the force of the objection that 'legal reasons' should reduce *either* to prudential reasons, on one hand, *or* moral reasons, on the other. However, it is not clear that Hart, or a modern follower of his approach, needs to concede this point. Why should one assume that one has a *moral* obligation to do as the law says, simply because the law says so? While it may once have been the accepted view that just legal systems create such general moral obligations to obey their enactments, many theorists today have offered strong arguments against such a general obligation.[25] The alternative view is that law *sometimes* creates moral obligations, and that this is a case-by-case analysis, relative to the individual citizen, the particular legal rule, and the coordination problems or expertise claims that may be involved.[26] Also, some theorists have added, there are good reasons to avoid constructing one's theory of the nature of law around the view that law generally does create, should create, or even claims to create moral obligations.[27]

Even John Finnis, the foremost theorist working today within the Natural Law tradition, rejects the idea that law makes moral claims, and accepts the view that law creates only 'indefeasible legal obligations',[28] which are then slotted into

> a flow of general practical reasoning – by good citizens in terms of the common good … by careerists in the law in terms of what must be done or omitted to promote their own advancement towards wealth or office, and by disaffected or criminally opportunistic citizens in terms of what they themselves need in order to get by without undesired consequences (punishment and the like).[29]

Similarly, for those who accept the law as giving them reasons for action, why should we assume that these reasons are moral reasons? For example, with etiquette or chess, we understand how a practice can give reasons that are not

[25] eg MBE Smith, 'Is There a Prima Facie Obligation to Obey the Law?' (1973) 82 *Yale Law Journal* 950; J Raz, *Ethics in the Public Domain* (Oxford, Clarendon Press, 1994) 325–338; WA Edmundson, 'State of the Art: The Duty to Obey the Law' (2004) 10 *Legal Theory* 215.

[26] Raz, *Ethics in the Public Domain* (n 25) 325–38; D Enoch, 'Reason-Giving and the Law' in L Green and B Leiter (eds), *Oxford Studies in Philosophy of Law* vol I (Oxford, Oxford University Press, 2011) 1–38.

[27] F Schauer, 'Positivism Through Thick and Thin' in B Bix (ed), *Analyzing Law: New Essays in Legal Theory* (Oxford, Clarendon Press, 1998) 65. Even Finnis states: 'very strictly speaking, the law does not claim to be morally obligatory' and law 'does not … make a moral claim': J Finnis, 'Reflections and Responses' in J Keown and RP George (eds), *Reason, Morality, and Law: The Philosophy of John Finnis* (Oxford, Oxford University Press, 2013) 553, 554. Finnis clarifies that this reflects in part the fact that even in the central case of law, any 'moral obligation created and imposed by law is defeasible, and defeasible not only by injustice in its making or content but also by competing moral responsibilities of particular subjects on particular occasions …': Finnis, 'Reflections and Responses' 555. He elaborates: '[T]o hold that the law claims to be morally obligatory *non-defeasibly* … would be to hold that the law – even in the central case of law – embodies a moral error, and asserts (albeit implicitly) a moral falsehood': Finnis, 'Reflections and Responses' 554–55.

[28] Finnis, 'Reflections and Responses' (n 27) 555–56.

[29] Finnis, 'Reflections and Responses' (n 27) 555.

moral reasons. Perhaps law similarly gives reasons that are not *moral* reasons but are merely *legal* reasons.

To tie this part of the article with the first part, when do legal systems create legal obligations? Is there any connection with citizens' choices or decisions? One analysis appears in a recent work by Kenneth Einar Himma (where he is offering a reading of Hart's legal theory).[30] Under this analysis, *a legal system* exists when officials accept the foundational rules of the system, but questions remain open about citizens' obligations. Himma argues that theories of legal obligation should track the usual understandings and practices of legal officials and citizens or face a strong burden of justifying deviation from those usual understandings and practices. Himma is concerned in particular with the conventional understanding that the law creates (legal) obligations for all citizens – regardless of whether those citizens accept the law or not. He argues that a legal system creates legal obligations for its citizens when the citizens *acquiesce* to the system of norms – a passive acceptance of the norms combined with a willingness to conform generally to those norms – and this is combined with coercive enforcement of the norms. The difficulty with this analysis is that it is not clear that it leaves any independent content to the claim that citizens have a legal obligation, other than the fact that they are in a functioning legal system. Returning again to the point of the first part of the article, we need to remember the gap between the descriptive (perhaps sociological) fact of an 'efficacious' legal system, and any *normative* reading of that descriptive fact.

Returning to the question of law and morality: it has become common for legal theorists to claim a close connection between the two.[31] And in this category I include not only the traditional natural law theorists, some of whom offer a moral test for what counts as valid law, but also Robert Alexy, who argues that all legal systems claim (moral) 'correctness',[32] and Joseph Raz, who argues that law, by its nature, claims moral authority (though Raz is also quick to note that he thinks that legal systems' claims to moral authority are usually mistaken).[33]

This purported connection between law and morality is often presented in contrast to older theories that emphasised power and sanction: for John Austin, law is essentially the command of a sovereign, where 'command' means that the sovereign is willing and able to impose a sanction if the directive is not followed.[34]

[30] Himma, 'A Comprehensive Hartian Theory of Legal Obligation' (n 22).

[31] Raz, *Ethics in the Public Domain* (n 25) 325–38; L Green, 'Legal Positivism' in EN Zalta (ed), *Stanford Encyclopedia of Philosophy* plato.stanford.edu/entries/legal-positivism (2003) § 4; R Alexy, *The Argument from Injustice*, BL Paulson and SL Paulson, trans (Oxford, Oxford University Press, 2002).

[32] See eg Alexy, *The Argument from Injustice* (n 31) 34–39.

[33] See Raz, *Ethics in the Public Domain* (n 25) 199–204.

[34] Such theories, especially Austin's, were also distinctive for reducing law to or equating law with factual descriptions (like a habit of obedience, and an ability and willingness to impose a sanction) (see J Austin, *The Province of Jurisprudence Determined* (Cambridge, Cambridge University Press, 1995)). Most theorists view the effort to reduce law to the factual rather than the normative as doomed to failure, but that is a debate for another day.

For some theorists, the existence of a sanction is essential to law, even if a sovereign is not. Robert Cover argued that '[l]egal interpretation is either played out on the field of pain and death or it is something less (or more) than law'.[35] Similarly, Frederick Schauer has maintained that even if coercion is not 'essential' or 'necessary' to law – in the sense that one can imagine a system that was 'legal' that lacked coercion – in the real world, legal systems are always associated with coercion, and this is important for understanding law and legal systems.[36]

Why should one assume that law makes moral claims (let alone that law by its nature *always* makes such claims)? As with all claims regarding the relationship of law and morality, the difficulty is that both terms in the equation – 'law' and 'morality' – are hard to define, and all likely definitions will be controversial. As already mentioned, Hart pointed out a similar objection when responding to Lon Fuller in their famous debate in the *Harvard Law Review*. Fuller had argued that legal interpretation often displays no sharp separation between 'is' and 'ought', with statutes (and other legal texts, like contracts and wills) often being interpreted not only according to the clear meaning of the text, but also in line with the lawmaker's or drafter's purpose.[37] Hart responded that there were many kinds of 'ought', and many of these forms of normative reasoning had little to do with morality.[38] Nazi Germany had its own demonic objectives, which judges could further by interpreting statutes one way rather than another; this is an 'ought', but not one we would likely call truly 'moral'. At a more mundane level, one could well imagine statutes that either sought to promote corporate profit-making or treated corporate avarice as an evil to be fought; in both cases, a judge could apply the statute in ways that furthered either of those (contrary) purposes (one's moral or political beliefs will determine which one of those views one considers moral, and which one not). Hart's own example was of the failed poisoner who states with regret that he should have used a second dose, reminding us again that normative language is appropriate whenever one speaks of a purpose, however immoral or amoral the objective.

The advantage of the approach discussed in this article – that the normativity of law is a matter that individuals choose, assume, or presuppose (or not) – is that it accounts for the normative nature of law, at least in a thin way, without the requirement of substantial metaphysical assumptions or controversial moral claims.[39]

[35] RM Cover, 'Violence and the Word' (1986) 95 *Yale Law Journal* 1601, 1606–1607.

[36] eg F Schauer, *The Force of Law* (Cambridge, Mass, Harvard University Press, 2015).

[37] LL Fuller, 'Positivism and Fidelity to Law – A Reply to Professor Hart' (1958) 71 *Harvard Law Review* 661.

[38] Hart 'Positivism and the Separation of Law and Morals' (n 18) 612–14.

[39] None of this is to deny the important point made by many natural law theorists (and some legal positivists), that one important aspect of legal rules and legal reasoning is the way law operates as or within a form of practical reasoning, the reasoning both citizens and legal officials use to determine how to act.

To take a naïve position for just a moment: we all know the difference between law and morality. We do not confuse the two. Law is made up of the rules the government promulgates – many of them guiding behaviour directly through imposing sanctions on actions the government wishes to discourage, and other rules affecting behaviour in more subtle ways by imposing selective tax benefits or payments due, or by offering legal enforcement to certain contracts, trusts, wills, and so on. Morality, by contrast, involves the rules and principles for how one should live one's life.[40] For those for whom morality is a secular matter, morality is not tied to any institution, and the only sanctions are those that come from the reproach of one's peers or from self-reproach. For those who have a more religious approach to moral matters, law and morality may seem similar in some ways: there may be institutions which clarify what that religion's morality requires, moral rules may be thought to be the directives of a law-giver, in this case a divine law-giver, and the believer may think that there are punishments for transgression, in this world or in a world to come. At the same time, sharp differences remain: religious morality purports to show us timeless truths, while legal rules are always relative to a particular system that is tied to a time and a place, and legal rules are changed by the fallible choices of fallible law-makers. Consider the same comparison from a different, more analytical direction: when a legal system says 'do X' or 'don't do Y', the basic meaning is that certain things are to be done or not done, because authorised officials have so declared. By contrast, when the same prescriptions ('do X', 'don't do Y') are moral, the understanding is that individuals have reasons to do or not do certain things, and that those reasons have no necessary connection to any (non-divine) speaker or official.

As part of Leslie Green's analysis that '[n]ecessarily, law makes moral claims on its subjects' (part of his list of ways in which he states that there are necessary connections between law and morality, contrary to some understandings of legal positivism's 'separability thesis'),[41] Green explains that law 'make[s] categorical demands' upon citizens, and that these demands require citizens 'to act without regard to our individual self-interest but in the interests of other individuals', and that these criteria together constitute 'moral demands'.[42] I do not find this definition of morality (or this characterisation of law's demands) persuasive. Even putting aside, for the moment, Hart's essential point that law does not merely command, it also empowers,[43] legal rules do not make the same sort of (implied

[40] Of course, there are also differences of focus, in that a legal system necessarily focuses primarily on 'externals' – how one acts, rather than on the virtue or error of our thoughts and feelings. At the same time, this difference can be overstated, as the law *does* concern itself with 'internals' to an extent, as when it punishes *intentional* or *malicious* actions more than accidental/negligent actions.

[41] Green, 'Legal Positivism' (n 31) § 4.2.

[42] Green, 'Legal Positivism' (n 31) § 4.2; *cf* J Coleman, 'Beyond the Separability Thesis: Moral Semantics and the Methodology of Jurisprudence' (2007) 27 *Oxford Journal of Legal Studies* 581.

[43] Hart, *The Concept of Law* (n 9) 27–33; Hart, 'Positivism and the Separation of Law and Morals' (n 18) 604–606.

or express) claims as do moral rules: they do not, as moral rules do, (purport to) reflect universal and unchanging moral truths, nor do they always purport to be integral aspects of the Good, as moral rules do.

Joseph Raz offers a somewhat different explanation of why he believes that law's claim to authority is a moral claim: 'it is a claim which includes the assertion of a right to grant rights and impose duties in matters affecting basic aspects of people's life and their interactions with one another'.[44] I am not sure that this will go much further towards persuading those not already persuaded that law's claims are moral claims. Many normative systems, including those of etiquette and even fashion, seem to involve claims of 'rights to grant rights and impose duties'. And while it is true that law, like morality, covers 'basic aspects of people's life and their interactions with one another', this does not seem sufficient to turn claims on behalf of law into moral claims.

I do not mean this to be a dispute about the proper way to define morality; in any event, such disputes are unlikely to get far beyond one person's 'that seems right to me' evoking 'but it does not seem right to me' by another. I think it is sufficient to the perspective I am trying to elaborate that few of us confuse morality and law. We may be inclined to overestimate the moral merits of the law, but we still do not confuse the two. Who besides a strong believer in a Sharia legal system thinks that law is essentially an instantiation of morality, grounded in divine command or otherwise?[45] It is true that the early common law judges in England (and commentators on the common law from that period) sometimes cited 'Reason' with a capital 'R' as the justification for why the common law rules were the way they were,[46] but even legal figures from that period did not conflate or confuse law with morality. For example, in English (and later American) common law, there was no legal obligation to rescue another, however easy and low-risk the rescue might be,[47] and there was no legal obligation to keep one's promises (only those promises that were supported by 'consideration' – that is, that were part of an exchange). In these, and many other cases, the common law judges distinguished what individuals had a moral obligation to do and what their (common law) legal obligations were.

While I think that most people do not conflate law and morality, some very able theorists seem to be advocating just such a merger. For example, Mark Greenberg argues that 'when the law operates as it is supposed to, the content

[44] Raz, *The Authority of Law* (n 10) 315–16.

[45] One might add Immanuel Kant, on one reading of his 'Doctrine of Right': I Kant, *The Metaphysics of Morals*, M Gregor (ed) (Cambridge, Cambridge University Press, 1996/1797); see also A Ripstein, *Force and Freedom: Kant's Legal and Political Philosophy* (Cambridge, Mass, Harvard University Press, 2009). I am grateful to Micha Glaeser for pointing this out.

[46] Those same judges also frequently characterised their actions as declaring existing law, while modern observers would describe their decisions as making new law or modifying existing law.

[47] eg EJ Weinrib, 'The Case for a Duty to Rescue' (1980) 80 *Yale Law Journal* 247.

of the law consists of a certain general and enduring part of the moral profile'.[48] This claim seems related to, but is in fact distinct from, the views of traditional natural law theorists (like John Finnis), who argue that human law, when consistent with the natural law, can frequently change our moral reasons for action. Greenberg is going further, by arguing that law is in fact (part of) morality.

Greenberg's way of using the label 'law' in his works thus differs sharply, not merely from the views of legal theorists caught up with 'the Standard Picture',[49] but also from the way of speaking of both legal practitioners (lawyers, prosecutors, judges, etc) and citizens who are not legal practitioners. This deviation from conventional ways of speaking leads immediately to the question: is Greenberg claiming that we have all been mistaken about the nature of law, and he is correcting a significant and collective error (one that would be both widespread and lasting many centuries)? Or is his claim different: that if we were to look at our practices more carefully and reflectively, we would see that the Moral Impact Theory[50] more accurately reflects what we have really meant all along when we have spoken about 'law'? Either position would entail a difficult burden of proof, and Greenberg has yet to produce the necessary argument(s).

An approach put forward by David Enoch explains a way of understanding the connection between law and morality that does not require us to think of the law as making a moral claim or as being some sort of subset of morality. Enoch's argument is the legal enactments and other actions by legal officials can act as 'triggering reasons', giving us reasons to act under the moral reasons for action that we already have.[51] This parallels a more common observation that law may make more articulate or determinate our general obligations: for example, our obligation to drive safely entails driving on one side of the road, and the law selects which side, and at a safe speed, and the law chooses a particular limit; also, we have an obligation to support the basic needs of society and help the poor, and the state specifies what percentage of one's income goes for those purposes through taxes. Legal rules sometimes – not all legal rules, and not all the time – work effectively as salient solutions to coordination problems, and make more determinate otherwise vague moral obligations.

IV. Conclusion

This article has offered controversial positions on two central questions of legal theory: first, that the *normativity* of law depends on the choice of citizens; and

[48] Greenberg, 'The Standard Picture and its Discontents' (n 17) 57; Greenberg, 'The Moral Impact Theory of Law' (n 17).

[49] Greenberg, 'The Standard Picture and its Discontents' (n 17).

[50] Greenberg, 'The Moral Impact Theory of Law' (n 17).

[51] Enoch, 'Reason-Giving and the Law' (n 26).

second, that legal normativity is *sui generis* and not merely a form of or subset of morality.[52] Ultimately what is at stake in these topics is the nature of law, the connection between law and morality, and the nature and grounding of obligation. These are obviously large issues, and one should not assume that any discussion will resolve them suddenly or to everyone's satisfaction. It is enough if the present reflections add something to a long-standing discussion that needs to be continued.

[52] As noted, both positions can be traced back to earlier theorists: the first derives from Hans Kelsen's works, and the second from HLA Hart's works. I do not mention these eminent names to hide behind their authority – though I do not mind if their stature at least prevents a quick dismissal of these views as simply absurd.

4

The Problems of Legal Normativity and Legal Obligation

KENNETH EINAR HIMMA

I. Introduction

Mandatory legal norms are thought to provide reasons for action. The characteristic way in which legal norms provide reasons for action is through mandatory legal norms (ie a law that *requires* some act or acts) creating a legal obligation that binds subjects and thereby provides them with a reason for doing what the norm requires. The problem of legal normativity, for my purposes, is concerned with explicating how legal norms provide reasons for action; since mandatory legal norms characteristically regulate behaviour by defining legal obligations, a conceptual theory of law must successfully explain what a legal obligation is, by nature, and how it binds subjects by providing reasons for action.

In this essay, I argue that the only account of legal obligation that can succeed is one that holds that legal obligations bind by providing prudential reasons for action.[1] Then I consider two conflicting views. First, I reject the claim that it is a conceptual truth that mandatory legal norms provide moral reasons for action; this view is widely rejected, as it should be, by legal theorists and by normative political philosophers.

Second, I consider the possibility that mandatory legal norms merely 'purport' to define legal obligations and hence reasons for action. That is, on this view, mandatory legal norms neither *necessarily* define legal obligations nor provide reasons for action; they simply purport to do both, leaving open the possibility of a legal system consisting of laws that never define obligations or provide reasons for action. I argue that this view, given the proper understanding of the relevant kind of reason for action, is inconsistent with the very legal practices and

[1] KE Himma, 'A Comprehensive Hartian Theory of Legal Obligation: Social Pressure, Coercive Enforcement, and the Legal Obligations of Citizens' in W Waluchow and S Sciaraffa (eds), *The Nature of Law: Contemporary Perspectives* (Oxford, Oxford University Press, 2013).

self-conceptions of practitioners that construct the content of our concepts of law and legal obligation.

II. The Problem of Legal Normativity

The conceptual functions of law are generally thought to be to guide and regulate behaviour. The concepts of guiding and regulating behaviour are related but somewhat different notions. In its ordinary usage, the notion of guiding is an epistemic notion. One guides by informing persons of what they should do. The notion of regulating behaviour involves a normative dimension; to regulate is to prescribe behaviour. Guiding behaviour, as the term is understood here, is a descriptive enterprise: it is the answer to the question 'what does the law say about doing X?' Regulating behaviour is a normative enterprise: it provides the answer to the question 'what should I do under the law with respect to doing X?'

Thus, the conceptual functions of law have two distinct but related dimensions: the first is largely epistemic, while the second is largely normative. The epistemic function of law (ie the guiding function) can succeed only by informing a person of what the law requires her to do. Thus, to guide A to do *p* is to inform A that the law requires that she do *p*. Not everyone, of course, needs to look at a statute or case law to know what the law requires; I suspect everyone knows that the law prohibits murdering people. In less obvious cases, one might need to consult the law or a lawyer to ascertain what her obligations are under the law. But in such cases, the epistemic function is informative, and hence descriptive.[2]

The second function of law is normative (ie the regulative function) and involves exercising some degree of, so to speak, control over a person's behaviour by giving her a reason to comply. Accordingly, to perform the normative regulative function, the law must give subjects a reason to do what the law requires; if the law requires that A do *p*, it must give A a reason to do *p*.

Accordingly, the conceptual function of law is, in part, to inform people (especially, citizens) what they should do when they do not know what to do and, in part, to give them reasons for doing what law requires so as to keep the peace.[3] But the problem of informing people what to do is not a problem of explaining legal normativity because the function of informing is purely epistemic. The real

[2] This should not be construed to deny that the epistemic function of law also involves providing reasons to believe, but once one is justified in believing an authoritative legal system is in force, which would be justified on the basis of various observable practices in the society, the relevant reasons to believe what law says about what law requires have antecedently been provided. The same reasons that lead me to believe that the law prohibiting murder tells me that murder is prohibited also justify my believing that the law requiring me to take reasonable precautions to avoid injuring someone through my negligence requires me to take such precautions. Those antecedent reasons justify me in believing that a legal system is in force in the relevant jurisdiction.

[3] See KE Himma, 'Law as an Artifact: Does Law Have a Conceptual Function?' in KE Himma, L Burazin and C Roversi (eds), *Law as an Artifact* (Oxford, Oxford University Press, forthcoming 2018).

problem of legal normativity, then, is the problem of explaining how law can give people reasons to act.

But notice that the regulatory function of law logically presupposes that one point of the law is to try to change behaviour at times; when a behaviour is undesirable, the law prohibits it in an attempt to prevent people from behaving that way. When a person does something differently because of law, her behaviour has been changed by the law. At the most basic level, the problem of legal normativity, then, is to explain how law can change behaviour by providing reasons for action.

It is crucial to note here that we are talking about the conceptual function of a legal system, and not the function of a rule of recognition. The rule of recognition is primarily an ontological rule. The conceptual function of a rule of recognition is to define the criteria that constitute a rule as a legally valid norm of the system; it is normative only as to the persons serving as officials who are bound by any duty-creating rules by virtue of taking the internal point of view towards the rule as creating legitimate standards that govern their behaviour as officials. Citizens need not take the internal point of view towards the rule of recognition.

Although any rule that constitutes a norm as a legally valid norm of the system provides information that might enable officials or citizens to identify which rules are valid rules of the system, the conceptual point of a rule of recognition should not be considered an epistemic function – and certainly not one that provides an algorithm that resolves any dispute as to the content of law. Experience tells us that there is no such algorithm for answering hard questions of law. Beyond this, HLA Hart is clear that citizens need not know the content of the rule of recognition in order for it to define a legal system.

The problem of legal normativity involves exploring both how the rules of recognition and primary legal norms guide the relevant class of subjects by providing reasons for action; it not concerned with how law informs citizens. The problem of legal normativity, then, requires answers to the questions of both how the rule of recognition provides reasons for officials to act and how the primary rules provide citizens with a reason to do what law requires – and, again, has nothing to do with how law guides behaviour by informing citizens of their legal obligations. The problem of legal normativity is concerned exclusively with explaining how law provides reasons for action.

This should not be thought surprising. We are rational beings who act for reasons. We do not act without reasons; when we do something, it is for a reason – whether a good one or a bad one. When people start to do things for no reason at all or against the obvious reasons, it is reasonable to think something is psychologically wrong with them that requires medical or therapeutic intervention.

The problem of legal normativity, then, is really just a matter of explaining how law can give reasons. How can the law change a person's reasons for action and hence her motivations for doing this or that? The problem of legal normativity is, therefore, to explain the mechanism by which the law can potentially change a person's behaviour.

III. The Problem of Legal Obligation and Its Logical Relation to the Problem of Legal Normativity

The problem of legal obligation is distinct from – but related to – the problem of legal normativity. The law, as Hart, Dworkin, and Raz have each pointed out, uses terms like 'obligate' and claims,[4] through its officials, to create obligations that are legal in nature. By this, I mean that the law creates obligations that are different from moral obligations, although legal obligation and moral obligation are surely conceptually related as two instances of 'obligation'. The problem of legal obligation, then, is to explain whether and how law can create legal obligations that, in some sense, *bind* people. The problem is to explain the 'nature' of legal obligation.

The relationship between these two defining problems of conceptual jurisprudence is as follows. The problem of legal normativity is the problem of explaining how law gives reasons to do things. But the mechanism by which law characteristically gives reasons to do things is by creating legal obligations. It is the very nature of an obligation *of any kind* that an obligation provides a reason for action. The problem of legal normativity is, then, the problem of explaining how legal obligations bind subjects by giving reasons for action.

The reason an obligation provides might be defeated by other reasons and hence is not necessarily decisive or the winning reason. A legal obligation, other things being equal, is defeated by a conflicting moral obligation, while a prudential obligation, if there are any, is usually defeated by a conflicting legal obligation (at least in legal practice, if not necessarily as a matter of practical rationality). But to say that a person, A, has an obligation to do *p* is to say that A has some reason, however weak, to do *p*. That is just the kind of thing that an obligation is. Thus, to solve the problem of legal normativity requires solving the problem of legal obligation. Once we understand how law creates legal obligations, then, and only then, can we understand how law creates reasons for action.

There are two steps, then, toward solving the problem of legal obligation. The first is to explain the nature of legal obligation. It should be obvious that we cannot understand how law provides reasons for action by creating legal obligations unless we understand what legal obligations *are*. So the first step in solving the problem is to give an explication of what legal obligations are, by nature.

The second step in solving the problem of legal obligation is to identify the kind of reasons that legal obligations provide. Once we understand what legal obligations are, by nature, we can see how they can provide reasons to act. What these reasons are, however, will be determined by what a legal obligation is. Legal obligations *bind* persons; thus, the issue is to identify the relevant reasons that would

[4] I mean 'claim' here in a metaphorical sense, as opposed to a literal sense.

count as *binding* persons – a notion that is a conceptual prerequisite for a norm, of any kind, to create an obligation. Again, it bears emphasising that the problem of legal obligation is conceptually linked to the problem of legal normativity; solving the latter problem requires solving the former problem.

In this connection, it is worth noting what is required to explain the normativity of obligations. It is part of the very nature of any kind of obligation that it binds you in the following sense: you must satisfy your obligations, other things being equal, regardless of how you feel about it. Obligations make behaviours required and non-optional. For example, if charity is merely morally good but not morally obligatory, then it is morally good for you to give to charity, but it is not morally wrong if you do not. This is the hallmark of the notion of being non-optional: *p* is legally/morally non-optional if and only if it legally/morally wrong not to do *p*. Obligations are not optional once you are obligated. They 'bind' you in the sense that you are, in some sense, accountable for not doing what you are obligated to do regardless of your reasons for not complying.

As this point is absolutely crucial in understanding the nature of obligation, it is worth quoting HLA Hart on it:

> The figure of a *bond* binding the person obligated, which is buried in the word 'obligation', and the similar notion of a debt latent in the word 'duty' are explicable in terms of these three factors, which distinguish rules of obligation or duty from other rules. In this figure, which haunts much legal thought, the social pressure appears as a chain binding those who have obligations so that they are not free to do what they want. *The other end of the chain is sometimes held by the group or their official representatives, who insist on performance or exact the penalty.* (emphasis added)[5]

Here it is worth noting how difficult the problem is of explaining how moral obligations can be binding in this sense. It is utterly mysterious as to how objective moral standards could bind in this important respect. One can hold that moral standards bind by providing exclusionary reasons, but then the question is how is it that moral standards provide such reasons.[6] To my knowledge, no one solution to the problem of explaining the binding quality of moral obligations has succeeded.

Of course, different types of obligations arise from different sources, and hence one would expect that the mechanism that explains how an obligation binds subjects will be different depending on what kind of obligation it is (for example legal, moral, or prudential). As we will see, the problem of explaining how legal obligations bind is somewhat easier than the problem of explaining how objective moral obligations, if there are any, bind.

[5] HLA Hart, *The Concept of Law*, 2nd edn (Oxford, Oxford University Press, 1994) 87. It is worth noting the role authorised coercive enforcement mechanisms play in the notion of being bound by an obligation in the italicised portion of the quote.

[6] See J Raz, *Practical Reason and Practical Norms* (Princeton, NJ, Princeton University Press, 1990).

IV. The Distinction between Subjective and Objective Reasons

There are two relevant distinctions regarding reasons that should be discussed at the outset. The first is between subjective and objective reasons. Subjective reasons refer to the agent's internal reasons for performing an act. For example, your desire to eat defines a subjective reason. It is wholly mind-dependent and provides you with your subjective motivation for eating something. Subjective reasons are 'internal' because they are linked to passions and desires but not *necessarily* to objective rules of rationality, which apply to you regardless of your feelings. Your subjective reasons can be very bad reasons. Maybe you decided to rob a bank because you want the thrill of committing a crime; that, obviously, is a very bad reason that leads you to do a stupid thing. Or we can have false beliefs that motivate us to do something; those beliefs also are bad reasons.

Once we understand that there can be bad and good reasons, we can understand the concept of an objective reason. There are certain objective standards, on this widespread view, of practical rationality that express values with respect to whether a reason is a good or bad reason. Obviously, we do not always act according to good reasons, as when we act against moral reasons.

There is a second distinction of interest here: the distinction between explanatory reasons and justificatory reasons.[7] Explanatory reasons explain an act, while justificatory reasons justify an act. There is a subjective and objective dimension to each of these kinds of reasons. A subjective explanatory reason would be a reason that the agent believes contributes to explaining her act in some circumstance but the agent might be incorrect with respect to which reasons actually explain the relevant act; in this case, the objective explanatory reason is different from the subjective explanatory reason. Perhaps what explains her act is something in her subconscious of which she is not aware; such an explanation is, for our purposes, plausibly characterised as an explanatory reason.

There is a similar dualism with respect to justificatory reasons. A subjective justificatory reason would be a reason that an agent believes justifies her act; such a reason might be moral or it might be prudential in character. An objective justificatory reason would be a reason that, from an objective perspective, actually succeeds in justifying the agent's act – whether it be a prudential reason, moral reason, or some reason that takes into account all of the relevant reasons.

The relationships among these various types of subjective and objective reasons are unclear but that is not important here; what is important is this: the reasons we are concerned with in solving the problems of legal obligation and legal normativity are objective justificatory reasons – ie those reasons that are good

[7] J Lenman, 'Reasons for Action: Justification vs. Explanation' in EN Zalta (ed), *The Stanford Encyclopedia of Philosophy* (Winter 2011 edition), available at http://plato.stanford.edu/archives/win2011/entries/reasons-just-vs-expl/.

reasons and should motivate us, as a matter of normative practical rationality. There are four related reasons for this.

First, there is no real problem of legal obligation when it comes to subjective reasons of any of these kinds (motivations, explanatory, or justificatory). It is utterly trivial to explain how law could provide subjective reasons. People can decide to act on the most foolish reasons whatsoever. For example, one can obey the law because one believes that obeying the law prevents cancer or because one fetishises the law. Anything can provide an internal reason; one just has to have the right desires and logically appropriate beliefs, which, of course, can be false. As David Hume once said, 'reason is the slave of the passions'.

Second, the assumption that obligations provide only subjective reasons implies that mandatory legal norms do not necessarily obligate. Mandatory legal norms do not necessarily give rise to internal reasons in everyone. I have never killed anyone but not because it is illegal. The illegality of murder has nothing to do with why I have never killed. Indeed, if any part of the reason you have never killed someone is that it is illegal, there is something wrong with you. The reason should be, as an objective matter, that human life is sufficiently valuable that you would never kill an innocent person. The reason should be for reasons of altruism and morality, assuming these are distinct types of reasons, and not because the law requires it. Whether the altruistic and moral reasons really motivate you, those are the reasons that *should* motivate you – and those are objective reasons.

Third, it is simply foolish to think that law could require any sort of subjective reasons for complying with the law; whether someone conforms to the law because it is the law is utterly irrelevant with respect to the regulatory purpose of law. The regulatory purpose of law is to provide reasons for doing what law requires, and it can accomplish this only by providing reasons that would characteristically matter to those disinclined to obey law in order to *induce* them to act otherwise. The regulatory purpose of law is to ensure behaviour conforms to certain norms, regardless of why the behaviour conforms to norms. What that purpose does require, however, is that it provide some sort of reason for action that should as an objective matter, and characteristically does as an empirical matter, induce people to behave within the law when they might be subjectively disinclined to do so.

Fourth, and most importantly, explaining legal obligation exclusively in terms of subjective reasons makes it impossible to explain how law is *binding*. Obligations bind by requiring or prohibiting certain acts, making those acts or abstentions mandatory. It is worth recalling Hart's remarks on the resemblance between being obligated and being chained to a fence: 'The figure of a *bond* binding the person obligated, which is buried in the word 'obligation', … appears as a chain binding those who have obligations so that they are not free to do what they want'.

It is absolutely crucial to note that Hart's remarks preclude the possibility of explicating the nature of legal obligation in terms of subjective reasons. After explaining the relationship between the binding quality of obligations and the metaphor of a chain, Hart explains that one must avoid the mistake of thinking that the binding quality of obligation can be explained in terms of subjective reasons:

> Natural and perhaps illuminating though these figures or metaphors are, we must not allow them to trap us into a misleading conception of obligation as essentially consisting in some feeling of pressure or compulsion *experienced by those who have obligations.* The fact that rules of obligation are generally supported by serious social pressure does not entail that to have an obligation under the rules is to experience feelings of compulsion or pressure. Hence there is no contradiction in saying of some hardened swindler that he had an obligation to pay the rent but felt no pressure to pay when he made off without doing so. To *feel* obliged and to have an obligation are different though frequently concomitant things.[8]

Hart takes the position, then, as he must, that obligation cannot be explained in terms of subjective reasons precisely because the bond is an external one that may or may not generate subjective reasons. The obligation can be there even when the subjective reasons are not.

In this connection, a point about conceptual methodology should be made. As Hart, Raz, and others have pointed out, it is our social and linguistic practices that construct the content of our concepts. Our social concepts are manufactured through certain relevant social practices; in the case of law, these will be linguistic practices and the core legal practices that inform them. Thus, the relevant social practices, legal and linguistic, are the touchstone for evaluating an account of the nature of legal obligation. There is nothing even remotely controversial about this: there is simply no other plausible possibility.[9]

This implies that we cannot be, as Raz puts it, 'systematically mistaken' about the content of our social concepts.[10] Since our practices construct our concepts and hence fix or determine the content of our concepts, an account of a concept must largely harmonise with our practices. We can be mistaken about some things, but there is a limit to how mistaken we can be if our practices determine the content of the concept. The suggestion that legal obligation can give rise only to subjective reasons means that legal obligations do not bind in any meaningful sense – and this is the kind of mistake that a theory of legal obligation simply cannot make. If it were true that legal obligations do not bind, then it would be difficult to explain why legal systems are created to regulate behaviour so as to keep the peace. Whatever else law is, it must be reasonably contrived, as a conceptual matter to do that, and law can be reasonably contrived to regulate behaviour only if law creates obligations that provide the right kind of reasons.

The problems of legal obligation and normativity ultimately amount to this, then. The problem is to explain legal obligation in terms of objective reasons in a

[8] Hart, *The Concept of Law* (n 5) 88.

[9] See KE Himma, 'Immodest and Modest Conceptual Analysis: Interpreting Dworkin's Methodology for his "Third Theory" of Law' in WW and S Sciaraffa (eds), *The Legacy of Ronald Dworkin* (Oxford, Oxford University Press, 2016).

[10] J Raz, *Ethics in the Public Domain* (Oxford: Clarendon Press, 1994) 216–17.

manner that enables us to understand how legal obligations are binding – again, in something like the sense that being chained to a fence is binding. Perhaps there is some interesting problem concerning how obligations give rise to internal reasons, but that is a problem of legal sociology or psychology and not of conceptual jurisprudence.

V. A Non-Orthodox Account of the Nature of Legal Obligation

To fully secure the points made in the last section, it is worth discussing an opposing view. Brian Bix argues that people are not under a legal obligation in the jurisdiction in which they live unless they choose to be; as he puts the point, 'citizens do not (in a sense) have "legal obligations" – even as regards legal systems that are efficacious and are generally just – unless and until those citizens have (in a sense) so chosen'.[11]

On Bix's volunteerist view, the mechanism by which one becomes subject to legal obligations is the largely the same as the one by which one becomes subject to a contractual obligation – namely, by voluntarily undertaking the obligation. Just as, other things being equal, one must voluntarily take on a contractual obligation to be bound by it, one must voluntarily undertake any legal obligations at all. Presumably, this means that an individual must consent to be bound by the mandatory legal norms of a legal system, as it would be odd to think that one can pick and choose among the laws which laws one is obligated by.

The primary objection to Bix's analysis is that it is unable to make sense of the non-optional nature of legal obligations. It is true that one can put oneself under a legal obligation by making a choice, such as is done when one enters into a contract. It is also true that, more generally, there is something resembling a choice to put oneself under the obligations of the law of a particular jurisdiction insofar as one chooses to remain within the geographical boundaries of that jurisdiction (although it is not true that people can simply leave one country for another).

However, the idea that people can choose to be under a legal obligation within the jurisdiction in which they live is problematic for a number of reasons. First, it is inconsistent with what seems to be a clear conceptual truth about law and legal obligation: law defines legal obligations that bind all those within the relevant jurisdiction. The denial of this implies that the very practices that construct our social concept of law are systematically mistaken – and, as we have seen, that is incoherent given the accepted methodology of conceptual analysis.

Second, it is hard to make sense, even for those who have 'chosen' to be obligated, of how obligations could bind in the relevant sense. If one must opt in to

[11] B Bix, 'The Nature of Legal Obligation': see ch 3 above.

being obligated by choice, then one can opt out at any time. But that is inconsistent with the idea that one is bound. To be bound to do X is to make X non-optional and, for someone who has chosen to be obligated to do X, all she has to do at any time is retract her acceptance to be released from having to do X. It is hard to see what the meaningful sense of 'bound' is, given our general practices involving all kinds of obligations, when one can simply opt out. This is not a claim that could be plausibly made of *moral* obligation, and it can no more be plausibly made of *legal* obligation, without distorting the more general concept of obligation to a point beyond recognition.

Here it is important to understand that a choice is not a commitment. Making a choice is a necessary condition for making a commitment, but making a choice is not a sufficient condition for a making a commitment. Unilateral choices can be withdrawn or counteracted at any time without the consent or approval of any person, as when I choose to let you into my home and then choose to terminate your permission. The same is true of unilateral commitments, if one is tempted to interpret Bix's notion of 'choice' as implying a commitment. It simply does not matter whether we are talking about a choice or a commitment: if it is unilateral, it can be changed or withdrawn entirely. I might unilaterally commit myself to being your servant, but in the absence of some other socially or morally salient considerations, that commitment can be withdrawn. In the absence of some other salient characteristic that would create a commitment that is sufficiently durable because it cannot be withdrawn, Bix's explication of obligation cannot make sense of the notion of being bound.

Indeed, this distinguishes ordinary legal obligation, on Bix's account, from contractual obligations. One cannot unilaterally unbind oneself from a contractual obligation; indeed, a valid contract is binding on the parties precisely insofar they cannot unilaterally withdraw from its requirements. It is this feature of contractual obligation that renders the required acts non-optional or binding. In contrast, it would appear that, on Bix's view, one can opt in and opt out of being subject to the requirements of a legal system as one sees fit. It is hard to understand how this could plausibly express what it means to be obligated – under the law or any other set of valid norms.

Finally, Bix's analysis implies a systematic mistake with respect to another paradigm legal practice – again, something that is not possible given the fact that our paradigmatic practices construct the content of our concepts. A breach of a legal obligation furnishes the legal justification for imposing sanctions; that is a paradigmatic feature of our practices. A failure by a person *P* to behave in a way that breaches a legal obligation that binds *P*, as a conceptual matter and as a matter of substantive law, implies that there are no legal remedies for that behaviour. The law does not authorise the imposition of a legal consequence for a behaviour that does not breach a legal obligation; or, to put it a different way, a legal obligation cannot, as a matter of paradigmatic legal practice, be correctly enforced against someone who is not under the obligation. This means that in any lawsuit the court would have to ascertain whether the legal obligation has been chosen. This is radically inconsistent with core legal practice in every paradigm of a legal system we have known.

The problems arise with respect to Bix's theory of legal obligation because he misconceives the nature of legal obligation as binding only in the sense of providing internal subjective, presumably expressed, motivations – and what a person's attitudes are towards the law are a contingent matter. To recall Hart's remarks on the issue:

> Natural and perhaps illuminating though these figures or metaphors are, we must not allow them to trap us into a misleading conception of obligation as essentially consisting in some feeling of pressure or compulsion *experienced by those who have obligations*. The fact that rules of obligation are generally supported by serious social pressure does not entail that to have an obligation under the rules is to experience feelings of compulsion or pressure. Hence there is no contradiction in saying of some hardened swindler that he had an obligation to pay the rent but felt no pressure to pay when he made off without doing so. To *feel* obliged and to have an obligation are different though frequently concomitant things.[12]

Now, one can, if one wants, study the subjective responses of persons to mandatory legal norms that define legal obligations. But that seems to be a project for legal sociology and legal psychology precisely because these subjective responses can vary from person to person. Indeed, a person's subjective responses can vary from law to law. I always have a subjective reason to pay taxes; I'm afraid of the IRS. But I could not care less about jaywalking prohibitions. If there is no cop at an intersection to give me a ticket, I am not going to waste the precious moments of my life waiting for the little green man to permit me to cross.

Perhaps one can argue that the problem of legal obligation has been misconceived by Hart and others. While I am inclined to doubt that any such argument could succeed, this much should be clear: an argument that shows that the predominant view of the problem is misconceived *must be given*. And that problem is considerably more challenging that any theoretical inquiry, sociological in nature, into how people respond internally to the law in terms of the subjective reasons the law does or does not provide. Although I think there is much of value in Bix's provocative insightful paper, this is an issue that would simply have to be addressed to get the rest of the analysis of the ground. While there are many insights in the paper that deepen our understanding of the human response to legal obligation, it seems to me that Bix's views are not really about the *nature* of legal obligation at all – because they misunderstand the nature of obligation simplictur.

[12] Hart, *The Concept of Law* (n 5) 88.

VI. Explaining Law's Normativity in Terms of Basic Reasons: Moral and Prudential Reasons for Action

It is taken for granted that, as a conceptual matter, law is normative in the sense that it provides reasons to do what the law requires. Although it is not always clear how properly to understand this claim, one plausible interpretation is that laws giving rise to legal obligation provide prima facie reasons for doing what law requires. As prima facie reasons, these reasons are defeasible; however, the normativity of law seems to entail that law provides some kind of reason for action, even if the reason the law provides can be defeated by other reasons.

To assume otherwise, again, is to make it difficult to understand why societies would adopt a legal system as a means of regulating behaviour. It seems a conceptual truth that legal systems are reasonably contrived to do the job of regulating behaviour, something they could not do if mandatory legal norms do not provide objective reasons for action. Although these objective reasons may be defeated, as a matter of normative practical rationality, by other conflicting objective reasons, such as moral reasons, law could not be the type of tool for regulating behaviour unless mandatory legal norms provide some kind of prima facie objective reasons for action.

In addition to the distinction between objective and subjective reasons, there is another distinction that arises with respect to the relevant types of reasons law characteristically provides – the distinction between basic (or atomic) reasons and compound reasons. However conceived, the structure of reasons seems to resemble the structure of sentences, as defined by sentential logic. In sentential logic, there are two kinds of statement: basic (or 'atomic') and compound statements. A basic statement is one that does not contain any logical connectives; it cannot be reduced to some more basic statement by removing connectives. In contrast, a compound statement is composed of one or more statements conjoined by one of the available logical connectives; if A and B are basic statements, then ~A, (A v B), etc are compound statements. Likewise, there are at least some reasons that are *basic* (or atomic) in the sense that they cannot be reduced to, or constituted by, other more basic reasons. On this view, there are some reasons that cannot be constructed out of other reasons.[13]

Of course, I do not wish to assume too much here. It might be that no class of reasons can be reduced to more basic reasons of another class. If so, then all reasons are basic in the sense described above. Either way, there is a distinction to be made; the only difference between the two classes is that in one the set of compound reasons is non-empty and in the other the set of compound

[13] No claim is made here about the metaphysical structure of compound reasons, if there are any such things. But if there are not, then the only reasons that remain will be basic reasons and combinations of basic reasons.

reasons is empty. Accordingly, it is not otiose to attempt to identify the classes of basic reasons.

According to a common view that began with Immanuel Kant, the class of basic reasons is limited to two types: moral and prudential. As Kant conceived it, prudential reasoning is concerned with maximising happiness, while moral reasoning is concerned with acting according to universalisable maxims that can be derived from rationality and that trump prudential reasons.[14] Expressed in more modern terms, prudential reasons are concerned with maximising the agent's self-interest, while moral reasons are concerned with satisfying the overriding requirements of morality (or 'categorical rationality', as translations of Kant typically put it). It is a commonplace that if there are compound reasons, they are constructed out of these more basic materials.

There are not many other plausible candidates for basic reasons. Perhaps one could argue that altruistic reasons (ie reasons for action that derive from concerns about the welfare of other persons) are basic. It is not utterly implausible to think that one could care about another person for reasons that are neither prudential nor moral in character; although, unlike prudential concern, we are hardwired only with a *capacity* for altruistic concern, which is usually cultivated and developed in a person through proper parenting practices. This capacity, once developed, is deeply expressed in our behaviour towards other persons.

Likewise, it is plausible to think that there are basic aesthetic reasons for action which dictate that we expose ourselves to artistic expression, as well as commit ourselves to creative artistic activities intended to elicit aesthetic experiences in other persons. One might glean such a view from the popular slogan 'Art for art's sake'.

For our purposes, it makes little difference. First, it should be quite clear that aesthetic reasons, even if atomic, will have nothing to do with providing reasons for following the law; at most, they provide reasons for viewing and creating art – both of which, while important for human wellbeing, are utterly irrelevant for our purposes. Second, if altruistic reasons are basic in the sense described, it is sufficient, for our purposes, to consider them as included within the realm of moral reasons. Thus, for our purposes, it is reasonable to think that the two classes of basic reasons are prudential and moral.

Notice that there is no plausible reason to think that legal norms are the source of basic reasons other than prudential or normative.[15] While there may

[14] H Richardson, 'Moral Reasoning' in EN Zalta (ed), *The Stanford Encyclopedia of Philosophy* (Winter 2014 edition) available at http://plato.stanford.edu/entries/reasoning-moral/.

[15] Scott Hershovitz argues that the very project of conceptual jurisprudence is problematic because it falsely presupposes that mandatory legal norms generate novel legal reasons for action: S Hershovitz, 'The End of Jurisprudence' (2015) 124 *Yale Law Journal* 882. Hershovitz, on my view, is correct in thinking there are no such reasons, but there is simply no ground for believing that this is presupposed by the very project of conceptual jurisprudence. In this connection, it is worth noting that Hershovitz cites no one who unambiguously accepts this claim. While his analysis is nuanced and well-reasoned, his critique refutes a view that no one seems to hold.

be theorists who have gestured in that direction (and I know of no one who has unambiguously held that position), that is largely a matter of solving the problem of legal normativity by implausible fiat. To be candid, this is simply not a position that can be given a plausible defence; law is a social construct contrived for basic reasons that are *antecedent* to any reasons law itself could create.

As a logical matter, it should be clear that a system of new norms that is constructed out of only two types of basic reason could not possibly give rise to a new kind of basic reason. Whatever reasons legal norms give rise to will have to be a either a basic reason or a compound reason, if such there be, constructed out of basic reasons that reflect the reasons for implementing a legal system.

This means that law's normativity will ultimately have to be explained either in terms of basic moral or prudential reasons or in terms of compound reasons (whatever, if anything, those would amount to) that are constructed out of these basic moral and prudential reasons. Insofar as a law is normative, it tells subjects what they ought to do, and true statements about what subjects ought to do define reasons. As Raz puts this important point, 'statements of the form "x ought to φ" are logically equivalent to statements of the form "There is reason for x to φ"'.[16] And the characteristic form in which law provides reasons for action is through directives that create legal obligations; as Hart puts the point, 'where there is law, there human conduct is made in some sense non-optional or *obligatory*' (emphasis added).[17] The question of law's normativity, then, will ultimately come down to explaining what kinds of reasons a legal obligation provides; and this account will ultimately require explaining legal normativity in terms of only moral and prudential reasons.

Law as such, then, provides a certain kind of reason for action that might be distinctive to law in some respect, but that reason must ultimately be explained in terms of moral and prudential reasons, since these are the only possible sources of basic reasons. As we will see, this creates trouble for the view that some conceptually possible legal systems do not authorise coercive enforcement mechanisms for any violations.

To begin, no conceptual account of legal reasons can succeed if it explains legal reasons, in the relevant sense, even partly in terms of moral reasons for action. It is a commonplace – among anyone not holding the most implausibly strong natural law view – that law as such does not provide even prima facie moral reasons for action.[18] The point doesn't originate with Raz, but he accepts it and, indeed, argues

[16] Raz, *Practical Reason and Practical Norms* (n 6) 29.

[17] Hart, *The Concept of Law* (n 5) 82.

[18] It should be noted that the strong natural law theorist has a related problem. It might be that it is a conceptual truth that only properly promulgated norms that satisfy moral constraints are legally valid and hence law, but that does not imply that the norms that are applied by officials and enforced against subjects actually satisfy those moral constraints. For this reason, officials can be mistaken in thinking what they enforce as law really is law. Accordingly, the corresponding issue for the strong natural law theorist is whether there is a prima facie moral reason to obey what officials apply and enforce as law. Since officials are not morally infallible, they may apply what does not pass the requisite moral tests and

for a much stronger sceptical view about law and moral reasons. As he describes the view:

> I shall argue that there is no obligation to obey the law. I shall suggest that there is not even a prima facie obligation to obey it .... I shall argue that there is no obligation to obey the law even in a good society whose legal system is just.[19]

Raz is not just arguing that law as such does not give rise to prima facie moral obligations to obey.[20] He argues for the stronger position that there is not even a prima facie moral obligation to obey the law of a *reasonably just state*.

Although Raz uses only the language of moral *obligations*, the considerations that Raz adduces also apply to moral reasons that do not rise to the level of obligations. Clearly, the law of Nazi Germany did not give rise to even prima facie content-independent moral reasons to obey law. Either way, it follows that whatever law's normativity is, it cannot be explained in terms that imply law *as such* provides moral reasons for action.

The only other type of basic reason is the one to which the authorisation of coercive enforcement mechanisms appeals: prudential reasons. Coercive enforcement mechanisms do not necessarily involve what are called 'sanctions', which are thought of as punishment. They can involve mechanisms that enforce – or withhold enforcement of – civil remedies. And they need not be available for every violation of law.

However, in every existing legal system of which we know, the judge has the power to impose a contempt 'sanction' on defendants who fail to comply with a court order allowing the judge to incarcerate the defendant, not as a punishment, but as an inducement to comply. Now the prospect of being incarcerated may not strike every individual, subjectively, as providing even a prima facie reason to avoid it; however, the authorisation of such enforcement mechanisms is reasonably contrived, and characteristically regarded, as a prudential disincentive to do whatever it is that would trigger such a consequence.

No more than that is needed. The issue is not whether everyone does, as an empirical matter concerning subjective reasons, regard avoiding coercive

mistakenly enforce what is not law, as an objective matter, against subjects. Thus, it might be that, on the strong natural law theorist's view, people have a conclusive moral reason to obey what objectively satisfies the relevant procedural and moral standards; but there is little reason to think there is even a prima facie moral reason to obey the pronouncements of morally fallible officials concerning what is law. One cannot solve substantive problems of moral legitimacy simply by moving the content of concepts around.

[19] J Raz, *The Authority of Law* (Oxford, Clarendon Press, 1979) 233. Raz does not actually use the term 'moral' in the above passage, but he is clearly referring to moral obligations. His targets here are theories of moral legitimacy that take the position that there is a content-independent general *moral* obligation to obey the law in reasonably just states. The position that there is no legal obligation in such states is utter nonsense. Although much of Raz's theory is certainly counterintuitive from the standpoint of the core legal practices that construct the content of our concepts, it would be uncharitable in the extreme to attribute such a silly position to him.

[20] Although Raz is referring to moral obligations, the considerations that Raz adduces also apply to moral reasons that do not rise to the level of moral obligations.

enforcement mechanisms as a prudential reason for doing what the law requires; it is surely possible for it to be in a person's interest to put herself on the business end of such mechanisms. The issue is, rather, one of practical rationality: whether, as a general matter, one should regard the avoidance of such mechanisms, by itself, as a prima facie reason, *even if decisively defeated by other reasons*, for doing what the law requires. The answer to that seems obviously affirmative: avoiding coercive mechanisms is something that should be avoided in the absence of special circumstances that would make it prudentially rational to incur the consequences of the application of these mechanisms to achieve greater benefits.

This is why coercive enforcement mechanisms are reasonably contrived, and characteristically regarded, as reasons to do what law requires. Even if the probability of an encounter with these mechanisms is very low, the fact that one must even consider the probability of such an encounter shows that the very authorisation of such mechanisms is relevant with respect to deliberations regarding what one ought to do, as a prudential matter. That is, the needed recourse to the probabilities shows that the authorisation of coercive enforcement mechanisms provides a prima facie prudential reason for action; probabilities are commonly used by self-interested agents – often in ways that seem morally dubious or prudentially confused – to try to assess the strength of the prima facie reason provided by the authorisation of such mechanisms relative to the strength of other reasons.

It bears reiterating that the relevant kind of reason is an objective reason for action. It is a trivial matter of objective standards of practical rationality that the authorisation of coercive enforcement mechanisms – or the legal *possibility*, as opposed to *probability*, of their application to a non-complying defendant – provides an objective reason, though not necessarily decisive, to obey the law. Failure to distinguish between the relevant types of reason and indicate which of the relevant types is the correct reason has been the source of much mischief in conceptual theorising about law.

Indeed, it is sometimes, from the standpoint of objective practical rationality, prudentially advantageous to break the law. I am a serial illegal parker because it is economically advantageous. The cost of getting a parking ticket provides a prudential disincentive for parking illegally and hence provides a reason for not parking illegally. The benefit is that parking illegally saves me considerably more money than it costs because I rarely get a parking ticket. But, without more knowledge of the specifics of a situation, the authorisation of a fine, by itself, provides a prudential reason for doing what law requires. More than this cannot be needed to justify the claim that a legal system provides objective prudential reasons for doing what the law requires by authorising coercive enforcement mechanisms for violations. No more than this seems presupposed by the relevant legal practices themselves or assumed in the views of those officials and practitioners whose views and practices construct the content of our legal concepts.

Consider, in contrast, an alternative account of what objective reasons law might provide in the form of Scott Shapiro's theory of legal obligation.

According to Shapiro's account, X is legally obligated to do *p* if and only if, from the legal point of view, X is morally obligated to do *p*.[21] Assuming that 'the legal point of view' is constituted by some set of acts or beliefs of officials, the question is: what kind of objective reason could a legal obligation, thus conceived, provide to comply with its requirement?

None that can be explained in terms of the two basic reasons. In the absence of some sort of consequence for flouting the 'legal point of view' that is characteristically regarded, without more, as undesirable from the standpoint of self-interest, the claim that an act is legally obligatory, on Shapiro's analysis, provides no *objective* prudential reason to comply. Although it is possible for a person to fetishise anything (including the beliefs of legal officials) and hence regard anything as a *subjective* reason for action, the beliefs of persons who simply happen to have the status of legal officials, without more, cannot, as an objective matter of practical rationality, provide an objective prudential reason for action. Further, in the absence of some reason to think these legal officials have a special moral insight (which is obviously not a conceptual requirement for law), the claim that an act is legally obligatory, on Shapiro's analysis, provides no moral reason for action for anyone.

The denial, then, that the authorisation of coercive enforcement mechanisms is a necessary feature of a legal system leaves the theory of law unable to give a plausible account of law's normativity that coheres with core understandings that officials and legal practitioners have about the practices in which they engage that construct our concept of law.[22] The claim that the authorisation of coercive enforcement mechanisms provides what would characteristically be regarded, other things being equal, as providing reasons for action is an important feature in its favour – even if those reasons are prudential in character.

Raz acknowledges, as he *must*, that coercive enforcement mechanisms provide an objective reason for action, but argues that 'it is a reason of the wrong kind'.[23] The problem, on Raz's view, is that a prudential reason of this kind is just a first order reason, while it is a conceptual truth that 'mandatory [legal] norms … are exclusionary [or, as he put it subsequently, 'pre-emptive] reasons as well as first-order reasons'.[24]

This is not a topic that can be addressed in much depth here, but Raz's view is presumptively problematic. First, if this is grounded in an intuition, it is far from one that is universally accepted; many theorists, including Stephen Perry, deny

[21] S Shapiro, *Legality* (Cambridge MA, Harvard University Press, 2011) 232. Many have attributed in conversation this view to Raz, but he confirmed in an email (on file with the author) that he disagrees with this view.

[22] It should not be thought surprising that Shapiro's theory of legal obligation inherits problems from other areas of his thought. Shapiro also denies that law is essentially coercive. Once a theorist has taken a conceptual position on coercion (or on the nature of legal obligation), that position will have logical implications that constrain what can be said about other legal concepts.

[23] Raz, *Practical Reason and Practical Norms* (n 6) 161.

[24] ibid.

that it is a conceptual truth that law provides pre-emptive reasons. Second, if this is not grounded in intuitions, it cannot validly be inferred from the way in which law is enforced. Law is clearly enforced in an exclusionary fashion in the sense that it is enforced against the subject regardless of the desires that explain her non-compliance. But to infer a claim about what reasons law provides, as a conceptual matter, from a claim about how law is enforced – indeed, a contingent one, on Raz's view – is straightforwardly fallacious. Whatever other arguments Raz might have would have to be examined separately, but it remains noteworthy that Raz's view falls well short of enjoying a consensus among legal theorists.

Nevertheless, as Raz acknowledges, the authorisation of coercive enforcement mechanisms provides an objective prudential reason for action in every existing legal system of which we have ever known. And nothing in law apart from some sort of presumptively unpleasant consequences, such as are entailed by the application (or non-application, in some circumstances) of coercive enforcement mechanisms, can do that work. I suppose one could take the position that an informal social ostracism might take the form of such prudential considerations, but it cannot be part of the nature of law that subjects express disapproval of other subjects for violating law any more than it could be part of the nature of law that subjects accept their legal system as legitimate. Further, it simply makes more sense to think of a system of rules backed only by informal social disapproval as 'pre-legal' than as 'legal' in character.

One can, of course, deny that law as such provides reasons, and claim instead that law merely 'purports' to provide reasons for action. There are a number of concerns with this familiar view. To begin, the enforcement of law presupposes that law provides some kind of reason for complying. The violation of a valid legal norm provides the *legal* justification for applying the relevant coercive enforcement mechanisms to the party in violation. The violation of a legal obligation provides the grounds for invoking the application of these coercive enforcement mechanisms, but that makes sense only insofar as the existence of a legal obligation – at least, one backed by a coercive enforcement mechanism – is viewed as an objective reason for action.

But it is not just that legal practice presupposes that valid legal norms provide reasons for action (and do not merely purport to do so); it is rather that the associated practices are paradigmatic – regardless of whether one takes only existing legal systems as paradigmatic or includes conceptually possible legal systems. Given this, and that it is utterly uncontroversial in legal practice that mandatory legal norms create legal obligations, the view that law merely purports to provide legal obligations or reasons is inconsistent with a practice that is as central to law as any other suggests that, if true, officials are systematically confused about a concept that is formed by their beliefs and practices – something which cannot happen, on Raz's view. More argument, of course, would be needed to fully make out the case for this result, but this is sufficiently plausible that this result cannot simply be dismissed as false.

Significantly, at the end of his career, Hart changed his position on the nature of legal obligation to one that conforms to one argued for here. In a 1991 interview, in response to a question as to whether he would revise any part of the *The Concept of Law*, Hart replied, 'here are some topics of major importance where my exposition is not only confused but incomplete and important'. The most important problem, on his view, was that he failed to give an adequate account of legal obligation:

> The most important of these topics is that of legal obligation. The main source of my error here is the account which I gave … of the general idea of obligation. This account … wrongly treats obligations of all kinds as arising from social rules which are accepted by the majority of the members of a social group as guides to their conduct and standards of criticism, and are sustained by general demands for conformity and pressure on those who deviate or threaten to deviate. Plainly such an account could at best fit only those obligations which arise, in what I have called a regime of 'primary rules', from *custom-type* rules. But as the rest of my book was concerned to show, in a developed legal system where there are courts and a legislature and constitutional secondary rules of recognition and change, legal obligations frequently also arise under *statute-type* rules enacted by a legislature and applied by courts. Such enacted rules may not be accepted by ordinary members of a society and may not be supported by general social pressure on those who deviate or threaten to deviate. Nonetheless they are recognized by the courts as valid rules of the legal system which courts have to apply to cases coming before them because they satisfy the criteria of validity provided by the secondary rule of recognition which the courts and officials of the system of accept. *But my account of obligation … fails to give any explanation of how it is that legal obligations arise from such enacted legal rules.*[25]

This remarkable passage calls attention to significant mistakes made by common interpretations of Hart. It was often thought that Hart's remark that social obligations are accompanied by social pressure was not any part of his account of the nature of social obligation; rather, the thought was that social pressure was simply an indication that a rule was obligatory – despite the obvious fact that such an interpretation left Hart without any resources to explain the normativity of legal obligation.[26]

Accordingly, Hart admitted that he needed to give 'a fresh account of the general idea of obligation', where he, like Kelsen, made clear that 'the idea of a legitimate response to deviation in the form of demands and pressure for conformity is *the central component of obligation*'.[27] Here it should be clear that: (1) he is now giving a conceptual account of legal obligation as it binds citizens through primary norms; and (2) the central feature of that account is the authorisation of formal coercive mechanisms.

[25] HLA Hart, 'An Interview with Hart' in LD d'Almeida, J Edwards, and A Dolcetti (eds), *Reading H.L.A. Hart's The Concept of Law* (Oxford, Oxford University Press, 2015) at 502–503.

[26] See Himma, 'A Comprehensive Hartian Theory of Legal Obligation' (n 1), for a thorough discussion of this problem.

[27] Hart, 'An Interview with Hart' (n 25) 503.

To fully secure this important point, it is helpful to reproduce Hart's lengthy remarks in the interview that express this intent more clearly and precisely to eliminate any remaining doubts about a theory of obligation that is, to be candid, the only plausible possibility if our legal practices construct the content of our legal concepts. As Hart put the point:

> This revised account of obligation under a simple regime of custom-type rules can be extended to the more complex case of a developed legal system where legal obligations are imposed by statute-type rules enacted by a legislature. Such enacted rules may not be generally accepted by ordinary members of a society, but are recognized as valid rules of the legal system by courts … . *Such enacted rules imposing obligations need not be and frequently are not supported by general social pressure, but are supported by ancillary rules permitting or requiring officials to respond to deviation with demands and coercive measures to secure conformity.* These responses will not be merely predictable consequences of deviation (and indeed may not always be predictable) but will be *legitimate* responses to deviations, since deviations are permitted or required to make them.[28]

As should be clear, Hart has adopted a theory of obligation that closely parallels the account I developed earlier[29] and implicitly acknowledges that the relevant type of reasons that law provides are objective prudential reasons defined by a prudential interest in avoiding the coercive mechanisms of the law. Given the obvious relationship between the problem of legal normativity and the problem of legal obligation, he has pretty much endorsed the thesis for which I have argued in this paper.

VII. Summary and Conclusions

The case for thinking it is a conceptually necessary feature of law that it authorises coercive enforcement mechanisms for some violations of law is supported by two facts about paradigmatic legal practices. First, it rests on the centrality and ubiquity of these mechanisms in every existing legal system and the equally ubiquitous practice among paradigmatic legal systems of equating the notion of an actionable cause with the availability of a remedy that can be coercively enforced. In every legal system ever known to exist, one of the most salient features of legal practice is that the system authorises coercive enforcement mechanisms to induce subjects to do that deemed socially desirable or to refrain from doing that deemed socially undesirable. As our core practices define *our* legal concepts, it is reasonable to take law's reliance on coercive enforcement mechanisms as paradigmatic and hence as a necessary constituent of a legal system.

[28] Hart, 'An Interview with Hart' (n 25) 504.
[29] ibid.

Second, it rests on the inability of a conceptual account of law that treats coercive enforcement mechanisms as inessential to explain legal normativity. Once the authorisation of coercive enforcement mechanisms is taken out of the picture, it is hard to see what prudential rational considerations could arise from legal directives that should function as a reason to obey the law. But the normativity of law cannot be expressed in terms of moral reasons because, as Raz concedes, law as such does not even give rise to prima facie reasons to act.

5

Non-naturalism, Normativity and the Meaning of *Ought*: Some Lessons from Kelsen*

GEORGE PAVLAKOS

I. Introduction

It is remarkable how relevant Kelsen's scholarship still is in today's philosophical environment. His theoretical reflections span such depth and breadth of philosophical reflection that remain topical even amongst the most sophisticated scholarly debates of our time, capable of offering many an insight, even for questions that extend beyond the strict confines of legal theory, into meta-ethics, epistemology and even metaphysics.

Due to the enormous volume of Kelsen's work, however, it is not always easy to extract the gist of his thought, not the least so because the changes that his philosophical views have undergone over the many years of Kelsen's life,[1] render it difficult to reconstruct them in a manner free of contradiction. It seems to me that serious engagement with the Kelsenian oeuvre in a contemporary context would have to live up to three tasks: aim to subject Kelsen's philosophical ideas to careful reconstruction; demonstrate their effectiveness with respect to many a contemporary legal theoretical puzzle; and, finally, supplement them in a number of significant ways, with a view to restoring his arguments into a robust and coherent

* Research and writing of the paper has been partially supported by the Grant Agency of the Czech Academy of Sciences through a project on 'The Role of the Principle of Proportionality in the Decision-Making Process of Courts' (grant ID: 15-23955S). An earlier version of the paper was read at a one-day workshop on *Normativity and the Law – A Kelsenian Perspective*, which took place in November 2009 at the Law School, University of Leicester. For helpful discussion on several of its ideas I owe many thanks to Stanley Paulson and the other participants of the Leicester workshop as well as to Andreas Takis.

[1] For a periodisation of the various phases in Kelsen's work, see SL Paulson, 'Towards a Periodization of the Pure Theory of Law' in L Gianformaggio (ed), *Hans Kelsen's Legal Theory. A Diachronic Point of View* (Torino, 1990) 24; SL Paulson, 'Four Phases in Hans Kelsen's Legal Theory? Reflections on a Periodization' (1998) 18 *Oxford Journal of Legal Studies* 153; C Heidemann, 'Review article. Norms, facts, and judgments. A reply to SL Paulson' (1999) 19 *Oxford Journal of Legal Studies* 345.

system of thought, one whose heritage might well prove decisive in the jurisprudential debates to come.

In this paper I wish to focus on one particular aspect of Kelsen's philosophical programme. I am referring to non-naturalism, the tenet that is inexorably intertwined with the development and elaboration of the pure theory of law, Kelsen's most prominent and everlasting intellectual achievement.[2]

In what follows, I shall argue that Kelsen's endeavour for non-naturalism is incompatible with a strict separation between the legal and the moral domain. Famously both tenets, that of non-naturalism and that of the strict separation of law and morality, were put forward as complementary components of the purity thesis. To that extent I argue that the purity thesis is characterised by an insurmountable tension, which can be resolved only if one of its components is dropped. To make things clear from the outset, my claim rests on the assumption that non-naturalism is synonymous with, or at least constitutes a condition of, practical normativity in general. In other words, it is not possible to redeem a full-blooded normativity, unless one establishes that normative items (be they norms, reasons or what have you) are non-naturalistic through and through. However, so I argue, insofar as normativity pertains to the moral as well as the legal domain, it is incoherent to treat legal obligation in a non-naturalistic manner, while leaving out moral obligation, as Kelsen emphatically does.

It is only under a deeply problematic understanding of normativity that one can maintain a distinction between the different domains of practical reason, as Kelsen does. In addressing those problematic aspects of Kelsen's account, I will avail myself of a full-blooded conception of non-naturalism, demonstrating that Kelsen's own version of non-naturalism falls largely short of it. On the face of it, I shall demonstrate that Kelsen assumes a naturalistic psychology at the basis of his understanding of any type of normativity, one that forces him to introduce an artificial distinction between law and morality, on pain of condemning law to inertness. Having said all this, I will emphatically welcome Kelsen's insight of a non-naturalist normativity and attempt to suggest an alternative account. In a nutshell the argument is as follows.

Kelsen advances a new ideal of legal science with an eye to retrieving legal knowledge as purely normative, by purging it from any non- or extra-legal elements (II). His contention is that a key requirement for arriving at pure legal knowledge is that naturalistic explications of normativity be blocked appropriately (III). With an eye to undertaking the task of banning naturalism he devises, in a neo-Kantian spirit, a new epistemic category for cognising law *qua* normative or reason-giving realm, viz the category of (peripheral) imputation (IV). Imputation, to the extent that it applies peculiarly to law but not to morality,

[2] The question of naturalism in Kelsen's work has prominently occupied Stanley Paulson. See especially SL Paulson, 'The Very Idea of Legal Positivism' (2011) 102 *Revista Brasileira de Estudos Políticos* 139; SL Paulson, 'The Question of Normativity in Hans Kelsen's Pure Theory of Law', MS pre-circulated at the workshop 'Normativity and the Law – A Kelsenian Perspective' (School of Law, University of Leicester, 18 November 2009), on file with author.

rests on a misunderstanding of the nature of normativity and fails to deliver the requisite full-blooded non-naturalism (V). Failure to deliver a full-blooded non-naturalism leads to a fragmentation of the normative 'ought' into several domains, each of which is grounded on its own peculiar category of imputation (VI). A final section brings together the earlier lines of reasoning and offers a succinct restatement of the argument (VII).

II. Purity

Famously, in postulating knowledge of the law, which is purged from all foreign elements, Kelsen introduced the *purity thesis*. He took the purity thesis to resist any instance of mixing up non-legal with legal materials. Just to avail myself of one amongst many characteristic passages:

> It characterises itself as a 'pure' theory of law because it aims at cognition focused on the law alone, and because it aims to eliminate from this cognition everything not belonging to the object of cognition, precisely specified as the law. That is, the Pure Theory aims to free legal science of all foreign elements. This is its basic methodological principle.[3]

This thesis was developed to comprise not only purity from non-normative, or 'ought'-irrelevant materials, but – what is more – purity from other, non-legal versions of the 'ought'. Along these lines, Kelsen maintains, we should strive to steer clear the legal-ought from other variants of the 'ought': moral, aesthetic or otherwise. In effect, when put like this, the purity thesis asks us, first, to distinguish between different types of non-naturalistic fact (assuming that all 'ought'-facts are non-naturalistic) and, second, to keep legal non-naturalistic facts intact from other (ie moral) non-naturalistic facts.

It would follow that a central contention of the pure theory of law and its revolutionary methodology is the thesis that normativity requires a non-naturalist epistemology (and metaphysics).[4]

III. Non-Naturalism

I turn next to explore the (necessary) link between normativity and non-naturalism in terms that are broader that Kelsen's own enterprise. I argue that the

[3] H Kelsen *Introduction to the Problems of Legal Theory*, 1st edn of *Reine Rechtslehre*, BL Paulson and SL Paulson trs (Oxford, Clarendon Press, 1992) 7.

[4] Accounting for Kelsen's purity claim in detail would require a lengthy detour into a voluminous body of work that spans many years. Kelsen's most important ideas are to be found in: Kelsen, *Introduction to the Problems of Legal Theory* (n 3); *idem, Hauptprobleme der Staatsrechtslehre*, 2nd edn (Tübingen, JCB Mohr, 1923); *idem, Der soziologische und der juristische Staatsbegriff: kritische Untersuchung des Verhältnisses von Staat und Recht* (Tübingen, JCB Mohr, 1922).

success of any non-naturalistic programme can be measured against its capacity to elucidate our normative reasons in a non-psychologist manner. In a nutshell, the conclusion arrived at is that only such types of non-naturalism succeed, which manage to explicate our normative reasons as having motivational power *independently* of any psychological mental states.

Stanley Paulson's seminal reconstruction of Kelsen's own effort to reconstruct normativity, bears witness to the importance Kelsen placed on a non-naturalist explication of legal normativity in particular, but also normativity more generally.[5] Yet Kelsen was not alone in his struggle against naturalism. Another fine example of a non-naturalist explication of (moral) ought-facts comes from GE Moore. The relevance of Moore's thought for Kelsen goes beyond the mere fact that they were contemporaries. Both thinkers work and write in a philosophical environment of widespread non-naturalism that spans the so-called normative sciences (from logic to law). What is more, both thinkers, each from his own angle, pursue a non-naturalistic programme with respect to practical normativity. Finally, there is even textual evidence that Kelsen not only was aware of Moore's main theses, but also approved of them.[6]

Painting with a broad brush, Moore's non-naturalism can be summed up in two key claims:

(i) first, the *non-analysability thesis*:[7] this is the semantic contention that evaluative concepts in general (and in particular the concept 'good' which Moore takes to be the most basic evaluative concept) cannot be subjected to non-circular analysis through any non-evaluative concept. Thus, any effort to analyse 'good' as, say, 'pleasurable' would be circular because it would require a new reference to 'good' in order to retain its normative or evaluative significance;

(ii) second, the *open-question argument*: this argues for the metaphysical thesis that normative properties are not reducible to non-normative properties. The following observation is adduced as evidence for this claim: any exhaustive description of an object/situation in terms of non-evaluative properties leaves open the question which evaluative properties the same object/situation has. So even if I am in a position to describe exhaustively my teacher, I will still not have answered the question whether she is a good teacher.[8]

[5] See n 2.

[6] Kelsen refers to Moore's *Principia Ethica* in the second edition of the *Pure Theory of Law*: H Kelsen, *Reine Rechtslehre. Mit einem Anhang: Das Problem der Gerechtigkeit*, 2. vollständig neu bearbeitete und erweiterte Auflage (Wien, Franz Deuticke Verlag, 1960) 5, 11.

[7] I am using this term to summarise Moore's semantic arguments that may be taken to include the so-called 'naturalistic fallacy', which Moore uses to denote the impossibility of inferring an evaluative conclusion from non-evaluative premises.

[8] In later work Moore develops his two theses in more explicit non-naturalist terms. In particular in his *Ethics* he points out that attributing the meaning of evaluative terms to non-evaluative psychological states leads to unstable truth values for evaluative statements and cannot explain the possibility of moral disagreement: if the truth-value of the same evaluative sentence varies with the speakers,

Moore's version of non-naturalism is particularly useful for exploring the nature of normative reasons (or reasons for action). In what follows I shall refer to 'normative reasons' or simply 'reasons' to denote any action-guiding item, thus introducing a somewhat wider scope in the discussion of normativity. Also, I shall not strive for an accurate reconstruction of Moore's own ideas but merely use what can be coined a broadly Moorean framework to develop a non-naturalist understanding of reasons, which will be useful for present purposes.

One may argue that non-naturalism with respect to normativity presupposes something like the following:[9] what motivates us to act, ie our motivating reasons (and hence the normative meaning of the concepts we use to relate to them) does not derive from any mental states (ie naturalistic entities), but is identical to our normative reasons. Normative reasons are what our mental states are about, when those explain our behaviour.[10] Typically our mental states are about facts, in some appropriate sense of the word. It follows that: I have a reason to Φ not because of the fact that I am in a particular mental state, but because of the very fact[11] my mental state is about.

Switching to the level of discourse (as to remain within the confines of the method of conceptual analysis, one most favoured by Moore): reasons for action are embedded in truth-evaluable entities, ie propositions,[12] as opposed to propositional attitudes, ie beliefs, desires or volitional states in the broad sense. Let us avail ourselves of concrete examples.

First, a case of a motivating reason *qua* motivational state:

(MS) *The reason that I take an umbrella is my belief that it rains.*

Conversely, this is what we get when motivating reasons are identical with facts:

(NR) *The reason that I take an umbrella is (the fact) that it rains.*

Switching to the more complex case of a normative fact, the contrasting types of reason take the following form:

(MS) *The reason I help the needy is because I believe/intend/desire that helping the needy is good.*[13]

(NR) *The reason I help the needy is because (of the fact that) helping the needy is good.*

then it becomes impossible to explain how two speakers who affirm and deny the same sentence are disagreeing, rather than talking about different things. See GE Moore, *Ethics* (Oxford University Press, 1912; repr. 1961) 50–82.

[9] The formulations that follow owe a lot to D Parfit, 'Normativity' in R Shaffer-Landau (ed), *Oxford Studies in Metaethics*, vol I (Oxford, Oxford University Press, 2006) 325.

[10] Parfit, 'Normativity' (n 9) 365.

[11] For the ontological status of such facts see sections VI and VII.

[12] Further if a proposition is true, then a fact exists.

[13] Obviously, there is an asymmetry between beliefs and desires. A belief's content depends on the truth-value of the proposition – whereas for desires this is not the case. That said, a belief itself is still not a motivating reason *qua* normative reason; only the true proposition (fact) that corresponds to it is.

It would follow, then, that the general 'structure' of non-naturalist motivating reasons is:

> The fact 'that Φ',

NOT

> The fact of my believing/desiring/etc 'that Φ'.

Thus, a full-blooded non-naturalism with respect to reasons requires that our motivating reasons be not the psychological states of having a belief/intention or desire, but the actual facts our beliefs, desires etc are about. Such facts constitute our normative reasons and, further, deliver the salient meaning or content of ought statements – and we should stick to that.

In summing up: a distinction between motivational states and motivational reasons must be drawn. In a naturalistic outlook, motivating reasons are exhausted by motivational states. In a non-naturalistic outlook motivating reasons are independent of any mental states (ie propositional attitudes such as belief, desire etc) and identical with the facts that constitute our normative reasons. This I take to be the point of a full-blooded non-naturalism.

IV. Imputation

I rely next on Stanley Paulson's interpretation of imputation.[14] To put it succinctly, the category of imputation delivers two results in one go: first, it transforms subjective volitional states (acts of will) into objective meanings (norms, or normative reasons). Second, it does this by connecting 'material facts' in a *subjectless* way. It is this subjectless-ness which caters for the purification of normative contents from subjective states of the will (for an answer whether it succeeds, see section V below).

(Peripheral) imputation should be considered as Kelsen's effort to flesh out the meaning of ought statements.[15] Although imputation is a category of cognition, it takes an active role in determining the content of ought statements, for it purports to lead to knowledge of volitional materials *qua* non-naturalist, normative items, or what Kelsen calls the objective meaning of an act of will.

What should be emphasised it that Kelsen, in putting forward the category of peripheral imputation, is proposing a criterion of knowledge with respect to norms, not directly a criterion for specifying the content of such norms. However, given his definition of norms as the objective meaning of acts of will, it is pertinent

[14] See Paulson, 'The Question of Normativity in Hans Kelsen's Pure Theory of Law' (n 2) 53–55.
[15] In the present context I shall be focusing on the notion of peripheral imputation.

to remark that for it to succeed, imputation should deliver the following outcome: it should capture (legal) ought statements as meaning something over and above the subjective meaning of the act of will that corresponds to each of them. Assuming the content of any sentence is given by a proposition that corresponds to it, the following should apply: the proposition that determines the meaning of the norm-sentence should not be individuated by the volitional state of the agent who issues the relevant act of will, but by the normative fact that exists when the proposition is true. This should be the case even if, syntactically speaking, the sentence expressing the subjective meaning of the relevant act of will and the one expressing the norm (ie the objective meaning of the same act of the will) are identical.[16]

V. Psychologism

So far it has been assumed that non-naturalism is only relevant for an account of reasons if it serves normativity, not vice-versa. To revert to the terminology I introduced in section III: non-naturalism is capable of delivering normativity if – and only if – it can flesh out our motivating reasons as being exhausted by our normative reasons, while blocking the path of explanation that links them to motivating states.

There is a strong presumption that Kelsen never managed to rid his conception of normativity of psychologism and arrive at a full-blooded non-naturalism. Due to limitations of space, I cannot trace down in detail Kelsen's psychologism. However, I shall try to give an overview of its central structure, by focusing on some of his later writings.[17]

Let me take stock before I begin my exposition. We saw that, in Kelsen's jargon, a norm (normative reason) is supposed to be the objective meaning of a subjective act of will. This objective meaning is retrieved or established through the projection of the category of imputation on the relevant subjective acts of will of particular individuals. It is important to note at this point that the projection of imputation is the task of legal science, which is called upon to organise the bulk of brute volitional facts, which generate social authority, into objective knowledge.

[16] See H Kelsen, 'Norm and Value' in O Weinberger (ed), *Hans Kelsen: Essays in Legal and Moral Philosophy* (Dordrecht, D Reidel Publishing Company, 1973) 276, 276n.

[17] In comparing materials in Kelsen's work that stem from different periods I am potentially opening myself to the charge of doing injustice to his ideas. On a widespread view, Kelsen's later writings reflect strong philosophical concessions, which he had to undertake in order to render his legal philosophy more accessible to American lawyers. On this view, central amongst these concessions was the abandonment of neo-Kantianism for a less sophisticated legal realist approach. Even if true, this view should not lead one to assume that someone with Kelsen's intellectual stature would have defended ideas he held to be less than optimal just for the sake of popularity. In any event, my analysis corroborates, even if indirectly, the point of the received view in demonstrating that Kelsen – given his non-naturalist intuitions – ought to have followed a different philosophical path. However, my line of argument purports to attribute error to Kelsen on philosophical grounds, not as a result of pragmatic expediency.

A re-formulation of those ideas in the light of section III might run as follows: non-psychologism would require that the category of imputation remain sufficient for singling out facts that determine the content of the relevant normative sentences, as opposed to some volitional states. Assuming that that, which expresses the objective content of a normative sentence, is a norm, then what one needs to establish is that norms are motivating reasons *qua* normative reasons as opposed to motivational states. Thus, it would follow that Kelsen's notion of the objective meaning of an act of will (ie the norm) ought to meet the requirements for normative reasons, as those were set out earlier.

Let us see whether imputation can contribute to the 'objective meaning of an act of will' in the above sense of pointing towards a normative reason as opposed to a mental state. Take a normative sentence as uttered by legal science:

(Normative sentence or NS) 'If X parks illegally, X will be fined'.

There are two meanings/contents that may attach to this sentence; a subjective one and an objective one. Let us already relate the subjective meaning with a motivational state (MS) and the objective one with a normative reason (NR):

MS: the fact that someone wills that 'NS'.

Here the mental state <someone's willing NS> determines the content of NS.

NR: The fact that (NS).

Here the <fact that NS> determines the meaning of 'NS'.

Since we are talking about (objective and subjective) meanings we can restate the same ideas by staying at the level of semantics: in (MS) what determines the content of 'NS' is the propositional attitude that corresponds to the relevant mental state [ie some version of expressivism].[18] In (NR) what delivers the content of 'NS' is a proposition, in other words an entity capable of truth-evaluation (ie mind-independent). In any case the point is that the true proposition/normative fact that is our normative reason ought, *by itself*, to be capable of motivating action, without need for supplementation by any additional volitional element.[19]

[18] For the most authoritative discussion of expressivist semantics to date, see M Schroeder, *Being For* (Oxford, Oxford University Press, 2007).

[19] To bring this point home, compare with Neil MacCormick's idea of a hermeneutic standpoint, which stands between Hart's internal and an (extreme) external standpoint (see DN MacCormick, *HLA Hart* (London, Edward Arnold, 1981) at 34–40). Pace MacCormick, the hermeneutic standpoint enables one to make statements of reasons (rules) even in the absence of approval of/commitment to their content, which is otherwise required by Hart's internal standpoint. MacCormick explains the possibility of the hermeneutic standpoint through a distinction between cognitive and volitional capacities. While Hart's internal standpoint requires both capacities to be present, the hermeneutic standpoint obtains just on the basis of agents' cognitive capacities. However, if our reasons (rules) can become objects for cognition antecedently to any approval or commitment, then arguably no additional volitional gloss will be required in order to explain their normativity. This point is argued persuasively by N Stavropoulos, *Objectivity in Law* (Oxford, Clarendon Press, 1996) 57–60, who characteristically states: 'preference comes analytically too late to make a difference' (58–59).

Now, the objection I level at Kelsen is that imputation does nothing to guarantee that the meaning of 'NS' is not actually determined by some mental attitude, which forms the content of the one or the other mental state. In other words, Kelsen's 'objective meanings of acts of will' fall short of being normative reasons in the sense a full-blooded non-naturalism would require.

Showing that Kelsen introduces two incompatible views on normativity and argues for their mutual interdependence can drive the objection home. On the one hand Kelsen contends that normative reasons (norms) cannot coincide with any mental states of the subjects or the authors of the law. In 'Norm and Value',[20] Kelsen draws a distinction between judgements of objective value and those of subjective value. In his words, the former describe the relationship between an object (behaviour) and an objectively valid norm, while the latter describe the relationship between an object and the fact that some individual is in one or the other volitional mental state. Kelsen takes judgements of subjective value to be judgements about (naturalistic) reality, while he denies that for judgements of objective value. This is consistent with non-naturalism: for if judgements of objective value were statements of naturalistic fact, then the purity of law's normativity would be indefensible.

On the other hand, Kelsen seems to maintain that normative reasons (norms) are not sufficient for motivation, but instead require an extra layer of motivational force in order to motivate action. In his essay 'Law and Morality'[21] he seems to advocate the view that no normative order can do away with men's psychological states as motives for their acts and omissions. Given this constraint he urges:

> If it (i.e. a social order) is to be effective, it can only create the inclination or interest to behave in accordance with the social order, and to repudiate the inclinations [...] which would operate if it were absent.[22]

In another prominent essay entitled 'Why Should the Law be Obeyed?'[23] Kelsen argues that the law generates reasons for action to the extent that it 'adopts' or 'authorises' subjective volitional facts:

> The subjective meaning of the acts by which the norms ... of positive law are created is, necessarily, that these prescriptions ought to be obeyed. But ... why is their *subjective* meaning considered to be their *objective* meaning as well? ... Why do we interpret the acts by which positive law is created as having not only the subjective but also the objective meaning of binding norms?[24]

The point here seems to be that a norm has motivational capacity only to the extent that the subjective meaning of an act of will is adopted in full by the objective

[20] In Kelsen, *Essays in Legal and Moral Philosophy* (n 16) 280–81.
[21] ibid 83–94.
[22] ibid 85.
[23] In H Kelsen, *What is Justice? Justice, Law, and Politics in the Mirror of Science: Collected Essays* (New Jersey, The Law Book Exchange Ltd Union, reprinted 2000) 257–65.
[24] ibid 257.

formulation of the norm. Here the relationship between motivating and normative reasons is inversed: rather that determining fully the motivating reason, the norm *qua* normative reason requires some motivational state in order to develop its action-guiding force.

In either of the above cases Kelsen appears to be arguing that social norms require, for the part that they are capable of regulating action, some psychological state on behalf of the addressee. This proves precisely that there exists no objective meaning *qua* normative reason to regulate action but that, instead, normative reasons require to be supplemented by some motivational state on behalf of the addressee. However, in the light of our earlier analysis, this is precisely the trap of naturalism: to introduce a distinction between what is a normative reason and what motivates its addressees. No sooner does Kelsen allow the gap between reasons and motivation to open, than norms *qua* objective meanings cease to be normative reasons in a full-blooded sense.

This is a crucial point in the course of my argument, so allow me to ponder a little longer on it. I argued that the objection that Kelsen fails to flesh out non-naturalistic normative reasons can be levelled against him by pointing to two incompatible conceptions of normativity, which are at work in his writings. We now need to spell out in more detail where the incompatibility lies.

The point is this, more or less: if objective meanings (norms) were normative reasons, then we wouldn't need to be helping ourselves to motivating states in order to explain their normativity. The fact that Kelsen so does, points to the further fact that norms remain, as far as their action-guiding power is concerned, tied down to the subjective will of their authors. When a subjective will is directed at the addressee of the relevant norm, there is no (objective) normative reason to direct the addressee's action but only the psychological state of the author, which, naturally, is destined to remain opaque to the addressee.[25] On the face of it, a new psychological state needs to be evoked to fill the normative gap. The fact that Kelsen requires reference to the addressee's motivational universe shows precisely that the issue of motivation has at no point in his theory been elevated above the level of naturalist facts, to comprise objective normative reasons. Instead continuity in normativity is ensured, by seeing to it that, at every point in time, someone's (either the author's or the addressee's) psychological state can be plugged into the content of the norm.

A rather bleak picture emerges from the conceptual landscape just sketched: norms-as-action-guiding items never remain connected to the same content but attach in random order to different motivational states, which may coincide with one another only as a matter of ex post serendipity, not of ex ante necessity. This implies that in the Kelsenian universe obligations *simpliciter* are a rare phenomenon, since as a rule, all obligations are confined to particular contexts.

[25] In this context relevant are all the problems arising from the continuity of norms: 'is there a norm when the sovereign changes?' 'Is there a norm that extends beyond the physical presence of its author?', and so on – Kelsen of course recognises all these problems and argues that their solution is possible only by evoking the norm's objective meaning: see his 'Norm and Value' (n 16) 281.

If my interpretation follows through, then Kelsen's conception of normativity is strongly naturalistic and tends to point to a multiplicity of (psychological) grounds of normativity. Given the variety of psychological triggers that may motivate agents, it follows that it is possible that the content of our normative reasons becomes unstable as we move between domains (law, morality, etc).

It is my conjecture that Kelsen's anxiety to avoid this conclusion led him to appeal to external facts of social coercion, which uniquely are capable of aligning together the otherwise disparate subjective volitional states of agents, with a view to ensuring mutually compatible responses by them – at least within each particular normative domain. On this understanding peripheral imputation ends up emphasising the type of social coercion that is peculiar to each distinct domain of social normativity.

This, however, would be falling short by a large margin of the ideal of non-naturalism, as it was first introduced by Kelsen and further explored in this paper, ie the postulate that imputation generate genuine normative reasons out of raw psychological data. No sooner has imputation lost its grasp on normativity, however, than the theorist has to resort to some external trigger in order to account, if not for normativity, at least for its verisimilitude: in other words the condition under which agents appear to be acting in concert, as if guided by shared normative reasons. Owing to the fact that coercion (or the threat of it) can play the role of such a trigger, it comes as no surprise that Kelsen believed that only law could retrieve the objective meaning of an act of will: because law has at its disposal such an intense form of physical coercion that it can steer the behaviour of its addressees in the same direction, despite their diverging psychologies.

But if all this holds true, then things become even bleaker. We end up with the strongest imaginable form of relativism with grave consequences for truth and objectivity with respect to normative reasons for action: every agent is given a free pass to appeal to her own *private* normative reasons *qua* psychological states, in quoting the familiar relativist motto: 'true for me', 'true for you' and so forth!

Before I move on I would like to take on board a possible objection to my analysis. The objection states that my analysis is entangled in a category fallacy: far from being interested in reasons for action the pure theory refers to epistemic criteria for 'shaping' legal knowledge, criteria that are able to turn raw volitional materials into legal knowledge. Let us use a metaphor to drive the objection home: what Kelsen says is that in order to generate legal knowledge in the first place, we need something like a legal 'epistemic container' which can be filled with whatever raw (volitional) materials are available to experience. The purpose the container serves is to 'shape' those contents into distinctively legal-normative meaning. But all it takes for it to work is just that the container be made out of 'legal' material – its contents can be even the crudest naturalistic, psychological facts one can think of. This is an important objection – not impossible to meet, however: for the container to be capable of producing non-naturalistic knowledge, it ought to bestow practical/normative, or 'ought'-related meaning on its contents. If the container is merely a 'form', incapable of 'adding' any layer of meaning to its volitional contents, then those contents will be free to determine the content of the relevant ought-items out of their own resources.[26] And given that those resources are purely naturalistic, then the meaning of the ought-facts will simply be the meaning of those subjective acts of will that constitute the contents of the container in the first instance. Thus, in Kelsen's terminology, we will never manage to ascend from the subjective meaning of an act of will to its objective one.

For yet one more time, this shows that non-naturalism is a position that does not stop at the epistemic level, but goes all the way down to the nature of what it is to be a reason for action. The reason for that is that the incentive for introducing non-naturalism is precisely the idea that normativity cannot be reduced to naturalistic items because of its practical or action-guiding core. Thus, unless Kelsen adopted a full-blooded non-naturalism, his purity thesis would collapse anew to one or the other form of naturalism.

VI. Fragmentation

Kelsen's failure to develop a full-blooded non-naturalism with respect to normative reasons leads to a dilemma: save for removing altogether morality from the normative realm – which would be absurd even by Kelsen's own lights – two alternatives remain for accounting for the normative content of morality vis-à-vis that of law.

The first argues that the same category of imputation applies to both legal and moral norms. I shall set this option aside, given Kelsen's explicit resistance to it (via the purity thesis).[27] The second alternative argues for separate categories of cognition for legal and moral ought-facts. Let us call these respectively Imputation-law and Imputation-morality, or, for the sake of brevity, I-L and I-M.

The second alternative seems to be more in line with Kelsen's own intentions. In 'Why Should the Law be Obeyed?'[28] we read that each of the normative disciplines (theology, the study of natural law, etc) has its own basic norm:

> However in this respect there is no difference between legal positivism on the one hand and the natural-law doctrine or theology on the other […] Just as the basic norm of legal

[26] In fact Kelsen seems to retain a volitional-motivational layer about normative reasons: in his view it is our inclinations that at the end of the day constitute our normative reasons – see his 'Law and Morality' in *Hans Kelsen: Essays in Legal and Moral Philosophy* (n 16) 84–85; also see his 'Why Should the Law be Obeyed?' (n 23), where he seems to argue that the law gives reasons by authorising subjective volitional facts in virtue of organising them into a formal structure (ie peripheral imputation).

[27] There is another, trivial sense in which legal and moral reasons may coincide: Kelsen argues that moral and legal norms have a common structure in virtue of being social rules that constitute relative values – in this formal sense, submits Kelsen, law can be deemed to be moral: see 'Law and Morality' in *Essays in Legal and Moral Philosophy* (n 16) 86–89; and especially at 90: '… the concept of law (…) fall(s) under that of goodness. For the concept of "goodness" can only be defined as that which "ought to be", as that which accords with a norm'.

[28] See n 23.

> positivism is not issued by the legal authority but is presupposed in juristic thinking, the basic norms of the natural-law doctrine and of Christian theology are not issued by nature or by God but are presupposed as hypotheses by these doctrines.[29]

Despite being sanctioned by Kelsen, this alternative is saddled with serious shortcomings: if I-L and I-M are in place, a serious risk of fragmentation of normative meaning is at play. Even though the introduction of two forms of imputation is likely to limit the radical fragmentation of normative meanings, which would otherwise arise from the association of reasons with mental states under conditions of naturalism, not all risk of fragmentation of normative reasons will have been eradicated. For the existence of even just two separate categories of normative knowledge would cause normative meaning to vary with the context. Thus, depending on whether I-L or I-M is at work, the same normative sentence could be affirmed and negated simultaneously, which of course would be tantamount to a logical contradiction.[30]

Some more detail needs to be added with a view to the possibility of logical contradiction. Affirming and denying the same sentence may, on occasion, remain free of contradiction: this is the case of sentences involving indexical terms. When Mary says, 'I am a woman' she makes a true statement; were the same sentence to be uttered by John, however, it would be false. Is there an inconsistency in affirming that the sentence 'I am a woman' can be simultaneously true or false depending on the speaker's point of view? Surely few would disagree that there is none. It is part of the very meaning of indexical terms that they be understood in this way. This is illustrated, after all, by the fact that, in reporting the speech of the other, John and Mary would not disquote on 'I,' although they would in reporting their own speech.[31]

Things become more complicated when non-indexical terms (for example 'know', 'ought', 'good' and so on) are treated as indexicals. The claim here is that uttering the same sentence in different contexts would affect its truth-value. Here is a typical example: 'Mary knows that the world was not created yesterday'. On the view presented here, uttering this sentence in the context of a seminar of epistemology would make it false. Contrariwise, the same sentence would remain true in any other ordinary context. It follows that 'know' can coherently exemplify two different contents: 'know (high)' in the epistemological context and 'know (low)' in ordinary contexts. To those defending this view, the case of 'know' is the same as the case of 'I' earlier; hence, there is no contradiction in reporting that Mary both does and does not know that the world was created yesterday. But surely this strikes one as odd. If for no other reason than the fact that, other than in the case of indexical terms, in reporting the utterance about Mary, we would intuitively

[29] ibid 263.

[30] More precisely, what is contradicted is the law of the excluded middle, ie the postulate that a sentence be either true or false, no third, 'middle', truth-value being possible.

[31] T Williamson, 'Knowledge, Context and the Agent's Point of View' in G Preyer and G Peter (eds), *Contextualism in Philosophy* (Oxford, Clarendon Press, 2005) 91.

feel inclined to disquote on 'know'. For it would be strange to assume that 'know' includes in its meaning the context of assessment in the same manner that 'I' or other indexical terms do. Thus, in contrast to the indexical case, the existence of two distinct contexts of assessment of 'know' would lead to a violation of the law of the excluded middle.[32]

To get back to Kelsen: in introducing (two at least) distinct categories of imputation – which we called I-L and I-M respectively – Kelsen runs a similar risk of violating the law of the excluded middle; for I-L and I-M make available two separate contexts of assessment which may assign contradicting truth-values to the same normative sentence. Take the normative sentence: 'No one should profit from one's own wrongdoing'; assuming that this turns out false as uttered in a legal context and true as uttered in a moral (or other non-legal) context, then it would be correct to report that '*No one should profit from one's own wrongdoing* is true and false'.

One way for Kelsenian positivism to escape such undesirable effects would be to avail itself of *semantic contextualism*. In a nutshell, this is the view that the context of uttering the same (normative) sentence may cause it to vary its truth-value without contradiction. What would be, under normal circumstances, a violation of the law of the excluded middle is explained away by the fact that different normative contexts allow different evaluations of the same sentence.[33] Here is how:

Contextualism aims to avoid contradiction by claiming that a given sentence expresses different propositions as uttered in some different contexts. As uttered in the moral context 'No one should profit…' expresses proposition P; conversely, as uttered in a legal context the very same sentence expresses proposition Q. This is a remarkable construction: for although the utterance of the sentence in the moral context amounts to the negation of the same sentence, when uttered in the legal context, the *proposition* it expresses in the moral context is not the negation of the *proposition* it expresses in the legal context. To put it differently, the apparent contradiction that manifests itself at the level of sentences does not translate to a contradiction at the level of propositions; hence, there is no violation of the law of the excluded middle, as it might have appeared at first glance. This gives the contextualist view its great advantage over some crude form of relativism. While the relativist answer is that different speakers hold different claims to be true *relatively* to them, the contextualist solution is compatible with the possibility of objectivity: even if the same sentence may be evaluated differently in different contexts, propositions are as absolute as you like.[34] For the negation of 'No one should profit…' in the moral context amounts to the negation of proposition P; however non-P is not the negation of Q, or the proposition expressed by 'No one should profit…' in the legal context – in other words, the apparent contradiction

[32] ibid.

[33] Notice that context refers only to the point of view and of the circumstances of evaluation of a sentence: in other words, changing context does not entail switching worlds. See Williamson, 'Knowledge, Context and the Agent's Point of View' (n 31).

[34] Williamson, 'Knowledge, Context and the Agent's Point of View' (n 31).

dissolves. With it, we gain insight into a pluralistic understanding of thought, action and the world. As regards normative contexts, in particular, contextualism opens up the possibility to account coherently for the pressing need to accommodate the various different normative points of view that pertain to contemporary ethical, moral and legal debates without making any detrimental commitments to relativism. On the face of it is coherent to report that '*No one should profit from one's own wrongdoing* is true and false'. Or at least this is what Kelsenian positivism *qua* contextualism would have us believe.

Alas, this view comes at a relatively high price: a sentence and its negation can consistently co-exist only if they exemplify distinct propositions, ie only if they express different meanings. But then those who utter them are simply taking past each other. In the end coherence comes through eschewing communication between agents or even between different time-slices of the same agent. How does this consequence play out in the domain of normative reasons?

The fragmentation of normativity runs against a fundamental intuition we have about reasons: that normative reasons ought to count as such for the agent involved in a practical problem. If it were the case that each of the normative disciplines, by employing its own cognitive category, is at liberty to bestow diverging contents on the reasons one has, then how are we to decide about which reasons we actually have? Whereupon the following question arises: 'how can something be a reason for action if it doesn't count as one for the agent?'

What is at issue here is the wider problem that has been raised under the heading of the *normative question*:[35] this submits that no reason can be cognised independently of the agent's point of view, on pain of losing its normative status. For something acquires the status of a reason for action by remaining relevant to the practical problem of the agent.[36] Further, 'remaining relevant' means to be capable of offering a justified solution to the practical problem in question, where justification is a notion that is agent-relevant in a deep sense, ie in depending on the reflective capacity of agents to assess reasons from the first person perspective. It follows that contextualist reasons or reasons from a point of view are no longer concentrating on the relevant practical problem for the agent, but go amiss of their purpose to constitute normative reasons. Insofar as positivist reasons for action adhere to a contextualist account (ie they are reasons from a point of view) they will fail to become reasons for action proper (as in: reasons *simpliciter*).

Kelsen would seem to resist such an agency-centred conception of normative reasons. Indeed, we saw that a key element of his conception of peripheral imputation was its subjectless character. True enough, the motive behind his 'subjectless construction' was to attain to the condition set by non-naturalism to abstract from any psychological features of subjects. While this is a legitimate requirement,

[35] See C Korsgaard, *The Sources of Normativity* (Cambridge, Cambridge University Press, 1996).

[36] See the similar vocabulary in Williamson, 'Knowledge, Context and the Agent's Point of View' (n 31).

it should not lead us to run together subjectivity in the sense of psychological nature with another, more valuable, conception of subjectivity: that of reflexive agency. No explanation of causation, let alone imputation, may succeed without addressing that latter notion of subjectivity: in other words, without demonstrating what renders normative cognition relevant or pertinent to practical agency.

Conversely, a successful account ought to link normative knowledge to the standpoint of reflective agency. While a detailed exploration of the standpoint of agency would escape the scope of this paper, its main contours may be spelled out in brief:[37] remaining within a broadly Kantian framework[38] the standpoint of agency involves the claim that any form of normative knowledge is grounded on the reflective capacity of *anyone* who is an agent to give and demand reasons. Notably, this standpoint is immune to naturalism, because it involves a capacity that does not pertain to the psychology of any particular biological subject, but to the constitution of persons as having the identity of a reason-appreciating agent. As such, the standpoint succeeds in respecting a full-blooded non-naturalism without losing hold of the practical relevance of normative cognition.

VII. Conclusion and Summary

Despite Kelsen's intention to offer a full-blooded non-naturalism as the basis of a theory of normative cognition, his concept of imputation has been shown to be wanting for the task at hand. The category of imputation, much as it aspired to drawing a clear line between states of the will and normative reasons, did not provide sufficient resources for conceiving reasons as objective items (facts), free from psychological elements. Instead Kelsen's theory of normative cognition was directed, misleadingly, to a different kind of purity: that of the separation of law from morality. I have argued that this concession is indicative of the failure to deliver normative knowledge proper, for any workable notion of (normative) purity can only aim to insulate normative from non-normative materials and not, as in Kelsens's case, create a segmentation between the various aspects of normativity. Conversely, I suggested that full-blooded non-naturalism would require, far from the abolition of a strict separation between law and morality, an account of normative reasons that cuts across the various facets of the practical domain. In concluding, I have hinted at the fact that such an account must rest on a unified practical standpoint: the standpoint of practical agency.

[37] For a more detailed exploration of the standpoint of agency see G Pavlakos, 'Practice, Reasons and the Agent's Point of View' (2009) 22 *Ratio Juris* 74 and G Pavlakos, 'Law, Normativity and the Model of Norms' in S Bertea and G Pavlakos (eds), *New Essays on the Normativity of Law* (Portland, Hart, 2011) 246.

[38] I am referring here to Kant's practical philosophy, which Kelsen famously left out of his theory of normative knowledge.

PART III

Norms as Reasons for Action

6

Norms, Reasons, and the Law

ANDREI MARMOR

I. Introduction

Legal philosophers tend to talk about the normativity of law as if it is a central aspect of law that we need to explain, often assuming that there is a single underlying question about it. I think that this is a mistake. Part of what I want to show in this paper is that there isn't really anything unique to the normativity of law.[1] But this will follow from something more fundamental that I want to explore here, which is the nature of norm following. I want to show that different kinds of norms provide reasons for action in different ways. And those different kinds of norms are present in law as well, suggesting that the normativity of law is both complex and multifarious, yet not, I will argue, essentially different from normativity in other domains.

It is, actually, quite remarkable how many social, legal, and other institutional norms we follow, literally obey sometimes, on a daily basis.[2] Before going to work you dress in conformity with some norms of fashion or, at least, of propriety. On your way to work you obey traffic regulations, perhaps you greet an acquaintance you meet in some conventional manner; at work you follow norms and regulations of your institution, you probably follow some norms of etiquette and civility in dealing with your colleagues, and then, perhaps in the evening you go out to a restaurant, and there follow some conventions of dining in public, tipping the waiter, etc. And in the background of all this there are more fundamental norms we follow, such as various norms constituting juridical relations that we encounter on a daily basis, determining, for example, what is mine and what is yours, what I need permission to use and what I can use without asking anyone, etc. Life is norm-governed through and through. But what is it to be governed by a norm or to follow a norm? Is it something like taking the norm to be a reason for your action? How can we make sense of that?

[1] I do not intend to exempt myself from this mistake; in some of my previous writings I may have given the impression that there is a central question about the normativity of law.

[2] Of course, in using language we follow norms of various kinds, but I will not be concerned with linguistic norms in this paper. I have done that elsewhere, see my Social Conventions: From Language to Law (Princeton, Princeton University Press, 2009) chs 4 and 5.

Let me begin by saying a few words about what I mean by 'norms'. We can think of norms as a subset of rules of conduct. There are all sorts of ways in which rules can figure in our practical and moral deliberation, without those rules being norms.[3] Rules, in other words, can be abstract deontic quantifications over action types. I will stipulate here, however, that norms are the kind of rules which have some social or institutional reality to them. A norm can be a rule enacted or directed by some person or institution in a position of authority; or it can be a social rule, one which is followed, and considered to be binding in some respects, by a certain population in a given context. Many social norms are conventions, others may not be. But all social norms reflect the collective attitudes of a certain population to some rule following behaviour they exhibit. Whether institutional or social, I assume here that norms are the kind of rules which have a social reality to them; that if we talk about a norm, or say that 'there is a norm that so and so …', we should be able to answer the question: Whose norm is it, when, and where? And then my question is going to be: how can norms, social or institutional, give us reasons for action?

Let us assume that a reason for an action to φ, is a fact that counts in favour of φ-ing. This is not saying much, of course, but I will not try to say here much more than that. For our purposes it is enough to accept the common view that reasons for action can be understood in causal terms, as the kind of facts that figure in a causal explanation of someone's action (often called motivational reasons), but that they can also be understood normatively. That is, in terms of facts that actually count in favour of an action, the kind of facts that would be needed to respond to the question of why one should or ought to do it, not why one actually did. Thus, unless otherwise indicated explicitly, I will use reason for action in this second, normative sense.[4] So what is it for a norm to be a reason for action? Obviously, it has to be a fact of some kind, and it has to count in favour of doing (or not doing) something. Now, given the narrow understanding I assume here about what norms are, they are clearly facts of social or institutional kind. We can say, for example, that there is a norm to do such and such here, but not there; or that there used to be a norm but it is no longer in force, and things like that. Thus, intuitively, we can regard a norm as a reason for action when the fact that there is a norm inevitably figures in an explanation of why one ought to do something. Before I expand on this, we should note another familiar distinction. Something can be a reason for action without being the complete reason. The fact that it is raining outside is a reason for me to take the umbrella when I go out; but it is not the complete reason

[3] I am not suggesting that there is uniformity of usage in the literature about this. Norms of rationality, for example, would not be norms in the sense I use the word here. And some philosophers use the concepts of norms and normativity very broadly, aiming to cover the domain of practical reasons quite generally. See, for example, R Wedgwood, *The Nature of Normativity* (Oxford, Oxford University Press, 2007).

[4] On the distinction between normative and motivational reasons see, for example, J Dancy, *Practical Reality* (Oxford, Oxford University Press, 2000). Note, however, that I take no sides here in the debate between internalists and externalists about reasons for action.

to take the umbrella. The complete reason would need to list more facts, as it were, such as my desire not to get wet, perhaps the fact that it is not too windy outside, and so on and so forth.

Now let us return to the idea that a norm is a reason for action if and only if it inevitably figures in an explanation of why one ought to do something. This is a fairly robust condition. It is meant to capture the intuitive idea that a norm is a reason for action for an agent when the agent must refer to the existence and content of the norm as part of their complete reason for action. The relevant practical reasoning must contain as one of its premises something like: I ought/have reason to do it 'because it is a norm that …'. Let me call this the condition of normativity. It is a robust condition because it actually fails with respect to a certain type of norms, namely, it fails when the norm in question summarises or formulates reasons for action that exist independently of the norm. Saying that I do something (partly) because there is a norm that requires me to do it is sometimes the wrong kind of normative explanation for your action.

Suppose, for example, that your friend tells you that they do not cheat on their spouse because there is a norm against it. You might think that your friend is a faithful spouse, perhaps, but for the wrong kind of reasons. You are not supposed to cheat on your spouse because cheating is wrong, not because there is a norm to avoid cheating. The norm, if there is one, only summarises or formulates reasons that are there anyway, so to speak, regardless of the norm in question. So it may well turn out that most moral norms actually fail the condition of normativity.[5] In giving an account of the complete reasons against, say, murder, rape, physical assault, deceit, etc, there is no need to refer to norms. If there are any norms in play, they only summarise or formulate reasons for action that are there anyway. Now compare this to cases in which the condition of normativity clearly obtains. For example, suppose you account for your reasons to stop your car at a red light; your complete account of the reasons for action is impossible to give without referring to the traffic norm in play here. Or think about your reasons to move the bishop diagonally playing chess. Surely a reference to the rules of chess is an essential part of it. If the rule was different, you would have a different reason.

The idea that basic moral norms fail the condition of normativity may sound more exciting than it should. Perhaps rule consequentialists would have us believe, or act as if we believe, that moral rules meet the condition of normativity. I'm not a fan of this idea, but my thesis here is not meant to rule it out. Remember that we are talking about the kind of rules of conduct that have a certain social reality to them, not about abstract rules we can formulate on any grounds whatsoever. Now of course, this does not exclude moral rules from also being norms. If there is a population that exhibits widely shared pro-attitudes towards a moral rule, then of course the moral rule is also a norm, a social norm, and it would be a social norm

[5] Not necessarily all; some social conventions may have a limited role to play in our moral reasons for action. See my *Social Conventions* (n 2) ch 6.

regardless of the truth or soundness of the norm's content. In any case, my arguments in this paper are focused on social and institutional norms, not on moral rules or moral principles. I want to show that there are four main kinds of norms, and that there are some interesting differences between them in the ways in which they can contribute to the subjects reasons for action. I turn to this taxonomy now.

II. Codifying Norms

Countless social norms we follow in our everyday lives, many of them legally codified norms, are essentially formulations of beliefs about the kind of things that ought (or ought not) to be done. Norms against murder, rape, theft, corruption, etc, are all the kind of norms that purport to generalise (perhaps sometimes simplify) and subsume under rule-like formulations sets of reasons for action that apply to us, regardless of their normative codification. Of course, nothing guarantees that such norms get the reasons right; they may or may not. But either way, their function is to summarise or codify in rule-like formulations reasons that are there anyway. The codification, legal or social, is not meant to add anything to the reasons that apply to the subjects regardless of the codification. Legal rules and social norms codifying prohibitions on murder, rape, and theft, for example, are meant to capture and formulate exactly the moral reasons that count against murder, rape, theft etc. Such rules aim to get things right, as it were. And the interesting conclusion is that the more such norms get things right – the more accurately they capture the reasons in play – the more they fail the condition of normativity, that is, the less difference they can make to the subject's reasons for action. As noted earlier, when a given norm aims to capture reasons that apply to you anyway, referring to the norm as your reason for action would be a case of acting on the wrong kind of reason. We should avoid murder, rape and theft, etc, because it is wrong to do those things, not because there is a norm prohibiting them. The norm itself plays no reason-giving role in such practical deliberations.

The fact that countless legal and social norms fail the condition of normativity does not mean that they are pointless or have no useful functions. There are a variety of functions such norms can serve. Consider, for example, a legal norm codifying the prohibition on theft. And assume it gets the reasons against theft right, that is, assume that the norm captures accurately the relevant reasons against theft, their circumstances of application, their limits, etc. The first and foremost social-political function of such a norm is to form an antecedent to the justification of penal reaction. Punishment is conditional on doing wrong; by formulating the wrong in a codified manner, we make it easier to justify, and publically more transparent, that the penal reaction, when applied, is applied properly, in reaction to a wrong committed. Generally speaking, and this goes beyond legal codification, one of the functions of norms codifying preexisting reasons is to render social and legal reaction to violation of the norm easier to justify publicly. Such norms serve functions of transparency and publicity. Codifying norms may also serve educational functions, perhaps facilitate certain forms of social cohesion, and they may even serve epistemic functions in making reasons easier to keep in mind and internalise. The one function such norms cannot serve, however, is to give us reasons for action. At best, they just remind us of reasons we have anyway.[6]

The interesting cases, however, are those in which the social or legal norm that purports to codify preexisting reasons gets those reasons only partially right. Then the question is whether the wrong part of the norm, as it were, can have any normative import. And I think that the answer is that sometimes it can. Let us take a very schematic example. Suppose there is a norm that purports to capture an obligation to avoid actions of type X. Assume that there is a moral obligation to avoid actions of type X, that is, assume that X is a category of actions one ought to avoid. But now suppose that the relevant social or legal norm gets the definition of X only partially right. It defines X as 'Y', and assume the truth is that Y overlaps substantially with X but includes some action types that are not X, and excludes some that are. Suppose Xi is not included in Y. It stands to reason that notwithstanding the omission of Xi from Y, one should not do Xi. But now suppose that Y_2 is an action type included in Y but not in X. In other words, according to the relevant reasons in play, there is no reason to avoid Y_2. Does it mean that social or legal norm notwithstanding, one has no reason to avoid Y_2? That is far from clear and would hugely depend on the circumstances. Since social and legal norms serve many functions beyond the direct-reason-giving one, there may well be reasons to comply with the norm even if it misidentifies the right reasons for action. Setting a bad example for others is a familiar type of consideration that might be in play; erring on the side of caution, saving deliberation time, etc, are other familiar considerations. I am not suggesting that any of these kinds of considerations can give you a reason to do something that you would otherwise have good reasons to avoid. But in marginal cases, when the reasons in play are not all that clear cut, such considerations may tilt the balance in favour of norm-following.

III. Reason-instantiating Norms

One of the most familiar types of social norms we follow in our everyday lives are those that instantiate or concretise preexisting reasons for action, when those reasons underdetermine the particular modes of conduct that would be properly responsive to the reasons. Let me call them reason-instantiating norms. In previous work I argued that all social conventions are of this nature. Conventions are norms underdetermined by their underlying reasons.[7] Examples are abundant. Consider, for example, our greeting conventions. Greeting is supported by reasons

[6] See D Enoch, 'Giving Practical Reasons' (2011) 11 The Philosopher's Imprint 4.

[7] See my Social Conventions (n 2) chs 1 and 2.

for manifesting respect to others by signalling some form of recognition. How to signal such recognition and how to express the relevant kind of respect in this context is hugely underdetermined by the reasons for doing so. The greeting convention fills out this gap; it give us a reason to do it this way rather than another (for example saying 'Hi' instead of jumping up and down or whatever).

Needless to say, underdetermination by reasons, by itself, does not explain the need for a norm, social or institutional. There has to be another practical reason to have some normative regulation in place. The fact that the reasons for greeting an acquaintance underdetermine particular modes of greeting does not explain why would we have a convention about it. There has to be some additional practical need for some uniformity of conduct. The need to resolve a recurring coordination problem is certainly one such type or reason. But I doubt that coordination is the only type of practical need that explains normative regulations of this kind. Perhaps there is some need for coordination that explains the greeting conventions we have. However, I doubt that the convention to bring a bottle of wine (or something similar) to the host of a dinner party is the kind of norm that is called for by the need for coordination; there is not much to coordinate here. You are expected to bring something for the dinner party as a token of appreciation to the host. The reason in play here clearly underdetermines what exactly you should bring. In this case, perhaps not much would be lost if there was no social norm about this at all. But, at least in my social circles, there is one, and its function, I assume, is to smooth social relations, reduce the chances of awkwardness and misunderstandings, and to reduce deliberation costs.

Though I argued that all social conventions are norms underdetermined by their underlying reasons, not only conventional rules have this function. Many institutional norms, often explicitly enacted, have this feature as well. Countless legal and bureaucratic norms, for example, serve the function of rendering concrete and specific reasons that leave the requisite conduct under-specified.[8] Think about rules that function to set a cut-off point in borderline cases of some regulatory rationale, such as setting a particular age limit for voting or for drinking alcohol, setting speed limits for driving, or deadlines for submitting official requests, etc. Or think about the kind of norms we have in the daily operation of institutions. In the law school there is need for somebody to make decisions, on a regular basis, about teaching allocations and schedules. It can be the dean, the associate dean, or a committee, for example. Each law school might have its norms about this. They all respond to the same reasons, but the reasons do not determine which option to choose. I hope that these examples are sufficient to show how prevalent these kinds of norms are, namely, norms that instantiate reasons where the reasons in play are such that they underdetermine the particular mode of conduct required.

Some of the examples mentioned above may attest to the fact that vagueness has something to do with the underdetermination of reasons. General reasons for

[8] This function of legal norms has long been identified; Thomas Aquinas called it determination.

action can be vague.[9] Consider the reasons for setting an age limit for voting in democratic elections. There is a very good reason to limit voting rights to persons with a certain level of cognitive maturity. Voters should be able to understand what voting is about and what is that they are asked to decide, etc. But maturity is a vague criterion, and it admits of borderline cases. We know who is clearly mature enough, who is clearly not mature enough, but there are bound to be borderline cases of maturity. Where and how exactly to set a desirable cut-off point – assuming there is a practical need for it – is underdetermined by the reasons in play here. And this phenomenon is prevalent; it actually explains a great many social and institutional norms we follow in our everyday lives.

To sum up: we would typically get a reason-instantiating norm when the reasons for a certain mode of conduct underdetermine the specific conduct required, and there is some additional reason to have a publicly available norm people can follow, that is, when there is a practical need for some concerted action under the relevant circumstances. I hope we can see that the combination of these two types of reasons, when present, explain how the condition of normativity applies to reason-instantiating norms. One would regard the norm as a reason for action, not because the norm constitutes the main reason in play, but because the norm adds the requisite specification of reasons that are otherwise not sufficiently determinate. In these cases, it makes perfect sense to say that I have a reason do this (rather than some other reason-responsive act) because there is a norm prescribing it. In other words, one's complete reason for action would have to cite the norm as one of the operating reasons for action.

IV. Constitutive Norms

One of the main functions of norms, both social and institutional, is to constitute certain distinct types of human activities. In previous work I argued that many social conventions have this feature and that they are distinct from coordination conventions.[10] There is no need to repeat those arguments here – the conventional nature of constitutive norms is not our present concern. Whether conventional or not, a great many kinds of social norms and, of course, countless institutional ones, including legal norms, have this constitutive function: their function is to create a distinct type of activity, a kind of activity that could not exist without the rules that make it the kind of activity it is. There is a considerable range of human activities constituted by some distinct normative framework, such as structured competitive games and sports, artistic genres, etc. In the legal domain, examples

[9] On vagueness in morality, see, for example, R Shafer-Landau, 'Vagueness, Borderline Cases, and Moral Realism' (1995) 32(1) American Philosophical Quarterly 83.

[10] See my *Social Conventions* (n 2) mainly ch 2.

include corporate entities and their functioning as such, perhaps even contracts,[11] arguably at least certain aspects of private ownership of property, legally constituted organisations and agencies of various sorts, to some extent, the institution of marriage,[12] and so on and so forth. The constitution of distinct types of legally-enabled activities is, actually, one of the main functions of law in a modem legal order. Each one of these activities is constituted by a complex set of interlocking norms, determining what counts as an act of this or that type, who has the legal power to do this or that, whose obligation it is to comply, what are the sanctions for non-compliance, etc.

I take it that all this is familiar. The difficult question here is to explain what the relation of constitution is, and how it affects reasons for action, in particular, how it explains the condition of normativity. Now, if we want to be very pedantic about this, we can acknowledge that rules or norms, by themselves, do not constitute anything. A certain social reality of following the rules is what constitutes the activity in question. Think about music. Scores do not make music; scores are instructions how to make it, and only when the orchestra follows the instructions do we get the music. Similarly, the rules of chess don't, by themselves, as it were, constitute the game. The rules define what counts as winning and losing, what are permissible and impermissible moves, etc. People play chess when they follow the rules. But here is the crucial point, which is meant to capture the idea that rules can constitute an activity: the idea is that we can only grasp the idea of playing chess as a rule-guided activity. Without the rules of the game, there is no game to play. And whenever people actually play the game, part of what they do, an essential part, is to follow the rules.

So the first step here is to see that there are types of human activities, like playing a competitive game or, for example, acting on behalf of a corporate entity, perhaps even forming a legally binding contract, where following some rules is an essential aspect of the activity, it is partly what the activity of that kind essentially is. And at least in this sense, it makes perfect sense to say that the rules enable the activity in question. Notice, however, that there is more to the constitutive relation than one thing enabling another. A shovel enables you to dig, but digging is not constituted by shovels. No doubt, in part at least, because you can dig without one; there is digging without shovels, there is no playing chess without the rules that determine what chess is.

[11] At least to the extent that they diverge from ordinary promises. How much contracts and promises diverge, and how much they should, is controversial, of course.

[12] Marriage is a very interesting case in which legal-institutional norms and social practices interact in complex ways; there are historical and cultural variations about the extent to which institutionalised norms actually constitute what marriage is, and how it is conceived by those who practice it. One of the interesting lessons from the recent advocacy of gay marriage and its widespread momentum is that the crucial role of legal norms and their constitutive function has been widely recognised. It is one of those cases in which people saw very clearly how legal norms have a constitutive function in shaping interpersonal relationships, even respect and self-esteem.

I don't think that we will make progress by trying to analyse in greater detail what the relation of constitution is. For our purposes, it is sufficient to understand the notion of A constituting B in terms of building blocks: A is constitutive of B, we can say, if A is an essential building block of B, that is, without A we could not have B. The key to understanding how norms can constitute an activity lies in understanding the latter notion, namely, the idea of an activity. Rules do not constitute an act, they constitute activities, and the distinction between the two is what explains, I think, the kind of constitutive norms we are after.[13]

Activities are types, not tokens. We often perform acts, as tokens of a type, within, or as part of, certain activities. Not all acts, however, have to be tokens of an activity-type. Running is an act, which may, or may not, form part of a larger activity. It can be part of, say, a sports competition or even, perhaps, the activity we call 'jogging', if you will. But one can also just run to catch the train, which is not an activity. What makes for an activity is the complex relations that obtain between different parts of it, such as different acts and attitudes, to something that has a meaning as a whole. An activity has semantics and syntax, as it were. By combining elements in certain ways we get new meanings. The role of rules and norms here is analogous to the role of norms in language: they provide the syntax and the semantics of the activity in question. This is just a metaphor, of course, so let's try to flesh it out a bit.

Consider a move in chess: say, you move the rook one square ahead on the board. You performed an act of moving a piece of carved wood on a checkered board. Saying that doesn't quite capture, of course, what you have done, which is, we presume, making a move in the game. To explain the latter we need some semantics; we need to have a sense of what the game is, what are moves within it, what for, what counts as winning the game, etc. Without grasping the meaning of these different acts within the game, and the meaning of the game itself, as it were, we cannot grasp the meaning of the move, as such, as a move in the game. All activities, I submit, have this complex structure of different parts making distinct contributions to something that has meaning for us, as a whole. And norms play a constitutive role here in providing both the syntax of the relations between the various parts, and how they combine to form meaningful structures, and in providing some of the semantics. It is impossible to explain the meaning of the moves, and their relations to other moves, without reference to the rules that define them.

You might think that I'm reversing an old metaphor here. It used to be the hallmark of the Oxbridge philosophy of language in the 1940s and 1950s to explain concepts and meanings by reference to the example of games. Here's a quotation from Ryle, as an example:

> … concepts are not things, as words are, but rather the functionings of words, as keeping wicket is the functioning of the wicket-keeper. Very much as the functioning of the wicket-keeper interlocks with the functioning of the bowler, the batsman and the rest,

[13] I have explained this argument in my Social Conventions (n 2) ch 2.

> so the functioning of a word interlocks with the functioning of the other members of the team for which that word is playing.[14]

So yes, in a way I am reversing the same metaphor. To the extent that language is like a game, games are also like language. They have rule-defined syntax and moves within the game have meanings in the functioning they contribute to other moves and to the game as a whole. Needless to say, not every activity is as clearly structured as a game of chess (or cricket, for that matter). Many human activities are a bit more intangible and diffusive, so to speak. But I think that all activities have some structure constituted by norms that define, to some extent, their syntax and semantics. It is true of social practices as well as institutional ones.

Consider, for example, the kind of activities we engage in in our academic institutions. We teach, we grade exams, we publish books and articles, we confer degrees, and so on and so forth. All these activities are made up of particular acts, of course, but the acts have the meanings they do only in relation to, and as part of, some social and institutional reality that is partly constituted by norms. We just cannot grasp or explain what it is to be a student, or to take an exam, or to confer a degree, or even to participate in a seminar, without the institutional and social norms that contribute to the meaning we assign to these roles and functions. And of course, the legal domain provides ample examples as well. Suppose you observe A giving an object to B and getting some other object from B. Whether A sold something to B (or vice versa) is for the law to determine; legal norms define what counts, legally speaking, as an act of sale. And they can only define it in relations to other kinds of transactions in the vicinity, such as a loan, or a rent, or a gift, etc.

Granted that norms have some constitutive function in enabling the kind of activities we engage in, how would they meet the condition of normativity? How can constitutive norms give us reasons for action? John Searle rightly observed, a long time ago, that constitutive norms typically have a regulative function as well.[15] A norm that stipulates, say, what counts as a touchdown in football, would also give you some guidance, it would also tell you what you need to do with the ball to make a touchdown. Similarly, a law that stipulates what counts as a legally valid contract would also guide you to ways of making one if you wish to do so. So the problem here is not to explain how constitutive rules can also guide action, it's partly what they stipulate. The question is what kind of reasons for action such norms can provide, and on what grounds. I think that the main answer is fairly obvious: whatever reasons we have for following any set of constitutive norms would have to be derived from the value of the kind of activity that the norms constitute. Constitutive norms enable a certain kind of activity that would not have been possible to engage in, as an activity-type, without the norms. Therefore, if and

[14] G Ryle, Dilemmas (Cambridge, 1954) 32. The quotation from Ryle is not meant to imply that I agree with Ryle's account of concepts. See my 'Farewell to Conceptual Analysis (in Jurisprudence)' in W Waluchow and S Sciaraffa (eds), The Philosophical Foundations of The Nature of Law (Oxford, Oxford University Press, 2013) 209.

[15] J Searle, Speech Acts (Cambridge, Cambridge University Press, 1969) 33.

to the extent that the activity in question is valuable for certain agents, its value for those agents would ground their reasons for following the constitutive norms in question.

Let me insert a clarification here. It is not part of my argument to reject Scanlon's buck-passing account of values.[16] Though I spoke as if I take it for granted that values have explanatory priority over reasons, my argument does not depend on such a view. It can be translated, as it were, to Scanlon type buck-passing account. We can say that whatever value people find in a given activity is entirely a function of the reasons there are to engage in that activity. Either way, buck-passing or not passing, my point is that the reasons to follow the constitutive norms are parasitic on the reasons to engage in the kind of activity they constitute or, if you prefer (as I do), on the values people find in the activity in question.

The result of this dependence relation between reasons to follow constitutive norms, and the values we find in the activities they constitute, is that the normativity in question is a conditional one: if and to the extent that A finds (or perhaps ought to find) an activity of type X valuable (or has reasons to engage in X), A would have a reason to follow the norms that constitute X. Thus, we can see that constitutive norms meet the condition of normativity conditionally. The reasons to follow constitutive norms depend on the reasons to engage in the kind of activity they constitute. I doubt that this is a surprising result. It should be rather obvious. And the conditional nature of the normativity in play here should be even less controversial upon realising that the values of different kinds of activities constituted by norms are of different types; some values or reasons are entirely dependent on subjective preferences, sometimes on matters of taste or inclination, while others might have a categorical nature. Some activities might be such that people have reasons to value them regardless of their own personal inclinations or interests. Either way, the reasons to engage in the activity or to value its practice is what provides the reasons to regard the constitutive norm as worth following.

V. Authoritative Norms

Many norms of conduct we follow in our everyday lives are institutionally enacted. They are products of some authoritative directive. The most prevalent directives are legal, of course. The law, in a developed legal system, regulates by way of authoritative directives almost every aspect of our lives. But the law is not the only social context in which we face norms purporting to regulate conduct by way of authoritative directives. For one thing, parental authority does the same; parents often aim to regulate the conduct of their children by way of setting norms they

[16] T Scanlon, What We Owe to Each Other (Harvard, Harvard University Press, 1998) ch 3.

expect the children to follow. And then there are countless sub-legal institutions and practices, such as corporations (or, more generally, employers), universities, clubs, NGOs, etc, where authoritative norms are ubiquitous. Needless to say, not every authoritative directive has to take the shape of a norm. Authorities can direct their subjects to perform a particular act. Parents and employers often do just that; they tell their addressee to do this particular thing or to refrain from doing that particular thing. Legal and other institutional authorities, however, tend to regulate by way of issuing rules, not instructions to do this or that. They lay down norms that purport to apply at some level of generality, both in terms of the norm's subjects and the type of act they regulate.

So let us take a simple model. Suppose A is an authority, issuing the following norm, N: All Xs who are F ought to φ in circumstances C. So now the question is what would have to be true of A and N for Xs who are F to have a reason to φ in C, in a way that meets the condition of normativity? That is, in a way that would account for the fact that X is to regard N as at least part of the reason to φ in C.

Following Joseph Raz, many philosophers assumed that the answer is simple and it all depends on whether A is a legitimate authority vis-à-vis X (at least those who are F, on matters of C). So the idea here is that if we can spell out the conditions for the legitimacy of practical authorities, we would have an answer to the question of how any putative authority's directive can make the practical difference it purports to make, that is, meet the condition of normativity. An authoritative norm can make this difference if A's authority is legitimate vis-à-vis the subjects whose conduct A purports to guide.[17]

With some qualifications, I will come to agree with that. But we shouldn't move too fast. Directives don't have to be authoritative. There is a great variety of cases in which the saying so of a person changes the reasons for action of another, and in a way that is very similar to the condition of normativity we are discussing here. In fact, the term 'directive' is used in speech act theory to capture the category of speech acts where the utterance is performed with the intention of giving the hearer a reason for action by way of recognising that the performance of it is part of the hearer's reason for action.[18] Examples are abundant: they include asking a question, issuing an invitation, making a request, adjourning a meeting, expressing consent,[19] etc. In all these cases, and many others, speakers intend to create a reason for action to the hearer by way of recognising this intention and recognising that the speaker's expression of the intention is at least part of the reason to

[17] Raz's theory of authority has been refined and modified over the years. Mostly I rely here on his original formulation of the theory in The Morality of Freedom (Oxford, Oxford University Press, 1986) chs 1–4.

[18] See K Bach and R Harnish, *Linguistic Communication and Speech Acts* (Cambridge, Cambridge University Press, 1979) 47.

[19] Consent usually waives a reason against doing something, rather than giving a reason for action. But I doubt that this is a significant difference.

comply. When I ask you a question (genuinely, of course, not a rhetorical question) I intend to give you a reason to answer, and by way of recognising that my asking it gives you such a reason. You may have had no reason to answer before I asked, and perhaps you have no reason to answer if somebody else were to ask the same question. But by asking you, that is, by performing the speech act, I clearly presuppose that my asking gives you a reason to reply. The same applies to invitations. You may have no reason to show up at my dinner party unless I invite you. By inviting you, under normal circumstances and assuming sincerity and all, I intend to give you a reason to come and I intend this reason to stem from the fact that I had actually expressed the invitation. 'Thanks, I was planning to come to your dinner anyway' is not normally a good answer to a dinner party invitation. Which is to say that the invitation is a directive: without it being expressed, the relevant reasons are not there (at least not the complete reason).

So I hope we can see that changing another's reasons for action by saying something is ubiquitous and certainly not confined to authoritative directives. Furthermore, notice that all directive speech acts presuppose some notion of standing, in the normative sense of it. When I invite you to the party, I assume that I have the relevant standing to do so; I can invite you to my party, not to Joseph's. Even asking an ordinary question assumes some notion of standing; it assumes that I can reasonably expect you to answer the question under the circumstances. And this kind of assumption may be wrong or misguided on occasion. (For example, when you present an intimate question to someone with whom you do not have an intimate kind of relationship.) Generally, then, when you perform a speech act with the intention of creating a reason for your addressee, at least partly by your performance of the speech act, you would presuppose that you are in some normative relation to the addressee that makes it reasonable to expect her to comply, that is, to gain that reason by way of your saying so. And of course, the relevant kind of standing depends on the kind of speech act performed and other normative and factual circumstances. Notice, however, that from the perspective of the addressee or the hearer, the reasons to regard the speech act as giving them the reason for action it purports to give would normally follow from a combination of two considerations: the question of whether the speaker does actually have the kind of standing his or her directive presupposes, and of course, from the specific content of the directive. Suppose, for example, that I invite you to Joseph's dinner party (not mine); perhaps you'd like to go to that party if invited, but you might think that I don't have the standing to issue the invitation. So my speech act would fail to give you the reasons to go on grounds of lacking the relevant standing here. But, of course, having the requisite standing does not guarantee that the hearer ought to accept the reasons for action the speech act purports to give; not every directive speech act gives you a reason for action. Some invitations are not welcome, some questions are too silly to answer, etc. In other words, we can distinguish between two ways in which the condition of normativity may fail, on a particular occasion, for a directive speech act: it can fail for lack of standing (call it standing-failure), or it can fail because the content of the directive is such that in the relevant circumstances it does not give the hearer the reason for action it purports to give (call this content-failure).[20]

Admittedly, the distinction between content failure and standing failure is not always very sharp. Consider, for example, requests from a friend. Normally, friendship is precisely the kind of relationship that gives you a standing to ask for a favour. But if the favour you ask for is much too burdensome, or perhaps such that your friend cannot possibly perform, your request may fail to give your friend a reason to comply; it's just too crazy or pointless, the friend might rightly think. So this would normally be a content failure. But suppose the request is not simply too burdensome; complying with it might get your friend into serious trouble. At some point we might think that you have no standing to make such requests, friendship notwithstanding. The distinction admits of borderline cases, no doubt.

Speech act theorists have long noted that performing a speech act of ordering or issuing a command presupposes an authoritative standing vis-à-vis the addressee. And that seems quite right.[21] However, one might suspect that orders or commands are not the only kind of authoritative directives we encounter, certainly not in legal and other institutional contexts. Laws and regulations often take the form or granting rights of various kinds, conferring normative powers, and such. These don't look like commands, as HLA Hart famously demonstrated.[22]

Let's take a step back: why is it that directives of a certain kind necessarily presuppose an authoritative standing vis-à-vis the addressee? What makes authoritative directives unique? The widely held response is that authoritative directives purport to impose an obligation on the addressee of the directive. Asking a question, issuing an invitation, making a request, and these kinds of directives, do not purport to impose an obligation. They purport to create a reason for action, but not of an obligatory kind. Authoritative directives, however, typically aim to impose an obligation. And that would seem to sit well with the assumption that in order to be able to impose an obligation on another by your speech act, you need to have an authoritative standing vis-à-vis the other. This doesn't mean, of course, that authoritative directives must be orders or commands. They can take a variety of forms; but the underlying normative function of authoritative directives is to impose an obligation. And this is not contradicted by the fact that authorities often grant rights or permissions, or confer powers; rights and powers involve imposing some obligations. By successfully granting somebody a right you also impose an obligation on somebody else to protect or respect the right in some sense;

[20] It might be worth noting that the distinction between content failure and standing failure is well recognised in administrative law. Standard challenges to administrative decisions can either take the form of a challenge to standing, alleging that the administrative agent in question had no standing to make the decision (ultra vires), or it can take the form of challenging the content of the decision as being patently unreasonable or unwarranted, in US law called 'arbitrary and capricious'.

[21] See Bach and Hamish, *Linguistic Communication and Speech Acts* (n 18).

[22] HLA Hart, *The Concept of Law*, 2nd edn (Oxford, Oxford University Press, 1994) ch 3.

by successfully conferring a power on somebody you also impose an obligation on another to comply with the power-holder's directives;[23] and so on and so forth.

All this would seem to lead to the conclusion that the question of how directive norms meet the condition of normativity that we are after, entirely depends on the relevant standing in question. If the directive norm imposes obligations, it must be an authoritative directive and thus presuppose an authoritative standing. And thus reasons to comply with the directive would depend on the authoritative relations between the relevant agents. If the authority is legitimate, its directives obligate those who are subject to the authority. And they obligate the subjects in virtue of the authoritative standing in play. Though this picture doesn't get things wrong, it is suspect in one respect: it would seem to imply that with respect to authoritative norms, the condition of normativity can only fail to obtain by virtue of a flaw in the relevant standing; content failure seems to be ruled out. If true, it would make authoritative directives unique in some crucial respect, compared with other kinds of directives. As we mentioned earlier, directive speech acts can fail the condition of normativity either by way of standing-failure or content-failure. Do we have reasons to think that authoritative directives are unique? And are they unique in a way that rules out content-failure?

Before I explore some options, let me acknowledge that Raz's view seems to be the exact opposite. According to Raz, authoritative standing is entirely a function of content. Namely, authorities gain the authoritative standing they have by virtue of the function they fulfil in guiding their subjects to comply with the correct reasons for action that apply to them.[24] My doubts about this aspect of Raz's theory of authority I have expressed elsewhere,[25] and I will not repeat those arguments here. I mention this here to clarify that the argument I explore below aims to put pressure on the opposite view, not on Raz's.

Perhaps the uniqueness of authoritative directives stems from what Raz called their preemptive nature. Consider for a moment the difference between an order and a request. When I request somebody to help me out with a certain task, I intend to give the addressee a reason to do something that he would not have had but for my request. My intention is to give him a reason for action, but not necessarily of the kind that is meant to replace other reasons for action that apply to him under the circumstances. 'I would have loved to help you but I'm really tired right now' is not necessarily an inappropriate response to my request. In other words, the idea is that it makes sense to assume that a request aims to add some reason for action that may not have been there prior to the expression of the request, but it does not necessarily aim to replace other reasons. An order, however, necessarily aims to do precisely that. It aims to create a reason that is there to replace at least some of the other reasons that apply to the addressee under the circumstances. According

[23] Granting a permission to φ is typically a case of withdrawing a prior obligation not to φ.
[24] Raz, *The Morality of Freedom* (n 17) ch 3.
[25] See my 'An Institutional Conception of Authority' (2011) 39(3) Philosophy & Public Affairs 274.

to Raz, authoritative directives in general, and not only orders of course, have this preemptive function, that is, the function to replace some of the reasons that apply to the subjects of the authority, and not only to be added to the balance of their reasons for action.

Raz gave us a very elaborate account of what it is for reasons to function in this preemptive sense: reasons for complying with an authority's directive are meant to be both of a pre-emptive nature and constitute protected reasons. The idea of preemption is the one I mentioned above:

> The fact that an authority requires performance of an action is a reason for its performance which is not to be added to all other relevant reasons when assessing what to do, but should replace some of them.[26]

Therefore, an authoritative directive constitutes what Raz calls protected reasons: a protected reason to φ is a 'first order reason to φ and an exclusionary reason not to fail to φ for a certain range of excluded reasons').[27] So, as far as I can tell, Raz explains the idea of preemption in terms of protected reasons. An authoritative directive is meant to replace some of the antecedent reasons for action in the sense that it provides the agents with a combination of first order and second order reasons: first order reason to do as instructed and second order reason to exclude certain types of considerations or reasons from potentially defeating the first order reasons.

Now there is, undoubtedly, something very compelling about Raz's account of preemption. Consider, for example, a father telling his teenage son: 'You can go out, but make sure to be home by 7'. Clearly father intends to give son a first order reason for action, that is, to be home by 7. But, additionally, father also intends son to have second order reasons to exclude certain types of potentially defeating reasons from counting against getting home by 7, such as a reason to go to see a movie later or a reason to have another spin in town. Not all potentially defeating reasons are excluded, of course. If there is an accident and son needs to take his friend to the hospital, for example, that would be OK – it would be the kind of potentially defeating reason that is not excluded.

As Raz made quite clear from the start, however, this combination of first order reasons for action and second order exclusionary reasons is not confined to authoritative directives.[28] Consider, for example, the reasons in play when you use a GPS navigation system to get from A to B; you have a first order reason to follow the direction indicated by your GPS, as well as reasons to exclude certain kinds of potentially conflicting reasons, such as your own sense of direction or best guesses which way to go (as my wife often needed to remind me). Similarly, if a friend asks for a favour, you may have both a first order reason to comply, and

[26] J Raz, Ethics in the Public Domain (Oxford, Oxford University Press, 1994) 198.
[27] J Raz, 'On Respect, Authority and Neutrality: A Response' (2010) *120* Ethics 298.
[28] J Raz, Practical Reasons and Norms (Princeton, Princeton University Press, 1990).

some exclusionary reasons, say, to exclude some reasons of minor discomfort from potentially defeating the reason to comply. In other words, protected reasons are ubiquitous, and it's not clear that they capture the unique force we normally attach to authoritative directives. What seems to be missing is the obligatory nature of reasons to comply. Protected reasons do not necessarily amount to an obligation. There is no obligation to follow your GPS instructions, even if it is the rational thing to do under the circumstances.

Raz was quite aware of this, and seems to have suggested that obligations involve certain kinds of reasons, those that are 'categorical reasons, that is, ones whose application is not conditional on the agent's inclinations or preferences, and so on …'[29] Whether Raz is correct about this, and in general, the question of how to explain the concept of obligation, is not our immediate concern. For our purposes, it would seem to be enough to accept that authoritative norms purport to create protected reasons for their putative subjects. And if the authoritative directive is legitimate, then we can say that the subject has protected reason to comply, that is, a first order reason to do as instructed and second-order reasons to exclude certain types of potentially conflicting reasons from defeating the first order reason for action. Now this would seem to meet the condition of normativity. It would seem to explain in what sense the subject of an authoritative norm would have reason to do something because the norm requires it.

Assuming that this is true, as far as it goes, we have not yet seen any reason to doubt that authoritative directives can fail for content-related reasons as well. As we noted earlier, the addressee's reasons for complying with an ordinary directive speech act are not only a function of the relevant normative standing presupposed by the speaker. Having the normative standing presupposed by a directive might be a necessary condition for giving the addressee the reason to do as directed, but it is not a sufficient condition. It also depends on the content of the directive, in the particular circumstances of its utterance, and the relevant reasons in play. And this should apply to authoritative directives as well. In other words, legitimate authorities can issue directives that fail the condition of normativity, they may fail the condition of normativity for reasons related to the content of the directive, even if they would not fail for lack of standing.

There is a possible counter-argument we need to consider. It is possible to argue that when A is a legitimate authority vis-à-vis B with respect to matters of type C, the issuing of a directive to B to φ (in C) necessarily creates a reason for B to φ, even if that reason is immediately and unquestionably defeated by countervailing considerations. Perhaps the directive is so silly or pointless or misguided that there is no reason for B to comply; but those would be defeating considerations, immediately outweighing the reason to φ. Notice, however, that if A's directive is authoritative, it must purport to give B a protected reason to φ. So it must be of the

[29] Raz, 'On Respect, Authority and Neutrality' (n 27) 291.

kind that also excludes certain reasons from potentially defeating the reason to φ. And then it becomes questionable that we must assume that any directive issued by an authority with the right kind of standing would necessarily create for the subject a protected reason for action.

To me it seems more simple and natural to maintain that authorities can fail to give their putative subjects any reason at all. I don't see how it would be different from other kinds of directives where standing is not the issue but the content of the directive is. Consider, for example, asking a good friend, who happens to be completely broke, to give you a huge loan to pay down your mortgage. The standing to ask for a favour you may have, but under the circumstances, the request is just too silly or pointless, it gives your friend no reason to do anything. Perhaps not even a reason to politely refuse. In fact, it may be the other way around; at least in some cases, expecting the addressee to come up with a defeating reason might be the wrong kind of expectation, even if the speech act is not subject to a standing failure. One can appropriately ask a partner to have sex, for example, but it is far from clear that the partner needs to have any reason to say no. In short, legitimate authorities may issue all sorts of directives that simply fail to give their subjects any reason for action. Authorities, legitimate or not, can issue directives that are silly, pointless, or downright immoral. Not every mistake of an authority renders it illegitimate or calls its legitimacy into question. Mistakes about the content of a directive are just that, mistakes, and they can be such that they give the subjects no reason to do anything. And if a directive gives you no reason to φ, there is no need to come up with a reason not to φ.[30]

VI. Is Law's Normativity Unique?

Having seen that different types of norms bear on our reasons for action in different ways, it is time to consider how all this plays out in the legal context. From the discussion so far I hope it is clear enough that all four types of norms we examined prevail in law as well. To recap, many legal norms aim to codify preexisting reasons for action. This is most evident in the central provisions criminal law and torts, perhaps even contracts (to the extent that contract law aims to enforce promises), in the cases of safety regulations, etc. Countless legal norms are of the reason-instantiating kind, particularly those that set cut-off points or precisifications for borderline cases of vague requirements. Then there are countless legal norms, or rather, clusters of norms, constituting various activities people can engage in, particularly in the corporate domain and related areas. Finally, all these norms are also authoritative and, thus, belong to the authoritative-norms category as well.

[30] I am not denying that there might be all sorts of secondary and auxiliary reasons to comply with authoritative directives even when they fail the condition of normativity. Reasons concerning setting a bad example for others, or undermining the authority's ability to regulate conduct in the area, etc, might still be in play.

Normally, the fact that one and the same norm functions in more than one way, say both constitutive and authoritative, is not particularly puzzling or problematic. One possible exception, however, might be the combination of codifying norms with the authoritative kind. One might wonder how can the same norm both try to codify preexisting reasons for action, that is, reasons that apply to us anyway, and at the same time make the demand authoritative. Raz's Normal Justification Thesis provides a good answer. Authorities are often in a very good position to help their subjects comply with reasons that apply to them anyway, regardless of the authoritative directive. Ordering you to do something that you have reasons to do anyway is quite rational and useful whenever it is the case that by complying with the order you are more likely to act according to the reasons that apply to you, than by trying to figure out, or act on, those reasons by yourself. And as Raz and others convincingly demonstrated, this condition obtains often enough.

So there is no contradiction in the combination of authoritative directives with norms of the codifying kind.[31]

Still, you might *think* that there is something problematic here. As we have seen, at least from the perspective of the norm-subjects, codifying norms fail the condition of normativity. If a norm codifies reasons for action that apply to you anyway, then citing the norm as a reason for your action would be an instance of acting on the wrong kind of reason. You ought to avoid assaulting a person because assault is wrong and ought not be done, not because the criminal code forbids it. But we have also seen that there are good reasons to have norms of the codifying kind, and it is not difficult to see that those reasons can be instantiated by authoritative directives. It is important to have a legally authoritative definition of what counts as a criminal assault, for example, to render punitive reaction to assault publicly transparent, to minimise misunderstandings, and such. Thus, even if the main provisions of, say, a criminal code, fail the condition of normativity, their authoritative nature is rational and serves all sorts of auxiliary functions.

The question I want to address in this final section is whether there is any general feature of law that renders its normativity unique. Raz suggested, a long time ago, that there is something that makes legal normativity unique, in that law necessarily purports to be supreme to any other kind norms that might apply to its subjects and claims the authority to regulate any kind or sphere of behaviour. In other words, the idea is that law claims to be the final arbitrator in determining what reasons for action apply to its subjects and in all possible domains of human conduct. Raz called these two features law's claim to be supreme and comprehensive.[32] Law's claim to supremacy, however, can be understood in two ways. In one sense, and I am pretty sure this is the one Raz had in mind, law's claim to supremacy is an attribute of a legal system in relation to other normative systems that might be practised in a given community. So the idea is that between

[31] See Raz, The Morality of Freedom (n 17) chs 3 and 4.
[32] Raz, *Practical Reasons and Norms* (n 28) 150–51.

different systems of norms that are regarded as binding by given population, such as law, religion, social customs, positive morality, and such, law essentially claims a normative superiority. But then, another sense in which we might think of law as claiming superiority over other normative considerations might be directly related to the kind of reasons for action legal norms purport to create; it is arguable that whenever the law tells you to do something, it purports to give you an all things considered reason to do it. So in this sense, supremacy of the law is to be understood as an attribute of legal norms, as such. I think that both of these theses about law's claim to supremacy are inaccurate, at best. Let me explain.

Raz's idea, which I am not sure he holds anymore, that legal systems necessarily claim comprehensiveness and supremacy conflates, I think, law with state sovereignty.[33] The emergence of modem states and the idea of state sovereignty clearly went hand-in-hand with these ideas of normative supremacy and comprehensive authority. The authority of a state was meant to be the supreme authority in the land, often allowing other normative systems to be in place but only by the authoritative permission of the state; and state sovereignty, at least in its ideal form, indeed acknowledged no inherent boundaries to its reach. But at least from an historical perspective, these ideals of state sovereignty are relatively novel, starting from, roughly, the sixteenth century, reaching their peak around the late nineteenth to first half of the twentieth century, and fading away in the last few decades. Legal systems were in place long before state sovereignty came on the scene. In other words, I seriously doubt that law's claim to be comprehensive and supreme is an essential attribute of law and legal systems. It is an attribute of a particular political ideal of state sovereignty, not of law.

Let me explore, however, a different sense in which law might be understood to claim supremacy. When the law imposes an obligation or some requirement, it also implicitly acknowledges, as it should of course, that one may have good reasons not to comply under the circumstances, perhaps deriving from a conflicting obligation or some other excuse. But the law always claims the authority to determine whether non-compliance was legally justified or not. In other words, the law always reserves itself the final say on what you should do or should have done all things considered. Consider a simple example: the law prohibits parking in a given space; this amounts to an obligation not to park there. But then there might be a conflicting obligation that applies to you, you may need to pick up your friend who is seriously ill and cannot make it to the car if it is parked far away. So you might think that the latter obligation prevails, and you park your car in the prohibited zone for a bit. Now the law may agree with you, or not, but it purports to be the final arbiter about your decision. The law claims to have the authority to determine whether you had a legally recognised defence, and it may agree with

[33] I have made this point in greater detail in my *Positive Law and Objective Values* (Oxford, Oxford University Press, 2001) at 39–42.

you or not, but in any case, it purports to decide whether, all things considered, you could park your car there or not. So it would seem that the law claims supremacy in the sense of claiming to give its subjects all things considered reasons for action, that is, at least from a legal point of view.

Let us try to be more precise here. Legal norms impose obligations of various kinds; all legal obligations include various explicit or implicit unless clauses that are meant to capture various exceptions or modifications of the relevant obligations under some circumstances. Since it is well recognised that not all justified exceptions to the application of norms can be predicted in advance, the law authorises someone (typically the courts) to make the final decisions about such matters.[34] Therefore, in each particular case, whenever the law has a conclusive verdict on what you have reason to do, it is a verdict about your reason for action all things considered; at least from a legal point of view, if you will.

Now, one way of understanding Raz's ideas about law's claim to superiority is precisely the sense in which the legal point of view, quite generally, claims superiority over any other kind of normative consideration. So we might think that when a final legal verdict on reasons for action conflicts with some other normative demand, such as a moral one, the law claims, and necessarily so, superiority over the moral considerations. But even if true, the claim to supremacy is not unique to law. After all, morality would also claim normative superiority to law; and the same can be said about religion, for those who take religion to give them reasons for action, or about conflicts between demands of morality and personal attachments. Normative points of view can genuinely conflict. There are many complicated issues involved here, no doubt, but I cannot see how law's claim to superiority over other normative domains, if it has such a claim, as it were, makes law unique in any way; all comprehensive normative perspectives might conflict with other perspectives and would naturally embody some claim to superiority – this is what makes it a conflict.

Let us put aside, then, the question of how the legal point of view compares with other normative domains, and focus on the way in which legal authority purports to give us reasons for action. I think that it is true that in some contexts the law purports to give its subjects an all things considered reason for action. But I think that this is more common than one might think. Authorities often intend, and not irrationally, to give their subjects all things considered reasons for action. Consider father's instruction to son again. When father instructs son to be home by 7, he may intend to give son an all things considered reason to do so. Think about the deliberative process here. It might go like this: father thinks that it is important for son to be home for dinner; there are reasons for this. Of course son might prefer otherwise, and he may have reasons for that. Father considers

[34] I explained this in greater detail in my 'Defeasibility and Pragmatic Indeterminacy in Law' in A Capone and F Poggi (eds), Pragmatics and the Law: *Philosophical Perspectives* (Dordrecht, Springer, 2016) 15.

the conflicting reasons that apply, and makes a decision. All things considered, he decides, son should be home for dinner. Thus by communicating his authoritative directive, father quite possibly intends son to have an all things considered reason to be home for dinner. After all, he considered all the reasons and concluded that being home for dinner is required. Now there are two caveats: first, if father is a reasonable person, he would realise that there might be relevant reasons he failed to consider. But notice that under normal conditions, the possibility of error is just that, a possibility, and would not be taken to affect the conclusiveness of the directive. For all I know 'I ought to φ' is, practically speaking, for me tantamount to 'I ought to φ'. Unless, of course, it turns out that I was wrong. But if I have no particular reason to suspect that I am wrong, I ought to φ.

The second caveat does have practical import: father would also know that some new and unforeseen reasons might come up or reveal themselves later. And it is always possible that a defeating reason may come up that outweighs, all things considered, the original reasons for the directive. In this sense, the all things considered reason he purports to give son is qualified: all things considered, son ought to φ, unless something comes up, presently unforeseen, that outweighs the reason for φ-ing. In other words, there is always an 'unless …' clause attached to a directive for action all things considered: unless a defeating reason comes up later, which is presently unforeseen.

Notice that all things considered judgments are typically qualified in this manner. Suppose I wonder whether I should keep a promise I made to X which turns out to be a more burdensome than I had initially predicted. Obviously I have reasons to keep my promise, and now it seems that I have reasons not to keep it, and I must make a decision: what is it that, all things considered, I have reason to do? Suppose I realise that all things considered I ought to keep my promise. It does not normally mean: keep my promise come what may, especially if the action required is in the future. It only means that within the domain of reasons that are reasonable for me to consider, those I can be reasonably expected to take into account right now, all things considered I ought to keep my promise. But the possibility that something might come up later, that I could not reasonably take into account right now, is something that we are normally aware of. All things considered 'I ought to φ' normally incorporates an implicit unless clause: unless something comes up that, all things considered, defeats the reason to φ. Of course it has to be the case that the defeating reason is not presently predictable; if it is, then its likelihood and possible impact should form part of the all things considered reasons.

Suppose it is true that authorities, sometimes at least, intend to give their subjects an all things considered reason to do as instructed. That still leaves it an open question of whether the subject has an all things considered reason to comply. Even if we assume, as we should for now, that son has an obligation to comply with father's directives, whether all things considered son ought to comply with father's instruction is a separate question. An obligation to φ does not entail an all things considered reason to φ. Obligations give us protected reasons, they give us a first order reason and second-order exclusionary reasons. But protected reasons are not all things considered reasons. So from the perspective of the subject, whether compliance with an authoritative directive is required all things considered, is a question to be answered on the merits of the case. In principle it is always possible that all things considered one should not comply with an authority's directive, even if the authority is by and large legitimate and its directives obligatory.

The conclusion I drive at here might have an air of paradox to it. It would seem that on the account I suggest, authorities may purport to achieve something that they cannot expect to accomplish; an authoritative directive to φ may purport to give the subject an all things considered reason to φ, but for the subject, the reason to φ cannot be an all things considered one, solely on the grounds that the subject was instructed to φ, even if the instruction is legitimate, as it were. Whether there is an all things considered reason to comply with an authoritative instruction is always an open question. So it seems that authorities, again, at least sometimes, purport to give their subjects the kind of reasons that subjects cannot be given. I doubt that this is as paradoxical as it seems, but there is certainly an essential asymmetry in the authority subject relations. Authorities may purport to give their subjects all things considered reasons, whereas subjects can only regard authoritative directives as giving them protected reasons.

You might think that the difference between trying to give you an all things considered reason to φ – when 'all things considered' is inevitably qualified to the domain of likely and foreseeable reasons (as it always is) – and trying to give you a protected reason to φ, is just too abstract; it has the feel of a hair-splitting distinction. So let us try to think about it by comparing two kinds of speech acts: compare a command or an order with a request of a certain kind, the kind of request that gives the addressee a pretty strong reason to comply. For example, suppose I am in a dire need of financial help and I ask my best friend to help me out with a modest loan, one that he can easily afford. This is the kind of request that would seem to give my friend a protected reason to comply. Once I made the request, he has a first order reason to give me the loan, and some second order exclusionary reasons, say, not to consider his immediate discomfort or embarrassment to count against the first order reason (after all, I am in a dire need of help and he is my best friend and all…). So the idea is that some requests may well give us protected reasons to do as requested. But this is still markedly different from a typical legal order. If the IRS issues a directive requiring me to make an advance on my taxes, it aims to do more than just give me a protected reason. It tells me to send in the cheque, all things considered. And if I fail to send in the cheque, the law clearly purports to determine whether my failure was warranted or not. But again, there is nothing all that unique to law here. Authorities often purport to give their subjects all things considered reasons for action, parental authority being one good example.

None of this was meant to suggest that the law necessarily purports to give its subjects an all things considered reason for action. In other words, I am not suggesting that this is an essential feature of legal directives. It is a feature of certain types of authority the law purports to exercise in certain contexts, mostly in the contexts of mandatory regulations, such as criminal law, safety regulations, tax law, etc. In many other domains, the law operates as a service provider, offering arbitration and enforcement services if certain conditions it sets out are met. Contract law, for example, does not tell the subjects how to make binding promises, and it certainly does not tell anyone to make a contract. It only conditions the adjudicative and enforcement services the law provides on the parties meeting certain conditions. If you want the law on your side, make sure to have a legally binding contract. In other words, the law is not always in the business of telling us what to do (or not to do). It is often just a service provider, and like any other service provider, it lays out its conditions for the service to be provided. Needless to say, this is hugely over-simplified. Many services the law provides are not easy to avoid. But that is true of countless other services we are offered: they are often not easy to avoid. Law's coercive aspect, though not unique to law, calls for an explanation of its own, one which would have to rely on a serious elaboration of what is the nature of coercion and what makes something coercive to begin with. Those are complex issues that go far beyond the confines of this essay.

7

Normative Reasoning From a Point of View

WJ WALUCHOW

I. Introduction

A central issue in the philosophy of constitutional law is the role judges play when interpreting and applying bills or charters of rights.[1] Such legal instruments invariably contain very abstract clauses referring to concepts of political morality, such as freedom of speech or expression, dignity, equality, due process, and the principles of fundamental justice. Judges often draw on such concepts in the process of reviewing official legislative and executive acts, a review process that sometimes results in a declaration that the latter are legally invalid, unconstitutional, or of no (legal) force and effect. These powers of constitutional review raise a host of questions as to their justification in societies dedicated to democracy and the rule of law. Among the most prominent of these is what I will call *the democratic challenge*, which can be summarised in the following question. How can we, as communities fully committed to the principles of democracy, tolerate a system that accords unelected, democratically unaccountable judges, the power to thwart the well-considered judgements of bodies elected by and accountable to the democratic communities they have been chosen to serve?[2] How can we tolerate judges (apparently) substituting their own, personal views about free expression, equality, and the principles of fundamental justice for the views of those whom we have supposedly chosen to decide such issues on our behalf? In short, isn't constitutional review under a charter of rights inconsistent with the fundamental tenets of democracy?[3]

There are a number of ways one might respond to the democratic challenge. First, one might simply reject the very possibility that constitutional review could

[1] For purposes of easing expression, I will refer only to charters.

[2] I say 'well-considered judgements' to rule out judgements that are, eg, the result of bribery and extortion, or that blatantly fail to respect well-established procedural requirements.

[3] Henceforth the term 'constitutional review' will be used to refer to review of this kind, ie, under a constitutional charter (or bill) of rights.

ever, under any circumstances, be justified. This was the option pursued by Jeremy Waldron, who famously argued that constitutional review is, in all but highly unusual circumstances, an affront to the fundamental democratic right to political participation.[4] A second possibility is to note the many contemporary political communities that embrace forms of constitutional review which do not grant judges the final say on the questions of political morality that typically arise under constitutional review. This is the route pursued by Stephen Guardbaum, who draws our attention to 'the new commonwealth model', embraced in different ways in countries such as England, Canada and, to a lesser extent, New Zealand and Australia.[5] Canada's section 33 'notwithstanding clause', to cite just one example, allows Parliament or a Provincial legislature to declare that its legislation will stand notwithstanding a court ruling that it violates one of a specified number of rights of political morality recognised in the Canadian Charter of Rights and Freedoms. In England, to cite another example, Parliament is constitutionally at liberty simply to ignore the Supreme Court's judgment that its legislation is incompatible with a provision of the UK Human Rights Act. Judges have an important say in England but, arguably, it is anything but the final say. I say 'arguably' because Parliament has, in practice, invariably reacted to a declaration of incompatibility by modifying or withdrawing the offending legislation, leading some to suggest that in practice England actually embraces *strong-form* constitutional review. This is the form of review practiced in the United States, where the Supreme Court is constitutionally empowered to strike down or nullify acts of the executive or legislature, thus giving them the final say on matters of constitutional law. A third possibility is to agree that constitutional review is undemocratic, but justified on other grounds, for example, justice and the enlightened pursuit of the rule of law.[6] A fourth possibility, one pursued by theorists like Samuel Freeman and Ronald Dworkin, is to show that even US-style, strong-form constitutional review is in fact consistent with the democratic principle.[7] In previous work, I have also pursued this fourth option by defending a theory under which the principal role of a judge is not to draw on her own first-order convictions in regard to the relevant matters of political morality that arise in constitutional review.[8] Rather, her role is to hold the community to *its own* fundamental moral convictions on these matters, convictions expressed

[4] See, eg, J Waldron, 'A Rights Based Critique of Constitutional Rights' (1993) 13 *Oxford Journal of Legal Studies* 19 and J Waldron, *Law and Disagreement* (New York, Oxford University Press, 1999).

[5] S Gardbaum, *The New Commonwealth Model of Constitutionalism: Theory and Practice* (New York, Cambridge University Press, 2013).

[6] See, eg, D Strauss, *The Living Constitution* (New York, Oxford University Press, 2010).

[7] See, eg, S Freeman, 'Constitutional Democracy and the Legitimacy of Judicial Review' (1990–1991) 9 *Law and Philosophy* 327; R Dworkin, *Taking Rights Seriously* (Cambridge MA, Harvard University Press, 1977) and R Dworkin, *Law's Empire* (Cambridge MA, Harvard University Press, 1986).

[8] By 'first-order moral conviction (or judgment)' I mean a personal moral conviction about what morality *really* or *ideally* demands in the circumstances in question. By 'first-order moral reasoning' I mean moral reasoning the aim of which is to substantiate the truth or validity of a first-order moral conviction. It is what we normally think of when we refer to someone having to engage in moral reasoning.

in what I call *the community's constitutional morality* (CCM).[9] CCM is not, as I conceive it, the personal morality of any particular person, such as a judge who helps decide a constitutional case. Nor is it the morality decreed by God, inherent in the fabric of the universe, or residing in Plato's world of forms. Rather, it is a kind of community-based, positive morality consisting of the fundamental moral norms and convictions to which the democratic community has actually committed itself and which have acquired some kind of formal, constitutional recognition. It is the political morality actually endorsed in a community's constitutional practices. In many systems, constitutional recognition of CCM norms includes (though it is not limited to) entrenchment in a charter of rights and, importantly, in the legislative history and jurisprudence that combine to flesh out the local, concrete understandings or Thomistic 'determinations' or specifications of those norms for that particular community.

With this conception of constitutional morality in hand, I set out to defend constitutional review against the democratic challenge. Put simply, my thesis was that CCM, owing to its social origin in the democratic community, is a source of entrenched, moral norms and convictions upon which judges can justifiably draw in constitutional review without compromising democratic legitimacy. Constitutional review typically involves the task of ensuring that legislative acts do not infringe the fundamental commitments of CCM. If this is its nature, then democratic legitimacy need not be compromised. Indeed, the judge, in ruling against a piece of legislation, may not be thwarting the democratic will at all. On the contrary, she may be taking steps towards implementing that will by enforcing the democratic community's own moral commitments against an action that conflicts with them.

Appealing to CCM in this way is not, of course, without its difficulties. As some critics have pointed out, we disagree strongly and widely about the demands of CCM, just as we do about virtually any moral matter.[10] Indeed, that's why cases of constitutional review arise in the first place. If everyone agreed on what CCM requires in individual cases, then very few – if any – cases would ever arise to be adjudicated by courts. And even when they did arise, everyone would agree on how they should be decided. But of course not everyone agrees, and this once again raises the democratic challenge. If people – judges included – disagree about what CCM demands, some thinking that the legislation in question offends its basic

[9] On what I mean by CCM, see 'Constitutional Morality and Bills of Rights' in G Huscroft (ed), *Expounding the Constitution: Essays in Constitutional Theory* (Cambridge, Cambridge Universtity Press, 2008) 65.

[10] See, eg, BW Miller, 'Review Essay: A Common Law Theory of Judicial Review' (2007) 52 *American Journal of Jurisprudence* 297; N Struchiner and F Shecaira, 'Trying to Fix Roots in Quicksand: Some Difficulties With Waluchow's Conception on the True Community Morality' (2009) 3 *Problema Anuario de Filosofía y Teoría del Derecho* 23; IB Flores, 'The Living Tree Constitutionalism: Fixity and Flexibility' (2009) 3 *Problema Anuario de Filosofía y Teoría del Derecho* 37; N Stoljar, 'Waluchow on Moral Opinions and Moral Commitments' (2009) 3 *Problema Anuario de Filosofía y Teoría del Derecho* 101; and L Alexander, 'Waluchow's Living Tree Constitutionalism' (2010) 29 *Law & Philosophy* 93.

commitments, and others believing that no such conflict exists, then one cannot point to consensus within the democratic community to defend constitutional review against the democratic challenge. Of course, as Ronald Dworkin repeatedly pointed out throughout his career, the mere fact of disagreement in no way entails that there is no fact of the matter in such cases – no truth about what CCM really requires upon which a judge could reasonably draw. Nor does it entail the absurdity of viewing the role of a court as attempting, as best it can, to discern what that fact is.[11] Nevertheless, it is undeniable that such disagreement threatens to undermine the *practical possibility* of democratic legitimacy. After all, how can the decision to apply a CCM norm in a particular way be reasonably viewed as reflective of the democratic will if there is so much dissensus and uncertainty about what it is? Will a judge in such circumstances not be forced to choose from among the possibly large number of different interpretations of the relevant constitutional norms on offer? And will she not ultimately end up having to ground her choice in what she, personally, thinks is the morally preferable option? What else could she do in such circumstances, short of simply declining to make a decision at all? Yet if this is so, the democratic challenge remains a powerful threat to the legitimacy of constitutional review. The judge will seemingly be forced to rely on her own first-order moral judgements about the rights of political morality under dispute in the case she must decide. And this, the argument goes, cannot be rendered consistent with the fundamental principles of democracy.

My aim in this paper is to challenge the soundness of this argument. My contention is this: even in those cases where the community reasonably disagrees about the commitments embodied in its CCM, a judge drawing on those commitments in a contentious case of constitutional review need not do so in a way that invites the democratic challenge. My defence will rest on a crucial, but often neglected, distinction between:

(a) interpreting a constitutional norm from the perspective of a judge's own, first-order moral judgements; and
(b) interpreting a constitutional norm from the perspective of the democratic community and its first-order moral judgements.

My argument will be this: even when interpreting contentious CCM norms inevitably requires the judge to make a hard moral choice based on moral reasoning, this need not be done in a way that offends the principles of democracy. Drawing on Raz's theory of detached normative statements and reasoning from a point of view, I shall argue for the following claims: (1) any moral reasoning that takes place in the process of constitutional review can be undertaken from the perspective or point of view of the democratic community and its CCM commitments;

[11] This theme appeared and played a prominent role throughout Dworkin's career, up to and including some of his most recent work. See, eg, R Dworkin, *Justice For Hedgehogs* (Cambridge MA, Harvard University Press, 2011), *passim*, but especially ch 5.

(2) this process can be undertaken by a judge without the unwarranted intrusion of her own, first-order moral convictions; (3) when undertaken from this point of view, constitutional review is consistent with democracy; and (4) this is so even when this activity requires a good deal of substantive moral reasoning and argument on the part of the judge – substantive reasoning and argument with which many will reasonably, and sometimes profoundly, disagree.

II. Reasoning From a Point of View

Joseph Raz observes that there are at least three points of view from which one can approach the expression of normative statements. First, a speaker can utter a normative statement which personally commits her to the view expressed. When Katharina says 'Kara did the morally right thing in keeping her promise to Maggie' she commits herself to the claim that Kara's action was, in fact, morally correct.[12] When I, being confronted with a valid law of a legal system to which I am subject and which I fully support, say 'It would be wrong not to pay my taxes', I commit myself to the normative view I express. My statement is an *internal statement* uttered from what Hart famously called 'the internal point of view'.[13] A second point of view, also noted by Hart, is of course 'the external point of view'.[14] This is where I do not myself express or assert a normative point of view but rather *describe* the point of view of other people, perhaps by describing their beliefs, attitudes and actions regarding some normative situation. When I say that the British not only habitually queue up while awaiting public transport, but believe that this is the right thing to do and are prepared to criticise anyone who deviates from that pattern of behaviour, I describe their normative behaviour, beliefs and attitudes – and I do so from the external point of view. I describe what Hart called the observance of a 'social rule' accepted *by them* from the internal point of view. But I do so in a way that in no way commits me to the normative view expressed in observance and endorsement, by them, of that rule. Analogously, if I say that, under South African apartheid law, it was wrong for white people to have sexual relations with black people, I describe the state of law in 1920s South Africa.[15] But quite obviously I don't commit myself in any way to the normative view described.

[12] Under normal circumstances we can assume that the statement is sincere. But even when it is not, the commitment is nevertheless expressed (if not endorsed).

[13] See HLA Hart, *The Concept of Law*, 3rd edn (Oxford, Oxford University Press, 2012) 89–91.

[14] ibid.

[15] The Immorality Act, 1927. Sexual relations between blacks and whites remained illegal in South Africa until 1985 when the Parliament of South Africa introduced The Immorality and Prohibition of Mixed Marriages Amendment Act, 1985. See CG Van der Merwe and JE Du Plessis, *Introduction to the Law of South Africa* (The Hague, Kluwer Law International, 2004).

In addition to these two points of view, there is, according to Raz, an important third alternative with its corresponding type of statement: the *detached point of view* and the *detached normative statements* expressed from that perspective.[16] Focusing now on law, Raz claims that 'A detached legal statement is a statement of law, of what legal rights or duties people have, not a statement about people's beliefs, attitudes, or actions, not even about their beliefs, attitudes, or actions about the law'.[17] In other words, the statement cannot be reduced to an external statement of the form: 'S believes that he ought to do x' or 'The legal officials of legal system y have enacted law L requiring x, and will therefore hold S accountable should he fail to do x'. But neither does the statement carry the full normative force that a legal statement uttered from the internal point of view usually does. This is because it does not commit the speaker to acceptance of the normative view it expresses.[18] A detached legal statement is *like* an internal statement in that it *uses* the law as a standard with which to evaluate and judge conduct. But it is different from any such statement in so far as its utterance does not commit the speaker to the normative view expressed. It does not, at least necessarily, express *his* particular view of the matter. Raz observes that this third kind of statement is characteristically used by individuals, for example lawyers, who are neither concerned with describing social practices from the external point of view nor with applying the law to their own behaviour. Rather, their aim is to inform others what they ought to do according to the law, and this information is conveyed from a point of view that is not necessarily that of the speaker.[19] She needn't believe that this is the point of view people should, all things considered, *really* take on the matter. As a result, the speaker who utters a detached legal statement merely needs to be able to identify the point of view so that the appropriate recommendation can be made from it. Most importantly, for our purposes, '[l]egal scholars – and this includes ordinary practising lawyers – can use normative language when describing the law and make legal statements without thereby endorsing the law's moral authority'.[20] Putting it another way, legal scholars – and this includes ordinary practising judges – can make legal statements without thereby expressing first-order moral judgements.

[16] Raz credits Kelsen with recognising the importance of detached legal statements. They are, Raz suggests, 'crucial to anyone holding his view on the meaning of "validity" and rejecting natural law at the same time': see J Raz, *The Authority of Law: Essays on Law and Morality* (Oxford, Oxford University Press, 1979) 155.

[17] ibid 153.

[18] ibid.

[19] ibid 155. Indeed, it could be conveyed by an anarchist lawyer who in fact rejects the law's authority completely. Normally, of course, lawyers endorse their legal system and its claims, and so their statements are internal ones. But Raz's point is that this is not necessary. It is possible to *use* legal standards to judge, evaluate and advise without actually endorsing the point of view they express. Think, here, of a progressive, liberal-minded lawyer in 1920s South Africa advising his client of his legal duties under The Immorality Act, 1927.

[20] ibid 156.

Detached legal statements, therefore, seem clearly possible.[21] But the possibility of uttering a detached statement is in no way unique to law. It exists within any normative context, including morality and religion. Raz writes:

> Imagine an orthodox, but relatively ill-informed Jew who asks the advice of his friend who is Catholic but an expert in Rabbinical law. 'What should I do?' he asks, clearly meaning what I do according to *my* religion, not yours. The friend tells him that he should do so and so. The point is that both know that this is not what the friend thinks that he really ought to do. The friend is simply stating how things are from the Jewish Orthodox point of view.[22]

So once again, it seems possible to know and state what should be done from a point of view one does not necessarily endorse. Now if the possibility exists here, that is, from the point of view of the Jewish Orthodox community and its religious commitments, then there seems no reason, in principle, to deny the possibility when we turn to the point of view of a democratic community and its fundamental constitutional commitments, ie, when we turn to the requirements of its CCM. Here too it seems possible to render a detached judgement without necessarily endorsing the view expressed – ie *without inserting one's own first-order moral convictions into the equation.* Just as the Catholic friend can, in a detached manner, discern and express what should be done from the point of view of his Orthodox friend, and just as a judge in a criminal case can, in a detached manner, discern and express what should be done from the point of view of the criminal code, a judge in a constitutional case should be able to discern and express what should be done from the point of view of the democratic community and its CCM commitments. If this truly is possible, then we seem to have a potentially decisive answer to the democratic challenge. Judges who engage in the process of interpreting and applying constitutional rights are not – at least necessarily – relying on their own, personal first-order moral judgements. They are reasoning, not from their own moral point of view, but from that of the democratic community. And there is nothing inherently undemocratic about that.

III. Objection 1: Application versus Interpretation

There are, no doubt, a number of objections that might made to this attempt to posit CCM as a basis from which detached judgements can be made. Among them is the following: it is one thing to express a detached judgement about the demands of norms whose meaning and application are presumably indisputable

[21] For criticisms of Raz's theory of detached legal statements, see L d'Almeida, 'Legal Statements and Normative Language' (2011) 30 *Law and Philosophy* 180. For further reflections on the theory, see K Toh, 'Raz on Detachment, Acceptance and Describability' (2007) 27 *Oxford Journal of Legal Studies* 403.

[22] Raz, *The Authority of Law* (n 16) 156.

(Raz's example). It is quite another to do so when all one has to offer is a highly disputable judgement about something as elusive and contestable as CCM norms. An unstated, though perhaps crucial, feature of Raz's example is that the identity and meaning of the norms drawn on by the Catholic friend are clear and obvious to anyone who is in the know. And so no judgement or reasoning, moral or otherwise, is required in order to express a detached – or committed – claim about what they demand. The Catholic friend simply has to *apply* the relevant norms, something *anyone* who had the requisite knowledge could quite easily do. But the same cannot be said when one turns to the norms of CCM and the role they are being asked to play in constitutional review. One cannot here offer a judgement from a detached point of view because one cannot identify and apply the relevant norm(s) in a way that calls for no fully committed, first-order moral reasoning and judgement. In Raz's example, the advisor need engage in no measure of first-order moral reasoning and judgement because he needn't consider which, among any number of contestable interpretations or understandings of the relevant norms, he ought to recommend to his friend. Nor need he weigh one norm against another before deciding what advice to give his friend. In other words, he need not engage in what we normally think of as normative *reasoning* or *interpretation*. But in the controversial constitutional cases in which CCM norms are said to figure so prominently, that is precisely what is required. The judge must *interpret* the relevant norms, *weighing* and *balancing* one against the other(s). Only then can any conclusions about how the case ought to be decided be drawn. But she cannot do any of these things – interpreting, weighing and balancing – without leaving her detached perspective behind and exercising good old-fashioned first-order moral reasoning and judgement that calls on her personal, first-order moral convictions. The judge, in having to interpret and weigh the very norms she is called on to apply to decide the case before her, will be forced to exercise the kind of full-blooded, highly contentious moral reasoning that invites the democratic challenge.[23]

This objection, if sound, is probably enough to undermine my attempt to ward off the democratic challenge.[24] But is it sound? This is far from clear. In order to understand better why this might be the case, let's shift our focus momentarily to Dworkin, a theorist whose views on constitutional review seem, on virtually identical grounds, as susceptible as mine to the democratic challenge. Just as judges may be forced to exercise first-order moral reasoning to discern the requirements of CCM, judges on Dworkin's model will be forced to exercise moral reasoning

[23] A version of this argument is defended by Stephen Perry in a number of articles, most notably S Perry, 'Interpretation and Methodology in Legal Theory' in A Marmor (ed), *Law and Interpretation: Essays in Legal Philosophy* (New York, Oxford University Press, 1995) 97; and S Perry, 'The Varieties of Legal Positivism' (1996) 9 *Canadian Journal of Law & Jurisprudence* 361. In those papers, Perry addresses the interpretation of the concept of law, not the interpretation of moral concepts, principles and values that find their way into constitutionals or bills of rights. But the argument would be much the same – as would my response to it.

[24] This is not to say, of course, that there might not be other avenues open to one who wishes to argue that constitutional review is consistent with democracy.

whenever they set out to offer the law its best constructive interpretation. So we might profit by briefly examining Dworkin's more familiar theory.

Let's begin by considering one important, though largely overlooked, respect in which Dworkinian constructive interpretation is undertaken from a decidedly detached point of view. As Dworkin always insisted in answering critics who claimed that his theory encourages judges to 'play fast and loose with the law', constructive interpretations, as he conceived them, must always *fit* the materials to be interpreted to some highly significant degree.[25] The historical materials that set the stage for constructive legal interpretation – statutes, judicial decisions, and so on – include elements the interpreter might very well wish, for first-order moral and political reasons, were not there to constrain her interpretations. But they *are* there and they *will* invariably restrict her interpretive efforts in highly significant ways. And importantly for our purposes here, they will serve to obstruct any attempt, by the interpreter, to impose her own, first-order moral views.

> [T]he brute facts of legal history will … limit the role any judge's personal convictions of justice can play in his decisions. Different judges will set this threshold [of fit] differently. But anyone who accepts law as integrity must accept that the actual political history of his community will sometimes check his other political convictions in his overall interpretive judgment.[26]

An instructive way of viewing Dworkin's fit condition is to see it as requiring that constructive interpretation be undertaken, not from the point of view of the interpreter and her own first-order moral beliefs, but from the point of view of a particular community with its own distinctive history of decisions and commitments within the realm of political morality. Interpretation must be undertaken from *that* point of view, just as the advice of the Catholic advisor must be offered, not from his own religious point of view, but from the perspective of the Orthodox Jewish community and *its* particular history of decisions, rules, doctrines, values and commitments. A committed Marxist judge could no more offer a plausible interpretation or construction of American property law, according to which private property amounts to theft, than the Catholic friend could sincerely advise his friend that he need not observe the Jewish Sabbath. This could not be a sensible interpretation *of American property law.* It would be nothing less than an expression of the judge's own, personal first-order moral views about how property should, in an ideal world, be distributed. One could, I suppose, refer to this Marxist take as an 'interpretation', one that potentially puts American property law in its ideally best

[25] John Mackie was one of the first to level this charge against Dworkin. '… I am tempted to speak of Professor Dworkin playing fast and loose with the law. The alleged determinacy of the law in hard cases is a myth, and the practical effect of the acceptance of this myth would be to give … a larger scope for what is in reality judicial legislation … [I]it would shift the boundary between the settled and the unsettled law, it would make what on another view would be easy cases into hard ones … [I]t would encourage judges … to rely upon their necessarily subjective views about a supposedly objective morality': J Mackie, 'The Third Theory of Law' (1977) 7 *Philosophy and Public Affairs* 15–16.

[26] Dworkin, *Law's Empire* (n 7) 255.

moral light. But it could not possibly count as an instance of Dworkinian *constructive* interpretation because it does not fit the relevant institutional history. Putting it in terms relevant to our current discussion, it is not made from the perspective of the American community and its history of moral commitments with respect to the proper distribution of property. It does not construct that history so much as suggest how it might, in an ideal world, have been better.

It is crucial to acknowledge, at this juncture, that this reading of the fit requirement is not in itself enough to rescue constructive interpretation from the grip of the democratic challenge. And this is because, as Dworkin was always fully prepared to acknowledge, there will often be no uniquely correct interpretation that adequately fits the materials to be interpreted. To be sure, a Marxist interpretation of American property law could not reasonably be thought to fit the relevant object of interpretation and would therefore be excluded as a sensible candidate. But there will inevitably be other plausible interpretations and each of these will surpass the 'threshold test' of fit.[27] For instance, certain rival libertarian interpretations, as well as others favoured by devotees of law and economics, are likely to survive the test and remain as plausible constructive accounts of the American community's commitments with respect to property. Hence it might be thought impossible in these cases to identify a unique point of view from which detached constructive interpretation could take place. On the contrary, there could only be a variety of such perspectives and their corresponding interpretations. And choosing from among these perspectives will inevitably demand of the judge the very kind of first-order moral reasoning and judgement that invites the democratic challenge. She will be forced to choose, from among the available points of view, the one *she* thinks is morally best, ideally speaking. In other words, the process of constructive interpretation will inevitably force judges to rely on their own first-order moral convictions. And so the democratic challenge once again rears its ugly head.

The same seems true of my construal of constitutional review as an attempt to discern, interpret and apply commitments revealed in a community's CCM. In what sense could the first-order moral reasoning the judge must undertake when it is uncertain what established norms of CCM norms require in the case at hand be properly viewed as detached? After all, detached judgement is supposed to be undertaken without any sort of first-order commitment. That seems hardly true when the judge chooses, from among rival interpretations of CCM norms, that which *she* judges to be morally best. Put simply, the choice here is made on the basis of premises *she* provides and to which *she* is committed, not her community.

[27] Dworkin, *Taking Rights Seriously* (n 7) 342. In terms used in early statements of his interpretive theory of law, Dworkin writes: '[N]o principle can count as a justification of institutional history unless it provides a certain threshold adequacy of fit, though amongst those principles that meet this test of adequacy the morally soundest must be preferred'.

While I must acknowledge the force of this last objection, I continue to maintain that the reasoning involved here can still sensibly be viewed as detached. After all, it is reasoning that remains significantly constrained by an historical record of which the interpreter may well largely disapprove. And it is reasoning that can lead to conclusions with which the judge herself strongly disagrees morally – which she would most certainly *not* make were she free to decide on her own terms. Think of a Canadian judge in the years immediately preceding the Supreme Court of Canada's landmark same-sex marriage case who personally found same-sex marriage morally offensive. Canada's CCM commitments may have been uncertain or indeterminate to some degree and left open a variety of possibilities for interpretation. But none of the available options were in accord with that particular judge's first-order moral convictions. That's because, the judge, in choosing what she takes to be the morally best option open to her, would still have been required to choose on behalf of her community and within the confines of premises *it* has supplied by way of *its* constitutional record.

So even when a judge must engage in contentious moral reasoning in choosing from among alternatives the norms of CCM appear to leave open, we may still sensibly view her as reasoning and choosing from a detached perspective, ie from a point of view defined by the substantive constraints imposed by the community's prior moral commitments. She is still working *from* these premises regardless of whether she might have preferred (morally) to work from very different ones. In other words, she is still reasoning, not from her own point of view but from the point of view of the *community* with its own set of moral beliefs and commitments. Judgement exercised from that point of view is no more a reflection of the interpreter's own, personal first-order moral convictions and preferences (what she thinks ought, ideally to be the case) than is our Catholic's advice to his Orthodox friend. Insofar as and to the extent that any moral judgement exercised is exercised from a perspective defined by the democratic community and its fundamental moral commitments, it is one which all reasonable citizens can and should accept as an expression of *their* sovereign democratic will, not that of the presiding judge.

IV. Objection 2: The Circumstances of Judging

As we have seen, a key premise in my Raz-inspired defence of constitutional review is that the contentious judgement required in cases of constitutional review can be generated from a detached point of view. Just as one can discern, interpret and apply the law of Apartheid South Africa without endorsing the norms applied, one can discern, interpret and apply the requirements of CCM without endorsing the point of view it represents. It might be thought, however, that this defence fails because it rests on a mistaken view of judging. In other words, the defence seriously misrepresents the perspective of judges when they decide cases, especially those involving constitutional review. In an early article, Raz observes that judges do not, at least typically, take a detached point of view towards their legal systems and their laws.

> Judges, if anyone, take the law as it claims it should be taken. They more than anyone acknowledge the law at its own estimation. To understand legal statements we should interpret them as meant by those who take them and accept them at face value, those who acknowledge the law in the way it claims a right to be acknowledged. The decisive argument concerning the meaning of statements of legal duties is that the law claims for itself moral force.[28]

If Raz is right that judges accept the moral force the law claims for itself, then their legal judgments (and the statements they make in asserting them) would appear to be anything but detached. On the contrary, they seem to be fully committed, first-order moral judgements and statements about what *really* ought, morally to be done. And so the kind of detached judgement required to defend against the democratic challenge to constitutional review is simply not available.

But is this so? There seems little doubt that judges in modern constitutional democracies are typically committed to the moral authority of their legal systems. For a variety of different reasons, they deem these systems as morally worthy of support and view the roles they play within them as endowed with morally legitimacy. But two points need to be stressed here. First, that judges typically take this view is clearly not necessary any more than it is necessary when one turns to lawyers. That is, the kind of moral commitment that judges seem typically to display is not essential to assuming the role of judge. As Hart observed long ago, there are many reasons why people become judges and agree to abide by the basic ground rules of the system, and only some of these have anything to do with morality.[29]

Second, and more importantly for our purposes, it is false that a judge who fully endorses and accepts the moral authority the law claims for itself, and who recognises and endorses a moral obligation to discern, interpret and apply its requirements in deciding cases, is necessarily committed to endorsing the point of view expressed by the law on any particular issue of moral significance. Judges who endorse the moral authority of the systems in which they serve such a vital role, often disagree morally with the individual laws and prior decisions they consider themselves bound, legally, morally and prudentially, to apply. They view their adjudicative role as bringing with it a first-order moral commitment to apply the law *as it is*, not as it ideally *ought to be* – and this is a law that they are required to discover in a way that is detached from their own, personal, first-order moral convictions.[30] It follows that a judge who accepts and endorses the moral authority

[28] J Raz, 'Hart on Moral Rights and Legal Duties' (1984) 4 *Oxford Journal of Legal Studies* 131.

[29] Hart, *The Concept of Law* (n 13) 202–203.

[30] Things are a bit more complicated than presented here. As discussed briefly below, in some cases, judges can be required, by the law itself, to change or develop the relevant law. That the law sometimes imposes this requirement may itself give rise to the democratic challenge. But that question is perhaps best left for another occasion.

of her legal system and its constituent constitutional practices may feel compelled to interpret and apply its commitments in ways she personally finds morally problematic. More specifically, she may feel compelled to reach a decision that accords with CCM commitments but that fails, from her own personal moral perspective, to be fully justified. From that personal perspective, the one she would be at liberty to assume were she queen of the world, it's perhaps not even close to being 'the best that it can be'.[31] But it's the best that it can be *as judged from the perspective of the democratic community and its own particular history of CCM commitments*. And this is the perspective from which judges are morally required to render their decisions in cases of constitutional review.

In the way of summary: if (a) the judge endorses her legal system and its constituent constitutional practices as morally worthy of acceptance, support and participation (as a judge); (b) accepts and endorses her role-defined moral obligation to decide in light of *its* demands when engaged in the process of judging; and if (c) what that moral obligation demands in a particular instance of constitutional review is a decision made from the point of view of the democratic community and its history of CCM commitments, then (d) she will consider herself morally bound (in a non-detached, ie fully committed way) to make a decision she might, in an ideal world, have much preferred to avoid. And if she always acts on this fist-order moral understanding of her judicial obligation she will, I suggest, do nothing that leaves her vulnerable to the democratic challenge.

So a judge may, from a fully-committed, moral point of view, accept a commitment to decide cases from a detached point of view which sometimes generates decisions with which she morally disagrees strongly. But what if her disagreement is so strong as to raise the question whether her moral obligation is overridden or defeated by a competing obligation to, say, pursue justice despite the law. In that instance, she will be faced with a dilemma: apply the norms generated by the system she morally supports, or decide in defiance of the law. The latter possibility brings with it at least three options. She might, for example, offer an interpretation of the relevant norms she believes accords better with her own view of what really ought to be the case in the circumstances in question. And if she pursues this option, she has two further choices to make: conceal the fact that she is not simply deciding in accordance with the law (including CCM) as she finds it, or come clean about what she is doing. In both instances, she will be engaging in what Jeff Brand-Ballard aptly calls 'lawless judging'.[32] On neither option, however, is she abiding by her normally decisive moral duty to reason and decide from the perspective of the legal system and its constituent CCM commitments. She will have decided that her moral duty requires, not that she seek justice according to the law and/or her democratic community's moral point of view, but that she seek justice in spite of the law and/or her community's moral commitments. Of course,

[31] Dworkin, *Law's Empire* (n 7) 229.

[32] J Brand-Ballard, *Limits of Legality: The Ethics of Lawless Judging* (New York, Oxford University Press, 2010).

in this particular instance, her moral choice does in fact leave her vulnerable to the democratic challenge. She will, in effect, be placing herself above the law by substituting her own, first-order moral views for those expressed from the point of view in terms of which she is expected to decide. In the end, and all things considered, this may well be the only morally responsible choice for her to make. But it is one that we should not attempt to sugar-coat by denying that it raises significant issues of democratic legitimacy.

The issues briefly addressed in the preceding paragraph bring to the fore one final question with which I would like to close. What could possibly justify adopting the role of a judge engaged in the process of constitutional review, given that it brings with it the moral duty to apply CCM whenever it is clear what it demands, and to reason from the perspective of the community's CCM commitments when matters are not so clear? After all, the stakes in virtually any legal case, most notably one involving constitutional review, are often extremely high. Whether someone lives or dies can turn on how a Supreme Court interprets the constitutional right to life, liberty and security of the person. The same will be true in a case in which someone is threatened with deportation to a country in which he faces certain torture. How could any responsible moral agent, charged with deciding cases such as these, agree to decide them, not from the perspective of what *is* morally right, but from the perspective of what is *deemed* morally right by her legal system and or community? How could a liberal-minded judge in Apartheid South Africa possibly agree to be bound by the norms and decisions of that community's CCM? In other words, does the view for which I have been arguing – that judges should assume a detached perspective in discerning, interpreting and applying CCM norms – not require that judges do something that no moral agent should willingly do: abdicate her moral autonomy and the responsibilities that come with it? Judges, after all, are moral agents just like the rest of us – agents who must never, under any circumstances, relinquish their moral autonomy.

This question is not, of course, one that is unique to judging. It arises in any context in which structures of authority enter the picture, bringing with them authoritative norms and pre-defined roles, duties and responsibilities. It arises whenever a person is required to act or decide, not in terms of his own independent judgement, about what ought to be, but on the basis of someone else's judgement regarding that question. It arises when accountants, doctors, nurses and MPs are required to abide by their professional codes of ethics. It arises when a soldier is required to follow an order that she finds unconscionable. Returning to law, it arises, not only in difficult cases where a judge is required to decide in a way that produces (what the judge takes to be) grave injustice. It even arises in far less dramatic, every-day situations, where judges feel the force of binding precedent, coming to a decision, not because she thinks it right but because the decision accords best with the earlier decisions of judges further up in the judicial hierarchy.

It is perhaps worth observing here that the law sometimes explicitly permits judges to avoid the pull of the law's own perspective and to settle matters as the judge sees fit. This happens when they are allowed to distinguish or overrule precedents on serious moral grounds the law has not itself envisioned or accommodated. Or when they are entitled to interpret a statute in a way that seems to fly in the face of established meaning so as to avoid an otherwise unpalatable result. English law once used a term to describe such circumstances: 'manifest absurdity or repugnance'.[33] In such cases, the law permits judges to assert their personal autonomy and depart from the otherwise required detached perspective.[34] But often, no such moral escape route is permitted and the judge will be faced with the difficult choices outlined in the preceding few paragraphs. A moral choice will be required – whether to apply, interpret, and ultimately decide and act, on grounds generated from a perspective other than her own, or to abandon that perspective and decide as she thinks best. And as with any situation involving such difficult choices, there are no easy answers – and certainly no easy answers that apply to any and all situations with which the judge may ultimately be faced. A position as serious and important as judging brings with it many occasions calling for hard moral choices.

V. Conclusion

In this paper I have defended constitutional review against the charge that it necessarily runs seriously afoul of democratic principle. In so doing, I drew on Raz's theory of detached normative statements and reasoning from a point of view. After arguing that discerning the requirements of a community's CCM commitments can be undertaken from a point of view other than that of the interpreter – even in cases where a judge's first-order moral beliefs must enter the picture – I went on to argue for the following claims: (1) constitutional review can be undertaken from the point of view of the democratic community and its history of CCM commitments; (2) this process can be undertaken by a judge without the unwarranted intrusion of her own, first-order moral convictions; (3) when undertaken from this point of view, constitutional review can be rendered consistent with democracy; and (4) this is so even when these activities require a good deal of first-order moral reasoning, judgement and argument on the part of judges.[35]

[33] See *Becke v Smith* (1836) 2 M&W 195 per Justice Parke (later Lord Wensleydale), which states: 'It is a very useful rule in the construction of a statute to adhere to the ordinary meaning of the words used, and to the grammatical construction, unless that is at variance with the intention of the legislature to be collected from the statute itself, or leads to any manifest absurdity or repugnance, in which case the language may be varied or modified so as to avoid such inconvenience but no further'.

[34] And as noted above (n 30), this may well give rise to the democratic challenge.

[35] This paper draws and expands upon an earlier one that explored similar themes. That earlier paper sought to show how, surprisingly enough, Raz and Dworkin could be brought together in an effective defence of constitutional review against the democratic challenge. That paper, entitled 'Constitutional Rights and the Possibility of Detached Constructive Interpretation', was published in (2015) 9 *Problema, Anuario de Filosophia y Teoria del Derecho* 23.

8

Legal Reasons and Upgrading Reasons

HORACIO SPECTOR

I. Introduction

A widespread conception of the normativity of law says that law gives subjects practical reasons to act in conformity with their norms as long as such reasons are connected with pre-existing reasons.[1] This thesis I call the *nexus thesis*. It can take on three different forms. First, on the *codification account*, authoritative legal norms publicly specify the content of prior non-legal reasons (for example, moral reasons). Accordingly, legal norms do not modify or change pre-existing reasons. The codification account fits a coercive model of law, according to which the function of law is to track prior non-legal reasons and supplement them with new reasons that derive from law's threats of punishment to be applied by a centralised coercive system.[2] One drawback of the coercive model is that it confines the normativity of law to the practical force of sanctions, ignoring the peculiar normativity of authoritative commands. It is a fact that most citizens see such commands, rather than their associated penalties, as reasons for their daily behaviour. In this paper, I am concerned with the reasons given to those citizens by the commands of a generally effective system of law. Prudential reasons generated by official sanctions are only relevant to my inquiry in so far as they contribute to law's general effectiveness.

Second, on the *triggering account*, legal norms give citizens reasons that derive from pre-existing conditional reasons by a logical operation. This operation is a form of detachment. Lawmakers activate or trigger latent conditional reasons by satisfying the antecedent of prior conditional reasons in order to give subjects reasons to conform to the consequent of those reasons by recognising lawmakers' intention to give them reasons to do so. For example, some legal philosophers hold that law can provide genuine reasons to perform actions that impact other

[1] H Spector, 'The Irrelevance of Ideal Morality to International Law' (2013) *Analisi e diritto* 209–10. I have called this view the 'moral justifiability thesis'.

[2] For the coercive model of law, see, for instance, F Schauer, *The Force of Law* (Cambridge MA, Harvard University Press, 2015).

people only if its norms detach reasons from prior conditional reasons. On this account, law's normativity is explained in connection with pre-existing conditional reasons.

I seek to explore a third account of the normativity of law. On the *multi-tiered account*, legal directives create new reasons for subjects to conform to their content because the relevant reason-constituting rules are supported by higher-order reasons. On this account, legal norms do not reproduce or trigger pre-existing reasons, but rather create new reasons in so far as they are plugged into prior higher-order reasons. Law's capacity to *constitute* autonomous reasons (ie reasons that are not identical with pre-existing reasons) is based on individuals' pre-existing *higher-order reasons*. That is, under social, economic and technical conditions that exceed the problem-solving capacity of social morality, individuals have reasons *to try to establish* a social condition that enables their peaceful and prosperous living together by incorporating new reason-constituting rules. Those higher-order reasons, which I call *upgrading reasons*, are not reasons to *perform* any particular action, but rather reasons to *intend* to reach a new form of social governance. Upgrading reasons tell individuals to see to it that a social governance system is effectively established in which new sources of reasons can help them realise their social propensities.

I assume that moral reasons depend on social morality in ways to be determined. By 'social morality' I mean a set of commonly accepted standards for cooperative social life whose general observance relies on social sanctions and anxiety-related mechanisms (guilt, remorse, etc).[3] The dependence of moral reasons on social morality is a complex matter that I cannot address in this essay. Moral reasons are authoritative beyond their social recognition, but, in the absence of their actual or at least presumed feasible recognition, moral reasons would be merely aspirational or utopian standards. All positive moral norms are social norms, but we are reluctant to call 'moral' those social norms that are not concerned with the fundamental features of human cooperation. True or objective moral reasons result from a process of deliberative adjustment of positive moral norms, but the nature of this process is not easy to break down. In any case, I don't mean that moral reasons are reducible to social morality. As I will suggest towards the end of this paper, I think that, just as natural law is a critical construction out of positive law, critical or ideal morality is a critical construction out of social morality. Therefore, both natural law and critical morality emerge from the adoption of a critical stance towards positive normative institutions. Positive law is the normative creation of a political association, and its critical or ideal norms reflect the status of the members of such association. In the enlightenment era, critical morality and natural law embrace a similar set of universalistic and egalitarian ideas, applicable to individuals and

[3] My characterisation of 'social morality' resembles the standard one in the literature: PF Strawson, 'Social Morality and Individual Ideal' (1961) 36 *Philosophy* 1; RB Brandt, *A Theory of The Good and The Right* (Oxford, Clarendon Press, 1979) 164–76; G Gauss, *The Order of Public Reason* (Cambridge, Cambridge University Press, 2011) 163–69.

citizens alike, making the distinction between the moral community and the political community often unrecognisable. However, I want to distinguish between the morality discussed in the *Groundwork* (critical morality) and the kind of public morality addressed in *The Doctrine of Right* (natural law).

In any case, depending on the circumstances, a legal system of social governance is more or less needed. Social morality has many limitations under complex social, economic and technical circumstances, and so the emergence of a new reason-constituting institution is needed to supplement social morality under those circumstances. Law is one system of social governance that supersedes social morality by introducing reason-constituting rules that award authorities the power to *give* practical reasons to subjects. Social norms (ie, social morality) and law (ie, positive law) are two systems of social governance that solve coordination and cooperation problems under different social conditions.

On the *multi-tiered account*, (justified) legal directives do not track or trigger moral reasons, because moral reasons are based on social morality, and it is precisely their limited usefulness in complex societies that explains the need to introduce a new form of social governance. Though legal norms constitute reasons that are autonomous from prior reasons (also from moral reasons generated by social morality), the constitutive capacity of law is grounded on higher-order reasons that tell individuals to try to establish an institutional system that establish new reason-constituting rules according to which reasons are given by content-independent authoritative pronouncements. That is, legal reason-constituting rules *upgrade* moral reason-constituting rules and, therefore, it is a mistake to say that legal reasons merely codify or trigger moral reasons. It is just the insufficiency of moral reasons that explains the emergence of legal reasons. It's more precise to say that legal reasons are *plugged into a hierarchy of reasons*. Therefore, both moral and legal reasons are plugged into higher-order reasons that are based on people's social inclinations.

In section II I will discuss the codification account. I argue that the codification account can only provide a partial explanation of law. I will show in section III that the triggering account is also defective, in that triggering reasons are optional reasons that fail to capture the practical difference between seeing to it that a political authority does not issue commands and following such commands. In section IV I propose a multi-tiered account, which echoes Hobbes's conception of the normativity of natural laws, according to which people have reasons to try to establish a form of social governance in which authoritative directives give subjects reasons that tell them to act cooperatively.

II. The Codification Account

There are two crucial problems that social morality and law must resolve for peaceful and prosperous social life to be possible. First, we have the *coordination problem*. Agents often have common or convergent interests but their successful cooperation requires salient coordination points that have to be set by social norms or legal norms, depending on the circumstances. Also, people don't have perfect factual knowledge. Social norms and legal norms encapsulate available practical knowledge or create procedures by which relevant beliefs should be assessed for coordination to be made possible. Second, we have the *cooperation problem*. This problem is typical of strategic situations in which rational agents cannot be expected to converge on the cooperative equilibrium without external assistance that modifies the payoffs in such a way as to convert the conflict game into a cooperative game. I will consider only two examples of the problems of coordination and cooperation: a stag hunt game and a prisoner's dilemma game. In the stag hunt game (see Figure 1), there are two equilibria that coincide with the scenarios of convergent behaviour: either both parties cooperate in hunting the stag, or each of them acts on his own and pursues the hare. Though this game has a cooperative equilibrium, that equilibrium cannot be guaranteed without assurance. Such assurance can be provided by social and/or legal norms. In the prisoner's dilemma game (see Figure 2), there is no cooperative equilibrium because the dominant strategies of both agents lead them to converge on a non-cooperative equilibrium. The game has no cooperative upshot. Under these conditions, cooperation would require external intervention capable of deterring the non-cooperative dominant strategies.

The codification account of the normativity of law assumes that law tracks prior reasons. Consider the authoritative legal reason *R**. On the codification account, *R** depends on the pre-existing reason *R* in that *R** tracks *R* by codifying it. The codification account has some plausibility because law sometimes codifies preexisting moral rules and provide for their application and enforcement by means of specialised institutional procedures. Though social norms can secure coordination in small social groups in which shirking can be cheaply detected, they are bound to be very costly or unsuccessful in large societies. Also, social

Figure 1 Stag hunt game example

		Player 2	
		Cooperate	Defect
Player 1	Cooperate	2, 2	0, 1
	Defect	1, 0	1, 1

Figure 2 Prisoner's dilemma example

		Player 2	
		Cooperate	Defect
Player 1	Cooperate	2, 2	0, 3
	Defect	3, 0	1, 1

norms may prove ineffective in fixing salient points of coordination. At some stage in social development, coordination by social norms is hindered by the uncertainty, imprecision and incompleteness of social rules, and a code of law becomes necessary to solve coordination problems. In this connection, HLA Hart says that social norms (which he calls 'primary rules') are often vague and ambiguous and may leave undefined how to settle particular conflicts.[4] In the same vein, Alexander and Sherwin emphasise that a code of law turns indeterminate and contestable moral obligations into objective and public obligations.[5] Sometimes it is assumed that the insufficiency of social norms derives from the selfishness or limited generosity of human beings. But even if human beings were angelically motivated, the absence of publicly-enacted directives and of settlement and arbitration mechanisms would deprive social norms of much of their usefulness in coordinating social interactions and facilitating social cooperation.[6] On this view, law codifies and institutionalises social norms and provides for their enforcement. In fulfilling this function, law reproduces the content of social norms with greater precision and certainty and establishes penalties to deter their breach.

The idea that morality often fails to guarantee coordination and cooperation goes back to Hobbes's account of arbitration in Chapter 5 of *Leviathan*. Hobbes highlights the insufficiency of establishing morality (which he calls 'right reason') as a yardstick for resolving disputes and the need to adopt arbitration for such purpose:

> … as when there is a controversy in an account, the parties must by their own accord, set up for right reason, the reason of some arbitrator, or judge, to whose sentence they will both stand, or their controversy must either come to blows, or be undecided, for want of a right reason constituted by Nature; so is it also in all debates of what kind soever: and when men that think themselves wiser than all others, clamor and demand right reason for judge; yet seek no more, but that things should be determined, by no other men's reason but their own, it is as intolerable in the society of men, as it is in play after trump is turned, to use for trump on every occasion that suit whereof they have most in their hand.[7]

Since the content of 'right reason' is contestable, it is of no aid for avoiding or solving conflicts. Hobbes thinks that arbitral judgments are needed to fix a coordination point. He says that individuals have a prior reason to prevent violence, and that this reason justifies the parties' subjection to the arbitrator.

Joseph Raz's theory of justified authority can also be understood in terms of the codifying function. Raz contends that the mark of a (justified) legal

[4] HLA Hart, *The Concept of Law*, 2nd edn (Clarendon Press, 1994).

[5] L Alexander and E Sherwin, *The Rule of Rules: Morality, Rules, and the Dilemmas of Law* (Duke University Press, 2001).

[6] G Kavka, 'Why Even Morally Perfect People Would Need Government' (1995) 12 *Social Philosophy & Policy* 1.

[7] T Hobbes, *Leviathan* (1651, Richard Tuck ed, Cambridge, Cambridge University Press, 1996) 32–33.

authority is its capacity to supply exclusionary reasons that are based on (or reflect) subjects' pre-existing reasons and that guide them to better conform with those pre-existing reasons.[8] In fact, Raz seems to agree with Hobbes when he says that '[t]he case for the legitimacy of any political authority rests to a large extent on its ability to solve coordination problems and extricate the population from prisoner's dilemma type situations'.[9] He says that the explanation of authority includes three normative theses: a thesis concerning the justification of authority; a thesis about the considerations that should guide the issuance of the directives by the authority; and a thesis that accounts for the impact that authoritative directives have on the practical reasonings of subjects. Together, the *normal justification thesis*, the *dependence thesis* and the *preemption thesis*, as Raz respectively calls them, constitute the service conception of authority.[10]

I believe that Raz's fundamental insight is that agents do not sacrifice their rational autonomy if they acknowledge the directives of an authority as exclusionary reasons on the grounds that they will better conform to reasons that apply to them anyway (regarding certain matters) by intending to follow the authority's directives than by relying on their own judgement in making decisions.[11] Acknowledging an authority in these terms would be just a way of exercising autonomy more effectively.

Raz articulates his fundamental insight by drawing on a distinction between an agent directly responding to reasons and an agent indirectly responding to reasons by obeying an authority's directives. His normal justification thesis says that an authority is justified with respect to its subjects if the latter are likely better to comply with the preexisting reasons that apply to them by following the authority's directives.[12] Raz seems to defend the codification account, that is, the view that a legal system gives subjects reasons to do as the system requires if its norms track preexisting reasons that apply to subjects independently of directives. Raz's dependence thesis holds that legal directives give reasons if they reflect content-dependent reasons. Authorities are useful, argues Raz, because they mediate between background, ultimate or content-dependent reasons and the concrete decisions that must be taken by people to whom those reasons apply.[13] The dependence thesis says: 'all authoritative directives should be based on reasons which already independently apply to the subjects of the directives and are relevant to their action in the circumstances covered by the directive'.[14] Thus, authoritative

[8] J Raz, *The Morality of Freedom* (Oxford, Oxford University Press, 1986); J Raz, 'Authority and Justification' in J Raz (ed), *Authority* (New York University Press, 1990); J Raz, 'Authority, Law and Morality' in *Ethics in the Public Domain: Essays in the Morality of Law and Politics* (Oxford, Clarendon Press, 1994); J Raz, *Between Authority and Interpretation* (Oxford, Oxford University Press, 2009).

[9] Raz, 'Authority and Justification' (n 8) 132.

[10] Raz, *The Morality of Freedom* (n 8) 38.

[11] Raz, *Between Authority and Interpretation* (n 8) 136.

[12] Raz, *The Morality of Freedom* (n 8) 53.

[13] Raz, *The Morality of Freedom* (n 8) 58–59; Raz, 'Authority, Law and Morality' (n 8) 299.

[14] Raz, *The Morality of Freedom* (n 8) 47.

reasons depend on preexisting moral reasons that independently apply to the subjects in the relevant situations. Indeed, the dependence thesis seems to fit the codification account in saying that an authority's directive to φ may give subjects reasons to φ if the directive reflects or mirrors reasons to φ that apply independently to subjects. Finally, the preemption thesis is a corollary of the former two theses. According to the preemption thesis, authoritative reasons displace rather than merely outweigh other potentially competing reasons.[15]

In Hobbesian spirit, Raz discusses the case of two persons who decide to refer their dispute to an arbitrator:

> Consider the case of two people who refer a dispute to an arbitrator. He has authority to settle the dispute, for they agreed to abide by his decision. Two features stand out. First, the arbitrator's decision is for the disputants a reason for action. They ought to do as he says because he says so. But this reason is related to the other reasons which apply to the case. It is not [...] just another reason to be added to the others, a reason to stand alongside the others when one reckons which way is better supported by reason. The arbitrator's decision is meant to be based on the other reasons, to sum them up and to reflect their outcome.[16]

The arbitrator's decision is supposed to be based on other reasons (ie dependent reasons) and to replace as well the reasons that the parties could have (ie preemptive reasons).[17] For Raz the arbitration award is authoritative because: (1) it is meant to be based on other reasons the parties may have; and, consequentially, (2) it preempts those other reasons. According to Raz's normal justification thesis, the parties ought to acknowledge the authority of the arbitrator because by complying with his decision they are likely better to respond to their reasons than by following their own individual judgements.

However, Raz denies that authoritative pronouncements are practically inert. He contends that the dependence thesis does not rule out the *practical difference thesis*, according to which legal norms impact in non-redundant ways subjects' practical reasoning. In coordination and cooperation cases authorities can 'make a difference while acting on dependent reasons'.[18] Raz claims that, in coordination cases, 'once the directive is issued, individuals have reasons to take the action it requires which they did not have before because now there is ground to expect that the convention would be formed'.[19] Therefore, Raz does not merely embrace the codification account.

Consider again the prisoner's dilemma (Figure 2). Players have a dominant strategy, which leads them to a collectively suboptimal pattern of behaviour. In prisoner's dilemma situations, authoritative directives make a practical difference as well. Raz says that 'in these cases while people have reason to act in a certain way,

[15] ibid.
[16] Raz, *The Morality of Freedom* (n 8) 41.
[17] ibid 41–42.
[18] ibid 51.
[19] ibid 50.

given the situation they are in, they also have reason *to change the situation*, though they are unable to do so by themselves' (emphasis added).[20]

Raz's account of the practical difference thesis might seem self-contradictory. If an authority makes a practical difference, she is creating a new practical reason and such practical reason cannot be based on prior practical reasons if 'based on' has a merely reproductive sense. According to Raz, the dependence thesis 'speaks of authoritative directives being based on or reflecting reasons which apply to the subjects in any case'.[21] But this framing of the dependence thesis is ambiguous. To be sure, the requirement that authoritative directives be based on or reflect dependent reasons could be met by the authority if it enacts directives that reproduce the reasons which apply to subjects. But it might also be met if the authority orders an action that is justifiable by the reasons which independently apply to the subjects. However, in prisoner's dilemma situations people do not have reasons to act in cooperative ways. Actually, their (prudential) reasons prevail over other reasons that might apply to their predicament.

An authority can avoid a collectively irrational outcome by issuing norms that secure a cooperative equilibrium by modifying the payoffs of the players' strategies. Assuming that, before the authority's intervention, the players have defeated moral reasons to choose both individually and collectively irrational strategies, we might try to portray the intervention of the authority as 'just' changing the ranking of reasons that apply to the two players. Thus, the practical difference thesis might be understood as meaning that the authority can change the ranking of reasons, as something different from introducing new reasons. Yet the initial assumption of this approach is implausible. Do players have a reason *against* choosing the dominant strategy in a prisoner's dilemma situation? In other words, do they have reasons to follow a defeated or displaced reason? We might want to use this figure of speech in order to maintain the appearance of ranking reversal, but the dependence thesis could not be weakened so much as to require that the authority's directives be based on or reflect merely defeated reasons. According to the dependence thesis authorities must issue directives that 'correctly reflect the balance of reasons on which they depend'.[22] And telling them to act in accordance with a defeated reason is not a way of selecting directives on the grounds of the preexisting balance of reasons that apply to their subjects.

Raz acknowledges that the dependence thesis is ambiguous. He says, '[T]his can be taken to mean that the one proper way for authority to decide his actions is to ask itself what are the reasons which apply to its subjects and attempt to follow them'.[23] Raz goes on to assert that this is only one way of meeting the requirement of the dependence thesis but that all that this thesis requires 'is that its instructions will reflect the reasons which apply to it subjects, ie that they should require action

[20] ibid 50–51.
[21] ibid 51.
[22] ibid 60.
[23] ibid 51.

which is justifiable by the reasons which apply to the subjects'.[24] Raz concedes that sometimes the legislator 'has to act for nondependent reasons in order to maximise conformity to dependent reasons'.[25] At any event, Raz's account of the normativity of law is not clear, because it navigates between the codifying function of law and law's capacity to solve cooperation problems as well (for instance, the stag hunt and prisoner's dilemma games), that is, problems in which law cannot fulfil an assurance function by just reproducing or tracking preexisting social norms.

III. The Triggering Account

The triggering account emphasises law's impact on practical reasoning. Mark Greenberg has suggested that law is a subset of moral obligations that are created by the actions of legal institutions. Greenberg claims that law creates those moral obligations, which are at the same time legal obligations, by changing the relevant moral circumstances to which moral principles apply.[26] According to what he calls the 'standard picture' in legal philosophy, which equates law with the content of authoritative pronouncements, legal obligations cannot depend on moral obligations. He contends, however, that any legal obligation can be matched by a moral obligation if a subset of moral obligations depends on authoritative legal pronouncements. Thus, a subset of moral truths depends on the law if law 'arranges matters so that our legal obligations have the same content as our (new) moral obligations'.[27] Legal authorities can capitalise the force of moral principles by performing institutional actions that change the relevant moral circumstances and so generate moral obligations that also constitute *legal obligations*. Such moral obligations are only 'new' in that their specific content exceeds the content of the foundational principles, but in a deep sense they are just applications of pre-existing moral principles.

One way of rendering Greenberg's view more precise, with a low cost of distortion, I think, is to say that law activates or triggers latent or dormant reasons that lack practical force in the absence of the activating norms. On the triggering account, the function of legal authority is to activate *latent or dormant reasons*. Law does not track pre-existing moral reasons, yet it satisfies the antecedents of *conditional* moral reasons. Thus, the issuance of an authoritative directive may be a way of triggering or activating a prior conditional reason *R* by satisfying its antecedent and thereby detaching from *R* a new reason *R** that, strictly speaking, is independent of *R*.

[24] ibid 51.

[25] ibid 51.

[26] M Greenberg, 'The Moral Impact Theory of the Law' (2014) 123 *Yale Law Journal* 1288.

[27] M Greenberg, 'The Standard Picture and Its Discontents' in L Green and B Leiter (eds), *Oxford Studies in Philosophy of Law*, vol 1 (Oxford, Oxford University Press, 2011) 97.

The account of law's normativity in terms of law's capacity to trigger or activate dormant or conditional reasons is not new. For example, according to Howard Warrender, Hobbes thinks that legal directives activate or trigger pre-existing reasons grounded in natural laws.[28] On Warrender's interpretation, Hobbes takes it as evident that law's function cannot just be to reproduce reasons that already exist in the state of nature. Law would serve no purpose if it limited itself to matching reasons that already exist in noncooperative situations. Reasons based on pre-political obligations are dormant or latent while their validating conditions do not obtain. For Hobbes, as interpreted by Warrender, natural laws become binding law if they apply to a situation in which the validating condition of 'sufficient security' is satisfied.[29] When validating conditions do obtain (for instance, because the legal system sufficiently assures that other agents will behave cooperatively), those conditional duties are actualised and oblige agents to perform the specific actions conditionally demanded by those obligations. Therefore, authoritative coercive reasons allow reasons to cooperate to be detached from latent reasons. Now, in complex societies sufficient security can only be guaranteed if the legal system establishes an enforcement and adjudication system that is capable of securing that everyone follows cooperative strategies. On this model, positive law *activates* the pre-political system of duties by providing conditions of assurance that trigger the latent duties already existing in the state of nature. That is, natural obligations only become binding to agents if they have 'sufficient security', where 'sufficient' means good enough to solve the problems of cooperation. Therefore, according to the Hobbes/Warrender account, law's contribution to rational decision-making is made by detaching categorical duties from 'natural' conditional obligations.

Similarly, David Enoch proposes an account of robust reason-giving according to which legal authorities give reasons to subjects to φ by triggering latent or dormant reasons. For Enoch, authorities draw on latent reasons when they intend subjects to recognise their communicated intention that they φ and take such recognition as their reason to φ.[30] A latent or dormant reason can be represented in a conditional way: *if* the authority effectively requires cooperation, the parties have a reason to act cooperatively. Thus, agents have a conditional reason that can be formalised in this way:

(1) $L\varphi \rightarrow R\varphi$

In (1) '$L\varphi$' denotes the fact that a de facto effective legal authority (for example, one that guarantees 'sufficient security') tells subjects to φ, and '$R\varphi$' means that

[28] H Warrender, *The Political Philosophy of Hobbes, His Theory of Obligation* (Oxford, Clarendon Press, 1957).

[29] ibid 58–75.

[30] D Enoch, 'Giving Practical Reasons' (2011) 11(4) *The Philosopher's Imprint*; D Enoch, 'Reason-Giving and the Law' in L Green and B Leiter (eds), *Oxford Studies in Philosophy of Law*, vol 1 (Oxford, Oxford University Press, 2011); D Enoch, 'Authority and Reason-Giving' (2014) 89 *Philosophy and Phenomenological Research* 296.

subjects have a reason to φ. This statement is a *narrow-scope conditional* because the R-operator quantifies over the consequent. According to Enoch, the narrow-scope conditional reason asserted by (1) must be explained in terms of a *wide-scope conditional*.[31] In modal logics, a wide-scope conditional statement is one in which the modal operator ranges over the whole conditional; for instance, 'It's obligatory that (if you do *p*, then you do *q*)'. Accordingly, Enoch thinks that (1) must be explained on the basis of:

(2) R (L φ → φ)

As I said, this conditional is called 'wide scope' because the R-operator quantifies over the whole conditional. That is, the reason has an internal conditional content: to act cooperatively *if* the authority provides sufficient assurance.

Enoch appeals to a complex set of interrelated intentions to explain the particular form of reason triggering that is distinctive of authoritative directives. His account of authoritative 'robust reason-giving' includes a particular species of triggering reasons that is present in both requests and authoritative directives. Enoch says that robust reason-giving involves the authority intending to give subjects duties by communicating that intention to them so that the given duty depends in an appropriate way on subjects' recognition of the authority's communicated intention to give them the duty.[32] However, my critique of the triggering account does not depend on such complexities. I focus on the structure of wide-scope conditionals, that is, on reason-triggering per se.

Suppose the parties are now in a situation in which the if-clause of the conditional statement is true. That is, there is an authority that effectively assures cooperation by a socially recognised directive *D*. Then *D* triggers the latent reason *R*. According to the triggering account, *D* detaches a categorical reason from the preexisting wide-scope conditional reason. Now, wide-scope practical conditionals need special rules to allow detachment of a practical conclusion, because *modus ponens* cannot be applied to detach the consequent from such conditional. But how is the detachment possible, since *modus ponens* is useless for this purpose? Indeed, *modus ponens* can only be used when the additional posited premise ('*p*') replicates the antecedent of a conditional proposition ('if *p*, then *q*'). In this case, the replication is not possible because the operator R goes beyond '*p*'. Therefore, it is not possible to detach a practical conclusion from such a wide-scope practical conditional as 'R (L φ → φ)' without a special detachment rule. But Enoch does not supply such a rule.

On the triggering account, even in scenarios in which agents don't have a dominant cooperative strategy because the assurance problem is unsolved, they already have a conditional reason to act cooperatively *if* the authority successfully assures the relevant cooperative outcome. The authority secures cooperation by

[31] Enoch, 'Reason-Giving and the Law' (n 30) 6–8.
[32] Enoch, 'Authority and Reason-Giving' (n 30) 12.

giving the parties a reason to act cooperatively, and they do so by activating a prior latent reason.[33] For Enoch, cooperation relies on a reason being triggered or activated from a wide-scope conditional reason, namely, the reason [to act cooperatively *if* the authority effectively assures cooperation].

As I said, Enoch thinks that a latent or dormant reason can be represented in this way: 'If the authority effectively requires cooperation, the parties have a reason to act cooperatively'. He contends that this statement can be explained by a wide-scope conditional: 'The parties have a reason [to act cooperatively if the authority effectively requires cooperation]'. This position is untenable. Because in propositional logics 'If you do *p*, then you do *q*' is equivalent to 'You either don't do *p* or you do *q*', the wide scope deontic statement 'It's obligatory that (if you do *p*, then you do *q*)' is equivalent to 'It's obligatory that (either you don't do *p* or you do *q*)'. Therefore, if you have a conditional reason (to φ if *p*), you really have an optional reason to (either φ or see to it that not-*p*). However, an optional obligation to either act cooperatively or see to it that an authority does not secure cooperation is *not* the conclusion that an individual should draw from a prior reason if that conclusion is supposed to tell subjects to act cooperatively. In Enoch's sense, a triggering reason is a wide-scope practical conditional, that is, a disjunctive or optional reason. But the two options (ie, to act cooperatively and to see to it that an authority does not provide sufficient security) are *not* normatively on a par. To act cooperatively is the latent reason that agents have reason to actualise. In a situation in which there is an opportunity for an authority to secure sufficient security, agents have reasons to pursue that opportunity. Therefore, in Hobbes's jargon, reasons deriving from the natural laws are not just wide-scope conditional reasons. On the contrary, agents have non-optional reasons to try to establish an authority that ensures cooperation. The point of authoritative requirements is then not to trigger preexisting reasons, and the parties' reasons cannot be represented by a preexisting reason to [act cooperatively *if* the authority effectively requires cooperation].

I have said that in stag hunt and prisoner's dilemma situations (assuming away the authority of social morality and law), agents do not have (non-optional) reasons to act cooperatively. Therefore, the authority cannot reflect such prior reasons. Raz's dependence thesis cannot explain the function of authority in securing coordination and cooperation in such situations. In effect, an authority's function cannot be conceived of as that of reflecting or tracking preexisting reasons. However, the dependence thesis might be interpreted as an application of the triggering account. Yet, as I have argued, the triggering account does not represent well what Hobbes thinks about people's reasons in the state of nature. A more detailed exploration of Hobbes's conception can guide us into a better account of the normativity of law.

[33] Enoch, 'Reason-Giving and the Law' (n 30) 5; Enoch, 'Authority and Reason-Giving' (n 30) 4–5.

IV. The Multi-tiered Account

Hobbes believes that agents have categorical, non-optional reasons to leave the state of nature and enter into an authoritative regime of social governance in which authorities' pronouncements create binding obligations. Hobbes points out that, though reasons associated with natural laws are prior to the legal and political order, such reasons do not obligate in the usual sense. Hobbes calls them obligations *foro interno*. Obligations in *foro interno* do not require performance of concrete actions, but rather require that individuals be willing to establish an associational scheme in which peace can be secured and maintained. Hobbes's point is that agents in the state of nature have a *subjective reason* to try to establish and maintain an institutional regime in which political authorities can give subjects reasons to act in cooperative ways. Obligations *in foro interno* are not conditional (narrow-scope or wide-scope) obligations, but rather subjective obligations to search for a covenant that sets up a political authority capable of guaranteeing peace. Genuine *objective obligations* are in turn imposed by political authorities. Those are obligations in *foro externo*.

Hobbes's theory suggests how we might represent the rational choice of individuals who treat authoritative directives as reason-giving. Rather than focusing on conditional reasons, we focus on agents' higher-order reasons. Thus, we portray agents as having higher-order reasons to set up an institutional regime that turn authoritative pronouncements into reasons for acting in cooperative ways. We can say that lower-reasons deriving from legal directives are *plugged into* those higher-order reasons. The inference of practical conclusions is premised on higher-order reasons in this way:

(1) There is a reason to see to it that Lφ gives an exclusionary reason to φ

(2) L φ

Therefore, there is an exclusionary reason to φ

People have higher-order reasons to treat legal directives (ie, authoritative pronouncements) as exclusionary reasons. Those higher-order reasons, which I will call *upgrading reasons*, derive from agents' prior reasons to solve problems of collective action, for example, the assurance problem of cooperation. My narrative runs in these terms. Social morality is insufficient to facilitate cooperation under conditions of social complexity, and, therefore, a different kind of social governance is needed in which authoritative pronouncements give people exclusionary reasons to displace consideration of first-order reasons that might guide them to choose noncooperative strategies. Cooperative equilibria are obviously better than non-cooperative equilibria, and, therefore, under those conditions people have reasons to try to upgrade a non-political system of social morality to a political system of social governance that makes cooperative equilibria feasible. If the parties' endeavours to create a cooperative institutional regime are successful, the authorities' directives will give them exclusionary reasons. On the contrary, if those endeavours are unsuccessful, the parties will remain in a noncooperative equilibrium, and, as Hobbes says, they will not have a reason to act cooperatively. In complex societies, the coordination and cooperation problems require an authoritative reason-giving social organisation.

Upgrading reasons are reasons to treat L φ as an exclusionary reason to φ. In other words, the exclusionary reason to φ that derives from L is plugged into upgrading reasons. Now exclusionary reasons are second-order reasons that displace any other first-order potential reason not to φ. Since second-order reasons (ie, exclusionary reasons) are plugged into upgrading reasons, the latter are third-order reasons. The parties in a prisoner's dilemma or a stag hunt noncooperative equilibrium have a reason to upgrade their model of interaction to one in which they have exclusionary reasons that discard reasons for acting in noncoperative ways. Though the parties in noncooperative equilibria lack first-order reasons to act cooperatively, they do have a third-order reason to treat authoritative directives as exclusionary reasons (in case a generally effective authority issued such directives). Such upgrading third-order reason is justified on its causal consequences, that is, extrinsically. By responding appropriately to upgrading reasons people are capable of moving to a different scenario in which they have reasons to follow cooperative strategies. Therefore, individuals have a third-order reason to hold an authority as capable of giving exclusionary reasons if the reason-giving allows them to upgrade their practical situation to one in which cooperation is feasible. Unlike triggering reasons, upgrading reasons apply to agents in an indirect way. That is, legal reasons are not activated but rather plugged into upgrading reasons. Upgrading reasons tell agents to establish an authority and submit to it, but, as long as the reason-giving process is not socially recognised, authoritative directives don't give subjects reasons to act in cooperative ways.

In various social interactions that can be modelled as prisoner dilemma or stag hunt games there is no cooperative equilibrium, or the cooperative equilibrium cannot be reached because of lack of assurance. In those circumstances, each player has reason to maximise her payoff and to shun the cooperative strategy. Even if the cooperative strategy is required by social morality, in complex societies agents may lack reasons to behave morally. That is, if social sanctions are ineffective and there are no specialised institutions that provide assurance about each other's cooperative response, there are no reasons to behave morally. Thus, in a Hobbesian state of nature, cooperation cannot be the dominant strategy. However, even in those situations we might have higher-order reasons to treat legal authorities as reason-giving institutions. Agents will have reasons to cooperate if they have assurance that other agents will likewise cooperate. Authoritative reason-giving can provide that assurance and, therefore, facilitate cooperation in conditions of social complexity in which social morality has become unstable or insufficient.

The coordination and the assurance problems are not the only ones that explain the reason-giving feature of law. Social morality is a dynamic system in that its norms change over time. As long as that change is thought to go in the direction of progress, there is also moral progress. However, social morality lacks an institution specialised in reviewing and modifying social norms. Therefore, moral progress is very slow. For instance, moral attitudes towards slavery have changed, but only within the span of various generations. Even if morality is a changing system, its dynamics produce chronic moral lags.

While economic, demographic, environmental and technological circumstances change at a very rapid pace, social morality evolves slowly. Many of these changes make socially recognised norms inadequate or insufficient for regulating new forms of social coordination and cooperation. For this reason, social organisation requires a dynamic system of normative production. HLA Hart makes a similar point. He argues that a developed legal system allows changes in social norms ('primary rules') because they authorise individuals or collegiate bodies to introduce new norms. Such authorisation is given by a special type of secondary rules that he calls 'rules of change'.[34] Accordingly, one of the functions of law is to modify social norms so that the applicable set of normative requirements is better suited to facilitating coordination and cooperation under changing conditions of collective life. This I call the *updating function* of law. This function is parasitic on law's main function in securing coordination and cooperation. As circumstances change, traditional norms that facilitate coordination and cooperation prove inadequate, and we have to look for innovative norms that are better adapted to those new circumstances.

As a matter of fact, law keeps up a constant pace of normative updating that can match the speed of such economic and technological changes as those that take place in business law, intellectual property law, and internet law, for example. To fulfil this function lawgivers often create completely new rules that were present neither actually nor latently in the state of nature and that cannot be reasonably thought to reproduce or merely trigger pre-existing moral norms. An example in corporate law will clarify the point. One crucial issue is the regulation of collective decision making in general meetings of shareholders. In different jurisdictions, positive law establishes the voting rights of each shareholder depending on the class of his shares and the number of actual votes attached to those shares. Thus, in general meetings the democratic principle 'one person, one vote', which is attractive because of its allegiance to egalitarianism, is not applied. If business voting rights were assigned democratically, business corporations would be undercapitalised, for no large investor would be ready to let her assets be exploited by groups of numerous small investors. In areas such as corporate law and financial law it would be unreasonable to expect legal rules to track preexisting moral reasons to facilitate social cooperation or to solve new conflicts of interests. Now, on the multi-tiered account, an authoritative reason R^* is a new reason that does not necessarily track or trigger any pre-existing reason R. By contrast, R^* is given by pronouncements of the legal authorities in accordance with third-order *upgrading*

[34] Hart, *The Concept of Law* (n 4) 95–96.

reasons. The point is that the updating function of law also suggests that there are third-order reasons for authoritative reason-constitution that solves the problems of coordination and cooperation in dynamic societies. Such problems would persist and probably aggravate in the absence of a political authority.

The multi-tiered account assumes that authoritative directives give reasons for acting as they tell subjects to act. Is it not mysterious that authoritative enactments are capable of giving reasons? One objection against this account could run as follows. Reason-giving makes sense if there is an *intrinsic connection* between the reason-giving fact and the reason it gives. For instance, it is intuitively true to say that a child's starvation gives us a reason to help the child. By the same token, your request to your colleague to read your paper would give him a reason to do so if there is an intrinsic connection between your request and the reason it gives. However, your request to your colleague doesn't seem to give him a reason in the same sense. Similarly, if you promise your fiancée to go to the theatre, your promise gives you a reason to do as promised. However, your promise to your fiancée can only give you a reason to do as promised if the promise has an intrinsic connection with the reason it gives you. The problem is that, whereas the child-starvation-features of the relevant fact are intrinsically connected with the reason for us to help the child, the content of your request is not connected with the reason it gives your colleague because reasons given by requests are content-independent.[35] Similarly, regardless of the content of your promise (within certain limits), there is a reason for you to perform your promise. And the same point applies to authoritative requirements. Authorities give subjects reasons to do as required regardless of the content of what they tell subjects to do. In all cases of content-independent reasons, the intrinsic connection between a reason-giving fact and the reason it gives is absent, and, therefore, the multi-tiered account is confronted with a difficulty that does not impact the triggering account.

To answer the above abjection, we should notice that some reasons have no intrinsic connection with the sources from which they derive. For example, reasons to do φ as a means to pursue ψ are based on reasons to ψ. Such reasons to ψ may in turn be instrumental or noninstrumental. I want to emphasise that instrumental reasons to φ are not connected with the intrinsic features of φ, but with φ's causal consequences. For example, if I have a reason to lose weight, I have a reason not to eat an excessive amount of carbohydrates, but this reason is not related to the intrinsic features of eating an excessive amount of carbohydrates. By the same

[35] I doubt that reasons given by requests, promises and authoritative enactments are *totally* content-independent. Some content-dependence must be present for those sources to give reasons. For instance, if you ask your colleague to cover up your embezzlement, your request does not give him a reason. If you promise your fiancée that you will kill her former husband, the promise gives you no reason to kill. And if the legal authority orders you to torture a prisoner, the order doesn't give you a reason to do that. However, in cases in which requests, promises and enactments do give reasons, reason-giving is not explained by their content. Some contents just defeat the reason-generating power of requests, promises and enactments.

token, request-based reasons are related to the causal consequences of recognising requests as sources of reasons, but not to the intrinsic features of any service, nor necessarily to the intrinsic features of requesting that service. Therefore, we can have higher-order instrumental reasons. I don't think that requests give exclusionary reasons, and, therefore, I would regard such instrumental reasons as second-order reasons. It is more plausible to say that promises give exclusionary reasons to do as promised. If I promise to φ to my fiancée, I have exclusionary reasons to φ, but such reasons are not connected with the intrinsic features of φ, nor are they necessarily connected with the intrinsic features of promising φ. They are connected with third-order instrumental reasons that derive from further reasons to facilitate cooperative equilibria in our social life. Thus, the reasons for taking promises as sources of exclusionary reasons can be regarded as third-order instrumental reasons. According to the terminology I am suggesting, they are upgrading reasons justified by further reasons to live together with others in cooperative relationships.[36]

In a similar vein, upgrading reasons for recognising political authority as a normative source of exclusionary reasons are third-order instrumental reasons. The point is that the distinction between instrumental and noninstrumental reasons is orthogonal to the difference between levels or tiers of reasons. By distinguishing between the logical *level* of a reason (first order, second order, and so on) and its normative *source* (that is, whether it is an intrinsic or instrumental reason), it is possible to argue that there is an *upgrading* reason to see to it that Lφ gives an exclusionary reason to φ. Thus, the narrow-scope conditional

(1) $L\varphi \rightarrow R\varphi$

can be explained as deriving not from a wide-scope conditional but from an upgrading reason, because we have instrumental third-order reasons to recognise Lφ as a normative source of exclusionary reasons to φ. Such instrumental reasons are based on further reasons to solve problems of coordination and cooperation that exceed the problem-solving capacities of social morality. If we take (1) in isolation, it might seem mysterious that a fact that is different from φ can give people reasons to φ. This makes the triggering account appealing. However, I have argued that the explanation in terms of a wide-scope conditional reason is flawed. The multi-tiered account provides a better explanation. It is not mysterious to say that authoritative directives give exclusionary content-independent reasons that are different from the content-dependent reasons of social morality because we have upgrading reasons to take authoritative directives as giving those exclusionary reasons when social norms are insufficient as a problem-solving institution. Accordingly, upgrading reasons tell us to shift our form of social coordination and

[36] I believe that this explanation of how promises give reasons has Humean overtones. Hume also emphasised that the duty to respect promises is one of the conventions of justice that are needed to facilitate social life.

cooperation from a primitive social morality system to a more advanced political system that introduces both centralised and specialised agencies for establishing and updating norms in accordance with new social needs, as well as centralised and specialised agencies for arbitrating disputes about the application of the norms that derive from such normative sources.

The normative relation between reason-giving facts and reasons is not mysterious because such reasons are not merely entailed by those facts. On the contrary, upgrading reasons tell people that lacking a recognised authority is worse than following the exclusionary reasons that derive from problem-solving directives issued by such an authority. Instead of a naturalistic fallacy, we have a multi-tiered structure of reasons in which lower-reasons are plugged into higher-order reasons. If we have higher-order reasons to take some facts as lower-order reasons, the structure of reasons looks like a hierarchical legal system. Just as we have constitutional norms that enjoin us to take some directives enacted by the legislature as binding norms, we have upgrading reasons that tell us to take the directives enacted by the political authority as exclusionary reasons, which means that first-order reasons that might compete with such directives get displaced.

The multi-tiered account portrays the connection between law and morality in a different way. While the codification account says that law mirrors morality, and the triggering account holds that a set of moral standards react to legal directives, the multi-tiered account says that law and morality are two separate domains. Specifically, law substitutes social morality in complex societies. In fact, there is a reliable literature on the impact of social norms in solving coordination and cooperation problems in the absence of legal institutions.[37] Since social norms overlap with legal norms in contemporary societies, it is plausible to conjecture that social life was almost exclusively governed by social norms before the emergence of centralised political authorities. In close-knit social groups, social norms may be self-sufficient for preventing shirking behaviours, making legal institutions inefficient or superfluous. As the demographic, environmental and economic conditions of social existence change, law becomes an indispensable tool of social governance. While social norms exceed the domain of social morality, we tend to identify social morality as the subset of social norms that are backed by other-regarding preferences and upheld by such moral emotions as blame and remorse.

In social morality, practical reasons are constituted by relevant features of actions. So, for instance, the fact that someone is going to suffer as a result of one's φing constitutes a reason against φ. This is one of the many reason-constituting

[37] RC Ellickson, *Order Without Law: How Neighbors Settle Disputes* (Cambridge MA, Harvard University Press, 1994); EA Posner, *Law and Social Norms* (Cambridge MA, Harvard University Press, 2002); L Bernstein, 'Opting Out of the Legal System: Extralegal Contractual Relations in the Diamond Industry' (1992) 21 *Journal of Legal Studies* 115; A Grief, 'Contract Enforceability and Economic Institutions in Early Trade: The Maghribi Traders Coalition' (1993) 83 *American Economic Review* 525; LA Stout, 'Social Norms and Other-Regarding Preferences' in JN Drobak (ed), *Norms and the Law* (Cambridge, Cambridge University Press, 2006).

rules of social morality. Reason-constitution presupposes social recognition of reason-constituting rules, because social norms require by hypothesis social recognition, but social recognition is not a reason-constituting fact on its own. While practical reasons in social morality are constituted by relevant features of actions, law constitutes practical reasons on the basis of its authoritative pronouncements. Accordingly, the normativity of law can best be explained in terms of law's capacity to constitute reasons. This capacity is warranted by higher-order reasons that tell subjects and legal officials to treat authority's pronouncements as constituting autonomous practical reasons.

Both law and social morality claim authority over people's behaviour, and both must redeem that authority in the age of critical reason. The enlightenment project disenchants traditions and norms by regarding them as social artifacts that can be assessed from a critical perspective. Thus, both moral authority and legal authority must confront the fact that the source of norms is no longer authoritative on its own. Basically, with the enlightenment a new social institution emerged: *critical reasoning*. This institution underscores the equal status of all individuals and citizens in their rational capacity to accept or reject norms for their living together. As critical reasoning assesses social moral rules as applicable to all moral agents, *critical or ideal morality* emerges as a rational/critical transformation of social morality. In a similar vein, critical reasoning assesses positive legal norms from the rational perspective of all citizens, giving birth to *critical or ideal law*. Moral philosophy and political philosophy discuss the norms of critical morality and critical law (ie public morality). Now, since both critical morality and critical law have come to address normative problems by scrutinising socially recognised norms on the basis of abstract universalistic and egalitarian ideals, the distinction between those two domains has become blurred in contemporary legal philosophy. Therefore, critical or ideal law (natural law) is assimilated into ideal or critical morality and 'moral' becomes a catch-all term.

In any case, I don't mean that upgrading reasons must be moral reasons deriving from either social morality or critical morality. Though I should say much more by way of an analysis of the ways in which moral reasons are generated by social morality and critical morality, I think that my story is sufficiently clear for the goals of this paper. Upgrading reasons may encompass reasons of different sorts, and the distinction between prudential reasons and moral reasons may be inapplicable at this foundational level. Given the tendencies of human sociability, people have both self-regarding and other-regarding third-order reasons to recognise authoritative legal reasons as providing exclusionary reasons. Such exclusionary reasons, if upheld by an effective authority, are capable of solving the problems of social life, both statically and dynamically. I conclude that the nexus thesis is true, but the relevant nexus is more intricate than the codification account and the triggering account would suggest. The nexus goes through a multi-tiered structure of reasons that has some similarity with the hierarchical structure of advanced legal systems. I have suggested that the key to disclosing that structure is the idea of *upgrading reasons as third-order instrumental or extrinsic reasons*.

PART IV

Normativity and Legal Reasoning

9

Normativity of Basic Rules of Legal Interpretation*

BOJAN SPAIĆ

I. Introduction

The common view of legal interpretation is that this activity is guided by rules, specifically rules of interpretation, and that following those rules at least in some cases allows for determinate outcomes.[1] Some of those rules are codified in sources of law, some are thought of as being implicit in judicial practice, others are formulated within legal science and legal doctrine.

The function of interpretative rules is seemingly twofold. For one, it is often claimed that 'the 'proper meaning' of a legal text can be arrived at only if some rules of interpretation are followed'.[2] The primary role of rules of interpretation is to guide interpretative behaviour. For example, the rule stating that one should ascribe the plain meaning to a legal text when authoritatively interpreting it, directs the judge to: (a) identify the plain meaning of the text; (b) ascribe the plain meaning to the text. Secondly, '… judges present their interpretative decisions as based on rules, canons, maxims or methods of interpretation'.[3] In this second sense, rules are invoked to justify interpretative ascriptions of meaning to legal texts.[4] A rule

* I'm grateful to Ken Himma and Miodrag Jovanović for insightful comments on the first draft of the paper. The opportunity of engaging the topic of the paper was provided by the Alexander von Humboldt Foundation scholarship for research on the Institute for Public Law, Constitutional Law and Philosophy of Law of the University of Heidelberg, under the supervision of Martin Borowski.

[1] This is a starting point for many recent contributions to the literature on the topic: T Gizbert-Studnicki, 'The Normativity of Rules of Interpretation' in M Araszkiewicz et al (eds), *Problems of Normativity, Rules and Rule-Following* (Springer International Publishing, 2014); R Poscher, 'Interpretation and Rule Following in Law. The Complexity of Easy Cases' in M Araszkiewicz et al (eds), *Problems of Normativity, Rules and Rule-Following* (Dordrecht, Springer International Publishing, 2014); P Banas, 'Legal Interpretation as a Rule-Guided Phenomenon' and H Filipczyk, 'Blindly Following the Rules: Revisiting the Claritas Doctrine' both in M Araszkiewicz et al (eds), *Problems of Normativity, Rules and Rule-Following* (Dordrecht, Springer International Publishing, 2014).

[2] Banas, 'Legal Interpretation' (n 1) 256.

[3] Gizbert-Studnicki, 'Normativity of Interpretation' (n 1) 243.

[4] Gizbert-Studnicki explains that rules of interpretation can serve a heuristic purpose and a justificatory purpose. As a part of the heuristic purpose of ascribing meaning to a legal text, or interpreting law,

stating that one should ascribe the plain meaning to a legal text could be invoked to justify one ascription of meaning instead of the other. A judge could argue that he ascribed the meaning 'a plane figure with four equal straight sides and four right angles' to the word 'square' instead of the meaning 'the product of a number multiplied by itself' or the meaning 'a person who is conventional or conservative in taste or way of life', because 'a plane figure with four equal straight sides and four right angles' is the plain meaning of the word 'square'.

The multiplicity of rules of interpretation and their double role of guiding and justifying ascriptions of meaning to legal texts raise a number of important theoretical questions. The first concerns the identity and nature of rules that are supposed to guide legal interpretation. The second has to do with the fact that, for interpretation to be a normative enterprise, there have to be rules that either govern interpretation or guide interpretation – ie they have to be able to act as reasons for action.[5] In this paper I aim to do the following: in the first part of the paper, I identify some rules of legal interpretation that are considered to be basic, make the distinction between three kinds of norms – constitutive, regulative and instrumental – and give criteria for justifiably claiming that an activity was guided by a rule. Following the introductory classifications and criteria for being guided by rules, in the second part of the paper I distinguish between normativity of interpretation in the fundamental sense and normativity of interpretation in the derivative sense. I attempt to identify our commitments when we take basic norms of interpretation to be constitutive, basic norms of interpretation to be regulative, and basic norms of interpretation to be instrumental. I conclude that if we understand rules of interpretation as constitutive or instrumental they are not able to guide interpretative ascriptions of meaning, and that if we treat basic rules of interpretation as regulative they are unable to solve problems of legal indeterminacy.

II. Following Basic Rules of Legal Interpretation

A. Basic Rules of Interpretation

Theories of legal interpretation have formulated a number of rules that regulate legal interpretation. One of the recent studies on the topic identified as many as

they provide guidance to the process of interpretation. As a part of the justification of interpretation they are reasons for which an interpretation was adopted. Gizbert-Studnicki argues that issues related to heuristics pertain to the domain of empirical research, which should in principle be able to tell us if interpretations (as products of the process of interpretation) are guided by rules of interpretation ('Normativity of Interpretation' (n 1) 244).

[5] Rules *govern* a behaviour when the behaviour is 'subject to the regulation of an actual norm, whether or not the behaviour conforms to the norm'. Rules *guide* a behaviour when the 'behaviour conforms to a norm for the reason that the norm regulates the action in question': SJ Shapiro, 'On Hart's Way Out' in J Coleman (ed), *Hart's Postscript: Essays on the Postscript to The Concept of Law* (Oxford, Oxford University Press, 2001) 153. This paper is discussing the rule-guiding character of basic interpretative norms.

57 canons of interpretation of law, adding that this is only a third of the canons that can be found in common law adjudication.[6] Not all of the rules that are explicitly or implicitly present in judicial reasoning are considered to be of the same nature.[7]

Comparative studies on rules of interpretation have ascertained rules which are nearly universally invoked to justify interpretative 'discoveries' of meaning: (1) the *plain meaning rule*, stating that statutory provisions ought to be interpreted in accordance with the meaning an ordinary speaker would ascribe to it as its obvious, plain or common meaning; (2) the *systemic meaning rule*, stating that statutory provisions ought to be interpreted in light of the entire statute and other statutes regulating similar domains; (3) the *purpose of the legal text rule*, stating the statutes ought to be interpreted in accordance with the purpose of the statute and in the light of that purpose; (4) the *intention of the legislature rule* regulating that statutes should be interpreted in accordance with the intention of the legislature.[8]

These rules are familiar to anyone interested in legal interpretation not only as rules that are universally used to justify interpretations of legal text, but also as points of departure for contemporary doctrines of legal interpretation. Textualism takes the plain meaning rule to be fundamental in formulating a methodology of legal interpretation, intentionalism ascribes the same role to the intention of the legislator, and purposivism takes the purpose of the legal text rule to be crucial for interpretative endeavours in law.[9]

Because of their widespread use in judicial reasoning and their prominent role in all contemporary theories (descriptive accounts) and doctrines (prescriptive or normative accounts) of legal interpretation,[10] I will call those rules basic rules of interpretation.

[6] A Scalia and BA Garner, *Reading Law* (St Paul MN, Thompson/West, 2012).

[7] Gizbert-Studnicki makes a distinction between *strict*, *evaluative* and *mandatory* rules of interpretation. Strict rules yield definite interpretative outcomes. One such rule is: 'if the same word occurs more than once in the statute, the same meaning should be ascribed to each of those occurrences'. The second kind of rules instruct the interpreter to evaluate. An example of this rule would be: 'adopted interpretation should not be in conflict with fundamental constitutional values'. The third category mandates what the interpreter should take into account, such as the rule stating that one should 'take into account the legislative history of the statute': Gizbert-Studnicki, 'Normativity of Interpretation' (n 1) 243–44.

[8] N MacCormick and RS Summers, 'Interpretation and Justification' in N MacCormick and RS Summers (eds), *Interpreting Statutes* (Routledge, 1991) 512–15.

[9] In the tradition of legal theory and philosophy on the European continent, these rules have been formulated as canons of legal interpretation by the historical school of law, mainly by Friedrich Carl von Savigny. Savigny has closely followed the developments in general methodological hermeneutics in Germany: FK von Savigny, *System Des Heutigen Römischen Rechts* (Berlin, Veit und Comp, 1841) 213. The methodological hermeneutical tradition, which stretches across various fields of study like philosophy (Wilhelm Dilthey), history (Johan Gustav Droysen), and law (Emilio Betti), elaborated further some of those rules, reformulated them, introduced new ones and grounded entire methodologies of humanities on them. The main purpose of the rules within this strand of thought was to provide interpretation with a methodology that would allow for intersubjective verification of interpretative results. In common law jurisdictions, and especially in England, it is more common to talk about three basic rules of interpretation: the ordinary meaning rule, the golden rule and the mischief rule.

[10] 'Theories of legal interpretation' is used to denote descriptive theories of legal interpretation – theories about what is the nature of interpretation or how interpretation is conducted. 'Doctrines of legal interpretation' is used to denote normative theories of legal interpretation – theories about how

B. Taxonomy of Norms

A taxonomy of norms should – in principle – make it easier to account for the nature, normative status and the purpose of basic rules of interpretation. Unfortunately, there is little consistency in the usage of the terms 'rule' and 'norm' in the philosophical and legal literature. For the purpose of this discussion, I'll start with a basic classification of norms found in Georg Henrik von Wright's seminal work *Norm and Action*[11] and in John Searle's works *Speech Acts* and *Construction of Social Reality*.[12]

Talking about norms in the domain of law usually implies only the norms of one kind that von Wright and Searle identify as regulative norms (prescriptions). Regulative norms are usually expressed by ought statements, and their main characteristic is that they direct an activity that is already practised. A norm regulating the behaviour of students on university grounds is a regulative norm – it purports to guide a pre-existing behaviour in a certain direction. Such norms are, according to Wright, (1) usually prescribed by a person or a group of persons; (2) addressed to someone; (3) made known to the addressees; and (4) often followed by threat of sanction. Rules of law, customs, conventions, etiquette, fashion mostly fall within this category.

The peculiar character of the second kind of norms is that they are not prescriptive in the usual sense. Instead of regulating a pre-existing activity they define or constitute a new activity. The idea that there are norms that define an activity is in Searle's work expressed with the notion of constitutive rules.[13] This constitutive aspect of certain rules is most commonly explained by referring to games. The activity of playing a game is constituted by rules in the sense that there is no specific game if those rules are not observed by its participants. It would, for example, be senseless to talk about playing a game like football, chess, or bridge without grasping the rules that constitute the game in question. Moving on a field of grass with a ball might amount to an interesting and physically challenging activity, but that activity couldn't be characterised as football in the absence of rules regarding other players, ways to score, prohibitions of using hands during the game etc.

one ought to interpret. At the core of most doctrines of legal interpretation are descriptive claims about the nature of interpretation.

[11] GH von Wright, *Norm and Action: A Logical Enquiry* (Routledge, 1963). The full text of the book that was referenced in the paper can be found at www.giffordlectures.org/lectures/norm-and-action.

[12] J Searle, *Speech Acts* (Cambridge, Cambridge University Press 1969); J Searle, *The Construction of Social Reality* (New York, The Free Press, 1995). The terms 'rule' and 'norm' will not only be used to denote statements that are clearly prescriptive, but also, as is usual in philosophy and philosophy of law, statements that are called constitutive, as well as statements that are called instrumental (K Glüer and P Pagin, 'Rules of Meaning and Practical Reasoning' (1998) 117 *Synthese* 207, 215).

[13] Searle, *Speech Acts* (n 12) 33–35; Searle, *The Construction of Social Reality* (n 12) 28. Some legal theorists argue that as we could distinguish between 'dynamic rules', 'fact to fact rules' and 'counts as-rules', it is usual to reserve the term constitutive rules to the 'count as-rules' (JC Hage, 'Separating Rules From Normativity' in Araszkiewicz et al, *Problems of Normativity, Rules and Rule-Following* (n 1) 16–18).

To act in observance of those rules is to participate in the activity which is constituted by the very rules.[14] Searle authored the characteristic formulation of these rules: behaviour *X* (kicking the ball into the net) counts as *Y* (scoring a goal) in context *C* (playing football).[15]

The third type of norms is *instrumental norms (also called directives or technical norms).* Instrumental norms are statements of means for achieving a certain end. They too neither have a clear prescriptive character nor a clear descriptive character but instruct us how to act under the condition that we want to achieve a determinate goal. One will follow the instrumental norm contained in the part of the manual that comes with the TV set which explains how to mount the TV set on the wall, in so far as one's goal is to actually have the TV set on the wall. When we have determinate goals, instrumental norms tell us how to achieve those goals.

I will consider whether basic interpretative rules could fall under one of those categories or have some shared characteristic of some of those categories. Before that inquiry, it is important to establish what it means to say that rules guide behaviour.

C. Being Guided by Rules

The common presupposition that was mentioned in the introduction states that interpretation is a rule-guided enterprise. My intention in this part of the paper is to discuss the conditions that have to obtain in order to justifiably claim that an interpretative behaviour was guided by an interpretative rule. In other words, I'm not interested in whether rules are reasons for action that conform to a certain normative standard (justificatory reasons), or if they are good reasons for action, but only in the conceptual question about what does it mean to say that a behaviour was guided by a rule (explanatory reasons).[16] In order to ascertain the conditions for justifiably claiming that rules indeed guide interpretation, we have to answer the question about what it means to be guided by a rule.[17]

To start with, for me to justifiably say that an interpreter followed a rule of interpretation, the pattern of behaviour that the interpreter exhibits has to be in conformity with the pattern of behaviour prescribed by the rule. This condition

[14] In the domain of law constitutive norms create activities that otherwise would not exist in the absence of those norms, so that the activity would not be understandable with reference to the rules: see A Marmor, 'Norms, Reasons, and the Law', this volume. The version referenced in this paper is: A Marmor, 'Norms, Reasons, and the Law' (2016) *Cornell Legal Studies Research Paper* 16-19, available at SSRN: https://ssrn.com/abstract=2795220.

[15] Searle, *Speech Acts* (n 12) 35.

[16] That is, of course, not to say that this enterprise isn't valuable. Most literature, in fact, treats interpretative rules as rules that justify an interpretation under some justification criteria: Gizbert-Studnicki, 'Normativity of Interpretation' (n 1).

[17] In this part of the paper I will be following closely the explanation of what it means for a rule to guide action given by Kathrin Gluer and Peter Pagin in their 1999 paper 'Rules of Meaning and Practical Reasoning': Glüer and Pagin (n 12).

is not sufficient – we cannot justifiably say that a behaviour is guided by a rule by merely noticing that the behaviour is in accordance with the rule. There might be an existing rule that states that I should drink coffee every single morning, and it might actually be the case that I drink coffee every single morning. But I could be drinking coffee every morning just because I think that it helps me wake up, or because I like the taste. In these cases, the explanation of my behaviour doesn't have anything to do with the rule. Likewise, I could interpret the word 'fruit' to mean 'ripened ovaries of flowering plants', just because I heard it from someone, or because it was written on a wall in the suburbs of Belgrade, without any knowledge about a rule that states that I ought to interpret words in accordance with their plain meaning. To say that one was guided by the plain meaning rule it is at least additionally necessary that one was aware of the rule. The second condition for justifiably claiming that a rule guided the behaviour is, therefore, that *the rule was known to the agent.*

Even under the conditions of the existence of interpretative behaviour that conforms with the norms and interpreter's knowledge of the interpretative rule, the claim 'interpreter A was guided by the interpretative rule x' is still on shaky grounds in terms of justification. If I interpret the word fruit to mean 'ripened ovaries of flowering plants' that doesn't necessarily imply that I was guided by a rule that states: *One should always ascribe the plain meaning to words.* My interpretation could as well be guided by another rule, for example a rule that states – *I should always define words the way my mother defined them* – if the rule results in the same interpretative ascription of meaning, namely if it yields the result that 'fruits are ripened ovaries of flowering plants'. Both rules could be reasons to ascribe the same meaning to the word 'fruit' but one doesn't have to be guided by both rules (even if one could be guided by both).[18]

In order to justifiably claim that a rule acted as a reason for action it is necessary that it actually played a motivational role in the practical reasoning that led to interpretative action. To say that a rule motivated an interpreter is to say that the interpreter has ascribed the meaning to a legal text because the interpretative rule gave him a reason to ascribe the meaning.[19] Reasons that actually served as the interpreter's reason to ascribe a particular meaning to the legal provision are called operative reasons.[20] An interpretative rule explains the behaviour of the interpreter in so far as it is an operative reason for ascribing a specific meaning to the text.

Whether a rule was an operative reason in practical reasoning leading to an intention to act is not entirely an empirical matter. If, for example, following an interpretative rule allows for the ascription of multiple meanings of the same text,

[18] For a discussion about complete reasons see J Raz, *Practical Reason and Norms*, 3rd edn (Oxford, Oxford University Press, 1999) 22–25.

[19] Glüer and Pagin, 'Rules of Meaning and Practical Reasoning' (n 12) 208.

[20] ibid 209.

and one meaning is actually ascribed, we cannot justifiably say that the rule acted as the operative reason for the specific ascription of meaning. Reasons that are candidates for being operative reasons regardless of the actual performance of the ascription of meaning and regardless of whether the performance is based on that very operative reason are *basic reasons*.[21] For a rule to function as an operative reason, it must be possible for the rule to be a basic reason – it has to be able to motivate 'the agent to perform a particular action'.

Rules that are basic reasons for action fulfil what Andrei Marmor calls the *condition of normativity*.[22] To meet the condition of normativity a norm has to be able to provide a new reason for action. If the interpretative norm doesn't introduce a new reason for action, we can explain the interpretative behaviour without any reference to the norm. In other words, we could then say that the interpretative behaviour was regulated by the norm but not that it was guided by the norm.[23] So, the norm would meet the condition of normativity if and only if it provided a new reason for action and didn't simply reflect the pre-existing reasons for action.[24]

We can thus justifiably claim that an interpretation was rule-guided if the following conditions are satisfied: (1) the rule is known to the subject; (2) the behaviour of the subject has to be in conformity with the rule; and (3) the subject acted the way he acted because of the rule and not because of some other pre-existing reason. To act because of the rule means to be motivated by the rule to act in a certain way. An agent can be motivated by the rule if the condition of normativity is met – if the rule doesn't simply reflect pre-existing reasons for action but introduces a new reason for action.[25]

[21] ibid 209.

[22] Marmor, 'Norms, Reasons, and the Law' (n 14) 3.

[23] Shapiro, 'On Hart's Way Out' (n 5) 153–56.

[24] All rules that meet the condition of normativity are able to guide behaviour, but not all rules that guide behaviour are able to meet the condition of normativity. Marmor wants to exclude motivational reasons from his discussion by resorting to the justificatory idea of wrong and right reasons. He explains this in the following way: if someone avoids lying to a friend because there is a social norm mandating that we should not lie to friends, this social norm fails the condition of normativity because the agent refrained from lying for the wrong reasons. The right reason here is that we should avoid lying because lying is wrong: see Marmor, 'Norms, Reasons, and the Law' (n 14) 3–4. It seems that the condition of normativity is not met if we act in a certain way by following the norm if the norm is the wrong reason for action. The underlying claim here seems to be that only those norms that can serve as justificatory reasons, or the norms that can 'respond to the question of why one *should* or *ought* to do' something. Consequently, rules meet the condition of normativity only if they act as reasons for action if the action is undertaken because the rule states that it should be undertaken.

[25] Marmor claims that 'most moral norms fail the condition of normativity' on account of they being the wrong reasons for an action (Marmor, 'Norms, Reasons, and the Law' (n 14) 4). But if one was motivated by the rule that is in force in a society, the proper explanation of his behaviour would have to encompass the rule that was considered by her to be a reason for her action. It doesn't matter if the action can be accounted for in terms of other reasons, if the rule acted as motivation to act in a way.

III. Fundamental and Derivative Normativity of Interpretation

The exposition thus far narrowed the inquiry into the normativity of basic rules of interpretation to the question about the possibility of basic rules of interpretation to act as basic reasons for interpretative ascriptions of meaning. When we have a rule stating, for example, that the official should always interpret the legal text according to the plain meaning of the words and sentences, in order to say that the interpreter was guided by this rule it is necessary that the rule is a basic reason for the interpreter to ascribe to the texts their plain meaning.

Having in mind the basic rules of interpretation, the taxonomy of rules and considerations about what it means to be guided by a rule, the claim that interpretation is normative could be made out to mean at least two things. First, it could mean that interpretation is a normative or rule guided in the sense that there are certain rules that define or constitute the very activity of interpretation. In this sense interpretation is fundamentally normative because there would be no interpretation if some basic constitutive rules are not observed. To act in observance of a constitutive rule of interpretation is to interpret.

Second, the statement that interpretation is normative could be understood as the claim that basic rules of interpretation are either: (a) some enacted or agreed upon legal, social, conventional norms that purport to guide judges in ascribing determinate meanings to the legal texts; or (b) some instrumental norms that state the means with which a judge can achieve the ends of interpretation. In this sense interpretation is derivatively normative because the activity is guided by norms purporting to steer the discovery of meaning to the legal text in a certain direction.

A. Fundamental Normativity of Interpretation

i. Basic Interpretative Rules as Constitutive Norms

The first question to answer regards whether interpretation can be understood as fundamentally normative. This amounts to an inquiry about: (a) whether basic rules of interpretation can be understood as constitutive; and (b) what would the idea of the constitutivity of basic rules of interpretation entail.

Needless to say, contemporary doctrines of legal interpretation offer conflicting views on what legal interpretation is and how legal interpretation ought to be conducted. In these doctrines, basic rules of interpretation are often understood as strongly opposed to one another and even as mutually exclusive. While it certainly could be argued that these differences between doctrines are based on opposing ideas about the role of judges in contemporary legal systems, most theorists take the differences in approach to be of a more basic nature.[26] The underlying claim of the doctrines can be construed to state that one or more of the basic rules of interpretation is constitutive – the activity of determining meaning couldn't even be considered interpretation if the judges do not act with observance of the constitutive rule. The plain meaning rule, the intention of the legislator rule, the purpose of the legal text rule are not only considered more important than other rules of interpretation but are thought of as crucial for the very activity of interpretation.

Within *textualism*, the ordinary meaning rule is thought of as the 'fundamental semantic rule of interpretation'.[27] At the heart of this doctrine is the claim that the ordinary meaning rule is a rule that grounds the very possibility of justifiably claiming that an activity of understanding a text counts as interpretation. This is obvious in the distinction between interpretation and construction which is one of the pillars of contemporary originalism.[28] Interpretation is, in this view, an inquiry into semantic content or linguistic meaning, and everything that is outside the inquiry into the linguistic meaning doesn't count as interpretation but as construction.[29] Within textualist doctrines of interpretation, only the inquiry into the linguistic meaning of the authoritative legal text counts as interpretation (in the context of legal adjudication).

Intentionalist accounts of interpretation often share the same idea about basic interpretative rules. For intentionalists, to interpret is to inquire into the intentions of the person or entity that enacted a legal text. Consequently, the rule that states that interpretation ought to search for the intention of the author of the text is not, according to the common intentionalist view defended by Stanley Fish, simply one of the rules of interpretation – 'it *is* interpretation' itself.[30] Again, the idea would seem to be that there is a basic rule that constitutes interpretation, which could be formulated in the following fashion: inquiring into the intention of the

[26] Gizbert-Studnicki, 'Normativity of Interpretation' (n 1) 253.

[27] Scalia and Garner, *Reading Law* (n 6).

[28] This is not to say that originalist claims are construed in the way proposed in this this part of the paper. Originalism has become somewhat of an umbrella term for many interpretative doctrines in the United States (LB Solum, 'What is Originalism? The Evolution of Contemporary Originalist Theory' (28 April 2011) available at SSRN: https://ssrn.com/abstract=1825543), and one cannot discuss them without some (possibly problematic) generalisations that may leave out important details and elaborations of the doctrine by different authors.

[29] LB Solum, 'Interpretation-Construction Distinction' (2010) 27 *Constitutional Commentary* 99; BG Slocum, 'The Ordinary Meaning of Rules' in Araszkiewicz et al, *Problems of Normativity, Rules and Rule-Following* (n 1) 298. There are significant differences between theorists of legal interpretation in the exposition of the plain meaning rule, and there is a lot of literature covering the topic. My intention is not to give an overview of the changing positions.

[30] S Fish, 'Intention Is All There Is' (2008) 29 *Cardozo Law Review* 1109, 1112. Fish writes that presupposing intention is a condition of the very possibility of interpretation – in the absence of such a presupposition we couldn't presuppose that there was any meaning at all. Marks on the beach of Ada Bojana in Montenegro would, according to him, mean anything if we didn't presuppose that they were purposefully produced by an agent (ibid 1112). A similar claim is put forward in the textualist camp – basic canons of interpretation are sometimes regarded as 'presumptions about what an intelligently produced text conveys' Scalia and Garner, *Reading Law* (n 6). One of these basic presuppositions is, in Scalia's view, the presupposition that the words mean what they 'conveyed to reasonable people at the time they were written'.

author of the authoritative legal text counts as interpretation (in the context of legal adjudication).

The idea that basic rules of interpretation are constitutive of interpretation, and that they are mutually exclusive, is a prominent feature of the Anglo-American debate about interpretation. The tradition on the European continent is at first glance more inclined to consider basic rules of interpretation as complementary. Both legislation and legal theory suggest that there is a hierarchy between rules of interpretation structured in the following way: (1) the common or plain meaning within; (2) the legal system as a whole; (3) intentions of the legislator; (4) appeal to values instantiated in principles of the legal system; and (5) the sense of fairness of the judge.[31] This typical hierarchical relation between the rules can itself be made out to represent a second order rule that regulates the order in which the first order rules are to be applied, and which one of them should be given preference in case of conflicting results of interpretation. What is to count as a constitutive rule of interpretation depends on the understanding of the relation between basic rules. Even if we could, in principle, formulate a theoretical position in which constitutive rules of interpretation are all of the basic rules of interpretation,[32] the common theoretical position (and a position that is often supported by legislative enactments) is that the linguistic rule has a priority. Aharon Barak, to take just one example of a theorist who draws heavily from the European tradition, takes all of the basic rules of legal interpretation to be necessary to give an account of legal interpretation. Still, he insists on the primacy of the plain meaning rule, in the sense that the ascription of meaning to a legal text cannot in fact be considered interpretation if it crosses the boundaries of the plain meaning of the legal text.[33] Formulated in this way, the European tradition of interpreting and theorising about interpretation, shares the basic assumptions with Anglo-American doctrines.[34] The priority of the plain meaning rules shows that its status is similar to the status of the plain meaning rule in the Anglo-American tradition.[35]

The tacit premise of most current theorising about interpretation can, therefore, be formulated as the claim that a basic rule of interpretation is

[31] German tradition uses the idea of the 'limits of the wording' in order to distinguish between 'interpretation' and 'development' of law: see M Klatt, *Making the Law Explicit* (Oxford, Hart Publishing, 2008) 4–5.

[32] This was indeed claimed by E Betti in his *Interpretazione della legge e degli atti giuridici* (Milano, Giuffrè, 1971).

[33] A Barak, *Purposive Interpretation in Law* (New Jersey, Princeton University Press, 2005) 7.

[34] Gizbert-Studnicki analyses the debates about rules of interpretation is that the legitimacy of those rules is challenged *in abstracto* in American theoretical jurisprudence, while in continental theory and practice of interpretation there is at least a tacit differentiation between 'primary rules of interpretation' (linguistic, systematic or teleological) and 'secondary rules of interpretation' (presumably all the other rules which could, but are not necessarily connected to the primary rules: Gizbert-Studnicki, 'Normativity of Interpretation' (n 1) 252–53.

[35] Gizbert-Studnicki argues that we can account for this difference on a meta-theoretical level if we understand Anglo-American debates as challenges to the positions about first level rules of interpretation: Gizbert-Studnicki, 'Normativity of Interpretation' (n 1) 252.

constitutive of the activity of interpreting law.[36] The idea that some rules of interpretation are constitutive seems to capture something about the way judges treat rules of interpretation, for even in traditions in which there is a broader range of basic interpretative rules, those rules are considered as part of a hierarchy in which one rule, usually a rule about the plain meaning or the intention of the author, plays the role of the constitutive rule.

ii. Problems with Constitutivity of (Interpretative) Norms

The basic problem with this reconstruction of claims about basic rules of interpretation regards the nature of constitutive rules. Constitutive rules are supposed to serve a double function of constituting an activity and regulating that very activity. If we claim that some interpretative rules are constitutive, we would have to explain how those basic rules constitute interpretation and at the same time guide interpretation. But the two functions that are ascribed to constitutive rules are arguably not compatible – if constitutive rules can serve as reasons for action they cannot constitute an activity, and, conversely, if the rules constitute an activity they cannot serve as reasons for action.[37]

The incompatibility between the constitutive and the regulative function of constitutive rules is the main problem for treating interpretation as fundamentally normative. To see this, it is enough to remind ourselves that we identified the possibility to motivate an agent as one of the main conditions for justifiably claiming that the agent was guided by a rule. On the one hand, in their classic formulation proposed by Searle, constitutive rules cannot act as motivation. A constitutive rule stating that to kick a goal between the goalposts when playing football counts as a goal, doesn't motivate the player to follow the rule. It just tells the player what counts as a goal in the context of a particular game. Likewise, a rule that states that the inquiry into the plain meaning of a text is to count as legal interpretation in the context of legal adjudication doesn't motivate the interpreter to ascribe the plain meaning to the text. It just tells the interpreter what is to count as interpretation in the context of legal adjudication.

[36] There is an argument derived from the recent work in social ontology that claims that there is an important difference between constitutive rules and statements on constitution. Constitutive rules are, according to this view, characterised by the fact that they are not simple descriptive claims about an activity. In turn, we could call statements on constitution descriptive claims about an activity. Constitutive rules would thus create an activity, but statements of constitution would not be able to do so. See C Roversi, 'Acceptance is not Enough, But Texts Alone Achieve Nothing: A Critique of Two Conceptions in Institutional Ontology' (1912) 43 *Recthstheorie* 189–190. Fish, for one, is explicit that his idea of interpretation as the search for the intentions of the author is for the most part without any prescriptive significance. Intentionalism is to his mind just a descriptive theory of interpretation that doesn't tell you what you ought to do in interpreting the legal text: see Fish, 'Intention Is All There Is' (n 30) 1114.

[37] Glüer and Pagin, 'Rules of Meaning and Practical Reasoning' (n 12) 207; A Hattiangadi, 'Is Meaning Normative?' (2006) 21 *Mind and Language* 220.

If we understand basic rules of interpretation as constitutive norms, we would, seemingly, have to give up on the idea that they guide interpretation. Consequently, we would have to give up on the idea that interpretation is fundamentally normative. On the other hand, if these rules have the function of guiding interpretative enterprises in the sense that they give us reasons for believing, ie if they give doxastic reasons for ascribing a meaning to a legal text, they cannot be constitutive of interpretation, since the formation of the belief about meaning would have to be based on the very rule that guides the formation of a belief.[38] At least in their classical formulation, constitutive rules do not seem able to guide interpretative ascriptions of meaning and to constitute interpretation at the same time.

B. Derivative Normativity of Interpretation

i. Basic Rules of Interpretation as Regulative Norms

If basic rules of interpretation are not constitutive of the activity of interpretation they could still be regulative or instrumental, and interpretation could derivatively still be normative in the relevant sense. Andrei Marmor distinguishes three kinds of regulative norms: *codifying rules*, *reason-instantiating rules* and *authoritative rules*.[39]

The basic function of codifying rules is to make explicit collective beliefs about how we ought to act. Those norms don't give us new reasons for action; their role is to formulate reasons for action that are already present. For example, we have plenty of good reasons to act decently in relations with our co-workers even without an official text containing non-binding ethical guidelines for behaviour in the workplace.

The other possibility is that basic rules of interpretation are *reason-instantiating norms*. Marmor develops an account of these norms in order to explain *conventions*.[40] According to him, the common characteristic of all conventional norms is that they are reason-instantiating. The role of reason-instantiating norms is to shape reasons for action that already exist prior to their codification into a form that is clearer and more precise;[41] the need for those norms exists because the reasons for action that they instantiate are not clear or precise enough

[38] Glüer and Pagin, 'Rules of Meaning and Practical Reasoning' (n 12) 219.

[39] This is not to say that every of these norms satisfies the criteria of normativity. Marmor claims that in order for a norm to be a reason for action it is necessary that it figures in an explanation about why one ought to do something: Marmor, 'Norms, Reasons, and the Law' (n 14) 3.

[40] In the classical account of conventions authored by the philosopher David Lewis, conventions are understood as rules that solve large-scale coordination problems, that are arbitrary, and that require a large-scale convergence of behaviour. This idea was rightly dismissed by Gizbert-Studnicki, who relied on an account of conventions developed by David Lewis. It indeed seems implausible that rules of interpretation solve large-scale coordination problems: see Gizbert-Studnicki, 'Normativity of Interpretation' (n 1) 248.

[41] Marmor, 'Norms, Reasons, and the Law' (n 14) 4.

prior to codification.[42] For example, all of the rules that determine the boundaries of vague concepts in law, or the rules that determine what should one bring as a present to the hosts of a dinner party. In these cases, we have reasons for acting in a certain way – we have reasons to treat certain persons as minors, or to bring a gift to the hosts of a dinner party – but we do not have reasons for acting in a determinate way – to treat as minors all persons under the age of 18, or to bring a bottle of wine to a dinner party. The point of reason-instantiating norms is to make those kinds of activities determinate with the purpose of reducing the costs of deliberation about the appropriate behaviour.

The third kind of social norms that are products of authoritative directives and are called *authoritative norms.*[43] Authoritative rules are in the case of interpretation those rules that are institutionally enacted. Contemporary legal systems include a significant number of norms that are authoritative norms of interpretation but exhibit the characteristics of reason-instantiating norms. The primary institutional enactor of those rules in civil-law jurisdictions is the legislature. To mention just a few examples of basic rules of interpretation that have been enacted by the legislative bodies: the Austrian Civil Code from 1911 in Article 6 mandates that the statutes should be attributed only those meanings that are evident or plain and by regarding the relations between words, adding the intention of the legislator. The Italian Civil Code (1842) in Article 12 practically repeats the same formulations. The Vienna Convention on the Law of Treaties (1969) mandates the interpretation in accordance with the ordinary meaning.[44]

ii. *Indeterminacy of Basic Interpretative Rules*

At first glance, basic norms of interpretation could be simple codifying norms. We seemingly have reasons to inquire into the plain meaning of the legal text, into

[42] ibid 8. See A Marmor, *Social Conventions* (New Jersey, Princeton University Press 2009) 7.

[43] Marmor, 'Norms, Reasons, and the Law' (n 11) 11.

[44] The Austrian Civil Code from 1811 in Article 6 states 'Einem Gesetze darf in der Anwendung kein anderer Verstand beygelegt werden, als welcher aus der eigenthümlichen Bedeutung der Worte in ihrem Zusammenhange und aus der klaren Absicht des Gesetzgebers hervorleuchtet'. The Italian Civil Code from 1942 in the first paragraph of Article 12 states: 'Nell'applicare la legge non si può ad essa attribuire altro senso che quello fatto palese dal significato proprio delle parole secondo la connessione di esse, e dalla intenzione del legislatore'. On the international level, the Vienna Convention on the Law of Treaties from 1969, under the heading 'General rule of interpretation' in Article 31 states: '1. A treaty shall be interpreted in good faith in accordance with the ordinary meaning to be given to the terms of the treaty in their context and in the light of its object and purpose. 2. The context for the purpose of the interpretation of a treaty shall comprise, in addition to the text, including its preamble and annexes: (a) any agreement relating to the treaty which was made between all the parties in connexion with the conclusion of the treaty; (b) any instrument which was made by one or more parties in connexion with the conclusion of the treaty and accepted by the other parties as an instrument related to the treaty. 3. There shall be taken into account, together with the context: (a) any subsequent agreement between the parties regarding the interpretation of the treaty or the application of its provisions; (b) any subsequent practice in the application of the treaty which establishes the agreement of the parties regarding its interpretation; (c) any relevant rules of international law applicable in the relations between the parties. 4. A special meaning shall be given to a term if it is established that the parties so intended'.

the intention of the author, into the purposes of the text in order to determine the meaning of a text, even without an explicit norm that regulates such interpretative behaviour. A simple fact of a political order, like the separation of powers, can be reason enough to think that the acts enacted by the legislation have meaning and that we should inquire into that meaning and not simply ascribe any meaning to the text whatsoever. One of the conditions for justifiably claiming that a behaviour was guided by a rule is that the rule introduced a reason for action that was not present before. Codifying norms do not fulfil this criterion. To understand basic interpretative rules as codifying norms implies that we do not ascribe a meaning to the legal text because of a basic norm, but because of other facts that exist prior to codification. If the reasons for an interpretative behaviour are all present before the codification, basic norms of interpretation are simple prescriptive formulations of existing beliefs about what ought to be done. Basic rules could, in principle, be understood as the codification of some pre-existing reasons for action, but at the loss of their guiding function. Even if they do not guide action, codifying rules of interpretation can serve other important purposes. According to Marmor they can 'serve educational functions … facilitate certain forms of social cohesion … even serve epistemic functions in making reasons easier to keep in mind and internalize'.[45]

This leaves us with the possibility that basic rules of interpretation are either reason-instantiating norms or authoritative norms, or a combination of both. Since they introduce a reason for action that is new and somewhat different from the pre-existing reasons for action that they concretise, there is no doubt that that reason-instantiating norms are apt to guide behaviour. In this sense we could say that we already have reasons to ascribe, for example, the plain meaning to a text, and that the basic norm of interpretation makes this pre-existing reason more precise.[46] Authoritative norms, similarly, according to one common

[45] Marmor, 'Norms, Reasons, and the Law' (n 14) 6. If time spent in teaching students about those basic norms is any indication, this characterisation seems quite right. One brief note about the possibility of basic interpretative rules being codifying rules: If the interpreter was aware of the codifying norm, but was not aware of preexisting reasons for action, and his behaviour is in conformity with the rule, under the condition that this rule was also an authoritative rule, we could justifiably claim that this very rule guided interpretation since it is a rule that is in force for the interpreter, and is able to induce a pro-attitude in the interpreter in regards of following the rule.

[46] Already at first glance, it seems that some of the interpretative norms are norms that instantiated reasons that were underdetermined prior to their instantiating. One norm that comes to mind is the interpretative norm prescribing that 'the same words in a statute should be interpreted in the same way'. There are certainly some preexisting reasons for thinking that one word in a statute should mean the same thing, but the reasons that we have for thinking this are not determinate enough. The legislation process in contemporary states, for example, includes many expert commissions, commissions of the executive branch, commissions within the parliament. All of those actors in the drafting of the statute are able to add text, change existing text, delete text that was introduced by a previous participant in the legislative process. Given those facts, we could even have reasons to ascribe far less consistency to the meanings of the words used in the statute. Still there are reasons to treat the statute as an integral body of text, that is coherent and in which same words were used in the same way. It is usually thought that consistency in the usage of words relates positively to legal certainty. By introducing a reason

analysis based on the account of authority developed by Joseph Raz, not only give first-order reasons, but also give second-order or exclusionary reasons for action. This is prima facie evidence that they are able to be basic reasons for action.

Understood as either reason-instantiating rules or as authoritative norms, basic rules of interpretation can be basic reasons for action. Understood as reason-instantiating norms, basic interpretative rules should be able to significantly reduce the costs of deliberation about interpretative outcomes, facilitating the ascription of meaning to a legal text. Presumably, they are authoritatively enacted for the same purpose of guiding legal interpreters in 'finding the right solution to interpretative problems they face'.[47] The main role of basic interpretative rules understood as regulative norms would, therefore, be to facilitate the determination of meaning of a legal text, and to solve problems of indeterminacy of general legal texts by cutting costs of deliberation about meaning.

If this is true, then it is necessary that basic rules act not only as basic reasons but as reasons for the interpreter to adopt one interpretation and not the other. It seems reasonable to suppose that basic rules of interpretation fully achieve this purpose only in cases in which the rule leads to one single determinate meaning to the legal text. A rule is in fact an operative reason for action if – and only if – it explains why someone acted in one way and not in the other. Basic interpretative rules are not suitable to fully explain the outcome of interpretation, because, being instances of general regulative rules, they too face the problem of indeterminacy that they are supposed to solve – the employment of those rules is not sufficient to explain a unique outcome of judicial interpretation of texts.[48] To return to our simple example, the plain meaning of the word 'fruit' is not only 'the state of bearing fruit' but also 'ripened ovaries of plants'. The ascription of one of those meanings by a judge cannot be explained by referring to a basic rule of interpretation, and even if they are able to act as reasons for a class of ascriptions of meaning, they are not able to guide the interpreter to ascribe a single meaning to a text. Basic rules of interpretation understood as regulative norms can aid the interpreter in

instantiating norm that states that 'the same words should be interpreted in the same way' we at least try to reduce the amount of interpretative work that is to be done with the same words within a statute. An example of the norms of interpretation that fall under this category could be norms that regulate the conflicts of norms like – *lex posterior derogat legi priori*, or *lex specialis derogat legi generali*. We have some reasons in cases of conflict between law, often vague and imprecise reasons, to consider the law that was adopted at a later time to be binding, and to consider a law that regulates matters specifically to be binding. Those preexisting reasons are instantiated in norms of interpretation which in this way become some kind of conventional norms. We could of course always question the practical utility of those norms, but their general aim is to solve as uniformly as possible the problems of conflict between norms at the same level of generality (Marmor, 'Norms, Reasons, and the Law' (n 14) 8; Marmor, *Social Conventions* (n 42) 7.

[47] Gizbert-Studnicki, 'Normativity of Interpretation' (n 1) 244.

[48] JL Coleman and B Leiter, 'Determinacy, Objectivity, and Authority' in A Marmor (ed), *Law and Interpretation* (Oxford, Oxford University Press, 1997) 213–15. Of course, the indeterminacy thesis is true for all norms that can be complied with or violated by different behaviours. It is a predicament of all law that uses general terms to convey legal norms. The problem here is that the basic interpretative rules are second order rules that are supposed to solve the indeterminacy of first order legal rules.

identifying possible meanings, but are, however, unable to solve the problems that they are supposed to solve – namely the problems of significantly cutting the costs of deliberation about the meaning of a legal text.

This has been a common criticism of doctrines of interpretation for quite a long time. Hart was explicit in claiming that:

> Canons of 'interpretation' cannot eliminate, though they can diminish … uncertainties; for these canons are themselves general rules for the use of language and make use of general terms which themselves require interpretation. They cannot, any more than other rules, provide for their own interpretation.[49]

Likewise, Kelsen's conclusion about the rules of interpretation is that 'every method of interpretation developed thus far invariably leads merely to a possible result, never to a single correct result'.[50] At best, basic rules can provide us with multiple meanings of words or sentences, but the rule itself cannot be an operative reason for the ascription of meaning.[51] Recently, Richard H Fallon Jr argued that that 'textualism fails the test of relative determinacy in fixing legal meaning that many versions of textualism appear to set for themselves'.[52] The same argument is valid for intentionalist and purposivist theories, in so far as the idea of intention and objective purpose are subject to even more controversies than the idea of plain meaning, and can reasonably be construed to include a significant amount of time consuming and dubiously effective inquiries. In the end, even if we can say that authoritative rules of legal interpretation fulfil the criteria of being basic reasons, they do not solve the problem which give rise to interpretative rules in the first place.

iii. Basic Rules of Interpretation as Instrumental Norms

I now turn to the question of whether basic rules of interpretation can be understood as norms that state a means to an end. According to von Wright instrumental norms 'rest upon a causal relationship'. Von Wright gives the classical example of an instrumental norm: 'If you want to heat the house you should turn on the heating'. Basic rules of interpretation could be considered to be instrumental rules if they contain claims about the relation between certain interpretative actions and the end of interpretation – ascertaining the meaning of the text. Even if the basic rules often lack the usual means-end formulation characteristic of instrumental

[49] HLA Hart, *The Concept of Law*, 2nd edn (Oxford, Oxford University Press, 1994) 126.

[50] H Kelsen, *Introduction to the Problems of Legal Theory*, BL Paulson and SL Paulson trs (Oxford, Clarendon Press, 1992) 81.

[51] Note that this is not to say that the rule is completely useless in the context of discovery. After all even 'textualists' that purport to be strict construe the rule as to presume 'that a thoroughly fluent reader can reliably tell in the vast majority of instances from contextual and idiomatic clues which of several possible senses a word or phrase bears': Scalia and Garner, *Reading Law* (n 6).

[52] RH Fallon Jr, 'The Meaning of Legal "Meaning" and Its Implications for Theories of Legal Interpretation' (2015) 82 *The University of Chicago Law Review* 1235, 1285.

norms, they could be reformulated as instrumental rules.[53] We could, in principle, claim that the following is true: if an interpreter wants to determine the meaning of a text, he should inquire into the plain meaning/intention/purpose of the text.[54]

What is needed for rules of interpretation to be instrumental norms is that the interpreter ascribed a determinate meaning to a legal text because of those rules. Instrumental norms, however, share the same problem with constitutive rules – we do not do anything in the strict sense because of the instrumental rules, since instrumental norms are neither descriptive nor prescriptive. We follow instrumental rules because we want to achieve a certain end and we believe that we can achieve the end by resorting to the rule. So, instrumental rules themselves do not provide the necessary motivation for acting in a certain way. Their ability to guide behaviour is dependent on a pro-attitude towards the rule since they state: (1) a belief about the relevant meaning of the legal text; and (2) a belief about the means-end proposition. In this way, understanding basic rules of interpretation as instrumental norms deprives them of the possibility of acting as operative reasons for action.[55]

The second problem with treating rules of interpretation as instrumental norms is that the ends of legal interpretation are indeterminate. On the most basic level of analysis, interpretation is considered to have the end of understanding the meaning of an instance of legal text. But theorists of interpretation, especially in the hermeneutical tradition, have insisted that the ultimate end of interpretation is not cognitive (intellectual) – in the sense that it only tries to establish the plausible meanings of a legal text – but applicative – in the sense that its goal is to establish a meaning of the legal text in order to provide one with normative guidance.[56]

[53] John Searle includes the norms that von Wright calls technical or instrumental in the group of norms that he calls regulative. This is one of the results of Searle using the characteristic formulation of the rule as an indicator of the type of the rule. Regulative rules can in fact be formulated or paraphrased as imperatives, but that doesn't equate them with prescriptions in von Wright's sense.

[54] Beliefs about means-end relations can also serve as reasons for accepting certain constitutive or prescriptive rules of interpretation, both if one believes that the constitutive and prescriptive rules are means to a determinate end (most often a value like rule of law, legal certainty, efficacy etc). Even without believing that the prescriptive rule is a good mean to achieve a certain end, instrumental rules can still be followed. In these cases, it is enough that I believe that it is better that I follow the rule than to rely on personally examined reasons (Glüer and Pagin, 'Rules of Meaning and Practical Reasoning' (n 12) 225). For example, a judge could believe that some values are not best achieved by interpreting the legal text in accordance with an instrumental interpretative rule in a particular case, but he can still think that following this rule does, as a whole, yield better results in enough cases of interpretation, then if he was acting on his own reasons.

[55] Glüer and Pagin, 'Rules of Meaning and Practical Reasoning' (n 12) 225.

[56] In *Pure Theory of Law* Kelsen explains that the law to be applied is 'a frame within which several applications are possible, whereby every act is legal that stays within the frame': H Kelsen, *Pure Theory of Law*, M Knight trs (Berkeley, University of California Press, 1967) 354. The task of cognitive interpretation is to establish the possible meanings of the legal text, and the task of adjudicative interpretation is to ascribe one meaning to the legal text. In General Theory of Law and state the difference is explained in the following terms: 'the decision of the court can never be determined by a preexistent general norm of substantive law to such a degree that this general norm which the court applies is, as it were, reproduced only by the individual norm of the decision': H Kelsen, *General Theory of Law and State*, A Wedberg trs (Oxford, Oxford University Press, 1949) 146.

Hans-Georg Gadamer claimed that the applicative character of legal interpretation could serve as a model for understanding interpretation in general.[57] Emilio Betti similarly argued that what distinguishes legal interpretation from interpretation in other domains (literature, history, etc) is the fact that legal interpretation results in normative statements – we interpret law in order to understand how one ought to act. In fact, when we talk about legal interpretation from a theoretical perspective we are not only interested in the probable (plausible) meanings of the legal texts (cognitive interpretation), but also in the ascription of meaning to the legal text by an authoritative legal interpreter (adjudicative interpretation). The former consists in identifying the possible meanings of the text, and the latter kind consists in deciding which meaning is taken to be decisive in the case at hand.[58] The indeterminacy of ends is also reflected in disagreements about the role of judges in contemporary legal systems, resulting in long-standing controversies about the relations of the judge to the texts of constitutions, statutes and other legal texts.

Finally, even if the basic interpretative norms are instructions stating the means for achieving an end, we encounter the same problem that we encountered when discussing basic norms of interpretation as regulative norms. If we indeed believed that our tools for discovering meaning are basic instrumental norms of interpretation, the norms that are considered basic would seem to be inadequate for our purposes. A rule that tells the judge to assign the plain meaning is often, for reasons of ambiguity, vagueness, contestability etc. comparable to instructions to install the TV set that contain the directive to install the TV just like usual, or, perhaps even worse and somewhat dystopian, install the TV the way the company making the TV intended. While it would be possible that the instruction is enough in some cases, in cases that are semantically problematic it would not be of much use.

IV. Conclusion

I will end with some of the conclusions from the previous discussion: first, understanding basic rules of interpretation as *constitutive norms* seems to be in line with contemporary doctrines of legal interpretation. If they are understood as constitutive rules, basic rules of interpretation are not able to guide behaviour because they are unable to motivate interpretative action. At best, they can function as beliefs about the kind of meaning that is relevant for legal interpretation. Second, basic rules of interpretation could guide interpretative behaviour if they are conceived of as certain kinds of regulative norms. Since *codifying norms* do not introduce new

[57] H-G Gadamer, *Truth and Method*, J Weinsheimer and DG Marshall trs (New York, Continuum, 2006) 306–10.

[58] R Guastini, 'A Realistic View on Law and Legal Cognition' (2014) *First Genoa-Slavic Seminar in Legal Theory* 1–2 (on file with author).

reasons for action, basic interpretative norms can guide behaviour in so far as they are *reason-instantiating norms* or *authoritative norms*, or a combination of both. The fact that basic interpretative norms have the same problems of indeterminacy that they are aimed at solving means that they can hardly guide interpretation in ascribing one determinate meaning to a legal text. Finally, for the same reasons of generality and vagueness, basic interpretative rules can hardly be thought of as instrumental norms even if instrumental norms were able to motivate an interpreter to act in a certain way (which they are not). Discussing the normativity of legal interpretation seems to lead us to two equally sceptical conclusions. Either: (a) it cannot be justifiably claimed that basic rules of interpretation guide interpretative behaviour in law; or (b) basic rules of interpretation are borderline useless in ascribing a determinate meaning to the legal text.[59]

[59] We could, conceivably, take a different road and claim that what we call basic rules of interpretation do not in fact play a motivational role in our practical reasoning, but that they play a doxastic role: Glüer and Pagin, 'Rules of Meaning and Practical Reasoning' (n 12) 211.

10

Another Way to Meet Hart's Challenge*

ANDREJ KRISTAN

I. Introduction

Almost 60 years have passed since Oxford's HLA Hart famously challenged conceptual rule-scepticism with a set of arguments that sum up in a 'swift and devastating' refutation, as one prominent commentator observes.[1] His challenge, addressed to legal realism, was designed to demonstrate the superiority of Hart's own (conventionalist) theory of the normativity of legal discourse. It is not my goal to argue, as other critics have, that Hart was wrong in ascribing conceptual rule-scepticism to legal realism of one form or the other.[2] Instead, I am willing to bite the bullet and claim that Hart's arguments would not go through even if he was right about some legal theorists. Moreover, I intend to undermine his own solution to the challenge and thus put the pressure on his followers. To set the stage, though, we shall first revisit Hart's most developed argument against conceptual rule-scepticism: the argument from the fallibility of final judicial decisions. (I leave the treatment of two other counter-arguments aside until the end of the chapter.)

* Parts of earlier versions of this argument have been presented and discussed in scholarly meetings at the Universities of Belgrade, Buenos Aires, Graz, Carlos III Madrid, Mar del Plata, Milan, Oxford, Alberto Hurtado, and Uppsala. I have benefited greatly from those meetings, as well as from some comments made in private conversations. I would like to thank in particular Sebastián Agüero San Juan, Juan Pablo Alonso, Eugenio Bulygin, Pierluigi Chiassoni, Andrea Dolcetti, James Edwards, Alessandro Ferrari, Edoardo Fittipaldi, Francisco García Gibson, Riccardo Guastini, María Victoria Inostroza, Miodrag Jovanović, Patricia Mindus, José Juan Moreso, Esteban Pereira Fredes, David Plunkett, Pablo Rapetti, Jorge Rodríguez, José María Sauca, Torben Spaak, Bojan Spaić, Michel Troper, and Silvia Zorzetto.

[1] See HLA Hart, 'Scandinavian Realism' (1959) 17 *The Cambridge Law Journal* 233; HLA Hart, *The Concept of Law* (Oxford, Clarendon Press, 1961) ch 7 for the challenge, and B Leiter, 'American Legal Realism' in MP Golding and WA Edmundson (eds), *The Blackwell Guide to the Philosophy of Law and Legal Theory* (Oxford, Blackwell Publishing, 2005) 62 for its qualification.

[2] See, eg, Leiter, 'American Legal Realism' (n 2); E Pattaro, 'From Hägerström to Ross and Hart' (2009) 22 *Ratio Juris* 532; S Eng, 'Lost in the System or Lost in Translation? The Exchanges between Hart and Ross' (2011) 24 *Ratio Juris* 194; F Schauer, 'Legal Realism Untamed' (2013) 91 *Texas Law Review* 749; J Holtermann, 'Getting real or staying positive: Legal Realism(s), Legal Positivism, and the Prospects of Naturalism in Jurisprudence' (2016) 29 *Ratio Juris* 535.

II. The Argument from Fallibility

Hart's argument from fallibility has two parts.[3] Put briefly and non exegetically, the first part of the argument comes down to this: one cannot account for the fallibility of final judicial decisions if one embraces scepticism about the existence of the rules governing a case before the final court chooses the relevant sources of law and interprets them. In particular, one cannot account for the fallibility of final decisions if one adopts what is best labelled a *decision theory of law* – which may be described as stating that the law concerning an event is whatever concrete final judgment a court will issue when the event is litigated.[4] It follows from this theory that final judgments cannot possibly be incorrect from the legal point of view and Hart considered it a problem.

The view that the decision theory of law is problematic is quite intuitive but so is, for example, the geocentric view that the Sun revolves around Earth (which, as we all know, is patently false). It seems that Hart was well aware that one can make one's case only if the argument is based on reason and not on mere intuition. Accordingly, he put much effort in construing an example that would prove the need of separating the notions of finality and infallibility of judicial rulings. The fact that a ruling is final, he argued, does not entail that it is legally irreproachable, for if it did – and that is the second part of his argument – there would be no fundamental dis-analogy between the real-world adjudicative discourse and a made-up game he called 'the game of Scorer's Discretion'.[5] Here is what he had in mind.

In Hart's fictitious game, the score is what the scorer says it is. That is 'the scoring rule'. Moreover, there is no sign of criticism seriously addressed to the scorer for misapplications of the scoring rule. In legal settings, by contrast, genuine criticisms frequently invoke misapplications of the law even when they are addressed to final rulings. The existence of such criticisms indicates a fundamental difference between Scorer's Discretion and legal adjudication.

Hart thought that in order to explain the difference in question, one has no other option but to assume that the result of legal adjudication, unlike that of Scorer's Discretion, is bound by rules established in advance. On this assumption, criticisms of judicial rulings obviously make sense (that is, as reactions to their perceived violations of pre-existing rules), as does the distinction between the finality and infallibility of court rulings.

This is an attractive argument, which has been found conclusive in the eyes of many legal scholars who nowadays consider the decision theory of law

[3] For Hart's own formulation of the argument, see Hart, 'Scandinavian Realism' (1959) and Hart, *The Concept of Law* (n 1) ch 7.

[4] Compare this description with MS Green, 'Leiter on Legal Realists' (2011) 30 *Law and Philosophy* 383, where the express indication that we are talking about a *final* judgement is missing.

[5] See Hart, *The Concept of Law* (n 1) 142–46.

as a paradigm example of conceptual rule-scepticism manifestly implausible. Nonetheless, the argument is also doubly flawed, as I intend to demonstrate in the next two sections of this chapter.[6] On the one hand, it is flawed because Hart's view is not the only explanation of the obvious dis-analogy between legal adjudication and Scorer's Discretion.[7] On the other hand, it is also flawed because Hart's own distinction of the former from the latter gives rise to a contradiction. Namely, it gives rise to the conclusion that it is sometimes legally correct to do that which is not legally correct.

III. A Paradox of Hart's Fallible Finality

We shall see in detail in this section how the paradox arises from Hart's theory of the normativity of legal discourse. I will also add that, unlike some other paradoxes, this one is easy to resolve. The problem is, however, that the resolution of the paradox does not speak in favour of upholding Hart's view.

Let us consider a non-legal paradox just to set the tone of what will follow later on. I have picked the barber paradox reported by Bertrand Russell about a century ago.[8] The story goes like this: you can define the barber as one who shaves all those, and only those, who do not shave themselves. That is, the barber is who shaves all those who do not shave themselves and only those who do not shave themselves. Now, ask yourself, 'Who shaves the barber? – Does the barber shave himself or not? – This question makes the paradox emerge and here is why: If you respond that our barber shaves himself, then we shall conclude according to the definition given above that he does not shave himself (for the barber only shaves those who do not shave themselves). But, if you respond that the barber does not shave himself, then we shall conclude – again by our initial definition – that he shaves himself (for the barber shaves all those who do not shave themselves). This, of course, is paradoxical because – however you respond – you just cannot get it right. The lesson of this story, as reported by Russell, is that we cannot satisfactorily define the barber as one who shaves all those, and those only, who do not shave themselves. We cannot define the barber satisfactorily in this way because this definition gives rise to a contradiction. Contradictions do not exist in the real world, so a definition that leads to a contradiction is wrong. It is therefore wrong to assume that we can define the barber satisfactorily as he was defined in the beginning of this story.

I want you to bear in mind this non-legal paradox, because I believe that a deficiency similar to that of Russell's working definition of barber ought to be

[6] See already A Kristan, 'A Paradox of Hart's Fallible Finality' (2016) *Analisi e diritto* 339 (though some parts of the argument presented in this chapter supersede that version).

[7] One may wonder why we should bother to explain the difference between legal adjudication and some fictitious game, but I leave this objection aside.

[8] See B Russell, 'The Logic of Philosophical Atomism' (1919) 29 *The Monist* 355.

attributed to Hart's characterisation of final judicial decisions as 'fallible' or possibly incorrect from the legal point of view.[9] My argument is short and simple. It has three elements (a, b, and c). Assume there is (a) a legally incorrect final decision in (b) a system with the rule to the effect that it is legally correct to comply with final judicial decisions. The paradox consists in that it is then legally correct to comply with what is legally incorrect. In other words (c):

(c) It is legally correct to do that which is not legally correct.

The question is, what is the appropriate response to this apparently paradoxical conclusion? In what follows, we will briefly test three usual philosophical strategies to deal with any paradox. The first strategy consists in dropping some of the assumptions which figure as the premises to the paradoxical conclusion; the second one attempts to disambiguate the words which generate the paradox (for example, 'barber', 'legally correct'), whereas the third one consists in denying that the paradox exists.

By analogy with the lesson drawn from the barber paradox above, one could suggest that one of our initial assumptions – (a) or (b) – is wrong. However, none of these two moves would work for Hart. If he dropped the first assumption, (a), he would reject the very possibility of their being a final judicial decision that was incorrect from the legal point of view. This would go straightforwardly against Hart's view. Moreover, if he dropped the second assumption, (b), the resulting theory would be inapplicable to any system with a rule to the effect that it is legally correct to comply with final judicial decisions. The resulting theory would therefore be inapplicable to almost any legal systems properly so called, which would make it uninteresting for the purposes of legal studies in the modern society. Accordingly, we shall put this strategy aside and turn to somewhat more sophisticated ways in which paradoxes usually get resolved.

One promising strategy consists in disambiguating the phrase 'legally correct' as the culprit of the reflexive fallacy in (c): it is legally correct to do that which is not legally correct. In this aim, one might use the famous distinction between 'legal validity' and 'applicability'. Indeed, it is not uncommon that judges in one legal system, especially in the cases of private international law, apply the rules that have no legal validity in that very system. So, one might *also* say in our case that

(c) It is legally correct *qua* applicable what is not legally correct *qua* valid.

In other words, one could say that (sometimes) a legally invalid judicial decision is applicable. Apparently, this solves the problem. *Or not …* for to say that a legally invalid decision is applicable is to say that the act of application of a legally invalid decision is legally valid. Therefore, it is also legally valid to comply with such an act of application, and to comply with it is just to comply with a decision that is legally invalid. It is thus legally valid to comply with what is legally invalid, and so the paradox remains in place.

[9] Hart, *The Concept of Law* (n 1) ch 7, wording is different, but nothing substantial hinges on this.

An effective way to resolve the paradox through disambiguation is rather to hold that it is legally correct *all things considered* to do that which is not legally correct *all things considered, but one rule* (ie the one regarding the authority of final judicial decisions). While this avoids the paradox, it also goes against Hart's basic stance that final judicial decisions are possibly incorrect from the legal point of view. As it turns out, *all things considered*, they never are.

Another of the more sophisticated strategies worth exploring here is the most lawyerly solution to the problem. This solution is based on the observation that, strictly speaking, what I call 'Hart's paradox' is but a special type of inconsistency stemming from the legal system as the system is construed, and it is perfectly consistent, *not* paradoxical, to describe that inconsistency with (c). On the one hand, there is the rule that one ought to comply with final decisions (hereafter named R_{FIN}). On the other hand, there is a rule violated by the final decision in question (say, R_X). If the final decision did not violate R_X, then there would be no inconsistency between what follows for the case at hand from R_{FIN} and R_X, respectively. This is why the inconsistency is of a special type: it is contingent. The two rules only come into conflict when applied to a concrete case of a final decision violating R_X. This type of inconsistency is not so rare a phenomenon as to leave us perplexed in the way the barber paradox does.[10] Indeed, practising lawyers are trained to face such inconsistencies (among others). They solve most of them by means of the traditional meta-principles of preference, which are based on the criteria of hierarchy (superior rules prevail over inferior ones), specificity (more specific rules prevail over more general ones), and posteriority (subsequent rules prevail over earlier ones). So, let us check what these criteria say about our case. Given that R_{FIN} is part of the ideal of rule of law,[11] I take it that R_{FIN} clearly belongs to the highest level in the hierarchy of laws, and has the highest grade of generality, in the sense that it applies to all cases. Hence, the application of R_{FIN} ought to be given preference over the application of R_X in most cases, but not always. The opposite is true in the instance of R_X being posterior to, or less general than R_{FIN}, while having the same rank in the hierarchy.

On the face of it, this lawyerly analysis permits us to dismiss the 'paradox' as unworthy of serious consideration and to precisely identify the circumstances in which it is *safe* to speak of fallible finality without being over-scrupulous. But is it, really? Arguably, *it is not*. To see why not, we shall think of three possible scenarios with the rare circumstances just described. In the first (and the most unlikely) scenario, the fact that R_X ought to trump R_{FIN} is brought to the attention of a court that accepts the case for consideration. (I will say in a moment what

[10] See W Malgaud, 'Les antinomies en droit. A propos de l'étude de G Gavazzi' (1964) 18 *Dialectica* 18 (*l'antinomie accidentelle*) or R Guastini, *Interpretare e argomentare* (Milano, Giuffrè Editore, 2011) 107 (*l'antinomia in concreto*). See also T Mazarese, 'Antinomie, paradossi e logica deontica' (1984) 61 *Rivista internazionale di filosofia del diritto* 419 (*paranomia*).

[11] See, eg, *Brumărescu v Romania*, no 28342/95, § 61, ECHR 1999-VII, which started a clear and constant case law of the European Court of Human Rights on this point.

follows from this.) In the second scenario, the courts reject considering the case. In the third scenario, the issue is not even brought before a court. Now, in the first scenario the issue is resolved through (constitutional) interpretation operated by the courts in a new final decision. By that very fact, the previous decision, which violates R_X and has been hitherto protected by R_{FIN}, loses the status of finality. Therefore, it does not count as an example of a legally incorrect final decision even though it is erroneous, all things considered. In the second and the third scenario, however, the solution confirmed in our final decision prevails regardless of what ought to be the case by virtue of the meta-principles of preference mentioned earlier. This means that in the second and the third scenario, the characterisation of the final decision as legally incorrect has no legal consequence whatsoever.

To my knowledge, neither Hart nor his followers have offered a similar analysis to correct – and therefore to narrow – the usual scope of application of the notion of fallible finality. However, it appears that Hart would have accepted its conclusion. He explicitly admitted that it may seem 'pedantic' to distinguish, in cases of *res judicatae*, between finality and legal infallibility of the court ruling precisely because 'the statement that the court was "wrong" has no consequences within the system'.[12] Nonetheless, he decided to embrace the said conceptual distinction, as we have seen in the previous section, because he saw no other way of explaining the difference between legal adjudication and Scorer's Discretion. I will now show that another way exists. If my argument succeeds, it will give us an alternative account of the normativity of legal discourse that meets Hart's challenge without falling into legally irrelevant pedantry.

IV. An Alternative Account of the Normativity of Legal Discourse

The first aim of this final section is to distinguish legal adjudication from Scorer's Discretion in a way compatible with one's assumption of conceptual rule-scepticism and, in particular, with the decision theory of law. This means that my argument will be developed here under the assumption that final judicial decisions constitute the law for the cases in question just like the scorer's decisions do in the game of Scorer's Discretion. A fundamental difference between them will be drawn, however, in terms of a (pragmatic) presupposition that is constitutive of an interpreter's participation in the former but absent from any instance of the latter.

The second aim of this section is to make sense of the fallibility of final judicial decisions in a way that is compatible, again, with our previous assumption. Now, obviously, one cannot say that final decisions constitute the law for their respective

[12] Hart, *The Concept of Law* (n 1) 141.

cases and then explain the fallibility of such decisions in terms of violation of the very legal rules they constitute. Therefore, I will subscribe here to the view that final decisions are legally infallible or irreproachable and I will propose to separate the fallibility criterion for final decisions from the content of the law. In short, I intend to make sense of genuine criticisms of final rulings by reference to the aforementioned pragmatic presupposition, which is part not of the law but of the adjudicative discourse as a game-like social practice. Here is how we can do that.

Instead of assuming that the result of legal adjudication is bound by rules established in advance (unlike the result of Scorer's Discretion), the alternative account I am putting forward consists of pointing to the following (pragmatic) presupposition, which is constitutive of participation in legal adjudication but absent from any game of Scorer's Discretion: *Interpreters in legal adjudication purportedly agree with the lawgiver. Their decisions, or proposals thereof, are based on the sources of law and are not a mere fiat of discretion.*

To see the point, think of an umpire who, when publicly stating his decision, says that its content is in disagreement with every pre-existing authoritative pronouncement that is relevant to the case at hand. Such a disagreement would be conceptually impossible under the scoring rule ('the score is what the scorer says it is'), because there is no way for the scorer to break this constitutive rule of Scorer's Discretion, and by that very fact, step out of the game. By contrast, such stepping out is possible in legal adjudication. Were a judge to make the same statement as the umpire above – that is, were he to state, when he makes his decision public, that its content is in disagreement with every pre-existing authoritative pronouncement relevant for the case at hand (constitutional clauses, statutory provisions, judicial precedents, etc) – we would say that he is not acting as a judge. His decision-making speech act, I believe, would be deemed pragmatically infelicitous.[13] One promising explanation for this infelicity is that the judge denied the said presupposition of agreeing with the lawgiver. Because of such a step out, we would not be talking about a legally incorrect judicial decision. Rather, his decision would simply not count as judicial.

Based on these considerations, we can now explain the criticism of judicial rulings without assuming that these rulings are bound by rules established in advance. Therefore, we can also explain the criticism of such *final* rulings without embracing the problematic notion of (legally) fallible finality. Indeed, criticisms of judicial rulings make sense as expressions of a perceived presupposition failure of those rulings. In other words, they purport to show, contrary to the presupposition in question, that a given ruling is in fact in disagreement with the relevant sources of law (either because the relevant sources are thought to be different from those actually considered by the judge, or because the ruling is deemed incompatible with the sources that were rightly considered relevant).

[13] See JL Austin, *How to Do Things with Words: The William James Lectures delivered at Harvard University in* 1955, JO Urmson and M Sbisà eds (Oxford, Clarendon Press, 1962) 2nd Lecture.

Two more observations are in order. First, as you have seen, the presupposition in question is vague to the extent that it has borderline cases causing pervasive and intractable disagreements. Second, if the presupposition in question were semantic rather than pragmatic in character, the presupposition failure would affect the correctness of what is said.[14] But since we have to do with a pragmatic presupposition, the fact that this is not accepted by (some part of) the audience does not affect the ruling's correctness as such. This explains why you can also criticise final judicial decisions even if you accept, as the conceptual rule-sceptics do, that final judicial decisions cannot possibly be incorrect from the legally relevant point of view.

We have now arrived almost at the end of this chapter. With the aim of laying the basis for a solid theory of the normativity of legal discourse, I have suggested to avoid the drawback of Hart's theory and to face his challenge for the decision theory of law as the paradigm case of conceptual rule-scepticism. I have described the challenge as a set of arguments in the beginning, but so far we have only seen a refutation of the argument from fallibility. To meet the challenge, and thus rehabilitate the theory in question as a plausible theory of law, one would have to face at least two more objections.

The first additional objection starts by asking what the 'law' is on a given matter. On the decision theory of law, to ask 'What the law is?' is to ask 'How will the judge decide the case?' But even if the non-judicial uses of the former question may be understood this way, as Hart concedes for the sake of argument only,[15] its judicial uses cannot have that meaning. Otherwise, a judge who asks herself *what ought she do according to the law* turns out to be asking herself, *what will she do in fact*, which is clearly not the case.[16] As you may have perceived, though, this objection is a straw man fallacy. It is a straw man because it ignores that on the theory in question, the law concerning an event is the *final* ruling of the court – and the status of finality somewhat escapes the will of the judge of the case at hand. The judge who asks herself what ought she do according to the law is thus actually asking what ought she do in order for her ruling to be accepted as final. Accordingly, the question is not what the judge will do. The question is what the community will do. Will the community accept the decision as final or not? When the judge asks herself what ought she do according to the law, she is therefore asking what ought she do in order for the community to accept it as a final judicial decision. The first additional objection is therefore refuted.

[14] One example of a semantic presupposition is this: 'The set of bald monarchs includes the actual King of France' presupposes that there is actually a King of France. It is common to understand that the presupposing sentence is false not because the King of France is not bald but rather because the semantic content of the sentence in question presupposes incorrectly that there is actually a King of France. Here, the presupposition failure affects the correctness of what is said.

[15] See Hart, 'Scandinavian Realism' (n 1) 237.

[16] See Leiter, 'American Legal Realism' (n 1) 62 for one recent version of this argument.

The second additional objection against conceptual rule-scepticism consists in saying something along these lines: if there were no legal rules whatsoever before a competent authority chooses the relevant sources of law and interprets them in a final ruling, then it would be impossible to identify the competent authority in advance. However, in most cases, the parties and their lawyers have no problem identifying the competent authorities before getting to a final decision, and the theory in question cannot explain it. This, too, is often understood as a 'fatal' argument against conceptual rule-scepticism and, in particular, the decision theory of law.[17] But, to my mind, the argument is flawed and can be easily dismissed once we are aware of the presupposition mentioned in the first part of this section. Indeed, one need not refer to the law that identifies the competent authorities in concrete cases to explain successful identification of the competent authorities. Instead, the same can be explained by pointing to the sources of law which are commonly invoked as relevant in similar cases. The sources of law have this guiding function precisely because there is a presupposition to the effect that judicial decisions agree with the relevant sources of law.

That having been said, conceptual rule-scepticism and, in particular, the decision theory of law may have other flaws and even serious issues to address.[18] But they are not to be rejected on the basis of three arguments discussed above and usually deployed against them ever since Hart's challenge.

[17] A version of this argument has recently been used in Green, 'Leiter on Legal Realists' (n 4) 408.

[18] See A Kristan and M Vignolo, 'Assessment Sensitivity in Legal Discourse' (2017) 61(4) *Inquiry. An Interdisciplinary Journal of Philosophy* 394 for a recent analysis of its underlying semantics.

11

The Constraining Force of Analogies and the Role of the Judge

KATHARINA STEVENS

I. Introduction

Analogy plays an important role in the application and development of the law, especially – but not only – in common law countries where judicial decisions enter the law through the doctrine of precedent. However, scholars disagree about how far reaching the importance of analogy is. There is no consensus on whether reasoning by analogy stands behind all (or almost all) judicial decision making with precedents,[1] or whether it is restricted to decisions made with non-binding precedent-cases.[2] Nonetheless, it is widely recognised that the fact that two cases are analogous is often treated as a reason to decide the new case in accordance with the precedent-case.

Unfortunately, there is reason to doubt whether precedents can actually constrain judges when they make decisions based on analogies between cases. This is so because reasoning by analogy refers to similarities and differences between two cases, and similarities and differences can be found between *any* two cases. Judges who are allowed to use analogies to justify their decisions might therefore not be adequately restricted. They can always find some similarities and differences to support their decisions in either direction, no matter how idiosyncratic those decisions might be. Analogies might only be useful for giving the *appearance* of a legal justification for judicial decisions; they might not actually provide any *normative guidance* for judges when they decide cases. The problem, in Frederick Schauer's words, is that analogies might be 'always a friend, never a foe'.[3]

[1] See, eg, L Weinreb, *Legal Reason. The Use of Analogy in Legal Argument* (New York, Cambridge University Press, 2016).

[2] For example, G Lamond, 'Precedent and Analogy in Legal Reasoning' in EN Zalta (ed), *The Stanford Encyclopedia of Philosophy* (Spring 2016 edition) and G Lamond, 'Analogical Reasoning in the Common Law' (2014) 34 *Oxford Journal of Legal Studies* 567.

[3] F Schauer, 'Why Precedent in Law (and Elsewhere) Is Not Totally (or Even Substantially) about Analogy' in C Dahlman and E Feteris (eds), *Legal Argumentation Theory: Cross-Disciplinary Perspectives* (Dordrecht, Springer, 2013).

If this objection should turn out to be well founded, then the fact that analogies are widely used in judicial decision making should be worrying. After all, judges should decide cases according to legal reasons instead of their own hunches, at least as far as that is possible. Parties expect that the law will decide their dispute, not the personal opinion of the judge. But if analogies in judicial decision making cannot be anything but a smokescreen behind which judges are left to decide according to their own preferences, then they cannot be deciding based on legal reasons. Importantly, this problem does not only arise where judges use analogical reasoning to decide whether they are faced with a binding precedent. Persuasive precedents also have to be able to constraint judges to some degree in order to provide a way in which the law can influence judicial decisions. This is important even though the needed constraint only amounts to providing a legal reason that a judge has to outweigh with other reasons if she wants to resist deciding according to the precedent decision.

In this paper, I aim to provide some relief from this worry. I claim that in so far as judges respect their institutional roles, they are indeed constrained with respect to the decisions they reach when they reason analogically. I concede that arguers trying to convince an audience can use analogies as powerful argumentative tools that will be able to help them argue in either direction on a given subject. However, I argue that the institutional role of judges also determines the argumentative role they should play when deciding cases: judges are not supposed to reason as arguers, freely choosing tools to support their conclusions. Rather, judges are meant to fulfil the argumentative role of interlocutors, understanding and evaluating arguments for or against deciding their cases in a certain way. While analogies are always the friend of the arguer (though weak analogies can easily reveal themselves as unreliable friends) they might well turn out to be the foe of the interlocutor. Interlocutors are faced with the task of understanding and evaluating arguments, and therefore feel any argumentative force the analogy might have. Arguments by analogy, correctly understood, exert such argumentative force through their rhetorical properties. If we take into account both the role-specific restrictions that rest on judges and the rhetorical properties of analogies, then it becomes clear that precedents exert constraint, even where they are offered as source-analogues.

II. The Worry Explained

On first sight, comparing reasoning with precedent to reasoning by analogy seems like a good idea. It is hard to miss the analogy[4] between the way arguments by analogy are usually described, and the way the doctrine of precedent is usually described. A precedent-case that is similar to a present-case provides a reason

[4] Pun intended.

to decide the present-case in the same way as the precedent-case. Arguments by analogy work by asserting the similarity of two objects or situations in order to support the existence of a further similarity – or the claim that the two should be treated similarly.[5] It is hard not to be seduced by this, at least if we assume that arguments by analogy provide real justificatory support for a conclusion.

Unfortunately, there is a feature of reasoning with precedents that disturbs the ease with which we can compare it to reasoning by analogy: precedents *constrain* judicial decision making.[6] In an early paper on reasoning with precedent, Frederick Schauer brings this feature into focus in the following way: 'The previous treatment of occurrence X in manner Y constitutes, solely because of its historical pedigree, a reason for treating X in manner Y if and when X again occurs'.[7] A binding precedent gives a judge a sufficient reason to repeat the precedent decision in the present-case that is similar to it in all legally relevant respects.[8] An applicable persuasive precedent gives her at least an additional reason to reach the decision parallel to that in the precedent.[9] If reasoning by analogy is a plausible model with which we can understand reasoning with precedent, then we need to be able to show that reasoning by analogy can be the basis for this constraint. Analogies would have to provide judges with reasons, not just with the opportunity to pretend as if there were reasons. But it is not at all clear that they do. Indeed, there are legal theorists who doubt this very much.[10]

Larry Alexander and Emily Sherwin, for example, deny the existence of reasoning by analogy altogether: 'One cannot "reason" by analogy'.[11] The problem is that for some mental process to count as reasoning, it has to be possible to describe how it determines whether or not to treat something as a reason in the first place. But analogies operate over similarities. Which means that, in theory, the similarity of two cases is supposed to provide a reason (sometimes even a conclusive reason) for a judge to decide their present-case according to the precedent-case. But if any two cases will likely share many similarities as well as many differences, then a

[5] See, eg, LA Groarke and CW Tindale, *Good Reasoning Matters* (Canada, Oxford University Press Canada, 2008) 341ff.

[6] This difference has been highlighted for example by Frederick Schauer and Grant Lamond: F Schauer, 'Why Precedent in Law' (n 3); F Schauer, *Thinking Like A Lawyer* (Cambridge, Harvard University Press, 2012); G Lamond, 'Precedent and Analogy in Legal Reasoning' (n 2). Barbara Baum Levenbook emphasises that precedents bind even if their decisions are not justified: B Baum Levenbook, 'The Meaning of a Precedent' (2001) 6 *Legal Theory* 185.

[7] F Schauer, 'Precedent' (1987) 39 *Stanford Law Review* 571.

[8] And therefore – with respect to its legally interesting components – the same.

[9] The strength of this reason will depend on the kind of persuasive precedent. See Lamond, 'Analogical Reasoning in the Common Law' (n 2) for a discussion of the different degrees of strength persuasive precedent can exert.

[10] For example: Schauer, 'Why Precedent in Law' (n 3); L Alexander and E Sherwin, *Demystifying Legal Reasoning* (Cambridge, Cambridge University Press, 2008) but also, to some extent, D Hunter, 'Reason is Too Large: Analogy and Precedent in Law' (2001) 50 *Emory Law Journal* 1197, who sees analogy in the service of the reasoner rather than constraining her.

[11] Alexander and Sherwin, *Demystifying Legal Reasoning* (n 10) 65.

decision has to be made: are the two cases *overall* more similar than they are different? Or is it the other way around?

Usually, we determine that one case should be decided like another with recourse to principles and rules. If a rule applies to two cases, then both cases shall be treated according to the rule, and they are similar in so far as the rule applies to both of them. But reasoning by analogy is supposed to work directly from one case to the next, without the use of rules.[12] Therefore, the question remains how judges can determine, through reasoning by analogy, that two cases are similar in the right way. Or in other words: how can judges determine whether some similarities between cases are important enough to say that the decision in the precedent-case counts as a legal reason for deciding the present-case according to it – while other similarities are not important in this manner? Alexander and Sherwin fear that this happens simply through intuition.[13] The judge simply sees or feels that *these* two cases are similar in the right way. That would be problematic because it is highly obscure where our intuitions come from. There is no reason to assume that idiosyncratic beliefs, prejudices, even moods could not have a strong influence on what we intuitively believe to be the case. If judges simply intuit that two cases are overall similar or dissimilar, why should we trust that they make their decisions on legal grounds and not based on their own preferences?

This is then the problem as it presents itself: if reasoning by analogy is supposed to provide the basis on which to explain reasoning with precedents, it has to be possible to show that it can be constraining. We need to see that it is not just a fancy name for mere intuition, even without the use of rules or principles. This, as it turns out, is easier said than done.[14]

Taking a closer look at how reasoning by analogy is explained according to the (still) leading model in the cognitive sciences only seems to deepen the problem. According to this position, developed by scientists such as Holoyak, Thagard and Gentner, analogies work through the mapping of features from a source to a target.[15] Take, for example, the analogy 'People are like sheep'. Here, 'sheep' is

[12] That reasoning by precedent is based on, or has anything to do with reasoning by analogy is not a self-evident claim. Authors like Larry Alexander, Emily Sherwin and, to some extent, also Fredrick Schauer advocate a so-called rule-account for reasoning by precedent, according to which each precedent either provides a rule or follows one established in an earlier precedent. See Alexander and Sherwin, *Demystifying Legal Reasoning* (n 10), and Schauer, *Thinking Like A Lawyer* (n 6). I do not believe that these accounts work any better, but this is not the place to discuss their advantages and disadvantages. In this paper I am interested in the question whether reasoning by analogy *can* be constraining *if* it is to be taken as the basis for reasoning with precedents.

[13] Alexander and Sherwin, *Demystifying Legal Reasoning* (n 10) 68ff.

[14] For attempts, see eg, S Brewer, 'Exemplary Reasoning: Semantics, Pragmatics, and the Rational Force of Legal Argument by Analogy' (1996) 109 *Harvard Law Review* 923; E Levi, *An Introduction To Legal Reasoning* (Chicago, University of Chicago Press, 1967); Weinreb, *Legal Reason* (n 1); Schauer, 'Precedent' (n 7). As mentioned above, Schauer later adopted a rule-account of reasoning by precedent.

[15] See, eg KJ Holoyak and P Thagard, *Mental Leaps: Analogy in Creative Thought* (Cambridge, MIT Press, 1996); D Gentner, 'Structure Mapping – A Theoretical Framework for Analogy' (1983) 7 *Cognitive Science* 155.

the source analogue, used to say something about the target, 'people'. 'Mapping' describes the process in which features of the target-analogue are identified for features of the source-analogue and from now on treated as their respective equivalents. In 'People are like sheep', for example, we might want to map 'sheep live in herds' onto 'people live in social groups'. In analogical mapping, this process is guided by constraints on two levels. First, on the surface level, equivalents are preferred that have similar sensory properties (for example the analogues are both red) or can get sorted into the same categories, the narrower the better (for example 'is a mammal' is better than 'is a living thing'). And second on the structural level equivalents are preferred if not only the features, but also the relations between them, can be mapped from source to target. For example, the mapping 'sheep have lambs' and 'people have children' becomes stronger if we can also map 'sheep care for their lambs' onto 'people care for their children'. Once source and target have been aligned in this way, analogical inferences can be made. Such an inference takes a step from the existence of a feature in the source-analogue to the assumption that a similar feature exists in the target analogue. This step is supported by earlier successful mappings between aspects of the source analogue that are inferentially connected to the aspect of the source-analogue that is supposed to be transferred.[16] Once 'people' and 'sheep' are mapped – for example by connecting the docile and obedient nature of sheep to its equivalents in humans – transfers can be made of other sheep-properties that are inferentially connected to their being docile and obedient. For example: sheep will follow the barking sheep-dog, and if people are like them in docility and obedience then they will follow a confident, loud leader.

Importantly, which aspects of an object we concentrate on influences our overall understanding of that object, and this supports our ability to find and understand analogies. When drawing an analogy, we seek out and concentrate mainly on those features of the analogues that can be successfully mapped. For example, when drawing the analogy between sheep and people, we are mainly interested in the features these two could be said to have in common. With attention being a scarce commodity in the human mind, the attempt to understand an analogy makes differences step into the background of our thinking. Under the influence of the analogy, the mind forms a (possibly new) perspective on people, one in which they appear to us as sheep. We now concentrate on this new picture of people and might forget about their other qualities. The analogy could lead us, for example, to despair because we now think of people as creatures that cannot be trusted to oppose unjust authorities, just as sheep will let the sheepdog guide them to their death. It is worth stressing that in the process of analogical mapping, we reconstruct our understanding of one subject-matter according to our understanding of another. This means that analogies can offer us new understandings

[16] For an account of this from argumentation theory, see A Juthe, 'Argument by Analogy' (2005) 19 *Argumentation* 1.

of old subject-matters – understandings of them *as similar* to the chosen source-analogue. Thus, analogies do not simply rely on similarities we have already recognised – rather, they lead us to appreciate new ones.[17] This is why, with a little effort, we can construe ways in which even analogies that seem strange at first start to make sense. I am sure the reader can come up with a useful way to understand 'people are like bats', if she just gives it a try.

That analogies make similarities appear where we did not see them before is especially worrisome when we take into account that people pick their source analogues under a 'purpose constraint' – they pick them according to how they want to use them.[18] This means that arguers select source analogues that will make the target analogue appear in the light that they want to present it in. If, for example, I want to convince you that human beings are generally untrustworthy, I will pick the analogue 'wolf' rather than the analogue 'dog'. I do this because wolves, rather than dogs, are seen as untrustworthy in the common-understanding's eye. Further, I might pick 'snake' rather than 'wolf' because the stereotype of snakes attributes to them properties that are inferentially connected to untrustworthiness. The stereotypical snake is sly, selfish and smart, properties that – if mapped successfully – will support the transfer of the property 'untrustworthy'. When I present you with the analogy between snakes and humans, I prompt you to reconstruct your understanding of humans according to your understanding of snakes. Because that understanding is then in the foreground of your attention, I have made you more receptive to the idea that humans should be mistrusted.

But if this is the case, then it seems that only two conclusions about judicial analogical reasoning with precedents are possible. Either, like for example Hunter has done,[19] we take this to be a good reason to accept the claims of American Legal Realists. Then we might think that judges,[20] deep down, make decisions according to their own estimation of how the cases should be decided and use 'legal reasons' merely as smokescreens.

[17] See, eg, Max Black who has written on this in M Black, *Models and Metaphors: Studies in Language and Philosophy* (Ithaca, Cornell University Press, 1981). Donald Schoen describes an especially illustrative case where a metaphor (the sister of analogy) opened up new understandings: researchers could not understand why a new type of paintbrush with artificial bristles would not distribute the paint as evenly as natural-hair paintbrushes until someone suggested to see the paintbrush as similar to a pump. This directed attention away from the bristles and to the spaces between them, revealing what the problem was: see D Schoen, 'Generative Metaphor: A Perspective on Problem-Setting in Social Policy' in A Ortony (ed), *Metaphor and Thought* (Cambridge, Cambridge University Press, 2012).

[18] See, eg Holoyak and Thagard, *Mental Leaps* (n 15) and JE Hummel and K Holyoak, 'Distributed Representations of Structure: A Theory of Analogical Access and Mapping' (1997) 104 *Psychological Review* 427.

[19] Hunter, 'Reason is Too Large' (n 10).

[20] Especially in appeal courts. See Leiter's very helpful piece on American Legal Realism: B Leiter, 'American Legal Realism' in W Edmundson and M Golding (eds), *The Blackwell Guide to Philosophy of Law and Legal Theory* (Malden, Blackwell Publishers, 2005), as well as J Stone, 'The Ratio of the Ratio Decidendi' (1959) 22 *The Modern Law Review* 597 and K Llewellyn, 'Remarks in the Theory of Appellate Decision and the Rules or Canons about how Statutes are to be Construed' (1950) 3 *Vanderbilt Law Review* 395.

Or, if we want to preserve precedent-constraint, we deny that analogical reasoning has much to do with reasoning with precedent. Frederick Schauer comes to this conclusion in his rather unambiguously entitled paper 'Why Precedent in Law (and Elsewhere) is Not Totally (or Even Substantially) About Analogy'.[21] He argues against the importance of analogous reasoning in the law by pointing out that precedents constrain reasoners and often force them to make decisions they would otherwise have preferred not to make. In this, he claims, they are utterly unlike source analogues which the reasoner chooses according to her impression of whether they will be helpful in making a decision or persuading someone.

I think that there is a further way to react. It is possible to show that the very ability of analogies to make two subject-matters appear similar can be used as the basis on which the constraining force of precedents through analogical reasoning can be established. I argue that precedent can be constraining for judges, even if they reason analogously – but only where judges take their role within the legal system seriously. The normative force of analogy for judicial decision making is then dependent on the normative force of the judicial role.

III. Judges as Interlocutors

When talking about reasoning by precedent or judicial reasoning more generally, it is easy to imagine the judge as a lone thinker, wrestling with a problem all by herself. But this picture is rather undifferentiated. People reason under different circumstances, with different goals and – importantly – from within different roles that they need to fulfil. When judges reason about a case they should do this with a different goal and from a different role than if an attorney reasons about the same case. It is not easy to account for any of these factors when discussing reasoning with the lone thinker in mind. I believe that we can gain a bit more clarity when we introduce the concept of an argument into our deliberations.

We imagine the lone thinker as deliberating over reasons. However, reasons do not just appear in our heads with a big sign, identifying them as 'a reason' and as carrying a certain rational weight. A great part of the reasoning a judge has to engage involves discerning whether the precedent actually provides a legal reason with respect to the present-case at all. And even though we say that we 'give each other reasons' when we are trying to convince each other of one claim or another, what we really do is present arguments. An argument is not the same as a reason. If I present you with an argument for φ, then I have merely *purported* to give you a reason for φ. Whether I have actually given you a reason for φ is not clear; it depends on whether the argument is at least minimally good. For example, let us take for granted, for a moment, that it is a reason for you to drink orange

[21] Schauer, 'Why Precedent in Law' (n 3).

juice if someone with expertise on the subject claims that orange juice is healthy. Now imagine I present you with this argument:

> Albert Einstein said that orange juice is healthy.
>
> Therefore you should drink orange juice.

This argument has the general form of an appeal to authority. Let us assume that in presenting it, my general demeanour has indicated that I am trying to give you an expertise based reason to drink orange juice. But I have in fact not given you any such reason. Albert Einstein is not an expert with respect to the healthiness of drinks, and so the argument is very bad; it is so bad in, fact, that it presents no reason at all.

When it comes to presenting arguments in the *attempt* to give reasons for φ (or in the attempt to make someone *believe* that they have been given a reason), we can distinguish at least two basic roles: first, there is the one who composes and presents the argument for φ; the arguer. And then there is the one to whom the argument for φ is presented and who has to determine whether the argument does indeed carry a reason for φ; the audience.

Importantly, depending on whether someone approaches reasoning by analogy from the role of an arguer or from the role of the audience will make a big difference. Earlier, I imagined that I had the purpose of convincing you that human beings are generally untrustworthy. Under those circumstances, I would pick the source-analogue 'snake' rather than the source-analogue 'dog'. I described myself in the role of the arguer, choosing the structure and content of an argument I wanted to present you with. As an arguer, I experience great freedom when I reason analogically in order to form an effective argument. I know the conclusion I want to defend, and so I know both my target-analogue and what I want to claim about it. But I can choose my source analogue freely. I can pick snakes over wolves and wolves over dogs. Guided by my purpose of showing that humans are not trustworthy, I pick that source-analogue which will serve best to generate an understanding of humans that supports my conclusion.

Analogies are in general a preferred tool for arguers wishing to convince an audience. They are extremely effective at guiding others to adopt certain points of view, even at making them accept conclusions they might otherwise have rejected. For this reason, analogies are widely regarded as an effective rhetorical tool, and discussed as such in the literature on argumentation.[22] In argument, they are *persuasive*, because they have the *rhetorical* property of encouraging people to develop a point of view of a subject matter that is favourable to the arguer's conclusion.

[22] See, eg C Perelman, *The Realm of Rhetoric* (Notre Dame, The University of Notre Dame Press, 1982); L Bermejo-Luque, 'A Unitary Schema for Arguments By Analogy' (2012) 32 *Informal Logic* 1; L Bermejo-Luque, 'The Uses of Analogy' and E Fischer, 'Messing Up the Mind? Analogical Reasoning with Metaphors', both in HJ Ribeiro, *Systematic Approaches to Argument by Analogy* (Dordrecht, Springer, 2014).

The reason, though, why arguments by analogy are so rhetorically effective is because the freedom that the arguer feels in choosing the source-analogue does not exist equally for the audience. The audience does not choose the source-analogue, the target-analogue or the conclusion. They are provided with all three by the arguer. I tell you: 'Humans are like snakes, so they are untrustworthy'. And, importantly, if you want to determine whether the argument provides you with a reason to accept the conclusion, then you will have to try to understand the analogy under my pre-chosen purpose-constraint: you have to try and see *that* similarity between source and target which encourages an understanding of the target under which the conclusion becomes as plausible as possible. This means that you have to attempt mappings of aspects that are inferentially connected to the aspect marked by the conclusion as the one meant to be transferred. If I tell you: 'People are like snakes, so they are untrustworthy' – and you answer: 'I am not sure whether having two eyes makes you untrustworthy' – then you have not successfully rejected my argument. Instead, you just demonstrated that you did not understand it in the first place.[23] Only *after* you have understood the analogy as I meant it can you criticise it – by showing the unimportance of similarities, the importance of differences or by taking the role of the arguer and finding a different source-analogue. For a reasoner in the role of the audience, then, the analogical argument has a strongly guiding effect on the mind: by contemplating an argumentative analogy, the reasoner in the role of the audience opens herself up to the analogy's effects. She generates an understanding of the target that presents it as similar to the source in a way that supports the conclusion.

The difference between the way arguers and audiences relate to argumentative analogies makes the question what the argumentative role of the judge is interesting. In the next section, I will argue that judges, if they take their institutional role seriously, should adopt an argumentative role that is one variety of the basic role of audience: that of an interlocutor.

A. Are Judges Arguers or Audiences?

Judges operate and reason within an institutional framework that gives them a clearly defined, functional, institutional role. The judge is an adjudicator, making decisions with regard to normative questions that will usually have a considerable impact on the people these decisions are made about. As Lon Fuller explains, the adjudicative framework – in contrast to a negotiation or an election – is a framework for decision-making that gives a 'formal and institutional expression to the influence of reasoned argument in human affairs'.[24] And importantly, it is meant

[23] See Bermejo-Luque, 'The Uses of Analogy' (n 22) 8 for a discussion of this property of arguments by analogy.

[24] L Fuller, 'The Forms and Limits of Adjudication' (1978) 92 *Harvard Law Review* 353, 366.

to give the parties the opportunity to have their claims and arguments heard.[25] These claims and arguments, if the adjudicative system is not to be a mere sham, should be given influence over the ultimate decision: the judge is meant to base her decision, at least in great part, on her evaluation of the arguments that were presented to her by the parties. Of course, Lon Fuller is writing this with the adversarial system in mind, and goes on to defend the ideas of this system against its counterpart, the inquisitorial system.[26] And indeed, the roles of the judge in these two systems are importantly different.[27] However, I do believe that his basic idea about the foundation of the adjudicative framework as one meant to give influence to reasoned argument holds in both systems: in both systems it is realised by giving the parties the opportunity to argue their case and to present theories about how and on what legal grounds the case should be decided.[28] In both systems we find the ideal of judicial impartiality – the idea that the judge may not favour one party over the other before all evidence has been considered and all arguments evaluated.[29] Based on the institutional role of the judge, we can therefore say that

[25] ibid 365.

[26] This is an important point because precedent plays a role in both adversarial and inquisitorial systems. Generally, the adversarial system is associated with common law jurisdictions, while the inquisitorial system is associated with civil law jurisdictions. However, it has been argued that this connection is not necessary, and that either combination should be possible, if maybe difficult to achieve. See, eg, DA Sklansky, 'Anti-Inquisitorialism' (2008) 122 *Harvard Law Review* 1634. And while precedent plays a much more important role in common law jurisdictions, it is still important in civil law jurisdictions. See, eg, RW Emerson, 'Judges as Guardian Angels: the German Practice of Hints and Feedback' (2015) 48 *Vanderbilt Journal of Transnational Law* 709, 713.

[27] The adversarial system is characterised by a mostly passive judge who is provided with the facts and details of the case, the pleas, etc by the parties. See, eg, S Landsman, 'A Brief Survey of the Development of the Adversarial System' (1983) 44 *Ohio State Law Journal* 713. In the pure form of the adversarial system, the judge does not intervene, except in order to preserve orderly proceedings: she does not, for example, ask witnesses questions or point out mistakes. The role of the judge in the inquisitorial system is much more active: here the judge questions witnesses herself, investigates into the facts of the case and is empowered and – at least in Germany – obligated to point out where she believes parties are making mistakes or missing the opportunity to give an argument about an important piece of evidence. See, eg JH Langbein, 'The German Advantage in Civil Procedure' (1985) 52 *University of Chicago Law Review* 823; L Weinreb and JH Langbein, 'Comparative Criminal Procedure: "Myth" and Reality' (1978) *Faculty Scholarship Series* Paper 532; Emerson, 'Judges as Guardian Angels' (n 26).

[28] It is unlikely that a purely adversarial or inquisitorial system actually exists anyway. In the US, for example, judges give credence to *amicus* briefs. See BJ Gorod, 'The Adversarial Myth: Appellate Court Extra-Record Factfinding' (2011) 61 *Duke Law Journal* 1. They have been given leniency to take on a more managerial role in 'big' litigation (see J Resnik, 'Managerial Judges' (1982) *Yale Law School Faculty Scholarship Series* paper 951). In addition, they are empowered to explain basic legal requirements etc to *pro se* litigants (see J Steinberg, 'Adversary Breakdown and Judicial Role Confusion in "Small Case" Civil Justice' (2016) *BYU Law Review* 899). And modern inquisitorial systems have an important place reserved for party-advocacy through attorneys. In Germany attorneys have the opportunity to challenge witness and expert testimony: Langbein, 'The German Advantage in Civil Procedure' (n 27). Judges are only allowed to base their decisions on facts that parties have overlooked in their arguments if the record shows that the judge has given feedback regarding this aspect, giving the parties opportunity to weigh in on this aspect: Emerson, 'Judges as Guardian Angels' (n 26) 718.

[29] Fuller defends the adversarial system by arguing that it is designed to preserve judicial impartiality because it prevents judges from choosing their own theories early on and developing the case in that direction Fuller, 'The Forms and Limits of Adjudication' (n 24) 382–83. However, arguments have

of the two basic argumentative roles, the judge should *not* primarily assume that of the arguer. Especially in the adversarial system, but also in the inquisitorial system, the attorneys are meant to take on the role of arguers for the interest of their respective clients. The judge, on the other hand, is meant to stay neutral up to the point of decision. Even where she herself finds arguments for or against a client's case,[30] her main task is to determine the merit of these arguments – not to try to make the strongest case for a pre-chosen position. The institutional role of the judge therefore determines her argumentative role as a type of audience. What kind of an audience may vary from jurisdiction to jurisdiction and from court-level to court-level. It will depend on which questions the judge concentrates on – law or fact – and how much the judge is supposed to participate in the development of the case – whether she may, for example, ask questions of the witnesses, do her own research on factual questions or take the content of *amicus* briefs into account.[31] What is clear, however, is that the judge may not be an entirely passive audience in one important respect. Her institutional role charges her with making a decision based on her evaluation of the arguments for and against the case of either party. Therefore, she may not simply let arguments wash over her, deciding which ones appeal to her based on feeling or intuition. Rather, she has a role-based obligation to *evaluate* the arguments – to assess their merits and determine whether they actually succeed in providing support for their conclusion. Nor may she be a biased audience: she has to evaluate *each* argument, for either side, by the same process of reasoning, and she has to make a decision for either side based solely on the outcomes of these evaluations. In other words – rather than taking the role of a passive, malleable audience, she has to take the role of an active, engaged but disinterested audience. This role I will here call that of an interlocutor. Even if she enters an argument into the case herself, for example by taking a precedent into consideration that none of the parties has suggested, once the argument has entered her considerations, she has to treat it from the role of an interlocutor. This means, she has to evaluate it with the same process that she uses for the evaluation of other arguments instead of seeking to strengthen or weaken it with directed intention as a committed arguer would. The norms associated with the institutional role of a judge direct her to behave as an interlocutor towards arguments in her case.

been made that the adversarial system creates structural partiality in favour of those who can afford good attorneys – and inquisitorial systems have safeguards in place to preserve judicial impartiality. For example, in Germany either party can appeal a decision by showing that a judge neglected to point out a mistake or missing evidence and by showing how the party would have acted differently if she had been made aware: Emerson, 'Judges as Guardian Angels' (n 26) 726.

[30] As she is empowered to do in inquisitorial systems and, to some degree, also in many adversarial systems. Importantly for us, in the US judges have the right to take note of a pertinent precedent even if the parties overlooked it (they are not, however, supposed to introduce a precedent that is relevant to the case but would raise a new issue). See A Frost, 'The Limits of Advocacy' (2011) 59 *Duke Law Journal* 447, 456/479.

[31] See nn 26, 27.

B. The Argumentative Role of the Interlocutor

That judges should fulfil the role of interlocutor instead of arguer might seem like a mere restatement of the commonplace view that judges should be impartial and make their decisions based on legal reasons. But pointing out that judges should take the role of interlocutor towards the analogical arguments about their case is more than repeating the grand but unhelpful advice to stay impartial. Functional roles, like the one of 'judge' in the legal context and the one of 'interlocutor' in the argumentative context, are roles established to enable a division of labour for reaching a common goal. Such roles consist of clusters of norms, goals and expectations but also, importantly, of associated tasks and behaviours.[32] The role-norm that judges should be impartial means that they should behave towards legal arguments as interlocutors do. We should therefore ask how the role of interlocutor translates into the way an argument is handled. What, then, is it that interlocutors do?

Maybe the first answer that will come to mind is that an interlocutor has to evaluate the arguments she is presented with. She has to determine whether the argument actually supports the conclusion, whether it succeeds in providing her with a reason and how strong this reason is.

Importantly, this requires that she attempt to *understand* the argument first. In order to determine the weight of the reason an argument provides for a conclusion in comparison with those against the conclusion, she needs to know what this reason is. Even in order to be able to determine that an argument fails in providing any reason at all, she has to first make an attempt to make sense of the argument. More than that, I believe that she must attempt to understand the argument while employing the *principle of charity*.

It is relatively easy to see that an interlocutor needs to do her best to understand the argument. Otherwise she has no basis upon which she can decide whether it provides her with sufficient reason to accept the conclusion. But why does she need to employ the principle of charity? Audiences might engage with arguments for all kinds of reasons. They might take the role of an especially hostile opponent and pursue the goal to make the arguer look bad, for example. In this case, the audience does not need to understand the argument under the employment of the principle of charity. Instead, the audience needs to try and understand the argument in a way that makes it most vulnerable. The principle of charity, by contrast, asks us to understand an argument in such a way that it actually provides a reason to accept the conclusion. At least, it asks us to do so if that is possible

[32] See, eg, RH Turner, 'Role Theory' in JH Turner (ed), *Handbook of Sociological Theory* (New York, Springer, 2001); BJ Biddle, *Role Theory: Expectations, Identities and Behaviors* (Burlington, Elsevier Science, 1979).

without changing what is presented as the argument to such a great degree that it is replaced with another argument.[33] For example, imagine someone says:

> Banks are designed to keep your money safe.
>
> Therefore, you should put your money there.

In this case, the principle of charity tells you to choose the interpretation of the word 'bank' so that, if possible, the argument actually provides a good reason for its conclusion. This entails at least that you interpret 'bank' not as river-bank, which would not be a safe place at all, but instead as the money-handling-institute, which is actually a safe place to put money.

An audience who wants to make the arguer look bad has no reason to employ the principle of charity in such a way. After all, it is much easier to make fun of someone who suggests that river-banks are safe places to put money. However, an audience in the role of an interlocutor, who is interested in using the argument to determine whether she should accept the conclusion, has an interest in employing the principle of charity. This is so because she has an interest in considering all reasons available when determining whether to accept the conclusion. Therefore, such an interlocutor needs to begin her consideration of the argument by trying to understand it under the employment of the principle of charity.

Of course, merely understanding an argument charitably is not the whole task of an interlocutor. Even if an argument can be understood in such a way that it provides some reason for accepting its conclusion, that does not yet show that its conclusion should indeed be accepted. In addition, the argument also needs to be evaluated. Perhaps your country is in a major banking crisis, and therefore,

[33] I am here adopting Trudy Govier's conception of the principle of charity. 'Charity as a principle of interpretation [:] On a very generous principle of charity, not supported here, we would make out an argument to be as reasonable and plausible as we could, always giving the arguer the benefit of the doubt. On a more modest principle of charity, recommended in this text, we would avoid attributing to an arguer loose reasoning and implausible claims unless there is good evidence, in the presented speech or writing, for doing so': T Govier, *A Practical Study of Argument* (Belmont, Wadsworth Publishers Co, 2014) 55. Several scholars have pointed out that the question of what strength the principle of charity should have depends very much on the context, role and goal of the one applying it: T Govier, 'Uncharitable Thoughts about Charity' (1981) 4 *Informal Logic* 5; T Govier, 'On Adler On Charity' (1981) 4 *Informal Logic* 10; M Lewinski, 'The Paradox of Charity' (2012) 32 *Informal Logic* 403. It might be that an attorney only has to apply to principle of charity to an extremely minimal degree – just so much that she will not make herself ridiculous by interpreting the opposition so clearly uncharitably that no one will take her objections seriously. And depending on whether a judge is working in an adversarial or an inquisitorial system, she might want to apply the principle of charity somewhat differently: a judge in an adversarial system is supposed to play as little a role in the case as possible. Therefore, she may want to apply a principle according to which she chooses the interpretation that makes the argument stronger only if several equally well supported interpretations are available. A judge in an inquisitorial system is supposed to influence the development of the case in order to get to the best possible arguments on both sides. Therefore, she would apply a principle according to which she chooses the strongest interpretation of each argument, even if it less faithful to the original argument-formulation than another available interpretation.

even though banks are designed to keep money safe, they are currently failing at performing this function. That would mean that the argument overall fails at justifying the acceptance of its conclusion.

There are then two steps that an interlocutor performs. First, she tries to understand the argument while employing the principle of charity. Then, she evaluates the argument as she understands it now. The result is that the interlocutor does work in two directions. First, she works *for* the argument in an attempt to allow whatever argumentative force it might have to take effect on her, making sure that she will not dismiss the argument prematurely. Then, she works *against* the argument in order to make sure that the argument will not affect her more than it should, that she will not accept the argument's conclusion mistakenly. (Good) arguments constrain the reasoning of interlocutors because they have an obligation to accept the conclusion *if* understanding the argument charitably reveals that it provides them with a reason *and* the second step of evaluation does not reveal a stronger reason to reject the conclusion. Given that the main worry this paper deals with is whether precedents can provide judges with reasons when they are used as source analogues, I concentrate mainly on the first step.

IV. A Friend to the Arguer, A Foe to the Interlocutor

As I mentioned above, Frederick Schauer claims that reasoning by precedent cannot have much to do with reasoning by analogy because source analogues are 'always a friend, never a foe'.[34] What he means is that arguers are free to choose a source-analogue that will support the conclusion they wish to reach, so analogies will always be there to help them – but they will never constrain them. Replying to this worry, I argued that this is not true for the interlocutor, a special kind of audience who approaches arguments interested in determining whether they indeed provide them with a reason for accepting their conclusions. And judges, unlike attorneys, are obliged to approach arguments in the role of an interlocutor because of their institutional role within the legal system. A judge, then, who is confronted with the analogy between a precedent-case and her present-case, has a role-based obligation to allow the analogy to do its rhetorical, persuasive work on her mind. What this translates into is as follows.

According to the doctrine of precedent, a precedent-case that is similar to a present-case in a legally relevant way provides a legal reason for deciding the present-case according to the precedent decision. Arguments by precedent therefore support the claim that the two cases are legally relevantly similar. This means that in her role as an interlocutor, the judge has to make an attempt at understanding the analogy under the purpose constraint of finding the legally relevant

[34] Schauer, 'Why Precedent in Law' (n 3).

similarity between the two cases. In other words: she has to use the analogy in order to see the present-case as it would have to be understood if it really was similar to the precedent-case in a legally relevant way. She has to do this before she can make any decision about the applicability of the precedent to her present-case. Indeed, she has to do this even before she can start to think about relevant differences that might provide a reason for distinguishing an otherwise binding precedent (or against extending a persuasive precedent).

A. Similar in a Legally Relevant Way

This makes the question what it means for a similarity to be 'legally relevant' especially pressing. As I have argued at length elsewhere, it can be answered by paying attention to the role of the purpose constraint in analogical reasoning and the role of the judicial opinion in reasoning with precedent.[35]

In the judicial opinion, the precedent judge describes the precedent-case and presents reasoning that leads from the aspects of the precedent-case to her decision. In doing so, she determines which aspects are part of the precedent-case.[36] She then sorts these aspects into those that are irrelevant to her decision, those that are relevant and speak against her decision, and those that are relevant and speak for her decision. She also, by making the decision, determines that the aspects that were relevant and speak for her decision together outweigh the aspects that were relevant and speak against her decision.[37] Those aspects of the case that she determined to be relevant and speaking for the decision are integrated into the ratio decidendi or the *holding* of the case. The ratio decidendi of the case is the part of the opinion that that enters the law and is binding for later cases. In other words: by basing her decision on certain aspects of her case, the precedent judge determines that from the point of view of the law, the fact that the case possesses these aspects warrants the decision it received. Once the judge has made the decision and written her opinion, the aspects of the case she based it on are now not only the aspects she presents as relevant *to her*, in *her* reasoning, but also the aspects that are *legally relevant*.

[35] K Stevens, *Reasoning by Precedent – Between Rules and Analogies* (2017) *forthcoming*.

[36] The precedent-case is the case as it appears in the judicial opinion, not the case as it actually happened, out in the world. For example, by now some doubts have surfaced whether the car in *MacPherson v Buick Motor Co* 217 NY 382, 111 NE 1050 (1916) actually had a defect built in by the manufacturer, or whether its wheel broke simply because it was being driven too fast: see JA Henderson Jr, '*MacPherson v. Buick Motor Company:* Simplifying the Facts While Reshaping the Law' in R Rabin and L Sugarman (eds), *Tort Stories* (New York, Foundation Press, 2003). Nonetheless, the opinion is written about a case of manufacturer-negligence, and therefore it is a precedent concerning manufacturer negligence, whatever the actual state of the world was.

[37] Both Grant Lamond and Richard Horty pay close attention to the authority of the precedent judge to do this and develop their theory of reasoning by precedent based on it: see G Lamond, 'Do Precedents Create Rules?' (2005) 11 *Legal Theory* 1; JF Horty, 'Rules and Reasons in the Theory of Precedent' (2011) 17 *Legal Theory* 1.

Take, as an example, the case of *Vosburg v Putney*.[38] Here, the defendant, a 12-year-old boy, lightly kicked the plaintiff, a 14-year-old boy, in the leg. Even though the kick was so light that the plaintiff did not feel it, it ultimately resulted in the loss of the use of the leg. The court found for the plaintiff for assault and battery. Part of the court's reasoning establishes the special context in which the kick occurred as a legally relevant aspect of the case. It reads like this:

> [...] it appears that the injury was inflicted in the school, after it had been called to order by the teacher, and after the regular exercises of the school had commenced. Under these circumstances, no implied license to do the act complained of existed, and such an act was a violation of the order and decorum of the school, and necessarily unlawful. Hence we are of the opinion that, under the evidence and verdict, the action may be sustained.

Imagine a later judge, with her own present-case, trying to determine whether *Vosburg v Putney* gives her any reason relevant for deciding her case. Adopting the role of the interlocutor, she has to try to understand an argument by analogy between the precedent-case and her present-case. This means that she has to approach it under the purpose constraint so as to see the two cases' legally relevant similarities. These are those successful mappings between aspects of the two cases that have, as one of the two equivalent aspects, one of the aspects the precedent judge made legally relevant through her decision. The role of the interlocutor requires the judge to understand the analogy charitably. Therefore, the present judge has to find that understanding of the present-case which enables her to successfully map as many parts of the ratio decidendi onto aspects of the present-case as possible. She has to map her present-case onto the precedent-case as it is described in the opinion, taking care to attempt mappings for all those aspects that the precedent judge marked as relevant through her rhetorical choices.[39] The result is that she will create, for herself, that understanding of the present-case under which it most plausibly appears legally similar to the precedent-case. This allows her to identify the most plausible sense of the claim 'the two cases are similar in a legally relevant way'. And thereby, she also identifies the strongest reason the argument by precedent can provide her with for deciding her present-case in accordance with the decision in the precedent-case. If she wants to resist doing this, she has to do one of four things: first, she might identify an aspect in the precedent-case that was rhetorically marked as relevant and supportive of the decision, and for which no successful mapping can be made in the present-case. Second, she might identify an aspect in the present-case that speaks against the decision with a reason stronger than the reason provided through the argument by precedent. Third, she can point out that the precedent-case was wrongly decided

[38] *Vosburg v Putney* 80 Wis 523, 50 NW 403 (Wisc 1891).

[39] I should point out, here, that this includes also those aspects the precedent judge thought were relevant but spoke against the decision. As Lamond points out, these are aspects that the present judge cannot, anymore, use as a relevant difference based on which she can distinguish cases: Lamond, 'Do Precedents Create Rules?' (n 37).

(if she is dealing with persuasive precedent) or that she has the power to overrule and following the precedent's decision would lead to considerable disadvantages (if she is dealing with binding precedent). Or fourth, she might be able to show that there is a different precedent that – under the same evaluation in the role of an interlocutor – holds up better. If she is not able to do any of this, then she has to accept that the conclusion of the argument by precedent is valid; the two cases *are* similar in the legally relevant respect. Therefore she has to decide the present-case according to the precedent-case. In summary, because the institutional role of the judge obligates her to approach arguments by precedent in the role of an interlocutor, the precedent can become her foe, even if she treats it as a source analogue.

B. Does Analogical Reasoning make it Easier for Judges to Cheat?

So far, my discussion has shown that precedents can have a constraining effect on judicial decision-making, even if they are used as a source-analogue in an argumentative analogy. However, this works only if the judge takes her institutional role seriously and approaches the analogical argument by precedent as an interlocutor rather than an arguer. In this role, the analogy between precedent and present-case can influence her mind so that she can see how the two cases can most plausibly be understood as similar in a legally relevant way. This provides her with the strongest reason that, from her point of view, the precedent can give her to decide her present-case according to the precedent decision. The worry that analogical reasoning might not be able to constrain judicial decision making turns out to be unfounded, or at least mitigated: analogies can be foes after all.

But how safe is this? That analogies can only be constraining if the judge shows the integrity not to stray from her argumentative role implies that a judge who *is* willing to stray from this role can use analogical reasoning as a smokescreen after all. All I have shown is that honest judges, committed to fulfilling their obligations faithfully, will be able to use analogical reasoning in a way that provides them with constraint. But this constraint is only based on the 'unforced force of the better argument',[40] and arguments can deliver their reasons only if they are understood under at least a minimal *principle of charity*. They need the cooperation of those whom they are meant to constrain. Isn't *real* constraint something that will work even on those who are not motivated to cooperate? Shouldn't precedents leave judges *no choice* but to decide a certain way?

I think that this demand is unrealistic when it comes to reasoning with precedents (and also, though I will not discuss this, when it comes to legal reasoning in general). Some might think that precedent should constrain judges in a *stronger*

[40] J Habermas, *Between Facts and Norms: Contributions to a Discourse Theory of Law and Democracy* (Cambridge, MIT Press, 1996) 306.

manner than by just providing them with legal reasons derived from faithfully evaluated legal arguments. They might believe that a rule-based approach to precedent will establish a kind of inescapable force – such that judges will have no opportunity but to decide a certain way. According to such an approach, a precedent should be thought to provide a rule through its *ratio decidendi*. This rule can then be applied to cases through what McCormick calls the 'legal syllogism' – a modus ponens with the rule as the major premise and a description of the case as the minor premise.[41] Because the legal syllogism is a deductive syllogism that is either valid or invalid, judges have little choice but to acknowledge that the rule applies where it applies. Therefore, they also have little choice but to acknowledge the applicability of a precedent-case. Or so we might think. Unfortunately, the application of the legal syllogism is only straight-forward where the rule is clear. A rule that fits the legal syllogism will come in the form of a conditional, with a number of categories in the antecedent, and a legal consequence in the consequent. Only if the categories and their exact scope are known can the rule be applied deductively in all cases. For this to be the case, the rule would have to be formulated exceedingly clearly. Precedent opinions often do not even come close to this. Consider the formulation in *Vosburg v Putney* that I discussed above. In order to exactly determine the extension of the category of having 'no implied license', a considerable amount of interpretation of the precedent text is necessary. While there will be Hartian core-cases, the penumbra here is rather large.[42] Imagine a judge who gets presented with *Vosburg v Putney* as a precedent in their present-case: a schoolchild playfully pinched her friend *during a school-outing at the zoo* and accidentally caused nerve-damage. If she treats the argument by precedent as an analogical argument, she has to take up the role of an interlocutor. She will have to allow the analogy to work its rhetorical force on her mind, finding that understanding of the cases that presents them as most similar (how is the zoo-outing like the classroom?). Otherwise, she might miss the force of the argument altogether. But if she was to treat the argument by precedent as an argument from rules, her position is not much different. Given that much hangs on the interpretation of the passage from *Vosburg v Putney* cited above, the judge must realise that this passage is vague enough to allow for several rules. Some of these will and some of them will not apply. Again, she has to approach the case from the role of an interlocutor in order to identify and evaluate the feasibility of that rule which will make the argument by precedent a strong one. In either case, the normative constraint of the precedent depends on the constraint of the obligations associated with the judicial role.

[41] Eg, if a case x has properties n1, n2, n3 -> decision y should be reached. Case B has properties n1, n2, n3. Therefore, decision y should be reached in case B: N MacCormick, *Rhetoric and the Rule of Law* (Oxford, Oxford University Press, 2009) ch 4.

[42] HLA Hart, 'Positivism and the Separation of Law and Morals' (1958) 71 *Harvard Law Review* 593, 607–15.

This is the argument with respect to precedents whose opinions are underspecific. What about those precedents that provide clear categories? Here the legal syllogism can easily be applied. Won't this provide the judge with constraint much stronger than analogical reasoning can? No, because analogical reasoning is guided – among other constraints – by the surface-constraint, according to which equivalents have to be picked that fit into the same categories as the aspects in the source-analogue. Where the opinion clearly provides those categories, analogical reasoning, like rule-based reasoning, entails the application of these categories. Of course, a judge can wiggle their way out of this obligation. She might claim that the explicit wording of the opinion does not represent the precedent judge's intentions correctly, is unworkable, or simply a slip of the pen. But these strategies are also available to the judge who approaches precedents as providers of rules. In the end, precedent constraint depends on role constraint no matter which method of reasoning by precedent the judge chooses. Cheating is always possible. Precedents constrain judicial decision-making if it is understood as decision-making performed from within the boundaries of the judicial role. Judges who are willing to ignore these boundaries and approach their cases from the role of an arguer, out to find any apparent justification for the decision they want to make, will not be reined in through a change in reasoning method.

PART V

Legal Normativity beyond the State

12

What Makes a Transnational Rule of Law? Understanding the Logos and Values of Human Action in Transnational Law

VERONICA RODRIGUEZ-BLANCO

I. Introduction

Despite opposing voices[1] it is a shared view among legal and political philosophers that the Rule of Law is the most effective mechanism for controlling the coercion of the State and the arbitrary will that human beings can exercise upon one another. Different characterisations have been advanced to disentangle the nature of the Rule of Law, but two main conceptions can be identified: first, a thin perspective of the Rule of Law that establishes formal conditions for law-making and the exercise of government. These conditions, it is argued, are detached from human rights ideals, justice, freedom and other substantive values.[2] Second, a thicker conception

[1] See RM Unger, *Law in Modern Society: Towards a Criticism of Social Theory* (New York, Free Press, 1976) and D Kennedy '"The Rule of Law", Political Choices, and Development Common Sense' in D Trubeck and A Santos (eds), *The New Law and Economic Development* (Cambridge, Cambridge University Press, 2006) and 'Toward a Critical Phenomenology of Judging' in AC Hutchinson and P Monahan (eds), *Law's Rule – The Rule of Law: Ideal or Ideology* (Toronto, Carswell, 1987). They are sceptical of rules in general and therefore of the Rule of Law. For them there are no rules or principles of law because judges decide according to their biases, prejudices, social and historical perceptions and political ideology. Law is reduced to relations of power and therefore this scepticism also affects the Rule of Law, but mainly the Rule of Law conceived in a 'thin' or formalistic manner. See also M Horwitz, 'The Rule of Law: An Unqualified Human Good' (1976–77) 86 *Yale Law Journal* 561. Other criticisms come from communitarian fronts. For example, Michael Sandel considers the Rule of Law individualistic. However, this critique of Sandel arguably affects the thin conception of the Rule of Law only: see M Sandel, 'The Political Theory of the Procedural Republic' in AC Hutchinson and P Monahan (eds), *Law's Rule – The Rule of Law: Ideal or Ideology* (Toronto, Carswell, 1987).

[2] See Montesquieu, *The Spirit of the Laws*, A Cohler, B Miller, and H Stone trs (Cambridge, Cambridge University Press, 1989); AV Dicey, *Introduction to the Study of the Law of the Constitution* (Elibron Classics, 2005, originally published in 1889); F Hayek, *The Road to Serfdom* (London, Routledge, 2001); J Raz, 'The Rule of Law and Its Virtue' in *The Authority of Law* (Oxford, Oxford University Press, 1979)

of the Rule of Law that construes it as aspiring to moral ideals.[3] In the former conception the Rule of Law guides acts of government through managerial mechanisms, whilst in the latter view guidance though the Rule of Law is not the final end, but a by-product of the final end formulated as a moral aspiration.[4] Within this account the Rule of Law establishes right standards of conduct to be followed that enable legal practice to become closer to a moral ideal of conduct. According to common thought within the transnational perspective, if we correctly delineate the most appropriate conception of the Rule of Law then we are able to transpose the Rule of Law that is defended at the national level to the transnational level. But the appropriate solution at the transnational level is more subtle and complicated, and defenders of either conception overlook the most important premise of any sound argument that defends the Rule of Law and the Transnational Rule of Law, ie we need a correct understanding of human action and human compliance with rules, standards, regulations and principles (from now on RSRPs). This bottom-up approach is not alien in legal and political philosophy and has an established pedigree in Aristotle and Oakeshott, but is absent in much established thinking of transnational law.[5]

The emergence of transnational laws puts pressure on our most cherished legal and political concepts such as the State, legal authority and the normativity of law because these concepts have traditionally been shaped and theorised around the idea of State law and within the confinements of single jurisdictions. Furthermore, transnational laws, arguably, make superfluous the debate on the appropriate model of the Rule of Law because there is no State to control and therefore no coercion or arbitrary power to be liberated from. Actors in transnational contexts willingly accept and comply with rules, regulations, and principles

at 210–29; RS Summers, 'A Formal Theory of the Rule of Law' (1993) *Ratio Juris* 12; A Scalia, 'The Rule of Law as Law of Rules' (1989) *University of Chicago Law Review* 1175; R Posner, *Economic Analysis of Law*, 6th edn (Aspen Law, 2003) at 266–68, 541–42.

[3] See L Fuller, The Morality of Law (New Haven, Yale University Press, 1964); R Dworkin, A Matter of Principle (Cambridge MA, Harvard University Press, 1986) 12–13; J Finnis, *Natural Law and Natural Rights* (Oxford, Clarendon Press, 1980) at 270–81; N Simmonds, Law as a Moral Idea (Oxford, Oxford University Press, 2008); B Tamanaha, 'The Rule of Law For Everyone?' (2002) 55(1) *Current Legal Problems* 97; T Endicott, 'The Impossibility of the Rule of Law' (1999) 1 *Oxford Journal of Legal Studies* 1.

[4] For defenders of the thick conception of the Rule of Law the key argument is the need to make law intelligible. See EJ Weinrib, 'The Intelligibility of the Rule of Law' in AC Hutchinson and P Monahan (eds), *Law's Rule – The Rule of Law: Ideal or Ideology* (Toronto, Carswell, 1987).

[5] In transnational law the methodology is either socio-systemic, eg G Teubner, 'Global Bukowina: Legal Pluralism in the World Society' in *Global Law Without State* (Aldershot, Ashgate, 1996) and *Constitutional Fragment: Societal Constitutionalism and Globalization* (Oxford, Oxford University Press, 2012); R Cotterrell, 'What is Transnational Law?' (2012) 37(2) *Law and Social Inquiry* 500; W Twinning, *General Jurisprudence: Understanding Law From a Global Perspective* (Cambridge, Cambridge University Press, 2009); N Krisch, *Beyond Constitutionalism: The Pluralist Structure of Postnational Law* (Oxford, Oxford University Press, 2010) or neo-Kantian, eg see cosmopolitan claims in C Corradetti, 'Judicial Cosmopolitan Authority' (2016) 7(1) *Transnational Legal Theory* 29; S Benhabib, *Another Cosmopolitanism: Hospitality, Sovereignty and Democratic Iterations* (Oxford, Oxford University Press, 2006).

and, arguably, the 'coercion question' is therefore dissolved, making the inquiry for the most adequate account of the Rule of Law unnecessary. Why do we need, it might be argued, a transnational rule of law if there is nothing to control? Lex mercatoria[6] – which operates under conditions of 'raw agency' – illustrates the difficulties of the 'coercion question' and the Rule of Law. This means that agents or actors comply with regulations, customs and decisions because they are engaged with the ends of these regulations, customs and decisions, which they see as having good-making characteristics or values for them, or so I will argue. They willingly and freely comply with the set of rules, principles and regulations contained in lex mercatoria and since they do so, the idea of standards of conduct, such as the Rule of Law, does not add much to their already free action. However, contrary to appearances and to this common understanding of the matter, I will argue that the 'coercion question' is also relevant in the context of transnational law.

My aims in this paper are twofold. First, to demonstrate that, contrary to appearances, the 'coercion question' does in fact arise in transnational legal contexts once we properly understand the different features of coercion. Second, to defend a sound conception of the Rule of Law which will lead us to the heart of the correct question concerning the Rule of Law, ie what is the grounding that enables us to understand how participants of a legal practice comply with regulations, rules, directives, and principles (RRDPs)? Legal philosophers tend to defend one model of the Rule of Law over another assuming the truth of a certain view on human action and without much defence of this assumption. The method that I propose in this paper is the opposite. I propose to put the horse before the cart, ie to explain how human beings comply with RRDPs. This explanation will pave the way to understanding coercion at the transnational level. I will also argue in favour of a thick conception of the Transnational Rule of Law. The methodology that I defend establishes that a sound understanding of the Rule of Law entails posing the correct question about the Rule of Law, ie how participants comply with

[6] *Lex Mercatoria* is the set of principles and rules that guide the decisions of international commercial arbitration. The participants are non-State actors and State actors but not *qua* States, but *qua* parties to a commercial contract. States also are indirectly part of this *lex* via international treaties (see for example the Convention on the Recognition and Enforcement of Foreign Arbitral Awards, 1958, 'The York Convention'). The contemporary *Lex Mercatoria* includes established customary commercial practices, rules, principles and standards of different States, international organisations and special commissions (UNCITRAL, UNIDROIT, Principles of European Contract Law). See B Goldman, 'La Lex Mercatoria dans les Contrats et L'Arbitrage International: Realités et Perspectives' in *Clunet* (1979) and 'Lex Mercatoria' in *Forum Internationale* (1983); and CM Schmitthoff, 'The Unification of the Law of International Trade'(1968) *Journal of Business Law* 105. International arbitration law is the best example of *lex mercatoria*. It emerges as a result of landmark conflicts due to the nationalisation of oil companies in developing countries. See *Texaco Overseas Petroleum Co v Libya*, Int'l Arbitral Award, 104 J. Droit Int'l 350 (1977). As shown by international arbitration rules and principles, transnational law regulates specific activities across borders. Thus, *lex mercatoria* regulates international commercial activities only, but there are many regulations that aim to govern other transnational activities, eg insurance (European Standards Alliance), health (Food Standard Agencies and World Health Organisation), forest (Programme for the Endorsement of Forest Certification), banking (Basel Committee on Banking Supervision), advertising (European Advertising Standards Alliance).

the RRDPs of transnational law, and how law created by human beings is able to bind other human beings and guide them in their conduct.[7] The thought is that if we understand this basic question, then we can understand how the Transnational Rule of Law operates and why it is necessary. Finally, I discuss some possible objections to this view.

II. Understanding Human Action: The Medusa of Coercion

Coercion is characterised by two key features. First, coercion is typically defined as the exercise of violence, psychological or physical, and/or oppression or threats.[8] Second, coercion is defined by arbitrariness. This latter feature is less standard in the literature on coercion[9] but is amply studied in the literature on freedom of the will and practical reason. Coercion as arbitrariness implies that the person who ought to be able to choose and perform an action cannot choose and be guided by any rational standards because the reasons or logos that ground the action are confused, muddled, unclear or contradictory. In order to understand the latter feature of coercion we need to understand how voluntary action is possible and how we voluntarily engage and comply with RRDPs.

Aristotle[10] and Aquinas[11] accept that the individual (I) can be blamed or praised only for what the individual does voluntarily. They also accept that there are two types of voluntary action. First an action is voluntary if it springs from the will of the agent (V1), if, in other words, the agent is the origin of the action. The agent is the arché or principle of the action.[12] Second, an action is voluntary if the agent wills the end which she sees under the intelligible form of the good and deliberates about the means to obtain the end (V2). In the latter case we can say that there is full voluntariness and in this case a voluntary action overlaps with

[7] The importance of the 'internal aspect' of the agent or actor in the context of the Rule of Law has been highlighted by M Oakeshott, 'The Rule of Law' in *On History and Other Essays* (Indianapolis, Liberty Fund, 1999). However, his explanation of human action differs from the one I defend in this paper. For a point of view that emphasises the role of the actor in global law see, for example, M Zamboni, 'Globalization and Law Making: Time to Shift a Legal Theory's Paradigm' (2007) 1 *Legisprudence* 125.

[8] For an outstanding contribution of the idea of coercion in this sense in the context of law, see F Schauer, *The Force of Law* (Harvard, Harvard University Press, 2015).

[9] Exceptions to this trend are G Lamond, 'The Coerciveness of Law' (2000) 20(1) *Oxford Journal of Legal Studies* 39 and 'Coercion and the Nature of Law' (2001) 7(1) *Legal Theory* 35 and M Fowler, 'Coercion and Practical Reason' (1982) 8 *Social Theory and Practice* 329. For the standard view on coercion see R Nozick, *Anarchy, State and Utopia* (New York, Basic Books, 1974). See also T Endicott, 'Arbitrariness' (2014) 27(1) *Canadian Journal of Law and Jurisprudence* 49, who distinguishes arbitrary government from arbitrariness per se.

[10] Aristotle, *The Nicomachean Ethics*, 1109b30–34.

[11] Aquinas, *Summa Theologiae*, I–II, q.21, art. 2.

[12] Aristotle, *The Nicomachean Ethics*, 1110a16–20 and Aquinas, *Summa Theologiae*, I–II, q.6, art. 1 and art. 3.

an intentional action.[13] But is it the case that, on some occasions, V1 will be independent from V2? How can there be two types of voluntariness? The idea that the agent is the origin of the action (V1) is possible because the agent is able to grasp the end of the action in the form of good-making characteristics or values, and deliberates about the series of actions in terms of a series of reasons that lead to the planned end seen in the form of a good (V2). Let me explain. Aristotle insists that the starting point of any intentional action is the state of affairs or thing that the agent wants and that is wanted because it is presented to the agent as having good-making characteristics or as being valuable. For example, the man wants to have vitamin X because it is healthy. Furthermore, the practical syllogism is not limited to two premises and a conclusion, there can be many intermediate instances that are part of the syllogism. Unlike theoretical syllogism, practical syllogism is not a proof or demonstration of a true proposition, nor is it a proof or demonstration of what ought to be done or what we ought to do. It is a form of how and why we are bringing something about when we are actually bringing it about.

Anscombe presents us with an alternative analysis to practical syllogism and a different way to understand practical reasoning. Thus, the series of responses to the question 'Why?' manifests or reveals the practical reasoning of the agent and enables us to identify whether the action the agent is performing is intentional or not. However, she warns us, the why-question methodology is as 'artificial' as the Aristotelian methodology of practical syllogism.[14] When we act intentionally we exercise a kind of reasoning which is not theoretical and which is grounded on a desire for that which seems to the agent to be have good-making characteristics. You know the thing or state of affairs you are bringing about because you desire the thing or state of affairs you are bringing about, and you are able to desire the thing or state of affairs you are bringing about because you know practically the state of affairs. Your desire arises because you represent the thing or the state of affairs to be brought about as valuable or good. Volition and knowledge do not fall apart.[15] For example, if you are a painter you know how and why the shapes and colours on the canvas are what they are; it is because you desire and value the painting you will produce that it should be such and such a colour and shape. But it is also true that because you desire and value this and not that arrangement of colours and shapes, you are able to know it practically. Consequently, moral approbation is irrelevant for practical reasoning and for our practical engagement with the world.[16] This does not mean that there are no instances of objectively

[13] For a full development of this conception, see my book V Rodriguez-Blanco, *Law and Authority Under the Guise of the Good* (Oxford, Hart Publishing, 2014, paperback edition 2016). For a summary of the conception see V Rodriguez-Blanco, 'Practical Reason in the Context of Law' in D George and RP George (eds), *The Cambridge Companion to Natural Law Jurisprudence* (Cambridge, Cambridge University Press, 2017).

[14] E Anscombe, *Intention* (Oxford, Blackwell, 1957/2000) §41–42.

[15] ibid § 36.

[16] ibid § 37–38.

justified reasons for actions. On the contrary, we aim at getting it right and finding the genuine good-making characteristics or values that will provide meaning and intelligibility to the movement of our bodies. Therefore, the possibility of hitting the target of genuine good-making characteristics or values resides in our good characters and capacities. But to understand the basic structure of practical reason and the different scopes of agency, we do not need to begin from fully justified and objective values. Our choosing and deliberative activities are better understood in the progressive form. Therefore, I am the origin of an intentional and voluntary action because I can grasp the end and deliberate about the means as a series of actions that are intelligible because they are connected by underlying reasons (for actions).

One possible way of understanding that V1 and V2 might take separate paths, ie that there can be voluntary actions that are not intentional, is as follows. It can be argued that when an action is successful and the agent produces the end she intends, ie a state of affairs, object, artefact, or activity, then V1 and V2 coincide. However, if the end is not achieved we can say that V1 and V2 have become dislocated. The intended end is not achieved but another end is achieved *per* accidens and not per se. In this latter case, V1 results from V2, but V1 takes an independent form. In paradigmatic examples, the agent is forced by circumstances to change her plans to achieve an end that is not what she planned, but she is in some sense the origin (arché *or principle) of the action because the action is conceived and seen as a unity that is caused by her.*[17]

Let me put the following example to illustrate the point.[18] A captain might deliberate about the best route to take her ship and its cargo from Southampton to Venezuela, where the cargo needs to be delivered. She hires the best sailors, provides favourable wages, finds the best possible ship, and plans the best route that will take the ship, its cargo and the crew to the planned destination. The captain engages in this activity because she aims to earn money, and she aims to earn money in order to enjoy a month's holiday with her family. Let us recall, this is her first person deliberative stance. She sees this month of holiday as the end of her actions and as having good-making characteristics. When the ship sails close to Bermuda, however, there is a storm that endangers the life of the crew and the captain has no option but to throw the cargo overboard. The captain takes the decision to get rid of the cargo to save her life and the lives of the sailors. This is not what she had planned to do and it is not the end per se when she deliberated and acted upon her deliberations. The circumstances, however, lead her to this other end which in some sense is per accidens. She acts voluntarily because the action of hiring the sailors, agreeing to take the cargo to Venezuela and beginning the

[17] Here I assume the truth of agent-causation, which I do not have space to defend in this paper.

[18] See Aquinas, *Summa Theologiae*, SI IaIIae, Q6, where he says that this kind of action would be 'a mixed of voluntary and involuntary, but more voluntary'. See also Aristotle on mixed actions, *The Nicomachean Ethics*, Book III.

journey etc have an origin in her through her deliberations and the execution of her powers, but in one significant sense she did not deliberate about throwing the cargo from the ship. This action is voluntary because 'it springs from her will' but she did not plan or deliberate about it.

Let us suppose an alternative scenario where, in contrast to the former scenario where the plan is thwarted, there is no storm and the captain succeeds in her plan to take the cargo to Venezuela. In this case we can say that the captain had 'enhanced' control of her actions since she knew what she was doing and why, and there were no impediments to the intended direction of her actions and the production of the planned state of affairs, ie the delivery of the cargo. In the first scenario where the ship encountered a storm, the captain was in a position of reduced control because she could not deliberate, and circumstances obliged her to take a different route in her performance, ie to get rid of the cargo.

At the other extreme of the range of actions where V1 and V2 are located, we have actions that are neither intentional nor voluntary (V1) or (V2). This happens when we have been denied access to the reasons or logos of the action that is requested from us. Let us go back to our example of the storm. I am your captain and I do not tell you that there is a storm up ahead. When I tell you to throw the cargo overboard I do not provide any justification for this, I simply demand you throw the cargo overboard. This is a clear case of coercion as arbitrariness where I do not present you with the reasons or logos of the action, but merely demand that you act. Naturally, you do not understand why you are doing what you are doing and you do it purely because I said so. You have been deprived of your capacity as a chooser or deliberator and some authors might say that your dignity has been violated.[19]

How does this all apply to the 'coercion question' in the context of the Rule of Law and transnational law? In the context of national law, judges and legislators provide the necessary justification when the State exercises coercion and demands that citizens obey the decisions of courts and judges. Judges and legislators give reasons for action that justify why the law demands citizens to perform certain actions in specific circumstances. I have argued that citizens can be bound because legal reasons are formulated as genuine or as having believed good-making characteristics or values. In this way, the grounding of RRDPs are underlying reasons as good-making characteristics or values.[20]

[19] See Kant, who considers that dignity is grounded on our humanity and therefore capacity to choose our lives: I Kant, *The Metaphysics of Morals*, Mary Gregor trs (Cambridge, Cambridge University Press, 1996) 6:387, 6:392, 6:420, 6:462; *Groundwork for the Metaphysics of Morals*, A Zweig trs (Oxford, Oxford University Press, 2002) 4:435, 4:436; *The Critique of Practical Reason*, Mary Gregor trs (Cambridge, Cambridge University Press, 1997) 5:71, 5:87, 5:88. The dignity of humanity is the first step towards the most complete idea of dignity which is the 'dignity of personality'. See also my forthcoming article V Rodriguez-Blanco, 'Dworkin's Dignity Under the Lens of the Magician of Königsberg' in S Khurshid, L Malik and V Rodriguez-Blanco (eds), *Dignity in the Legal and Political Philosophy of Ronald Dworkin* (Oxford, Oxford University Press, 2018).

[20] See Rodriguez-Blanco, *Law and Authority Under the Guise of the Good* (n 13).

In the transnational context there is no apparent coercion, legitimate or illegitimate, of the State since there is no State at the transnational level. I argue, however, that whilst there is no coercion as violence or repression, there can be coercion as arbitrariness. For example, if the arbitrators in an international arbitration case do not provide coherent and adequate legal reasons grounded on values or genuine or believed good-making characteristics for their awards and decisions, or they demand certain conduct or an action to be performed by the parties grounded on muddled, incoherent or confused reasons, then we can say there is coercion as arbitrariness.

If this notion is sound, a transnational rule of law would serve as the quintessential mechanism to ensure that agents in the transnational legal context are not subject to the arbitrary will of another, because the transnational rule of law demands that reasons or logos as values or good-making characteristics are embedded in the creation of transnational RRDPs, and this enables agents in the transnational context to choose RRDPs because they are grounded in such reasons or logos.

But now the question that arises is 'What are the key features of a Rule of Law and Transnational Rule of Law that guarantee agent choice and liberate agents from arbitrariness?' This is the direction in which I now turn.

III. The Rule of Law and the Thick Conception of the Transnational Rule of Law

There are two contemporary theoretical views on the nature of the rule of law. First, a thin conception that establishes the set of conditions that are part of the doctrine of the Rule of Law and according to which the rules of law should be: clear; consistent with action; coherent; possible; public; non-retroactive; and constant. This set of conditions does not necessarily generate a legal system whose key feature is substantive justice.[21] According to the thin view this set of conditions is contingent upon the moral landscape of the specific legal system. In other words, these conditions can be equally present in either evil or benevolent regimes. Second, there is the view that the conditions are not only contingent upon and neutral to a just legal system, but that they embed a moral ideal that provides the conditions of possibility for any legal system to be just.[22] According to the latter, the conditions, albeit refined and conceptualised in more appropriate ways, give shape to and make possible a fundamental moral idea that is intrinsic to our understanding of what law is, ie the independence of one person from the will of another. Thus, legal rules and principles that are clear, consistent with action,

[21] Raz *The Authority of Law* (n 2) and M Kramer, 'The Big Bad Wolf: Legal Positivism and its Detractors' (2004) 49(1) *American Journal of Jurisprudence* 1.

[22] See Weinrib, 'The Intelligibility of the Rule of Law'(n 4) and Simmonds, *Law as a Moral Idea* (n 3).

coherent, possible, knowable, non-retroactive and constant enable citizens to guide their actions according to them under the warrant that these rules and principles are not the manifestation of the arbitrary will of officials, judges and legislators, but that they manifest a will possessing a certain logos as good-making characteristics or values. This is a crucial point, but difficult to understand. How can mere formal conditions generate the power of liberating us from an arbitrary will? Simmonds and Fuller carve out the idea of law as being purposive and Simmonds adds that it is purposive towards an aspiring moral archetype where the conditions above are fully fulfilled. (Note that the conditions are fulfilled only by degrees in defective legal systems.)

Both conceptions of the Rule of Law presuppose law created by the State. The emergence of transnational regulations, which go beyond the borders of State law, pose important questions about their legitimacy and normativity, ie about their capacity to create reasons for citizens at the transnational level. Transnational regulations seem to go – it is claimed – beyond the legitimacy that is provided by the Rule of Law. I would like to argue in favour of the possibility of a Transnational Rule of Law that meets the conditions adumbrated by the thick conception of the Rule of Law and explore the idea that the logos as values that underlie the rule of law enables us to be free from the arbitrary will of another person. In a similar way, in the case of a Transnational Rule of Law, the *logos as values* that shapes transnational interactions enables citizens in different States to be free from the arbitrary will of another person. My explanation differs from the one advanced by Fuller, Simmonds and Weinrib.[23] My proposal goes deeper into the nature of the logos as values of the Rule of Law and the distinction between arbitrary will and non-arbitrary will as being key to a conception of liberty. My proposal fully explains why the logos as values provides a warrant that the will of the arbitrator in the case of lex mercatoria and transnational law, and the will of officials, judges or legislators, in the national context, is not arbitrary.

Fuller points out that law is a practical craft and proposes that legislation and judging involve developing the skills for a practical craft. This idea should not be taken lightly. It invites us to reflect on the kind of creatures we are and how we produce things in the world and, more specifically, how the will can create something that is not arbitrary, but rather has a certain logos that is compatible with and appropriate to the kind of creatures we are. In previous work[24] I have argued that we are 'eudaimonic creatures' and that the authorship of the law and its key features, ie normativity and authority, are rooted in this condition. This means, following the Aristotelian and Thomistic traditions,[25] that in our condition of lacking we reach, interact the world and transform it following our visions, conceptions and imaginings of what good-making characteristics or values consist in.

[23] Weinrib formulates a similar thick conception, though he focuses on intelligibility, see n 4.
[24] See Rodriguez-Blanco, *Law and Authority Under the Guise of the Good* (n 13).
[25] See especially J Lear, *Radical Hope* (Cambridge MA, Harvard University Press, 2008).

We yearn and long for and desire certain things, sometimes apprehending what is correct, right and good, but sometimes catastrophically failing to grasp what is correct, right and good, though we still believe that what we desire and long for does possess good-making features. We do this not only individually but also collectively.[26] This condition is pervasive and makes the world intelligible beyond its pure materiality. Thus, a piece of music becomes more than noise, a speech becomes more than the vocal chords making sounds, a hammer is more than steel and wood assembled in a specific form, a cathedral is more than stone, mortar and glass, and a choreographed dance is more than a group of people moving their bodies. In a similar way the set of legal rules, directives and principles are not the sole expressions of the raw will of judges and legislators, nor mere social facts that become fully intelligible through examination of the beliefs and desires as mental states of judges and legislators. Judges and legislators create legal rules, directives and principles with the aim of bringing about a state of affairs, ie compliance with the rules, directives and principles that will either serve or produce good-making characteristics, albeit that they might be mistaken or merely believed.

RRDPs need to be intelligible to the addressee in order for him or her to follow and be guided by them and this intelligibility is only possible when the good-making characteristics or values appear in the scene of our longings, yearnings and desires. In other words, when they are present or knowable by us. Judges and legislators do not escape the 'eudaimonic condition' of humankind. What differentiates human actions from the actions of man and women? The latter actions possess an intrinsic aim formulated as a value or good-making characteristic. Other actions such as sneezing, itching your head or yawning are all human actions but not the actions of men and women. This suggests that when men and women transform the world they do it according to an order of reasons or logos that they understand and they do it under the rubric of 'actions of men and women'. This order of reasons or logos is not merely theoretical but is practical in the sense that it is directed to a future action, to something that will happen. The order of reasons or *logos* is known by the executor or agent of the action and he or she understands why one action ought to follow another until the good-making characteristics or specific value is achieved. The latter makes intelligible the order of reasons and its execution in the world. Thus, to make a cappuccino I follow certain procedures and/or possess the know-how to make a cappuccino. I switch on the cappuccino machine, put the coffee beans in the appropriate container, press the 'On' button, place the cup in the correct position, open the milk carton, pour the milk into the milk container to be frothed and finally add the milk to the coffee. There is a 'practical craft' in the process because the order of my actions cannot change

[26] See my forthcoming article V Rodriguez-Blanco and P Zambrano, 'One Myth of the Classical Natural Law Theory: Reflecting On the "Thin" View of Legal Positivism' (2018) 31 *Ratio Juris* 1, 9–32, for an explanation on how social practices define the particularities of the good or values. I rely on the idea of 'institutional transparency' advanced by GEM Anscombe in her article 'On Brute Facts' (1958) 18(3) *Analysis* 69.

if I wish to produce a good cappuccino. It has a natural practical character. The performance of any intentional action is parallel to a process of deliberation that involves the exercise of practical reason. This account of intentional action has been misunderstood or confused by contemporary understandings of intentional action which focus on intentional action as a mental state.[27]

It is arguable that the creation of the rule of law is also a 'practical craft', albeit one with a logos that can be the subject of discussion and re-conceptualisation. It requires that legal rules and principles are non-retroactive, knowable, clear, consistent in action, coherent, possible, public, and constant. Advocates of the thin view of the Rule of Law have argued that the formal conditions of the Rule of Law do not ensure a just legal system in any substantive way, and that the *logos* consists merely of rules of management that can lead to evil acts such as extra-legal violence. The notion of law as purposive gives us a hint towards a response to the thin view but does not seem sufficient and for a more fulfilling insight we need to go deeper into the nature of this *logos*. My proposal is as follows. What is missing from Fuller's account is the idea that this logos has a specific subject matter which are values or good-making characteristics and that our will yearns and desires good-making characteristics or values. This is the result of our 'eudaimonic nature'. Thus, if legal rules and principles are grounded on good-making characteristics or values then the consistency is not mere consistency of the will of legislators and judges, but consistency of good-making characteristics or values. If we look in further depth at the thin set of conditions that are part of the doctrine of the Rule of Law we can say that knowability concerns the knowability of values that are the basis for legal rules and principles; this does not only mean that the citizens of a state know the texts and words of court legal decisions and statutes, it must also entail that legal rules and principles are grounded on shareable values or good-making characteristics and are therefore knowable by the community. The non-retroactivity of law should also entail that the embedded values or good-making characteristics that ground the rules are non-retroactive. Clarity in the language of the legal rule, directive or principle entails that we correctly grasp the value or good-making characteristics that grounds the legal rule or principle since only in this way will it be possible to formulate in a clear manner RRDPs. The condition of possibility entails that the values are possible to realise and perform under specific social, psychological, cultural and economic circumstances. The condition of coherence requires that there is coherence in the values that ground the legal rules and principles, and the condition of constancy demands that grounding or underlying values and good-making characteristics of rules and directives, to the extent that this is possible, remain constant over time. Consistency in action requires that there is no discrepancy in terms of the values that are pursued by the law and the actions that guide officials.

[27] In Rodriguez-Blanco, *Law and Authority Under the Guise of the Good* (n 13) I extensively criticise this view and will, therefore, in this paper focus only on the account of intentional action under the model of the guise of the good only.

Let me provide a metaphor to better explain my point. A good cappuccino is not just the result of the movements of my body, the switching on of the machine, and the pouring in of coffee beans and milk and so on. To assert in an intelligible way that I am making a cappuccino is to understand; ie know practically why I am switching on the machine, filling the machine with coffee beans and milk and so on. Finally it is to understand that a cappuccino is a warming drink that will pep me up – emotionally and physically – during the day, ie the ends of the complex diachronic action provide the complete form or logos of my bodily movements. To understand what I am making entails understanding why I am making it. These two understandings are not independent when we reflect on them from the deliberative point of view or the point of view of the performer. Similarly, the legislator or judge creates RRDPs in the national context, and arbitrators, actors and regulatory bodies at the transnational level create RRDPs, following coherence in values, knowability of values, non-retroactivity of values, consistency in action being guided by the values, clarity in values, and constancy in values, to the extent that this is feasible, and the value is possible to realise. In other words, to understand that we are the authors of something called 'law' entails understanding why we create it. Judges and legislators at the national level, and arbitrators, actors and regulatory bodies at the transnational level, create RRDPs because we all yearn and long for values. But to achieve these values successfully in the world we need to ensure that an arbitrary will is not the creator or author of the law, but rather a will or intention that attains the *logos* as values. The thick conception of the Rule of Law and the Transnational Rule of Law hinders the intervention of a will that does not follow the underlying logos of RRDPs. It is the 'structure of values' or logos as values that ensures that I, as a citizen, will not be subject to the arbitrary will of another. Of course, as I have argued in previous works, the believed values or good-making characteristics might be mistaken, in error, badly characterised, or even evil.[28]

The power of the proposal lies in the idea that the logos of the Rule of Law and Transnational Law is able to direct us to the problem of the matter: the values to be pursued and subsequently we are able to choose whether or not to adopt the set of RRDPs. In other words, the logos enables us to see what the genuine or believed value truly is and it will be apparent to us what the genuine or believed value that grounds the RRDPs is. In the case of believed values that are not genuine values, the transparency of the logos enables citizens to make criticisms of RRDPs grounded on specific values.

The idea advanced in this paper is that the order of reasons or principles of creation lie with legislators and judges at the national level, and with arbitrators, actors or regulatory bodies at the transnational level, but the Rule of Law or Transnational Rule of Law make apparent the logos as values that reveal the order of reasons guiding the creation of RRDPs. Thus, to be more precise, the

[28] See Rodriguez-Blanco, *Law and Authority Under the Guise of the Good* (n 13).

idea is not that there is a moral ideal that we participate in and that by degrees we fulfil.[29] Rather, the approach is that legislators and judges at the national level, and arbitrators, actors and regulatory bodies at the transnational level, already have a set of values that they aim to foster and realise in their respective legal frameworks because we are 'eudaimonic creatures'. Consequently, the Rule of Law and a Transnational Rule of Law provide the best possible mechanism to guarantee the transparency and knowability of these genuine or believed values. When the conditions of the Rule of Law and Transnational Rule of Law fail then it is the transparency and knowability of the values that fail. Therefore, the Rule of Law and the Transnational Rule of Law can be substituted by any arbitrary value imposed by an arbitrary will. In other words, when the conditions of the Rule of Law and Transnational Rule of Law fail, the legislator or judge, arbitrator, actor or regulatory body is guided by his or her own arbitrary order of reasons, even a chaos of reasons, or for no reasons. The result is that the citizen or actor cannot guide his or her behaviour rationally and only illegitimate violence or coercion as arbitrariness force the citizen or actors to act and comply with the RRDPs.

When the conditions of the Rule of Law and Transnational Rule of Law are fulfilled, we still need to think hard about the kind of values that ought to ground RRDPs. The values that ground RRDPs and the logos of the Rule of Law and Transnational Law are not two different phenomena. On the contrary, the logos takes as its subject matter values and then brings the form of law to completeness. Analogously a piece of choreography is not only the bodily movements that follow a certain order, it is also the harmony, agility, grace and expression of the dance; we can still study the bodily movements but should not forget their subject matter, which is the harmony, agility, grace and expression of the choreographed piece. This thick conception of Rule of Law and Transnational Law opens the path for a new conception of Transnational Private Law and provides a framework of unity and intelligibility in the context of transnational law.[30]

I will further illustrate my core thesis with one key legal example, which is located at the intersection of Comparative European Private Law and a new European Contract law order. The German Federal Constitutional Court (*Bundesverfassungsgericht*) reached an interesting decision in the case of *Bürgschaft*.[31] In this case, a Bank offered a businessman a loan of DM 100,000 (€50,000) with the condition that his daughter would sign the contract as his guarantor. The daughter had no lawyer or financial advisor to assist her in understanding the duties that arose from the loan. Furthermore, she was asked to sign the contract and was given no explanation about her future obligations. She was told that the signed document was 'only part of the files'. The daughter, who was 21 and worked as an employee in a fish factory, accepted to act as surety for her father's debts. After few months, the father's business suffers financial difficulties and as a

[29] See Simmonds, *Law as a Moral Idea* (n 3).
[30] This is something I aim to explore further in future papers.
[31] BVerfG 19 October 1993, BVerfGE 89, 214 (Bürgschaft).

result he was unable to pay the loan to the Bank. The Bank claimed the total loan of DM 100,000 with interest from the daughter. The Federal Supreme Court reached the decision that anyone who has reached the age of majority knows that by signing the contract, she has bound herself to the duties expressed in the contract, in this case a surety contract. She appealed to the Supreme Court and argued that her constitutional right of autonomy had been violated. The Court decided that in cases where there is an imbalance in the bargaining power of the contracting parties, the Courts have the right to intervene on the basis of the general clauses of the Civil Code (*Bürgerlisches Gesetzbuch*, §138(1) and 242) concerning good morals and good faith.

Similar cases have emerged in England,[32] culminating in the decision of *Royal Bank Scotland v Etridge*.[33] The cases give origin to the doctrine of undue influence, which is a ground of relief from a contract on the basis of equity and the objective is that the influence of one person over another is not abused. The courts will investigate the manner in which the intention to contract was secured ensuring that unacceptable means, for example exercise of improper or undue influence, were not used by one party over another. Most of these cases arise from loans and mortgages given by banks or financial institutions acting as creditors and establishing relationships with wives or partners, who act as sureties, when the husbands or partners-debtors manipulate or exercise undue influence on them so that they enter into the transaction. Like in the *Bürgschaft* case, where the daughter's autonomy or self-determination has been violated, in the English cases the partners' or wives' autonomy or self-determination has been violated. In England, the bank will be put on inquiry if the transaction 'calls for an explanation' and the bank must take reasonable steps to ensure that the consent of the partner or wife has properly been obtained. It will be sufficient to show that the partner or wife has received advice from a solicitor. However, strong criticism has been advanced concerning this shift of responsibility from the bank to solicitors, since the only actions that partners and wives might eventually have is a claim on negligence for misstatements against the solicitor.

In the context of our discussion, the question that arises is how a European Private Law can be constructed if we are faced with these, at first glance, two very different approaches. The German approach is to argue in terms of self-determination and autonomy. The emphasis is to achieve substantive justice by invoking the protection of fundamental rights and good faith. The focus of English contract law is to rely on procedural justice, ie reasonable steps to ensure that the partner or wife has received advice. If we were to argue that a European Contract Law can be constructed on the basis of a Transnational Rule of Law where actors, as it has been shown in this study, will engage with the underlying *reasons as value*

[32] *Allcard v Skinner* (1887) 36 Ch D 145; *Lloyds Bank v Bundy* [1975] QB 326; *National Westminster Bank v Morgan* [1985] 1 AC 686; *Credit Lyonnaise Bank Nederland v Burch* [1997] 1 All ER 144; *Barclays Bank v O'Brien* [1993] QB 109.

[33] [2001] 3 WLR 1021.

or logos of the rules, then it would seem that the German and English contract law have separate and irreconcilable reasons as values or *logos*, ie substantive justice versus procedural justice. However, let us imagine the need to create legislation on undue influence at the European level. This new legislation would need to respect a European Transnational Rule of Law and preserve the publicity, knowability, clarity, non-retroactivity and consistency of the reasons as values or *logos* of both the German and English legal rules. The new legislation will need to look at the best ways to preserve *both* forms of justice, ie substantive fairness and procedural fairness, as the grounds to intervene in cases of undue influence and limit the sanctity of freedom of contract. In both jurisdictions, Germany and England, freedom of contract is limited by boundaries defined by ethical and moral considerations and the new legislation would require an act of imagination to reconcile two values and decide in a consistent manner accordingly. A European Transnational Rule of Law could not play its key function if it is about formal conditions independently of the underlying values as *logos* of the rules. The creation of legislation at the European Transnational level needs to both engage with the values as *logos* that underlies the different rules across Member States and be bound by a European Transnational Rule of Law that demands publicity of values, knowability of values, clarity of values, non-retroactivity in the application of the underlying *logos* of the rules, and consistency in the application of the underlying values or logos of rules across jurisdictions. In this way, agents or actors, including judges, will comply with the new created legislation because they are engaged with the ends or values of this new legislation.

IV. Possible Objections

A. The Conception Adumbrated in this Paper Contradicts the Quintessential Nature of the Rule of Law, ie the Pursuit of Different Ends and Values

It might be argued that the conception defended in this paper contradicts the reasons why we pursue any ends or goals. The Rule of Law, the objector might continue, is at the heart of the liberal project. But if legislators and judges, or arbitrators, actors and regulatory bodies create RRDPs following certain ends as good-making characteristics and values, and the citizen or legal participant follows these ends, then the citizen or legal participant is not really choosing her own ends.

However, the conception I have defended presupposes the view that ends are already given due to the kind of creatures we are and by virtue of the fact that we take part in certain social practices. Since we have a specific form of life, for example we eat, walk, love, play, have friends, write, think, mourn and so on, this form of life can only be understood if we understand the underlying grammar or logic of our activities (logos). By contrast, empirical investigations such as biological, chemical and physical research aim to discover their object of study. The inner logic of such investigations is not given to us in the ordinary practice of actions; we need to discover it. The case of human activities is at variance with this since the internal logic or grammar of our activities is given to us and defines the limits of what we can make intelligible. However, this view does not contradict the liberal idea that there is a plurality of ends that can be chosen and pursued according to our own life plan; it only proposes that there are limits to our choosing of ends and life plans. These limits are the limits imposed by our social practices and the underlying logos that demarcates rational from irrational action. It is a pledge of humility that recognises our human nature with its richness and limits. This entails that there is plenty of room for imaginative ways of living and participating in the plurality of ends as good-making characteristics or values. Individual purposes can flourish without this being a threat to human practical imagination.[34] The richness of a planned life is in the determination and creative combination of our joined values.

B. The Redundancy of Publicity

If values are embedded in the fabric of society, an objector might argue, then there is no need to make them explicit through the Rule of Law or Transnational Rule of Law; they are already public in our practices. We do not need the publicity of rules and their underlying values.

My response to this objection is as follows. There is a plurality of values and disvalues. All practices involve certain core values, but there is room for different interpretations of the core values of a practice. There is also room for divergence or distortions of the core values of a practice. The publicity of rules and their underlying values enable us to better understand – not only through practice but also reflection – the point of RRDPs. It also invites the participation of multiple and different cultural perspectives in the practice of compliance with RRDPs due to the pursuit of values. Consequently, it encourages diversity within unity.

C. The Transnational Rule of Law is Too Vague to Guide Behaviour

An objector might argue that the thick conception of a Transnational Rule of Law is too vague and therefore undermines its purpose, i.e. it does not enable us to predict behaviour and protect reasonable expectations in transnational law and, more specifically, in the private sphere.

[34] *cf* Hayek, *The Road to Serfdom* (n 2) 79.

This objection relies on an empirical conception of agency which presupposes that our intentions are mental events and that we can enact or recreate others' intentions to predict their behaviour. Elsewhere I have argued at length that this conception is parasitic on another model of human actions that relies on values and the good-making characteristics of our actions. I cannot fully engage with this objection here due to constraints of space, but I would emphasise that the position does not aim to eliminate agency construed on an empirical, economic or social basis. On the contrary, the idea is that the potential power of these explanations is parasitic on a more naïve and intelligible conception of human action that is not based on prediction and theoretical conceptions.

Legal actors who comply with transnational regulations need to recognise others. I have argued that in order to act and comply with RRDPs legal actors need to make intelligible the actions of others and this is only possible under the model of action that I have defended. For example, in the context of transnational arbitration, arbitrators are selected on the basis of their trustworthiness and credibility, and this is not dissimilar from the selection of judges. The arbitrator's capacities to follow lex mercatoria[35] and to advance the best possible interpretation of the underlying values of the different RRDPs embedded in lex mercatoria depend on his character as a trustworthy person. In this context, trustworthiness may be understood as a commitment to the underlying values of the fabric of RRDPs. Of course, as theorists we can create economic or social models that will enable us to predict the arbitrator's behaviour, but as legal actors in a practice we need to engage with the underlying values of the legal practice and the way that the arbitrator engages with such values.

D. The Thick Conception of the Transnational Rule of Law Undermines the Plurality of Goods Across Pluralistic Societies

This objection entails the view that in pluralistic societies, there is disagreement about values and therefore the thick conception of the Transnational Rule of Law presupposes that these disagreements can be dissolved.

The pluralism that I advocate is concerned with values as opposed to technical plurality,[36] and this brings about the danger that we can never reach consensus on matters of value. However, the model of human action that I defend as the basis of the Transnational Rule of Law takes the deliberative point of view as the privileged

[35] The correct function of a Transnational Rule of Law would need an ample use of the publicity requirement. In the context of international arbitration, for example, it would require the publication of arbitral awards.

[36] P Zumbassen and G-P Calliess in their book *Rough Consensus and Running Code: A Theory of Transnational Law* (Oxford, Hart Publishing, 2010) seem to advocate plurality in terms of technical standards. The model of conduct I defend relies on anti-hierarchical structures that emerge and grow from values.

position of human action and presupposes constant engagement and effort to make intelligible the position of the other as chooser. Genuine disagreements over values involves taking the matter at hand seriously[37] and earnest attempts to understand how different values can be manifested in legal and social practices. There is no ex ante solution that can guide us, and the process is one of constant construction.[38] To abandon our efforts to reach agreement and intelligibility is to abandon our rational capacities.

V. Conclusion

This paper began with a puzzle about the Rule of Law. If the objective of the Rule of Law is to protect citizens from the coercion of the State then a Transnational Rule of Law is unnecessary because at the transnational level there is no State and therefore there is no State to exercise coercion. I have shown that this puzzle is misleading, however, and relies on a misconception of coercion. Coercion is exercised not only through violence, oppression or threats, but occurs when legal actors are deprived of the opportunity to be choosers and – therefore – their access to reason is hindered. Consequently, I have argued, a Transnational Rule of Law that has as its subject matter values or good-making characteristics and ensures coherence, knowability, clarity and so on of values or good making-characteristics also ensures the availability of legal reasons to legal actors and shields actors from coercion as arbitrariness. Since we inherited via legal positivism a standard conception of the nature of law which is necessarily attached to State law, then any debilitated conception of the State as the source of law generates, it is argued, a soft conception of law. I have tried to show that this is a non sequitur. Law, soft or strong, is not only texts or words that are promulgated by the State and enforced by its organs; promulgated law also entails an underlying logos, which is translated as the reasons as values or good-making characteristics that ground RRDPs. This understanding of the law opens new avenues for the understanding of transnational and international law. I have shown that the former involves a logos as values that underlies RRDPs and has the form of an intelligible unity when legal actors adhere to the Transnational Rule of Law that ensures a framework of intelligibility and freedom as 'independence from the arbitrary will of another human being'. I have defended the thick conception of the Rule of Law and, a fortiori, of the Transnational Rule of Law because it is the only view that understands how we act in the context of the law and serves the key features of the human condition and human actions, ie our 'eudaimonic nature'.

[37] For a defence of this point, see my articles: V Rodriguez-Blanco, 'Genuine Disagreements: A Realist Reinterpretation of Dworkin' (2001) 21(4) *Oxford Journal of Legal Studies* 649 and 'Objectivity in Law' (2010) 5 *Philosophy Compass* 240.

[38] At the theoretical level a helpful metaphor is provided in 'Neurath's boat'. This metaphor also works at the practical level when we engage in actions and social practices.

13

Theorising 'Unidentified Normative Objects' of Global Regulatory Regimes

MIODRAG JOVANOVIĆ*

I. Introduction

At a recently convened symposium, marking the tenth anniversary of the development of the scholarship in the subject area of what has become known as 'global administrative law' (GAL), Weiler has noticed that 'GAL has become an attractive brand with which to draw attention to one's writing and hence is used whether appropriate or not'.[1] In that respect, one of the apparent challenges for the GAL scholarship is 'to explain which of the phenomena it studies are to be described as law'.[2] Interestingly enough, much of the contemporary theorising about the growing and diverging body of global regulatory regimes conspicuously avoids dealing 'with problems of their legal basis or taxonomical efforts to delineate their precise legal character'.[3] However, it would be erroneous to think that the mission of this scholarship will be completed if it manages to come up with criteria that regulatory instruments have to satisfy in order to qualify for the status of 'law'. If this were the case, a number of the existing regulatory instruments would remain under the radar, destined to be classified as 'unidentified normative objects' (UNO).[4]

This paper, thus, proceeds somewhat differently by, first, tackling the problem of normativity. If UNOs are really normative instruments, as they are commonly

* This paper is written within the project 'Identity Transformation of Serbia – Transformation of Serbian Public Law'. I owe special gratitude to Ken Himma and Veronica Rodriguez-Blanco for their invaluable comments and criticisms which helped me to improve the paper significantly.

[1] JHH Weiler, 'GAL at a Crossroads: Preface to the Symposium' (2015) 3(2) *International Journal of Constitutional Law* 463.

[2] A Somek, 'The Concept of "Law" in Global Administrative Law: A Reply to Benedict Kingsbury' (2010) 20(4) *The European Journal of International Law* 988.

[3] B Kingsbury, 'The Concept of "Law" in Global Administrative Law' (2009) 20(1) *The European Journal of International Law* 24.

[4] This is the label used by B Frydman, 'A Pragmatic Approach to Global Law' (2012) *Working Paper*, at ssrn.com/abstract=2312504.

taken to be, it is necessary to elucidate in what ways they can be said to display normativity and how, if at all, this is any different from the normativity of paradigmatic legal rules. In the first part of the paper, I will unload the two *how* questions of normativity. Whereas the first of them refers to the *epistemological* problem of how we are to ascertain normative statements (norms) and differentiate them from 'is-statements', the second one opens up the perspective of *practical rationality*, by asking how norms provide us with reasons for action. Although important, these two inquiries are not sufficient to ground a widely shared assumption that, in comparison to other norms, legal rules display special sort of normative force. It is the function of the *why* question to address the problem of sources of the alleged special normativity of law. By answering this question, one is supposed to reveal in what ways, if any, legal norms differ from other norms. The examination taken in the first part of the paper will eventually lead us to a rather unexpected and unorthodox conclusion that there is nothing special about the normativity of law. It will be demonstrated that law's normative force competes with the normative force of other normative orders, and that its higher level of efficiency should not be attributed to its special sort of normativity, but to the combined effects of law's normativity and its other typical features – institutionalisation, (coercive) guarantees, and justice-aptness These findings will be in the second part of the paper tested on the two paradigmatic cases of UNOs – regulatory instruments of the World Health Organization and the Basel Committee on Banking Supervision. This analysis will reveal that although the former qualify for the status of traditional international legal instruments, their degree of normativity – understood as the capacity to give rise to obligations – is very low. On the other hand, although the latter's instruments do not appear to pass the threshold of 'legality', they manage to display a surprisingly high level of normative force. Results of the undertaken analysis will, hopefully, bring more clarity to the burgeoning GAL literature.

II. Unpacking Normativity

Even those who challenge Hume's famous thesis on the gap between 'is-statements' and 'ought-statements' are ready to argue that, while 'not as clear as it might be', this thesis 'is at least clear in broad outline: there is a class of statements of fact which is logically distinct from a class of statements of value'.[5] But, in what sense one may speak of distinctiveness of normative statements?

A. The Two 'How' Questions of Normativity

In an attempt to unpack the concept of normativity, I propose to distinguish between the two *how* questions. First, one may employ the *epistemological*

[5] JR Searle, 'How to Derive "Ought" From "Is"' (1964) 73(1) *The Philosophical Review* 43.

perspective by asking *how we are to ascertain a normative statement.* The initial hunch is to rely on language of the respective statements. However, as is very well known, language may be indicative, but it is often not conclusive of one statement being normative. Alleged descriptive statements may contain a hidden deontic operator, such as in the statement: 'The National Assembly of the Republic of Serbia has 250 MPs'. One can easily discern that this is not a mere descriptive statement by the fact that it is part of a legal document, called the Constitution of the Republic of Serbia, and all the legal statements – so the common theoretical wisdom goes – are norms.[6] Hence, '[n]ormally, the context clarifies the exact meaning of such utterances. If it does not, it is always proper to require clarification'.[7]

However, the range of normative statements does not necessarily end here. Both Kelsen and Raz warn that we should take into account a special subset of statements, which although not being norms themselves, are aimed at representing and reconstructing existing norms.[8] Hence, when discussing the approach of legal science, Kelsen employs the expression 'rules of law in a descriptive sense' in order to denote statements of this discipline which are aimed at describing its object – legal norms.[9] This highly contentious phrase[10] is meant to encapsulate the epistemological project of the Pure Theory of Law, which expects to achieve the same kind of scientific objectivity as natural sciences.[11] Raz, in a similar fashion,[12] speaks of 'detached legal statements', which 'simply state what one has reason to do from the legal point of view, namely, what ought to be done if legal norms

[6] Raz challenges this view by arguing that not all laws are norms: J Raz, *The Concept of a Legal System: An Introduction to the Theory of Legal System*, 2nd edn (Oxford, Clarendon Press, 1980) 168–86.

[7] J Raz, *Practical Reason and Norms*, 2nd edn (Oxford, Oxford University Press, 2002) 84.

[8] Eng argues in favour of a *sui generis* concept of 'fused descriptive and normative propositions', which are paradigmatically used by lawyers in their *de lege lata* utterances. Eng says that '[d]escriptive and normative propositions can be more or less tightly interwoven so that it is more or less difficult to keep the propositions apart psychologically': S Eng, 'Fusion of Descriptive and Normative Propositions. The Concepts of "Descriptive Proposition" and "Normative Proposition" as Concepts of Degree' (2000) 13(3) *Ratio Juris* 237.

[9] 'The jurist, as the theoretical exponent of the law, presents these norms in propositions that have a purely descriptive sense, statements which only describe the "ought" of the legal norm. It is of the greatest importance clearly to distinguish between legal norms which comprise the object of jurisprudence and the statements of jurisprudence describing that object': H Kelsen, 'The Pure Theory of Law and Analytical Jurisprudence' (1941) 55 *Harvard Law Review* 51.

[10] This terminology was one of the subjects discussed during the famous meeting between Hart and Kelsen. At first, Hart was puzzled by the use of the aforementioned and alike expressions. Eventually, he was ready to concede to Kelsen's general idea: 'I do not think his terminology of rule and ought "in a descriptive sense" happy, but I do think he was wise to reject the alternative I proffered': HLA Hart, 'Kelsen Visited' (1963) 10 *UCLA Law Review* 716–17.

[11] As noted by Bulygin, Kelsen's 'concern was to shape a model of a legal science that would satisfy the requirements of this programme of a positivistic science, and to provide methodological foundations and conceptual tools for such an enterprise': E Bulygin, 'An Antinomy in Kelsen's Pure Theory of Law' in SL Paulson and BL Paulson (eds), *Normativity and Norms – Critical Perspectives on Kelsenian Themes* (Oxford, Clarendon Press, 1998) 301.

[12] He explicitly admits that his stance 'is closely related to Kelsen's view': Raz, *Practical Reason and Norms* (n 7) fn 3 to ch 5, 211.

are valid norms'.[13] Not only is this type of normative statement used more frequently than commonly thought, but it is not exclusively confined to law.[14]

Nevertheless, of the variety of normative statements, 'norms' are of particular relevance, in so far as they purport to guide human behaviour. In that respect, the *how* of epistemological perspective opens up an even more profound problem of explaining what Jellinek, in relation to legal norms, famously termed as 'the normative power of factual' (*die normative Kraft des Faktischen*).[15] How, if at all, can the factual act of uttering a statement provide this utterance with the behaviour-guiding force? Kelsen cannot be said to offer a full response to this question,[16] but he does provide us with an important epistemological clarification. He does so by pointing out that the 'norm', as 'the meaning of an act by which a certain behaviour is commanded, permitted, or authorised' has to be 'carefully differentiated from the act of will whose meaning the norm is: the norm is an *ought*, but the act of will is an *is*'.[17] This, however, does not entirely solve the puzzle. An utterance by a street bully, yelling in my direction – 'Do immediately ten push-ups!', also presumably contains a message that the required behaviour 'ought' to be conducted, just as does the traffic regulation requiring me to stop the vehicle at the red light. At this point, Kelsen introduces a further clarifying distinction between 'subjective' and 'objective' meaning of the act of will:

> 'Ought' is the subjective meaning of every act of will directed at the behaviour of another. But not every such act has also objectively this meaning; and only if the act of will has also the objective meaning of an 'ought' is this 'ought' called a norm ... That the 'ought' is the objective meaning of the act manifests itself in the fact that it is supposed to exist (that the 'ought' is valid) even if the will ceases to exist whose subjective meaning it is – if we assume that an individual ought to behave in a certain way even if he does not know of the act whose meaning is that he ought to behave in this way. Then the 'ought', as the objective meaning of an act, is a valid norm binding upon the addressee, that is, the individual at whom it is directed.[18]

Thus, only 'ought' in the objective sense of the word constitutes a 'valid norm'. For Kelsen, 'validity' is 'the specific existence of norms'.[19]

[13] Raz adds that 'they do not state this conditional. They do not state that if the law is valid that is what ought to be done. Nor do they state what ought to be done. They do not presuppose that the law is valid': ibid 175.

[14] Yet, Raz's claim about 'detached' normative statements was largely discussed in connection to legal context. In criticising it, D'Almeida notices that this claim 'has been accepted and incorporated in contemporary jurisprudence without much questioning': LD D'Almeida, 'Legal Statements and Normative Language' (2011) 30 *Law and Philosophy* 168.

[15] G Jellinek, *Allgemeine Staatslehre* (Berlin, Verlag von Julius Springer, 1929) 338.

[16] The reason for this stems from the fact that Jellinek's problem is maybe even more important for the *why* question of normativity, and in particular of legal normativity. As will be shown below, Kelsen's theory essentially does not try to address this *why* question, which amounts to the problem of the sources of (legal) normativity.

[17] H Kelsen, *Pure Theory of Law* (Berkeley and Los Angeles, University of California Press 1967) 5.

[18] ibid 7–8.

[19] H Kelsen, *General Theory of Law and State* (Cambridge MA, Harvard University Press, 1949) 30.

Raz notices that we are interested in norms 'either because they are prescriptive, practised, or valid, or possess some combination of these properties'. For him, to say that norms exist is to imply that 'they have one or more of these properties'. Yet, of the three mentioned properties, 'that of validity is beyond doubt the primary one'. This is so, because '[o]nly valid norms are valid or good reasons'.[20] Unlike Kelsen, however, Raz is primarily interested in the *perspective of practical rationality*. He says that '[t]he key concept for the explanation of norms is that of reasons for action'. By employing this perspective, one is interested in elucidating the second *how* question – namely, *how normative statements, and norms in particular, provide us with reasons for action*.[21] When put in this perspective, the *how* question reveals another set of puzzling issues. To begin with, one may wonder about the nature of the relevant sort of reasons. Williams famously distinguished between 'internal' and 'external' reasons for action. He says that the sentence of the type 'There is a reason for A to φ' (where φ stands in for some verb of action)' could plausibly be interpreted in the two contrasting ways. On the first reading, 'the truth of the sentence implies, very roughly, that A has some motive that will be served or furthered by his φ -ing, and if this turns out not to be so the sentence is false: there is a condition relating to the agent's aims, and if this is not satisfied it is not true to say, on this interpretation, that he has a reason to φ'. On the second reading, 'there is no such condition, and the reason sentence will not be falsified by the absence of an appropriate motive'. He calls the first 'internal' and the second 'external' reasons for action.[22]

Without here entering the complex and lively debate about these two sorts of reasons,[23] it is commonly argued, particularly among legal philosophers, that if (legal) norms necessarily provide us with reasons for action, these reasons can be only of the external nature. Furthermore, many authors are inclined to follow Raz's argumentation, according to which legal norms are 'exclusionary reasons' for action. According to him, legal norms are regarded as 'mandatory' norms which are issued by 'authority'.[24] While they are first-order reasons, ie reasons for performing or refraining from a certain act, they are also 'exclusionary reasons',

[20] 'Practised norms or prescribed norms can be called reasons only in the sense in which we refer to the reason for which a person performed some action'. Put differently, such a norm 'may not be a reason at all but some people believe that it is or intend others to take it as a reason': Raz, *Practical Reason and Norms* (n 7) 84.

[21] 'To my mind the main difficulty in explaining rules is to understand their relations to reasons for action': ibid 9.

[22] B Williams, 'Internal and External Reasons' in *Moral Luck – Philosophical Papers: 1973–1980* (Cambridge, Cambridge University Press, 1981) 101. Williams' ultimate position was that 'the only rationality of action is the rationality of internal reasons': ibid 111.

[23] For different aspects of this debate, see S Finlay and M Schroeder, 'Reasons for Action: Internal vs. External' in EN Zalta (ed), *The Stanford Encyclopedia of Philosophy* (Winter 2015 edition), available at http://plato.stanford.edu/archives/win2015/entries/reasons-internal-external/.

[24] Strictly speaking, only 'the valid legal norms of a legitimate legal system would give rise to exclusionary reasons for action, whereas the valid legal norms of an illegitimate legal system would merely 'purport' to give rise to exclusionary reasons': KE Himma, 'Practical Authority' 18 (on file with the author).

ie negative second-order reasons, that is, reasons to refrain from acting for some conflicting reasons.[25] Hence, whereas it might be contentious what is the role of mandatory norms in the process of our practical reasoning, one thing is clear – they preclude us from acting on some conflicting reasons.[26]

This alleged specificity of legal norms has to be contrasted with another widely shared assumption, according to which normativity is essentially the same across various normative orders.[27] It is often argued that the reason-giving nature of norms has the same logical form. Hence, Raz says that 'statements of the form "x ought to φ" are logically equivalent to statements of the form "There is reason for x to φ"'.[28] In the classical phase of his teaching, Kelsen fostered the claim that the concept of 'ought' was a general and an 'umbrella concept' (*Sammelbegriff*), 'which simply embraces all deontic modalities'.[29] However, in the last stage of his work, Kelsen seemed to retreat from this position by noticing: 'Although … the word "ought" can have different meanings, it does seem too far removed from ordinary usage to say, of behaviour that is empowered or is permitted, that one "ought" so to behave'.[30] Raz develops an argument along the similar lines. He says that '[i]t would be correct but highly misleading to state, in normal circumstances, that an act which in fact one ought to perform is permitted'.[31] Neither 'permissive norms'[32] nor 'power-conferring norms' can be classified as 'mandatory' norms, insofar as '[w]hat one ought to do depends on whether one desires or has other reasons for or against bringing about the relevant normative change'. Yet, they are 'normative and can be said to guide behaviour because of their contribution

[25] Raz, *Practical Reason and Norms* (n 7) 58–59.

[26] Himma notices that while Raz's 'exclusionary reasons do not preclude an agent from deliberating to determine what the balance of excluded reasons require', Hart fosters a much stronger, and, thus, 'strongly implausible view', according to which 'an agent who has a peremptory reason to do φ would be violating norms of practical rationality … simply by deliberating on – or weighing for herself – the class of excluded reasons': Himma, 'Practical Authority' 16.

[27] As pointed out by Spaak, 'there is only one sense of normativity, only one sense of "ought", so that although we may with good sense speak of the normativity of law or the normativity of morality, etc, there is no specifically moral or legal or prudential *type* of normativity, but only normativity plain and simple'. Spaak, 'The Normativity of Law' (n 24) 87.

[28] Raz, *Practical Reason and Norms* (n 7) 29.

[29] R Alexy, 'Hans Kelsens Begriff des Relativen Apriori' in R Alexy et al (eds), *Neukantianismus und Rechtsphilosophie* (Baden-Baden, Nomos, 2002) 186.

[30] H Kelsen, 'Validity and Efficacy of the Law' (1967) in C Bernal et al (eds), *Essays in Legal Philosophy – Eugenio Bulygin* (Oxford, Oxford University Press, 2015) 58, fn 6.

[31] Raz, *Practical Reason and Norms* (n 7) 89–90.

[32] Raz speaks of three different sorts of permissions. First, there are 'weak permissions', which are based on the absence of conclusive reasons for not performing the said act. Then, there are 'permissions based on exclusionary reasons' to disregard conflicting reasons. However, they do not play an important role in practical discourse. Finally, there is a third form of permissions: 'I am permitted to perform an act despite the fact that there are conclusive reasons for not performing it if I *may* disregard those reasons'. Raz calls them 'exclusionary permissions'. They 'differ from exclusionary reasons in that they do not entail that one ought to disregard the excluded reasons. They merely entitle one to do so': ibid 90.

to practical inferences, to the solution of practical problems'.[33] Moreover, these norms have the same structure as mandatory ones:

> A statement of permissive norm states that certain norm subjects have an exclusionary permission to perform the norm act when the conditions of application obtain. They differ from mandatory norms only in the deontic operator: the exclusionary permission operator replaces that of the exclusionary 'ought' coupled with a first order 'ought' which figure in statements of mandatory norms.[34]

Consequently, the normative function of guiding human behaviour can be achieved through the use of two quite different mechanisms – that of *ordering* (commanding and prohibiting) and that of *entitling* – and this is particularly true of law.[35] Yet, while the latter mechanism of granting *rights* does not lead to a moral squabble, because it is up to an addressee's will to trigger the normative function of a rule, the former mechanism of installing *obligations* opens up a far more intricate problem of accounting for the fact that law purports to impose some non-optional mode of behaviour on its subjects, ie to be 'binding'. In the rest of the paper I will focus on obligatory rules, ie directives, as a morally challenging mechanism of normativity.

B. The 'Why' Question of Normativity and the 'Exclusionary' Nature of Legal Rules

The common thread of the major legal theories in the positivist tradition is to make a direct link between the concepts of 'normativity', 'validity' and 'bindingness'. Hence, Kelsen holds that under the statement that a norm is valid 'we assume that it has 'binding force' for those whose behaviour it regulates'.[36] Raz comes to the same conclusion when distinguishing between 'requests' and 'orders'. The former 'cannot be said to be binding'. To utter '"I am asking you to do A and this is binding" is to say that I am not making a request but giving an order'. Thus, it makes sense to speak of 'a (normative) power to command', but it is senseless to speak of 'a (normative) power to request'. Raz concludes that 'an order can be binding because if valid it requires that its addressee shall act on it disregarding other considerations'. Put succinctly, 'it is binding by being exclusionary'.[37]

[33] ibid 106.

[34] Finally, these norms have the same dimensions as mandatory norms – they can be valid, practised, and prescribed, ie granted: ibid 96.

[35] Raz says that law guides our behaviour in two ways: 'either by affecting the consequences of a certain course of conduct in a way which constitutes a standard reason for avoiding that course of conduct, or by affecting the consequences of a certain course of conduct in a way which constitutes a reason for pursuing or avoiding it, depending upon one's wishes': Raz, *The Concept of a Legal System* (n 6) 169.

[36] Kelsen, *General Theory of Law and State* (n 19) 30.

[37] Raz, *Practical Reason and Norms* (n 7) 101.

As noticed, the universal mechanism of various normative orders through which they give us reasons to behave in a certain way is by installing obligations. Hence, rules of etiquette put us under an obligation to be the first to greet the older ones; moral rules put us under an obligation not to lie and cheat; religious rules put us under an obligation of worshipping; customary rules put us under an obligation of mourning for deceased loved ones, etc. Consequently, it is in the very nature of an obligation *of any kind* that it provides reasons for action. Moreover, obligation by its nature *purports to bind* subjects whose behaviour it regulates. As indicated, the first *how* question can be addressed by differentiating between a rule ordering certain behaviour and a mere request to do so. Kelsen's aforementioned distinction between 'oughts' in the subjective and objective meaning is of crucial help. Only an 'ought' in the objective sense is a valid norm. An act ordering certain behaviour will be a valid norm if it is as such certified by the tests provided by the given normative order, that is, if it satisfies conditions for membership in the given normative system. Despite all theoretical controversies, validity of legal norms is far more easily ascertainable than in cases of other normative orders. Paradigmatically, what one needs to do in order to determine the validity of a legal norm is to connect its emergence to a certain fact which counts as the formal source of law in the given legal system.[38] Does this fact alone warrant a further claim that, in comparison to other norms, valid legal norms not only purport to bind, but actually *are binding* for the subjects whose behaviour is regulated?[39] Presumably they are binding on account of being 'exclusionary' reasons, that is, on account of precluding other reasons from entering one's deliberation. This is a common way to address the second *how* question.

A full jurisprudential account of legal normativity, however, requires going beyond the two *how* questions and asking *why* law has this purported normative power. The *why* question has to do with *sources of legal normativity* and it is supposed to reveal in what ways, if any, legal norms differ from other norms. One may expect that jurisprudence, and particularly legal positivism, as a school of thought which insists on the autonomous nature of law as a normative order,[40] has already provided us with a satisfactory answer to the *why* question. It transpires, however, that this is hardly the case. In fact, both of the leading 20th century

[38] To be sure, this view is challenged by natural law theorists. As recently put by Murphy, 'Natural law jurisprudence … is the thesis that the existence and content of law depends … on normative facts.' That is, 'in spelling out the facts that make for the existence of law of a certain content, one must include some normative facts': MC Murphy, 'Two Unhappy Dilemmas for Natural Law Jurisprudence' (2015) 60(2) *The American Journal of Jurisprudence* 131.

[39] Raz says that 'a valid command (ie one issued by a person in authority) *is* a peremptory reason. We express this thought by saying that valid commands or other valid authoritative requirements *impose* obligations' (emphasis added): J Raz, *The Morality of Freedom* (Oxford, Clarendon Press, 1986) 37.

[40] A thesis about the autonomy of law can be raised descriptively, analytically and prescriptively. Phrased analytically, 'the question is whether law, by its nature, either *must be* or *cannot be* autonomous': BH Bix, 'Law as an Autonomous Discipline' in P Cane and M Tushnet (eds), *The Oxford Handbook of Legal Studies* (Oxford, Oxford University Press, 2003) 976. Legal positivists foster the former thesis.

legal positivists, Kelsen and Hart, failed for their own reasons to offer a full treatment of the problem of sources of legal normativity. Their failure aptly demonstrates the fact that legal positivism is in its elucidation of legal normativity torn up between the practical, behaviour-guiding dimension (norm) and the social component (fact) of law.[41]

Kelsen, for his part, makes a common jurisprudential mistake to treat the normativity of law as given. He escapes into a 'transcendental-hypothetical' *Grundnorm* as the ultimate ground of not only legal validity, but legal normativity as well. However, by making such a move, he 'confuses silencing a problem with solving it'. Instead of addressing the *why* question, Kelsen essentially 'invites us to stop asking'.[42] Delacroix rightly argues that the 'axiomatic status' of legal normativity needs to be challenged 'by putting forward an account of the context of social interaction that allows and conditions law's normativity'.[43] This is the task of the *genealogical* method. The point of this method 'is to bring out the artificial character of a certain kind of institution'. This method 'typically aims at those institutions that seem to be able to construct their legitimacy only by "forgetting" that they were brought into existence by a historical process'.[44] One may argue that Hart did propose exactly one such account by developing his 'fable of law's genesis'.[45] Yet, Hart's story of how the emergence of 'the legal' world managed to remedy the uncertain, static character of rules and their inefficiency in 'the pre-legal' era[46] does not take us all the way down to the solution of the *why* problem.[47] Hart did show us how law might get off the ground, by stressing the customary origin of rules and by pointing out that the most important rule – 'the rule of recognition' – is 'in effect a form of judicial customary rule',[48] but apart from telling us that it is the valid rule because it is accepted as such and practised,[49] he did not bother

[41] As pointed out by Bertea, the tension between the two dimensions 'is at the origin of the different accounts of the normative claim of law defended by the champions of analytical legal positivism': C Bertea, *The Normative Claim of Law* (Oxford, Hart Publishing, 2009) 12.

[42] L Green, 'Positivism and Conventionalism' (1999) 12(1) *Canadian Journal of Law and Jurisprudence* 36.

[43] S Delacroix, *Legal Norms and Normativity – An Essay in Genealogy* (Oxford, Hart Publishing, 2006) 102.

[44] ibid 100.

[45] J Gardner, 'Why Law Might Emerge: Hart's Problematic Fable' in LD D'Almeida, J Edwards and A Dolcetti (eds), *Reading HLA Hart's The Concept of Law* (Oxford, Hart Publishing, 2013) 82.

[46] HLA Hart, *The Concept of Law*, 3rd edn (with an Introduction by Leslie Green and a Postscript edited by Penelope A Bulloch and Joseph Raz) (Oxford, Clarendon Press, 2012) ch V.

[47] Delacroix believes that the genealogical approach is able to do that, because it 'is not actually interested in a "pre-legal hypothesis", but rather in a "suspension of legal normativity" hypothesis, referring to these intermittent periods of time where the political situation has led to overturning the existing legal order. These – relatively rare – moments provide for a helpful "laboratory situation" in which the provisional absence of legal order allows the legal theorist to observe, through the lens of history, the various factors deemed to contribute to the (re)construction of legal normativity': Delacroix, *Legal Norms and Normativity* (n 44) 143.

[48] Postscript to *The Concept of Law* (n 46) 256.

[49] This became known as 'the practice theory of rules'.

much to 'explain what kind of reasons people have for following a social rule'.[50] In that respect, his subsequent concession to the *conventionalist* account of social rules, in a passing remark,[51] can at best be seen as an invitation for an in-depth account of legal normativity along these lines. However, even the most developed accounts of that sort, such as Marmor's,[52] cannot but admit that the normativity of 'constitutive conventions', such as 'the rule of recognition', is 'conditional' and lies outside of the law itself – 'Conventional practices create reasons for action only if the relevant agent has a reason to participate in the practice to begin with'. Accordingly, if there is the obligation to follow the law it 'must come from moral and political considerations. The reasons for obeying the law cannot be derived from the norms that determine what the law is'.[53]

Raz seems to be aware of this and, thus, he offers a comprehensive 'externalist' account of the normativity of law.[54] According to it, elucidating sources of law's normativity requires unpacking the concept of authority. Raz argues that the 'normal' way to think of authority is to think of an actor (individual or institutional) claiming 'the right to rule', which triggers the correlative 'obligation to obey'.[55] This obligation 'is an obligation to obey if and when the authority commands, and this is the same as a power or capacity in the authority to issue valid or binding directives'.[56] This in turn raises the question of legitimacy of authority. Authorities are legitimate, according to Raz's 'normal justification thesis' (NJT), if they provide us service, by freeing us from the task of balancing a complex set of reasons for which we may lack sufficient expertise or information. That way, legal norms 'mediate' between us and the reasons that apply to us.[57] As a result, Raz's central thesis is tautological: law necessarily claims (legitimate) authority for being composed of

[50] 'Simply pointing to the fact that there *is* a regularity of behaviour, which seems to be suggested by Hart as part of the reason for following a social rule, is clearly the wrong answer': A Marmor, 'Legal Conventionalism' in J Coleman (ed), *Hart's Postscript – Essays on the Postscript to the Concept of Law* (Oxford, Oxford University Press, 2005) 197. Gardner similarly concludes that 'Hart did not get very far in his attempts to understand what makes norms into norms, or rules into rules': Gardner, 'Why Law Might Emerge: Hart's Problematic Fable' (n 45) 95.

[51] 'Rules are conventional social practices if the general conformity of a group to them is part of the reasons which its individual members have for acceptance': Postscript to *The Concept of Law* (n 46) 255.

[52] A Marmor, *Social Conventions – From Language to Law* (Princeton, Princeton University Press, 2009).

[53] A Marmor, 'The Conventional Foundations of Law' in S Bertea and G Pavlakos (eds), *New Essays of the Normativity of Law* (Oxford, Hart Publishing, 2011) 152.

[54] 'Externalist' theories 'do not explain the normativity of law from resources within the law itself. Rather, they locate the normativity of law in its relation to some other, nonlegal, body of norms, viewing law as heteronomous, as deriving whatever authority or action – guiding force law has from somewhere outside of itself': RA Shiner, 'Law and Normativity' in D Patterson (ed), *A Companion to Philosophy of Law and Legal* Theory, 2nd edn (Oxford, Wiley-Blackwell, 2010) 418.

[55] Raz, *The Morality of Freedom* (n 39) 53.

[56] ibid 24.

[57] Raz says that 'the normal way to establish that a person has authority over another person involves showing that the alleged subject is likely better to comply with reasons which apply to him (other than the alleged authoritative directives) if he accepts the directives of the alleged authority as authoritatively binding and tries to follow them, rather than by trying to follow the reasons which apply to him directly': ibid 53.

rules which are content-independent, exclusionary reasons for action; and, legal norms are mandatory in so far as they are issued by (legitimate) authorities.

Rodriguez-Blanco has recently challenged this view. According to her, Raz fosters a model of legitimate legal authority that connects legal rules and reasons for action, while simultaneously arguing that 'there is no need to evaluate the grounding reasons of legal rules to determine how they bind us'.[58] Contrary to his claim that it suffices that the agent *conforms to* reasons for action, without necessarily *acting for* reasons, Rodriguz-Blanco argues that practical agency requires acting for reason, and to act for a reason is to act *intentionally*.[59] Contrary to Raz's idea that 'we cannot reliably conform to reason unless much of the time we do so automatically and unthinkingly',[60] she advances the claim that, paradigmatically, we follow legal rules intentionally.[61] However, in conceiving intentionality, we need to abandon 'the standard view', according to which intentions are 'mental states'. This view cannot provide an adequate explanation of the fact that, when acting intentionally, 'we know the reasons why we are doing this or that, and this knowledge enables us to achieve the end of our action in a controlled manner'.[62] Rodriguez-Blanco, thus, argues that the primary explanation of an intentional act requires employing 'the guise of the good' model, which, by using the *why*-question methodology,[63] helps one to explicate her performed action (including the rule-following) in terms of the grounding reasons for action as good-making characteristics.[64] Put differently, to follow legal rules 'intentionally and not blindly' is 'to "tap into" the grounding reasons of legal rules'.[65] This eventually raises *the paradox of intentionality*: 'if we follow legal rules intentionally, then legal rules cannot be exclusionary reasons'. And vice versa, '[i]f we do not follow legal rules intentionally, then legal rules do not have a reason-giving character'. Consequently, 'either legal rules cannot be exclusionary reasons or legal rules do not have a reason-giving character'.[66]

[58] V Rodriguez-Blanco, *Law and Authority Under the Guise of the Good* (Oxford, Hart Publishing, 2014) 139.

[59] ibid 153.

[60] J Raz, *Engaging Reason – On the Theory of Value and Action* (Oxford, Oxford University Press, 1999) 94.

[61] There are certain actions that are at the edge of consciousness, which can be labeled as 'voluntary but unintentional'. However, these are not paradigmatic cases of actions when legal rules are followed: Rodriguez-Blanco, *Law and Authority Under the Guise of the Good* (n 58) 156.

[62] V Rodriguez-Blanco, 'Legal Authority and the Paradox of Intention in Action' in G Pavlakos and V Rodriguez-Blanco (eds), *Reasons and Intentions in Law and Practical Agency* (Cambridge, Cambridge University Press, 2015) 121.

[63] The why question methodology reveals the deep structure of our intentional actions and it can be explained in the following manner: 'I exercise my practical capacity and "practical reason shows itself" when I provide answers to the question "why"': Rodriguez-Blanco, *Law and Authority Under the Guise of the Good* (n 58) 177.

[64] She argues that '[t]o merely follow the authority's order *unintentionally*, though conforming to reason, is not to exercise our practical reasoning': ibid 159. For the full exposition of 'the guise of the good model', see ibid ch 3.

[65] Rodriguez-Blanco, 'Legal Authority and the Paradox of Intention in Action' (n 62) 122.

[66] Rodriguez-Blanco, *Law and Authority Under the Guise of the Good* (n 58) 157.

Rodriguez-Blanco believes that the authoritative nature of legal rules need not be achieved at the expense of their reason-giving character. Raz is at times explicit in stating that 'no blind obedience to authority is … implied' by his account. He says that 'acceptance of authority has to be justified, and this normally means meeting the conditions set in the justification thesis'.[67] However, Rodriguez-Blanco rightly observes that the key problem of Raz's approach, which is present in some other philosophical accounts of legal normativity as well, is that it employs the third-person theoretical perspective, thereby neglecting the first-person deliberative perspective of practical agency. That is, '[t]he moral puzzle of legal authority is formulated from the deliberative viewpoint, but the answer that Raz gives, ie rules as exclusionary reasons for actions, is from the theoretical perspective'.[68] The problems of justification of authorities and how their directives enter into practical reasoning of agents cannot be separated, 'because the justification of legal authority is *primarily* from the first-person perspective or the deliberative viewpoint'.[69]

This perspective, in turn, raises the question whether it is 'ever reasonable to exclude *entirely* from consideration an otherwise valid reason?'[70] A Razian response to this question would be that exclusionary nature of legal rules is necessary for them being authoritative. However, Rodriguez-Blanco believes that the 'the guise of the good' model is compatible with the authoritative nature of legal norms, insofar as 'we *can* act according to a presumption of the goodness of the rules and therefore a *presumption* of the authoritative force of legal rules'.[71] Acting according to a presumption implies acting 'as if something were correct or as if we have a justified belief'.[72] She argues that there are such reasons[73] that enable us to create a presumption of the goodness, ie legitimacy of legal authority.[74]

[67] According to Raz, this implies bringing into play 'the dependent reasons, for only if the authority's compliance with them is likely to be better than that of its subjects is its claim to legitimacy justified': J Raz, 'Authority, Morality and Law' in *Ethics in the Public Domain – Essays in the Morality of Law and Politics* (Oxford, Clarendon Press, 1996) 215.

[68] Rodriguez-Blanco, *Law and Authority Under the Guise of the Good* (n 58) 160.

[69] ibid 9, fn 10. This is in line with Green's 'perspectival' approach, according to which, '[a]s a social relation, authority is to be identified from the point of view of those who participate in it and for whom the relation has a special meaning': L Green, *The Authority of the State* (Oxford, Oxford University Press, 1988) 60.

[70] L Green, 'Legal Obligation and Authority' in EN Zalta (ed), *The Stanford Encyclopedia of Philosophy* (Winter 2012 edition), available at http://plato.stanford.edu/archives/win2012/entries/legal-obligation/. Delacroix pinpoints the same problem, by noticing that, according to Raz's account, law 'is meant to replace those reasons that a "reflective individual" would have found to lead her to the course of conduct required by law'. However, this raises the following question: 'What if … in balancing the various requirements that apply to her, the "reflective individual" found that abiding by the law actually takes her away from the path of 'right reason'?': Delacroix, *Legal Norms and Normativity* (n 43) 149.

[71] Rodriguez-Blanco, *Law and Authority Under the Guise of the Good* (n 58) 142.

[72] ibid 160.

[73] 'Reasons or pieces of insufficient evidence can create a presumption': ibid 160.

[74] There are two such reasons. First, authorities make claims about their legitimacy and moral correctness. And second, authorities make claims on complying with Fuller's eight desiderata of the Rule of Law: ibid 160–61.

Perry uses a somewhat different strategy for showing that a directive need not function as a second-order exclusionary reason in order to be authoritative. He introduces the concept of '*reweighting* reason' as 'a subjective second-order reason', which can be defined as 'a reason to treat a reason as having a greater or lesser weight than the agent would otherwise judge it to possess in his or her subjective determination of what the objective balance of reasons requires'.[75] He explains the nature of a 'reweighting reason' in the context of authority in the following way:

> I might take the judgment of the authority into account only to the extent of introducing an element of systematic bias into my practical reasoning; I would treat the case for the conclusion which is favored by the authority as being stronger to some specified degree than it actually appears to me to be. I would thus be deferring to the judgment of the authority only partially, in the sense that I would never permit my own judgment to be preempted completely by that of the authority.[76]

Perry is aware that that the idea of reweighting reason is incompatible with Raz's NJT, but he emphasises that it 'is nonetheless coherent in its own terms'.[77] And if the third-person theoretical perspective of Raz's service conception is inadequate to reconcile the reason-giving nature of legal rules with our practical agency, as it presumably is, then the room is open for 'reweighting reasons' in the conceptual framing of authoritative nature of legal rules.[78]

All this leads to a rather surprising and unconventional conclusion that there is nothing special about the normativity of law. According to it, law's normative force competes with the normative force of other normative orders. This, understandably, does not occur each time an actor is confronted with law's demands, because that 'would considerably diminish, and maybe cancel law's efficiency'.[79] And normally, a legal order is highly efficient. How is this possible? A satisfactory elucidation of this problem would require nothing less than a full-blown account of the concept of law. Suffice now to say that jurisprudential inquiries are often wrongly driven in the direction of claiming that the specificity of law as a normative order – including its high level of efficacy – can be best explained by reference to some special feature of the normativity of its rules. However, normativity of law cannot be adequately unpacked if one overlooks its other typical features[80] – that

[75] S Perry, 'Second Order Reasons, Uncertainty, and Legal Theory' (1989) 62 *Southern California Law Review* 932.

[76] ibid 932.

[77] ibid 933.

[78] *cf* Himma, 'Practical Authority' (n 24) 18. Alexander fosters a similar claim, that 'law cannot itself constitute a second-order, exclusionary reason to disregard all or any non-legal first-order reasons; what it can (and should) do is *demand* that it be responded to as if it had, and *perhaps claim* that it be regarded as having, *overriding normative weight*': L Alexander, 'Law and Exclusionary Reasons' (1990) 18(1) *Philosophical Topics* 5.

[79] On the other hand, 'the total absence of such deliberation would in turn transform legal rules into mere habits devoid of any normative meaning': Delacroix, *Legal Norms and Normativity* (n 43) 154.

[80] Under the prototype theory of law, 'concepts are not characterized in terms of necessary and sufficient conditions, but rather in terms of clusters of predicates. None of the predicates is per se necessary for the application of the concept. Some of the predicates are more salient than others, so that

it is a highly institutionalised order,[81] whose norms are guaranteed, most commonly, by means of coercion,[82] and whose rules are, overall, apt for inspection and appraisal in light of justice.[83] Authority of law, as persuasively demonstrated by Raz, decisively depends upon the legitimacy of law-creating and law-applying institutions. Recent studies in social psychology[84] lead to the conclusion that a sense of legitimacy of those institutions is an even more important factor than fear

individual items displaying them are more readily recognized as falling under the concept': A Peters and I Pagotto, 'Soft Law as a New Mode of Governance: A Legal Perspective' (2006) *New Modes of Governance Project, Paper No. 04/D11*, 12. This view, which is in a certain form endorsed by Frederick Schauer in his latest book *The Force of Law* (Cambridge MA, Harvard University Press, 2014), is harshly criticised. Green, for instance, says: 'If jurisprudence needs more attention to contingent, typical, truths about law, then it needs something else too. Before we can know what is typical we need to count. Before we can count we need to know that what counts as what. Counting-as is a matter of identifying necessary and sufficient conditions': L Green, 'The Forces of Law: Duty, Coercion and Power' Oxford Legal Studies Research Paper 12/2015, 3, available at http://ssrn.com/abstract=2588588. *cf* T Spaak, 'Schauer's Anti-Essentialism' (2015), available at http://ssrn.com/abstract=2539590. This is certainly not the place for solving this tremendously difficult methodological problem of jurisprudence. It should suffice to say in response to Green that, before knowing 'that what counts as what', we need to start from empirical observations about normal and typical, yet theoretically and practically relevant, features of phenomena we want to conceptualise. Himma has recently argued in favour of 'coercive enforcement mechanisms' as a 'conceptually necessary feature' of law. While not abandoning the traditional language of 'necessities', he, nonetheless, builds his case, among other things, on 'claims showing the ubiquity and centrality of coercive enforcement mechanisms *in every paradigm instance of law we have ever known*' (emphasis added). Put differently, he proceeds from what is normal and typical in and characteristic for known human (not angels') societies in order to conceptualise 'law' as a normative system: KE Himma, 'The Authorization of Coercive Enforcement Mechanisms as a Conceptually Necessary Feature of Law' (2015), 1, available at http://ssrn.com/abstract=2660468.

[81] 'Many, if not all, legal philosophers have been agreed that one of the defining features of law is that it is an institutionalized normative system': J Raz, 'The Institutional Nature of Law' in *The Authority of Law*, 2nd edn (Oxford, Oxford University Press, 2009) 105. On law as a 'normative institutional order', see generally N MacCormick, *Institutions of Law – An Essay in Legal Theory* (Oxford, Oxford University Press, 2007). Other institutionalised normative orders, such as religious one, tend to be highly efficient for those accepting their authority. This aspect cannot be discussed here in more detail.

[82] Coercion, understood in terms of physical force, is *stricto sensu* only a species of institutional guarantee. Jellinek rightly claims that 'an essential feature of the concept of law is guarantee, and not coercion, which is only a subspecies of guarantee. Legal norms are not so much coercive, but rather guaranteed norms': Jellinek, *Allgemeine Staatslehre* (n 15) 336–37. This point requires further elaboration which, due to the space restraints, cannot be offered here.

[83] As pointed out by Green, '[i]n view of the function of law … it necessarily makes sense to ask whether law is just'. That is, law is '*justice-apt*' abstract artifact, in so far as it 'is the kind of thing that is apt for inspection and appraisal in light of justice'. While '[t]his applies as much to the substance of law as it does to its administration and procedures', it 'does not entail that every individual *law* is justice-apt': L Green, 'Positivism and the Inseparability of Law and Morals' (2008) 83(4) *New York University Law Review* 1050.

[84] Bix has recently pointed out that social psychology might be more competent study discipline than jurisprudence for researching the alleged special normative force of law. He says: 'One might reasonably question whether we (whoever "we" might be in this case) do in fact believe that legal norms "provide [us] with special reasons for acting", separate from the prudential reasons associated with legal sanctions, or the general moral reasons that *some* legal norms might *sometimes* trigger … even if a significant number of people believe that law *qua* law gives them reasons for action, this may be a matter calling more for a psychological or sociological explanation rather than a philosophical one': B Bix, 'Kelsen and Normativity Revisited' in C Bernal and M Porciuncula (eds), *Festschrift for Stanley L Paulson* (Madrid: Marcial Pons, forthcoming) 18, available at ssrn.com/abstract=2287870.

of punishment in most people's law-abiding behaviour.[85] Only if one believes in the overall legitimacy of law-creating and law-applying institutions, '*can* [one also] act according to a presumption of the goodness of the [legal] rules'.[86] However, not everyone is ready to follow legal rules and, hence, the necessity for coercive guarantees. As famously pointed out by Hart, sanctions are required 'not as the normal motive for obedience, but as a *guarantee* that those who would voluntarily obey shall not be sacrificed to those who would not'.[87] In that respect, sanctions are only 'auxiliary reasons' for action, but nonetheless reasons.[88] Consequently, the higher level of efficiency of law is a result of the combined effect of the interrelated typical features of law – normativity, institutional nature, (coercive) guaranteeing and justice-aptness – and should not be attributed erroneously to the exclusionary nature of legal norms as reasons for action.[89]

III. On the Normativity of UNOs

A dominant approach in the GAL literature is the one which pays attention to the problem of legitimacy of the global regulatory mechanisms. The implicit assumption of this approach is that normative instruments through which global regulatory function is performed do not qualify for the status of 'law'. On this reading, 'legality' of those instruments is intricately connected to the capacity of regulatory regimes to satisfy some assumed legitimacy standards. For instance, despite claiming to foster a Hartian theory of law in conceptualising GAL, this is what Kingsbury essentially proposes when arguing that 'in choosing to claim to be law … a particular global governance entity or regime embraces or is assessed by reference to the attributes, constraints and normative commitments that are

[85] As put by Tyler: 'Leaders have legitimacy when people view their authority as being appropriate and proper, with the consequence that they feel obligated to defer to the decisions made by leaders with legitimacy and the policies and rules they create': TR Tyler, 'Psychological Perspectives on Legitimacy and Legitimation' (2006) 57 *Annual Review of Psychology* 393.

[86] Rodriguez-Blanco, *Law and Authority Under the Guise of the Good* (n 58) 142.

[87] 'To obey, without this, would be to risk going to the wall. Given this standing danger, what reason demands is *voluntary* co-operation in a *coercive* system': Hart, *The Concept of Law* (n 46) 198.

[88] Rodriguz-Blanco replicates Delacroix's point that '[i]f the majority of a population systematically follows legal rules because it fears those rules, and cannot understand or avow the grounding reasons as good-making characteristics of the legal rules, then those legal rules are part of a legal system that has marginal agency and fails to provide and engage citizens with the *logos* of the legal rule': Rodriguez-Blanco, *Law and Authority Under the Guise of the Good* (n 58) 199. It is important to recall that, in his discussion about 'necessary and natural' elements which constitute the minimum morality that makes a legal system possible, Hart sends essentially the same message. He says: if no one 'would have any reason to obey except fear' – and this would happen were the legal rules to deny even minimal 'essential benefits and protection' stemming from 'natural necessity' – than the legal system would 'sink to the status of a set of meaningless taboos': HLA Hart, 'Positivism and the Separation of Law and Morals' in *Essays in Jurisprudence and Philosophy* (Oxford, Clarendon Press, 1983) 81–82.

[89] I will have to say more about a prototype theory of (international) law in M Jovanović, *The Nature of International Law* (Cambridge, Cambridge University Press, forthcoming 2018).

immanent in public law'. The legitimacy standards of the 'publicness' criterion, thus, condition the legality of global regulatory instruments.[90] This is by no means an isolated attempt of this sort in the GAL scholarship.[91]

The approach taken here proceeds from the general concept of normativity. In that respect, even the harsh critics of GAL, like Somek, are not ready to deny that global regulatory instruments have *some* normative function. What they question is the tendency to use 'legality' as 'the default descriptor' for the normative nature of the given regulatory instruments.[92] However, when they raise this criticism they do so under the traditional assumption that the trade mark of the normativity of legal rules is its 'bindingness'.[93] The preceding analysis debunks a direct link between the concepts of 'normativity', 'validity' and 'bindingness', which opens the space for the re-conceptualisation of the oft-criticized notion of 'graduated', ie 'relative normativity'.[94] Namely, if the normativity of law does not exhaust in its bindingness, then there is room for gradation. This, in turn, enables us to shed new light on 'unidentified normative objects' of global regulatory regimes, 'whose legal character is uncertain or challenged, but which produce or aim to produce regulation'.[95]

In doing so, we need to be aware of the multifaceted character of the emerging 'global administrative space'.[96] It consists 'of separate regimes, which are connected into a network by piecemeal ties and cross-references'. This space 'is not the result of a unitary design and … does not embody a unitary structure'. Its distinctive features are the following: 'it is cooperative and non-hierarchical; it has no center; it does not develop according to a plan, but spontaneously and incrementally; it

[90] Kingsbury is fully aware that the 'publicness' requirement may sit uncomfortably with other elements of Hart's theory of law. He explicitly admits that this requirement 'seems much more consistent with Lon Fuller's view than Hart's': Kingsbury, 'The Concept of "Law" in Global Administrative Law' (n 3) 30. For this reason, Ming-Sung Kuo charges Kingsbury for reading Hart through Fuller's lenses: Ming-Sung Kuo, 'The Concept of "Law" in Global Administrative Law: A Reply to Benedict Kingsbury' (2010) 20(4) *The European Journal of International Law* 998. Somek is even more explicit when saying that '[o]wing to the stipulated nature of publicness, the amendment to the rule of recognition infuses GAL with a natural law component': A Somek, 'The Concept of "Law" in Global Administrative Law: A Reply to Benedict Kingsbury' (2010) 20(4) *The European Journal of International Law* 985, 990.

[91] Proceeding from an admittedly contested perspective of 'cosmopolitan constitutionalism', Savino has recently advanced a claim of 'conditional primacy', which implies that 'states acknowledge the primacy of global regulation *as long as* it incorporates the essential prescriptions of the global model of interest representation': M Savino, 'What If Global Administrative Law is a Normative Project?' (2015) 3(2) *International Journal of Constitutional Law* 494.

[92] Somek, for instance, does not deny 'meta-management' or 'managerial supervision' normative function of global regulatory instruments: 'The Concept of "Law" in Global Administrative Law: A Reply to Benedict Kingsbury' (2010) 20(4) *The European Journal of International Law* 985, 990.

[93] Hence, Somek notices that even the proponents of GAL admit of the fact that '[m]uch regulatory governance is taking its cue from non-binding rules': ibid 990.

[94] The earliest criticisms is raised in P Weil, 'Towards Relative Normativity in International Law?' (1983) 77 *American Journal of International Law* 413.

[95] Frydman, 'A Pragmatic Approach to Global Law' (n 4) 3.

[96] B Kingsbury, N Krisch and RB Stewart, 'The Emergence of Global Administrative Law' (2005) 68 *Law and Contemporary Problems* 18, 25ff.

creates a thick regulatory mass'.[97] Global regulatory instruments vary depending on the nature of the respective regime.[98] In order to illustrate the aforementioned reconstruction of the relation between the concepts of 'normativity', 'validity' and 'bindingness', I will use two somewhat paradigmatic, yet qualitatively different, examples of global regulatory regimes.

A. World Health Organization

According to the earlier elucidation of the concept of 'validity' of legal norms, some global regulatory instruments can be without much difficulty ascertained as 'valid' international 'legal' rules. This is so because their coming into being can be connected to one of the formal sources of international law enlisted in the Article 38(1) of the ICJ Statute. This is the case with the Constitution of the World Health Organization, which is a standard international treaty.[99] It stipulates, inter alia, that 'the Health Assembly shall have authority to adopt regulations' (Article 21), and that they 'shall come into force for all Members' (Article 22). Pursuant to these articles, the last revision of the International Health Regulations was adopted in May 2005 and they entered into force in June 2007.[100]

Does all this lead to the conclusion that the behaviour-guiding capacity of WHO's instruments warrant their 'binding' nature, that is, their ability to give rise to obligations? Put differently, can we speak of the WHO 'normative authority', understood as its 'power to shape or influence global rules and norms and to monitor compliance'?[101] Not necessarily. The last crisis with the Ebola outbreak is in that respect highly illustrative.[102] According to one commentator, this crisis

[97] S Cassese, 'Administrative Law without the State? The Challenge of Global Regulation' (2005) 37 *International Law and Politics* 677.

[98] Kingsbury, Krisch and Stewart differentiate between five global regulatory regimes: (1) administration by formal international organisations (eg UN Security Council and its committees); (2) administration based on collective action by transnational networks of cooperative arrangements between national regulatory officials (eg the Basel Committee on banking policy matters); (3) distributed administration conducted by national regulators under treaty, network, or other cooperative regimes (eg the exercise of extraterritorial regulatory jurisdiction); (4) administration by hybrid intergovernmental–private arrangements (eg Codex Alimentarius Commission on food safety standards); and (5) administration by private institutions with regulatory functions (eg International Standardization Organization on standards for various products): Kingsbury, Krisch and Stewart, 'The Emergence of Global Administrative Law' (n 96) 20–23.

[99] The Constitution was adopted by the International Health Conference held in New York from 19 June to 22 July 1946, signed on 22 July 1946 by the representatives of 61 States and entered into force on 7 April 1948.

[100] Available at http://apps.who.int/iris/bitstream/10665/43883/1/9789241580410_eng.pdf.

[101] This authority can be contrasted with 'the Organization's technical role (eg, providing medical or logistical advice on a vaccination campaign or monitoring and reporting on the global spread of an epidemic)': LO Gostin et al, 'The Normative Authority of the World Health Organization' (2015) 129 *Public Health* 7, 854.

[102] 'The Ebola epidemic presented an important test of the IHR, revealing flaws in the regulations and in the WHO more broadly': ibid 854.

'was a disaster for the International Health Regulations (IHR)', insofar as it 'highlighted dismal compliance with IHR obligations on building national core public health capacities'. During the crisis, 'WHO failed to exercise authority' and 'many member states violated the IHR'.[103] This has led the Ebola Interim Assessment Panel to assert in its Report that 'the global community does not take seriously its obligations under the International Health Regulations (2005) – a legally binding document'.[104] Moreover, the Panel stated that '[t]he Member States have a responsibility to act as global citizens'. Consequently, 'the Panel requests that the full IHR Review Committee for Ebola examine options for sanctions for inappropriate and unjustified actions under the Regulations'.[105] This recommendation is not a novelty, since the IHR Review Committee argued already in 2011 that the 'most important structural shortcoming of the IHR is the lack of enforceable sanctions'.[106]

The case of WHO's regulations can be assessed in light of Delacroix's distinction between 'law's capacity to guide behaviour' and 'law's ability to give rise to obligations'. Her account of legal normativity 'takes shape in the endeavour to articulate the "gap" between these two levels'. Thus, when confronted with the question – 'When are the reasons provided by law strong enough to give rise to an obligation?' – she comes up with the following answer:

> If one is to leave any room for the ideal of civic responsibility, the answer has to be framed in terms of moral legitimacy: law's claim to bind us, to impose an obligation upon us, succeeds if it is perceived as legitimate, if it is deemed to promote the ideals or values we want law to foster.[107]

Interestingly enough, in its appeal to the importance of following established rules, the Ebola Interim Assessment Panel refers to member states' quasi-civic responsibility. In following Delacroix's aforementioned statement, one might be inclined to conclude that the inability of WHO's regulations to secure high level of compliance has to do with its legitimacy deficit. At first glance, this seems to be unsatisfactory explanation, having in mind the fact that '196 countries across the globe have agreed to implement' them in the first place[108] and that the establishment of this international organisation 'with unprecedented constitutional powers' was met with 'the exalted expectations of the postwar health and human rights movement'.[109] On a closer look, however, the lower level of normative force of the WHO's legal instruments can be attributed to this organisation's failure to acquire full-blown 'normative authority'. This failure, nonetheless, has hardly anything to

[103] DP Fidler, 'Ebola Report Misses Mark on International Health Regulations', available at www.chathamhouse.org/expert/comment/ebola-report-misses-mark-international-health-regulations#sthash.8oAH9cMw.dpuf.

[104] World Health Organization, *Report of the Ebola Interim Assessment Panel*, 7, available at www.who.int/csr/resources/publications/ebola/report-by-panel.pdf.

[105] ibid 12.

[106] Quoted after, Fidler, 'Ebola Report Misses Mark on International Health Regulations' (n 103).

[107] Delacroix, *Legal Norms and Normativity* (n 43) 197.

[108] See www.who.int/ihr/publications/9789241596664/en/.

[109] Gostin et al, 'The Normative Authority of the World Health Organization' (n 101) 854.

do with the fostered 'ideals and values' of this organisation. Quite the reverse, the general moral ideal of this organisation – 'the attainment by all peoples of the highest possible level of health' – as enshrined in the Article 1 of the WHO Constitution, is universally endorsed by the global community of states.

This apparent lack of authority, thus, needs to be elaborated with reference to other typical features of law – institutionalisation and sanctioning. The institutional structure of the WHO is highly decentralised and subservient to its member states.[110] However, this feature as such is not decisive. Far more importantly, 'global determinants of health' as 'a political challenge'[111] are not currently working in the direction of a more globalised and self-contained regime of governance,[112] which would make an exit option for its members highly burdensome. The present overall situation is such that 'national politics drive self-interest, with states resisting externally imposed obligations for funding and action'.[113] In such a situation, the WHO is unable to exercise even a typical form of international law sanctioning, which Hathaway and Shapiro label as '*external outcasting*'. It is qualified as 'outcasting', because it 'involves denying the disobedient the benefits of social cooperation and membership'; and it is 'external', insofar as it is 'frequently carried out by those outside the regime'.[114]

Under the earlier mentioned prototype theory of law, whose one of the consequences is that 'boundaries between concepts are blurry',[115] the WHO regulations pass the threshold of legality, but they qualify at best for the status of international 'soft law'. Put differently, while being indisputably 'valid' international 'legal' instruments, in so far as they are grounded in the traditional sources of international law, their degree of normativity, understood as the capacity to give rise to obligations, is very low.[116]

[110] Notice that 'the Organization faces critical institutional tensions that significantly impair its functioning', only one of which is 'the WHO's decentralized structure' and 'excessive regionalization'. The other problems are 'a paucity of resources', 'earmarked funding', 'weak governance', and most importantly, that it is 'a servant to member states', insofar as they 'demand faithfulness to their often-conflicting demands': ibid 855.

[111] In its recent programmatic report, The Lancet-University of Oslo Commission on Global Governance for Health proceeds from the idea that 'global political determinants of health' can be defined as 'the transnational norms, policies, and practices that arise from political interaction across all sectors that affect health'. Furthermore, the Commission regards health 'as a political challenge, not merely as a technical outcome': The Lancet-University of Oslo Commission on Global Governance for Health, 'The Political Origins of Health Inequity: Prospects for Change' (2014) 383 *Lancet* 633.

[112] It is worth noting that the political agenda of this Commission goes beyond the establishment of a regime of the 'global health governance', which refers to 'the governance of the global health system – defined as the actors and institutions with the primary purpose of health', but instead urges for a 'global governance for health', which refers 'to all governance areas that can affect health': ibid 633.

[113] Gostin et al, 'The Normative Authority of the World Health Organization' (n 101) 859.

[114] O Hathaway and SJ Shapiro, 'Outcasting: Enforcement in Domestic and International Law' (2011) 121 *The Yale Law Journal* 258.

[115] Peters and Pagotto, 'Soft Law as a New Mode of Governance: A Legal Perspective' (n 80) 12.

[116] Most international legal scholars seem to envisage 'soft law' instruments in a similar fashion. Despite being critical of the idea of graduated normativity of international law, Weil says that it seems 'better to reserve the term 'soft law' for rules that are imprecise and not really compelling, since sublegal obligations are neither "soft law" nor "hard law": they are simply not law at all': Weil, 'Towards Relative

B. Basel Committee on Banking Supervision

Quite the opposite conclusion can be reached about the Basel Committee on Banking Supervision's regulatory regime. This body 'is a 'club' by design – small, homogeneous, and insular',[117] with the semi-open form of membership.[118] Pursuant to the opening article of its Charter, '[t]he BCBS is the primary global standard-setter for the prudential regulation of banks' (Article 1). According to its own wording, the BCBS 'does not possess any formal supranational authority. Its decisions do not have legal force'. Rather, it 'relies on its members' commitments' (Article 3). However, Article 5 specifies that BCBS members are committed not only to 'work together to achieve the mandate of the BCBS' (a), which is to 'strengthen the regulation, supervision and practices of banks worldwide with the purpose of enhancing financial stability' (Article 1), but also, and more importantly, to 'implement and apply BCBS standards in their domestic jurisdictions within the predefined timeframe established by the Committee' (e).

Despite the BCBS' self-proclaimed constraints, its regulations are globally implemented, even by countries which are not its members. Even more so, '[s]upervisors and banks outside the G10 countries, as well as inside, proved almost embarrassingly keen to adopt this new Basel standard, despite the fact that it was supposedly only designed for large international banks in developed economies'.[119] How are we to account for this 'enthusiasm' and 'acquiescence' with which Basel regulations were met 'in virtually every country'?[120] Proceeding from Guzman's 'reputational model' of 'compliance-based theory of international law',[121] Melissa Boey has recently dwelled on the idea that efficacy of the Basel Accords largely stems from states' unwillingness to suffer 'significant reputational penalties' for non-compliance.[122] However, this explanation is hardly compatible with Guzman's

Normativity in International Law?' (n 94) 415, fn 7. Besson argues that 'in terms of degree of normativity', international law 'now ranges from low-intensity or soft law to imperative law': S Besson, 'Theorizing the Sources of International Law' in S Besson and J Tasioulas (eds), *The Philosophy of International Law* (Oxford, Oxford University Press, 2010) 165. Chinkin, for her part, differentiates between 'legal' and 'non-legal soft law'. Rules in the first category are defined by their formal source (eg treaties), but they 'include only soft obligations': CM Chinkin, 'The Challenge of Soft Law: Development and Change in International Law' (1989) 38(4) *International and Comparative Law Quarterly* 851.

[117] MS Barr and GP Miller, 'Global Administrative Law: The View from Basel' (2006) 17 *The European Journal of International Law* 18.

[118] Article 5, para 4: 'In accepting new members, due regard will be given to the importance of their national banking sectors to international financial stability': Basel Committee on Banking Supervision, *Charter*, January 2013. www.bis.org/bcbs/charter.pdf.

[119] C Goodhart, *The Basel Committee on Banking Supervision: A History of the Early Years, 1974–1997* (Cambridge, Cambridge University Press, 2011) 190.

[120] ibid 190. To name just the example of my home country – despite not being member of the club, the National Bank of Serbia swiftly adopted in 2013 the Strategy for the Incorporation of Basel III Standards in Serbia.

[121] AT Guzman, 'A Compliance-Based Theory of International Law' (2002) 90(6) *California Law Review* 1823.

[122] Apart from this, she invokes other explanations as well. But this is the first one that she mentions: M Boey, 'Regulating "Bankerspace": Challenging the Legitimacy of the Basel Accords as Soft Law' (2014) 87 *Southern California Law Review Postscript* 102.

initial assumption that 'states negotiate over the content of the law and the level of commitment',[123] because the vast majority of countries that decided to implement Basel Accords had had no role whatsoever in framing these regulations.[124] Hence, it is necessary to employ a different strategy for elucidating the normative force of these regulations. It seems that it cannot be fully grasped without taking into account a peculiar form of the institutionalisation of this regulatory regime. Unlike the WHO, the BCBS is the case of an informal way of institutionalisation which came along with the rapidly 'globalised nature of bankerspace'.[125] Raz perceives this development of a growing limitation of states' independence in certain spheres of a globalised and interconnected world as a significantly new feature of international law. One of the corollaries of this development is that opting out of the given international regime would be if not 'very isolating' (like in the case of exit from more structured organisations, such as the United Nations),[126] then at least 'very costly'.[127] Consequently, to resort to the traditional source of authority of international law – state consent – as the plausible explanation of the normative force of the BCBS instruments would be a simplified and somewhat misleading solution. Boey fosters one such argument, thereby implying that legitimacy problems need not be opened at the international level. She says:

> As long as nations are able to make the conscious choice of whether to adopt Basel as law, the demand for democratic legitimacy need not arise at the international level, but can be satisfied at the national level through standard rulemaking procedures in respective jurisdictions. As private entities, banks are also able to determine whether they would like to apply Basel and be subject to Basel, as long as they remain compliant with the relevant binding laws of the states in which they operate.[128]

However, there is hardly any space for 'the conscious choice' if Boey herself admits that there is 'systemic risk [which] imparts the need for nations to harmonise their capital standards internationally, in order to prevent the rippling or domino

[123] Guzman, 'A Compliance-Based Theory of International Law' (n 121) 1846.

[124] Despite Guzman's argument that even 'soft law' instruments, such as 'memoranda of understanding, executive agreements, nonbinding treaties, joint declarations, final communiques, agreements pursuant to legislation' falls under the concept of 'international law', his reputational model is premised on the idea that only instruments which states explicitly or implicitly promised to follow could qualify for the status of law: ibid 1879–80. On this account, Basel Accords could not qualify even for the status of 'soft law'. Howse and Teitel criticise this and similar 'compliance-based' approaches for narrowing the perspective of international law: 'Looking at the aspirations of international law through the lens of rule compliance leads to inadequate scrutiny and understanding of the diverse complex purposes and projects that multiple actors impose and transpose on international legality, and especially a tendency to oversimplify if not distort the relation of international law to politics': R Howse and R Teitel, 'Beyond Compliance: Rethinking Why International Law Really Matters' (2010) 1(2) *Global Policy* 128.

[125] Boey, 'Regulating "Bankerspace": Challenging the Legitimacy of the Basel Accords as Soft Law' (n 122) 79.

[126] J Raz, 'Why the State' (2014) *Legal Studies Research Paper Series* 2014–38, at http://ssrn.com/abstract=2339522, 14.

[127] ibid 16.

[128] Boey, 'Regulating "Bankerspace": Challenging the Legitimacy of the Basel Accords as Soft Law' 111.

effect of any economic trouble'.[129] The risk could be labeled as 'systemic' only if the 'bankerspace' succeeded in gaining features of a functioning system. It transpires that it managed to do so, but not solely through the push and pressure of the world's wealthiest countries.[130] In addition, the BCBS has gradually strengthened its legitimacy credentials, by complying with some of the rule of law principles inherent in the administrative matters, such as procedural participation, transparency, review.[131] Consequently, although not qualifying even for the status of international soft law in the aforementioned sense of the word, Basel banking regulations managed to acquire significant normative force in terms of safeguarding the required behaviour of its norm-subjects. Moreover, measured by the level of compliance of the relevant norm-subjects, one may be inclined to conclude that BCBS instruments are regarded by relevant actors as 'binding', that is, as giving rise to obligations.

IV. Conclusion

In the aforementioned opening to the GAL symposium, Weiler sends the word of caution: 'When all issues of transnational or international governance become GAL' then the employed concept 'loses its explanatory power and methodological rigor'.[132] The aspiration of this paper was exactly to bring more analytical rigour in the treatment of UNOs of various global regulatory regimes. It tried to show that the obsession with 'law' as the 'default descriptor' (Somek) for various global regulatory instruments stems largely from the erroneous assumption about the special, ie 'exclusionary' nature of legal rules. Once the direct link between legal 'normativity', 'validity', and 'bindingness' is exposed as unsubstantiated, the path is cleared for a more nuanced discussion about the nature of different UNOs. On this reading, the 'legality' of a global regulatory instrument is primarily to be determined in terms of its 'validity' according to the established membership criteria, ie 'sources' of the given (in this case, international) legal order. This traditional jurisprudential approach contradicts some of the views expressed in the expanding literature on 'global law'. Neil Walker, for instance, argues that 'the authoritative basis for global relevance and resonance may not be understood and articulated in terms of specific source or pedigree *at all*'.[133] This is so because 'global law' is understood as

[129] ibid 102.
[130] ibid 103.
[131] ibid 106–109.
[132] Weiler, 'GAL at a Crossroads: Preface to the Symposium' (n 1) 463.
[133] 'For global law also refers to the emergence or to the prospect of the emergence of a trans-systemic and often explicitly inter-systematically engaged *common sense and practice* of recognition and development of jurisdictionally unrestricted common ground on particular rules, case precedents, doctrines or principles, or even with regard to background legal orientations': N Walker, *Intimations of Global Law* (Cambridge, Cambridge University Press, 2015) 20.

'adjectival rather than a nominal category'.[134] That is, 'a crucial definitional minimum' of 'global law' concerns 'a double sense of the global *appeal* of global law'. In the first sense, 'the global scale of global law is indicated by its destination rather than its source'.[135] In the second sense, 'global law' makes a global appeal in so far as it claims or assumes 'a universal or globally pervasive justification for its application'.[136]

A different venue for discussing the 'legality' of global regulatory instruments comes with a more thorough exposition of the sources of international law. Besson's analysis is of such a sort. She differentiates between '*formal* sources' of international law, *stricto sensu*, which refer to 'processes by which international legal norms are created, modified, and annulled', and '*probationary* sources', that is, 'the places where their normative outcomes, i.e. valid international legal norms, may be found'. Furthermore, international law-making processes can result in both 'complete legal norms' (*lex lata*) and 'intermediary legal products', such as legal projects (*lex ferenda*).[137] When it comes to the question whether the list of formal sources, enlisted in Article 38(1) of the ICJ Statute, is exhaustive, Besson cautiously remarks that there is a growing evidence of the 'coordinative practice' of various international actors 'over the extension of the triad of sources' – treaty law, customary law, general principles – 'to two further sources: unilateral law issued by states but most importantly by IOs … and non-conventional concerted acts issued by states'.[138] This certainly leaves enough room for arguing that some of the processes of global regulatory norm-making may be eventually recognised as formal sources of international law, which would, then, bestow on them the quality of 'valid legal' (be it complete or intermediary) products.[139] The most plausible channel of recognition would be through the practice of relevant international adjudicative bodies, whose decisions, despite being officially designated by Article 38(1) as a 'subsidiary source', do make 'the impact … on the development of international law [that] cannot be ignored'.[140]

[134] ibid 23.

[135] It 'purports to cover all actors and activities relevant to its remit across the globe': ibid 21.

[136] Global law's 'global reach is grounded in the claim or assumption that there are globally defensible good reasons for its invocation': ibid 22.

[137] Although the latter 'are not yet valid legal norms, [they] may be vested with a certain evidentiary value in the next stages of the law-making process': Besson, 'Theorizing the Sources of International Law' (n 116) 170.

[138] ibid 181.

[139] As noted by Boyle and Chinkin in their influential treatise on the making of international law, '[w]hile states retain their primary position within the international legal order, other actors contribute in a variety of ways to the development of the rules and principles of international law. These include intergovernmental organisations (IGOs) and other non-state actors whose actions in cooperating with, confronting and contesting state actions all play a part in the evolution of international law': A Boyle and C Chinkin, *The Making of International Law* (Oxford, Oxford University Press, 2007) 2.

[140] ibid 2. In the recent GAL literature one may find a further claim that 'ultra-state courts' can be qualified as 'GAL regulators'. This is a corollary of the process of 'judicial globalisation', which has gradually led to 'judicial regulation'. While this regulation can assume various forms, 'these are all characterised by the existence of a common denominator, the application of principles or rules in light of the absence or insufficiency of codified or legislative criteria' (307). These principles and techniques

As we saw, the degree of normativity that certain global regulatory instruments are capable of displaying is not necessarily related to the question of whether they pass the established test of 'legality'. Some indubitably international legal instruments, such as WHO's regulations, are of very low normative force, whereas other instruments with far more modest goals, such as BCBS' 'internationally harmonised global liquidity standards',[141] seem to provide weighty reasons for action of their norm-subjects. In both cases, however, one is able to trace what Walker calls the 'global appeal', which is 'expressed in the symmetry of subject and object'. This means that global normative instrument

> is, or should be, applicable to all who might be covered by its material terms regardless of location or association with a particular polity, because it is justifiable to all who might be covered by those material terms, or so it is claimed or assumed.[142]

The more globalised is the subject area of regulation, the more convincing is this 'global appeal' and the more institutionalised is the resulting global regulatory regime. But the processes are working in the opposite direction as well. Globalisation of the subject area is strengthened with the capacity of a regulatory body to exercise its power in line with some immanent justificatory standards, thereby acquiring the status of a legitimate authority in the given regulatory sphere.[143] A highly institutionalised global regulatory regime is the one from which the exit option for its norm-subjects is fairly burdensome and in which the typical form of international sanctioning – 'external outcasing' – can be extremely efficacious. When put in the much needed genealogical perspective, such a global regime, whose regulatory instruments display a high degree of normativity, has all the potential for transforming itself from a *prudential* standard-setter into an international *legal* regime.

form 'judicial doctrines' that are applied by 'ultra-state courts' in a global administrative space 'within which legal regimes enter into contact with one another'. In that respect, not only judicial doctrines are 'part of GAL', but they may also 'be defined as "global secondary rules"' in the Hartian sense of the word: E D'Alterio, 'Judicial Regulation in the Global Space' in S Cassese (ed), *Research Handbook on Global Administrative Law* (Cheltenham, Edward Elgar Publishing, 2016) 316.

[141] Basel Committee on Banking Supervision, 'Basel III: A global regulatory framework for more resilient banks and banking systems', December 2010 (rev June 2011) para 34.

[142] Walker, *Intimations of Global Law* (n 133) 22.

[143] See M Jovanović, 'The Quest for International Rule of Law and the Rise of Global Regulatory Regimes' (2015) 6 *E-Publica* 1–20, available at http://e-publica.pt/pdf/artigos/the-quest-for-international.pdf.

INDEX